Cracking the LSAT

By Adam Robinson and
Kevin Blemel
Updated by Mindy Eve Myers
and Robert Spruill

2006 Edition

Random House, Inc.
New York

www.PrincetonReview.com

The Princeton Review, Inc.
2315 Broadway
New York, NY 10024
E-mail: booksupport@review.com

Originally published by Villard Books, a division of Random House, Inc., 1989.

ISBN: 0-375-76478-X
ISSN: 1062-5542

Editor: Ruth J. Mills
Production Editor: Patricia Dublin
Production Coordinator: Jennifer Arias

Manufactured in the United States of America.

10 9 8 7 6 5 4 3 2 1

2006 Edition

ACKNOWLEDGMENTS

A successful LSAT program is a collaborative effort. We'd especially like to thank Tricia McCloskey, Jeff Rubenstein, Dan Edmonds, John Sheehan, Lindsey van Wagenen, Mark Sawula, Dave Schaller, Timothy Wheeler, Jim Reynolds, Omar Goodleg, Adam Frank, and Adam Landis for their suggestions and contributions. An extra thanks to contributing author Kevin Blemel, to Mindy Eve Myers, Bob Spruill, and Fritz Stewart for their expertise, and to Production Editor Patricia Dublin and Production Coordinator Jennifer Arias.

A very special thanks to Oliver Hart, professor of economics at M.I.T., and to Debora Davies and the folks at *Columbia Law Review* for their generous permission to quote an excerpt from an article by Professor Hart.

Finally, we'd like to thank all those who have taught us everything we know about taking tests—our students.

Special thanks to Adam Robinson, who conceived of and perfected the Joe Bloggs approach to standardized tests and many of the other successful techniques used by The Princeton Review.

ABOUT THE AUTHORS

Adam Robinson was born in 1955. He lives in New York City.

Kevin Blemel started working with The Princeton Review in 1994. Over the years, he has served as a teacher, tutor, and Master Trainer throughout the United States as well as in Bangkok, Thailand. In addition to creating written materials, Kevin has developed educational content for a Distance Learning program that provides web-based instruction. He makes his home in Austin, Texas, but can often be seen traveling here and abroad to feed his addictions to taking risks outdoors and to eating anything strange he can get his hands on.

CONTENTS

Dear Prospective Law Student:

Congratulations on your decision to purchase The Princeton Review's *Cracking the LSAT*. This self-study guide will help you achieve your highest possible score on the LSAT—arguably the most significant single factor in law school admissions decisions.

While most applicants understand the importance that the LSAT plays in their law school applications, many are unaware that the score they receive can have far-reaching consequences—often determining much more than just which law school they will attend. For example, many law schools consider LSAT scores when awarding merit scholarships and grants. Given that the average full-time *juris doctor* degree costs more than $150,000, a high score on the LSAT may well translate into tens of thousands of dollars in financial aid that can significantly reduce your law school debt upon graduation.

The LSAT purports to gauge your reading comprehension, reasoning, and analytical skills in an effort to predict your ability to survive a demanding law school curriculum. Those who hone their LSAT test-taking skills usually score the highest. Indeed, a strong LSAT score can be as much an indication of a strong work ethic as it is of intellect.

So invest the time and master The Princeton Review's proven test-taking strategies. While that investment begins with *Cracking the LSAT*, it should not end there. To truly benefit from this book, you should also visit The Princeton Review's website, www.PrincetonReview.com/cracking, to take advantage of the online resources available to purchasers of this book. There you will be able to supplement your self-study with free online exercises and tutorials, including additional practice questions and score reports based upon the practice tests you will take.

The Princeton Review's master instructors are devoted to sharing their wisdom and inspiration so that you can conquer the LSAT. *Cracking the LSAT* and its online supplement are the fruits of their efforts. I firmly believe that The Princeton Review, with its personalized instruction and test-taking techniques, is the very best way for you to prepare comprehensively for the LSAT.

Good Luck!

Sincerely,

Donald W. Macaulay, Esq.
President and Founder, Law Preview

Get More from *Cracking the LSAT* by Using Our Free Online Tools

Buyers of this book receive a free subscription to *Cracking the LSAT*'s **online companion course**, which features the latest in interactive tools for test preparation. Go to www.PrincetonReview.com/cracking to register for all the free services we offer to help you improve your test score and find the right law school. Once you've logged on, you'll be able to:

- **Take Extra LSAT Diagnostic Exams.** Get even more LSAT practice by taking full-length LSAT tests online. After each test, you'll receive a personalized score report that will show your strengths and weaknesses. You'll know exactly where you should be concentrating your preparation efforts.
- **Learn Key Test-Taking Skills Through Our Distance Learning Tools.** Some of the key lessons of *Cracking the LSAT* will be even clearer after you've spent a few hours seeing and hearing them presented online.
- **Analyze Your Performance on the Tests in this Book.** By logging onto our site and submitting your answers to the diagnostic tests in this book, you can get personalized score reports that will help you focus your energy on specific areas of weakness.
- **Research and Apply to the Best Law Schools for You.** Through www.PrincetonReview.com, our award-winning school search site, you can access our complete library of information about U.S. law schools, manage your application process, and even apply electronically.

YOU'RE IN COMPLETE CONTROL

Here's what you'll see once you've registered:

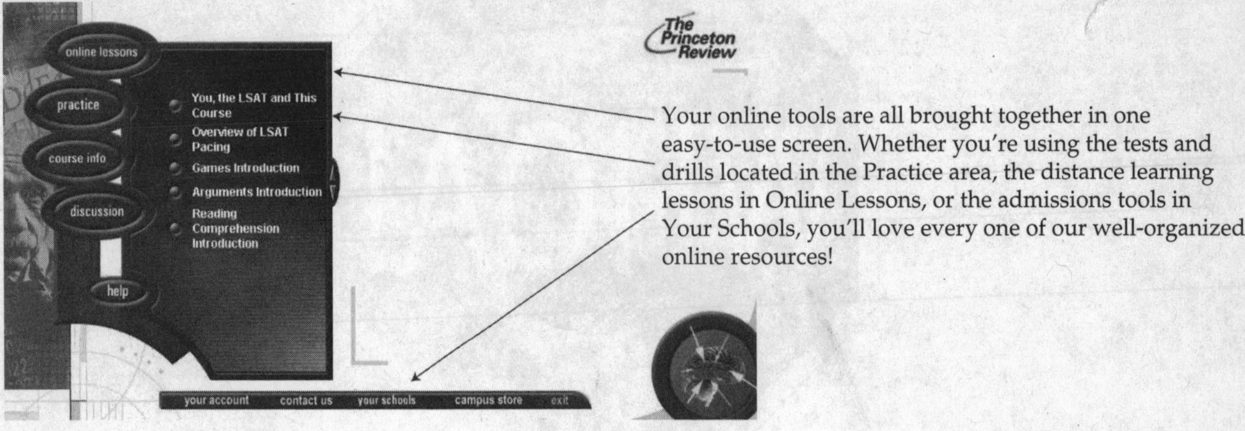

Your online tools are all brought together in one easy-to-use screen. Whether you're using the tests and drills located in the Practice area, the distance learning lessons in Online Lessons, or the admissions tools in Your Schools, you'll love every one of our well-organized online resources!

READING YOUR SCORE REPORT

After you take your extra diagnostic exam's, here's how to use your score report:

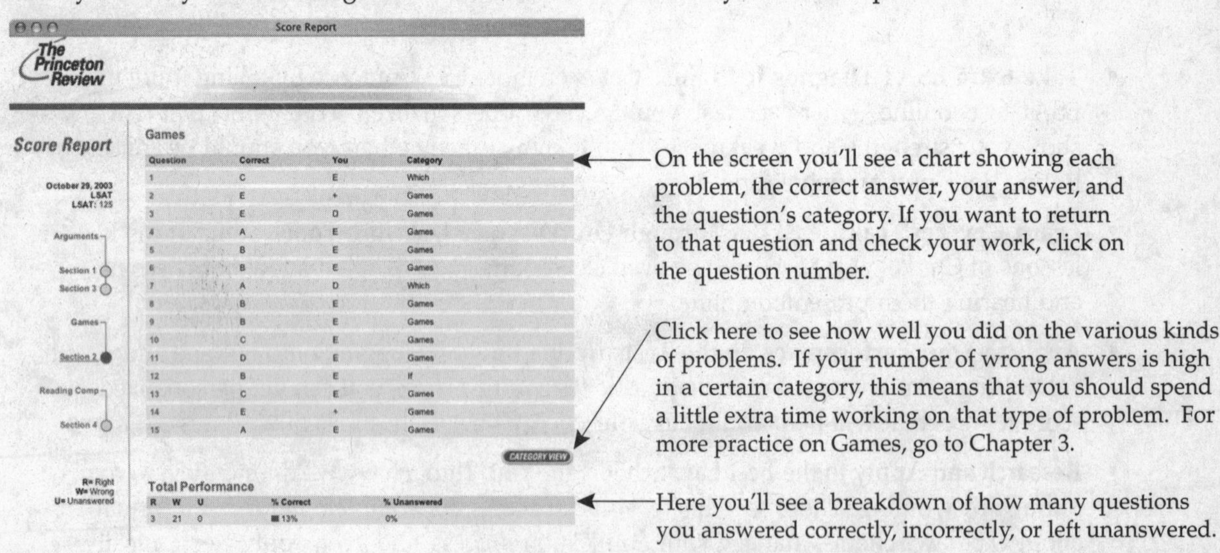

Question	Correct	You	Category
1	C	E	Which
2	E	*	Games
3	E	D	Games
4	A	E	Games
5	B	E	Games
6	B	E	Games
7	A	D	Which
8	B	E	Games
9	B	E	Games
10	C	E	Games
11	D	E	Games
12	B	E	If
13	C	E	Games
14	E	*	Games
15	A	E	Games

R	W	U	% Correct	% Unanswered
3	21	0	13%	0%

On the screen you'll see a chart showing each problem, the correct answer, your answer, and the question's category. If you want to return to that question and check your work, click on the question number.

Click here to see how well you did on the various kinds of problems. If your number of wrong answers is high in a certain category, this means that you should spend a little extra time working on that type of problem. For more practice on Games, go to Chapter 3.

Here you'll see a breakdown of how many questions you answered correctly, incorrectly, or left unanswered.

3

Games

WHAT IS A GAME?

The folks who write the test call this section the "Analytical Reasoning" section, but really the questions are just puzzles, so we call it the "Games" section. You are presented with the basic format and structure of the game in the *setup*, an initial paragraph that also provides the *elements*; you will be asked to determine the relationships between these elements. Following the setup will be a number of conditions, or *clues*, which put restrictions on how the elements can be manipulated and sometimes give you valuable information about the overall structure of the game as well. Finally, you will have a number of questions, each of which may introduce new restrictions or even occasionally change one of the original clues. Each question is independent of the others, although work completed for one question may help in eliminating answer choices on another question.

WHAT DOES THIS SECTION TEST?

Games test how well you can organize an incomplete set of spatial relations to extract information efficiently.

Games test how well you can organize information, understand spatial relationships, and make deductions from those relationships when presented with limitations on the arrangements allowed by the rules. They also reward you for being able to extract this information efficiently.

WHY IS THIS SECTION ON THE LSAT?

Games are designed to predict your ability to perform the kind of detailed analyses required of law students. They really just test how well you answer the games on the LSAT under strict time pressure. You won't do any of these in law school. And you certainly won't do these when you become a lawyer.

THE SECTION ITSELF

The Games section is made up of four games. Each game includes five to seven questions. The section has a total of 23 to 25 questions.

Before we begin, take a moment to read the instructions to this section:

> Directions: Each group of questions in this section is based on a set of conditions. In answering some of the questions, it may be useful to draw a rough diagram. Choose the response that most accurately and completely answers each question and blacken the corresponding space on your answer sheet.

These are the directions that will appear on your LSAT. As usual on the LSAT, the official directions are of little help. Review them now. They will not change. Don't waste time reading them in the test room.

THE GOOD NEWS

The good news is that with some rigorous practice diagramming games, you can radically improve your LSAT score. Many students have walked into The Princeton Review classes getting only a few games questions right, but they walk out scoring 75 percent or higher on the section. You can do the same, as long as you follow our step-by-step process and practice, practice, practice.

Games: General Strategies

Following is a list of general strategies that you should use when you are working the Games section. Make sure you take these strategies to heart.

Slow and steady wins the race

As in the Arguments section, you want to maintain a high level of accuracy on the games questions to maximize the number of points you get. Trying to rush through the section to make sure you'll finish every question isn't a productive approach. You will achieve the highest level of accuracy by using an approach that increases efficiency—not necessarily pace—without sacrificing your ability to be effective. As with arguments, you'll need to develop an approach that is best suited to your strengths. If you find you can't finish a Games section in the allotted time, don't fret; remember, you don't need to finish to get a good score. Through consistent practice, you will be able to move more quickly through the section without having to work so fast that you start to make careless errors.

Your mantra: *I will not rush through the games just so that I can finish. I will work to improve efficiency and accuracy, thereby improving my score.*

Survey the field

Remember, every correct answer on the LSAT is worth exactly one raw point toward your scaled score. It's quite possible that the two games that you should do first in a section may be the third and fourth games presented. Remember, the LSAT games and the questions attached to them are not arranged in order of difficulty. Therefore, you should look over all four games in the section and decide which ones are more approachable. We'll spend time later outlining what characteristics make a game more or less attractive.

Your mantra: *I will look over the Games section and rank the games before I begin working on them.*

Just do something

Keep working, keep moving forward, and don't ever just stare at a game in search of divine inspiration.

Your mantra: *I will keep moving forward.*

Transfer your answers after each game

As soon as you've finished working on all the questions on a particular game, transfer those answers to your answer sheet. This method has a number of advantages: It is the most efficient, it helps prevent careless errors, and it gives your brain a much needed change of task before you dive into the next game. When there are five minutes remaining in the section, fill in answers for all the remaining questions. Then you can go back and work on the remaining questions you have time for, changing the bubbles one at a time as you go.

Your mantra: *I will transfer my answers in a group after each game until five minutes are left.*

Take short breaks

After you've completed each game, take a short break. Not a nap, just ten seconds to take three deep breaths and ready yourself for the next game. Transfer your answers from that game, and then start the next game. You've cleared your mind, and you're ready to push on.

Your mantra: *I will use ten seconds after each game I complete to take some deep breaths and refocus.*

YOUR MANTRAS AND YOU

Here they are again.

> *I will not rush through the games just so that I can finish. I will work to improve efficiency and accuracy, thereby improving my score.*
>
> *I will look over the Games section and rank the games before I begin working on them.*
>
> *I will keep moving forward.*
>
> *I will transfer my answers in a group after each game until five minutes are left.*
>
> *I will use ten seconds after each game I complete to take some deep breaths and refocus.*

GAMES: SPECIFIC STRATEGIES

The directions for the Games section misleadingly state that "it may be useful to draw a rough diagram" when working the section. That's like saying it may be useful to train before running your first marathon. Actually, it is *necessary* to draw a very *detailed* diagram. Furthermore, you want to symbolize all of the clues that you are given.

Make it visual

Games are a visual exercise. Games test your ability to determine how various elements can be arranged in space. Therefore, words don't help you; images do. Your goal will be to translate all the words that you are given in the setup and the clues, and sometimes in the questions themselves, into visual symbols. Once you've done this, you won't need to (or want to) refer to that confusing verbal mess again.

The LSAT writers are banking on the fact that most test takers will try to organize all this information in their heads in their rush to finish. And they're right: most test takers do. But you'll also notice that when the bell curve gets played out, most test takers are lumped around the middle of the curve, getting only about half of the questions right. Coincidence? We think not. Don't be another statistic. Use your pencil, and draw it out rather than trying to work it all out in your head.

Be consistent

There are various ways you can symbolize and diagram the information that is presented to you in a game. We're going to show you what we've found to be the best and most efficient way to diagram and symbolize. Whatever method you choose, be consistent with your symbols and your diagram—don't mix and match. You'll get confused and wonder why you've gotten three answers that all look right for half the questions, and none that seem to work for the other half of the questions.

Be careful

Your goal is to translate all the information that you received from the setup and the clues into some sort of visual symbolization. However, if you don't read the clues carefully enough, you can wind up symbolizing something incorrectly. This will eventually lead to your diagram becoming a liability rather than an asset. So make sure you read the information slowly enough that you don't make mistakes in your symbolization.

Be flexible

The four games that you will see on the real LSAT may look slightly different from the games you have practiced on. Under the time pressure of test day, they may seem *completely* different. They won't be. Once you understand how games work and can recognize the basic structures the test writers use to build them, you can see how consistent they really are. Just stay calm and take a step back to evaluate the information. The details will change but the basic ingredients won't. Focus on the big picture. Focus on the similarities to other games you've already done. And get to work.

Don't simply stare at a game that seems confusing. Focus on the underlying similarities to games you've already seen, and get to work applying the process.

GAMES: A STEP-BY-STEP PROCESS

Just as in the Arguments section, The Princeton Review has boiled down the Games section into a step-by-step process. You will follow this process for every game that you do. Learn these steps, practice them rigorously, apply them consistently, and you'll improve your score. Sound good? Then let's go to it!

Step 1: Diagram and inventory

Your first step will be to determine the appropriate diagram for the game by evaluating both the setup and the clues. Remember that we want to translate all of the verbal information from the test into visual information on the page because this is really a test of *spatial* reasoning. You will be given enough information to understand the basic structure of the game. You will eventually assign elements and perhaps their characteristics to the places available in the diagram, so your basis for the diagram will figure out the underlying structure to which you will assign these elements. You will also want to list the elements next to the diagram, so that you'll have everything in one place and will be able to keep track of it easily. Don't rush through this step, because this is the core of your process. People often want to start scribbling a diagram as soon as something pops out at them from the setup. Take the time to evaluate both the setup and the clues, and you'll be well equipped for the rest of the process.

Step 2: Symbolize the clues and double-check

After you've drawn the core of a diagram, symbolize the clues listed below the setup. Once again, we'll convert the written clues into visual symbols. The clues should be symbolized in a way that is consistent with the diagram you have set up. The goal is to transform the clues into pieces that will fit into your diagram visually. Remember the three C's: Keep your symbols clear, concise, and consistent.

Never forget how important it is to symbolize everything correctly. Invest the few seconds it will take to be sure that your symbols match the information given in the clues. Be sure to go back over the information presented in the setup as well because some games may have longer, more complicated setups than others. A foolproof way to accomplish this is to *work against the grain*: Articulate what each of your symbols means and then carry that back up to the clues you were given. When you find a match, check off that clue. Once you're sure everything is all accounted for, you're finished. It's that simple.

Step 3: Look for links and size up the game
Now that you're sure you've got everything properly symbolized, it's time to make sure that you've made any *deductions* that you can from the information that was given. Look for overlap between the clues and the diagram, and among the clues that share elements, and see if there's anything else that you know *for sure*. For instance, does putting two clues together give you a third piece of information? Add your deductions to the information you already have. You'll notice that many deductions give you concrete limitations about where elements are restricted—where they *can't* go—rather than where they *must* go.

While you're looking for these deductions, you'll find that you're also learning how the game is going to work. Keep your eyes open for anything that seems as if it will have a particularly large impact on the outcome of the game. The most restricted places and the most restrictive clues tend to have the most impact when you start working the questions. The more you know about how the game will work, the more efficient you'll be at working through the questions.

Step 4: Evaluate the question task
Not all games questions are on the same level of difficulty. We'll show you which types of questions to attack first and why. As a rule, you should always look for specific questions that further limit the initial conditions of the game and provide you with more information. These questions can be done much more quickly than those general questions that don't provide you with any information. You should also make a point of either circling or underlining what each question asks you for. This will help you to determine the best approach to the question and the type of answer you'll need.

Step 5: Apply the strategy
Each question task requires its own strategy. Making sure that you use the proper strategy means saving time on a given question without sacrificing accuracy. Plus, by approaching the questions in an efficient order, you'll find that the work you've done on earlier questions will often help you to find the right answer on a later question.

Step 6: Use Process of Elimination
We know, you're sick of hearing about Process of Elimination. But get used to it. It will come in handy on Games, just as it did on Arguments. (Oh, and by the way, you'll use it in the Reading Comprehension section, too.) Of all the sections, Games is the one where the correct answer is concrete, not subjective as we saw previously in Arguments. Often, you'll find you know exactly what the answer is going to be. But even if you don't (which may well be the case on some tougher games), POE can help you avoid the frustration of trying out each answer choice and wasting lots of time on a single question.

Ready for Some Games?

Now let's see how the six steps work on a real game. Give yourself as much time as you need to apply the method to the following game. Focus on using the proper technique (feel free to have the steps written out next to you) and pay no attention to time—that will come later. Work the game using only the space available on the page. On the day of the test, you won't have any scratch paper, so you'll have to get accustomed to writing small and keeping things neat. Do the best you can, and then compare what you did to our explanation. After each game, we'll give you some extra techniques for approaching this section of the LSAT. You should work through each exercise fully before going on to the next game. By the end of the chapter, you'll know everything we do about how to tackle LSAT Games.

GAME #1: DAYS AND ENTREES

Don't worry about time yet. Just focus on the process. Your speed will increase naturally with practice.

A restaurant must choose its main dinner entree for each night of one week, beginning on Sunday and ending on Saturday. The possible entrees are beef, lamb, manicotti, pork, spaghetti, trout, and veal, each of which will be used on a different night. The following conditions must be met when determining the menu:

The lamb must be served either the night before or the night after the spaghetti is served.

The beef must be served either the night before or the night after either the pork or the trout is served.

The manicotti cannot be served the night before or the night after the veal is served.

The veal must be served on Monday.

1. Which one of the following is a possible menu in order from Sunday to Saturday?

(A) pork, veal, trout, lamb, beef, spaghetti, manicotti
(B) trout, veal, manicotti, beef, lamb, spaghetti, pork
(C) spaghetti, veal, lamb, trout, manicotti, beef, pork
(D) trout, veal, beef, pork, manicotti, lamb, spaghetti
(E) manicotti, veal, beef, trout, lamb, spaghetti, pork

2. If lamb is served on Saturday, which one of the following must be true?

(A) The spaghetti is served on Thursday.
(B) The beef is served on Tuesday.
(C) The manicotti is served on Thursday.
(D) The pork is served on Wednesday.
(E) The trout is served on Sunday.

3. If the trout is served on Thursday, the pork must be served on

(A) Sunday
(B) Tuesday
(C) Wednesday
(D) Friday
(E) Saturday

4. Which one of the following is a night on which the manicotti could be served?

(A) Sunday
(B) Tuesday
(C) Wednesday
(D) Friday
(E) Saturday

5. If beef is served on Saturday, which one of the following must be true?

(A) The trout is served on Friday.
(B) The pork is served on Thursday.
(C) The spaghetti is served on Wednesday.
(D) The lamb is served on Tuesday.
(E) The manicotti is served on Thursday.

Cracking Game #1

Step 1: Diagram and inventory

What we have here is seven days of the week and seven entrees. We learned this from the first paragraph, which is called the *setup*. We recommend using a grid in this situation to organize the information. In this case, we need to decide what goes on top of the grid—the days of the week or the entrees. We want the things that won't change order (our core) across the top of our diagram. Notice that the clues give us information about how the entrees can be organized in relation to one another. We are assigning elements (entrees) to places (days), so the days go on top of the grid.

Don't forget to list your elements near the diagram so that you'll have everything you need in one place.

Also, we have what is called a *one-to-one correspondence* in this game—there are seven places (days) and seven elements (entrees) that correspond to each of the places. In addition, we're told that each will be used, so we have to use all of them; one-to-one correspondence isn't just a matter of the number of each, but also whether all are used, or any can be reused. This is a good thing because it will limit the number of possible places to which the elements can be assigned. We have to use each element once and because we only have seven nights, we can't repeat any of the elements. That answers two questions you'll want to ask for each game you work: "Can we leave out any elements?" and "Can there be any repeats?" If the answer to either of these is yes, the game becomes more complicated. We'll talk more about this when we get to ordering the games later. In this game, the answer to both questions is no, so we should be able to tackle this one as long as we follow the steps.

In general, factors with a natural order (such as days of the week, rooms numbered 1 through 4, etc.) will act as the core of the diagram. For most diagrams, place what doesn't change on top of the diagram. For example: Nine people ride to work in three cars. The three cars don't change, but who rides with whom will change, depending on the question. So the cars would go across the top of the diagram.

Take a look at our diagram for this game:

Su	M	Tu	W	Th	F	Sa

Step 2: Symbolize the clues and double-check

Now that we've drawn a diagram, it's important that we symbolize the clues so that they fit into our diagram. We want to get rid of the words and transform the clues into visual puzzle pieces that fit into the framework that we've already drawn. Let's take a look at the first clue:

Draw excruciatingly exact symbols for the information given to you. Remember the three Cs for symbols: clear, concise, and consistent.

> The lamb must be served either the night before or the night after the spaghetti is served.

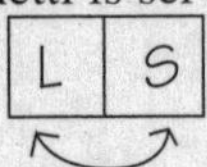

As you can see, we created a shorthand for each of the entrees, denoting them by their first letter (L = lamb and S = spaghetti). We then put these two letters next to each other to show that they must be *consecutive*. We then put a box around the two letters to show that this is a "block" of information that is fixed. Finally, we put the double-pointed arrow underneath the block to show that the order can be either "LS" or "SL."

The great thing about this piece of information is that it will occupy two of the seven possible spaces. Blocks are concrete, restrictive clues that limit the possible arrangements and will make your job easier, so look for them when you are reading over the clues and deciding whether to do a particular game.

> The beef must be served either the night before or the night after either the pork or the trout is served.

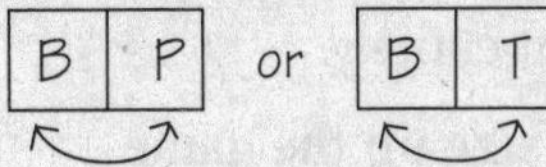

This is also good information, but not quite as good as the "LS" block. We do know that B (beef) must be next to either P (pork) or T (trout), so we drew two blocks, remembering to put the word "or" in between to show that it can be either of these two options. Note the double arrow again, indicating that it could either be "BT" or "TB" if T is next to B, or "BP" or "PB" if P is next to B. The good thing here is that B *must* be next to one or the other of these elements.

> The manicotti cannot be served the night before or the night after the veal is served.

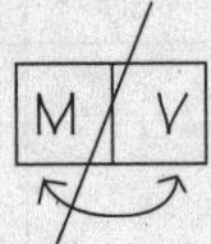

As you can see, this clue is telling us what we *can't* have. Here, we can't have the M (manicotti) next to the V (veal). So we drew another block, again with the double arrow underneath, and then we drew a slash through the block itself to indicate that this can never be true. We've just drawn our first *antiblock clue.*

The veal must be served on Monday.

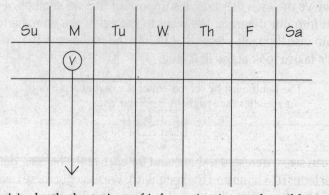

Su	M	Tu	W	Th	F	Sa
	(V)					

Not surprisingly, the best piece of information is saved until last. As you can see, this piece of information is so definitive that we were able to put it directly into the diagram. Whenever you have a clue that expresses a concrete relationship between an element and the diagram, go ahead and put it directly into the diagram. It will save time and your diagram will be better for it. Additionally, we circled the letter and ran an arrow down the appropriate column to show that veal will *always* be served on Monday, and nothing else will ever be.

As we mentioned, this is the time to compare your symbols to the clues and make sure nothing got mixed up in the translation from verbal to visual. This seems like a waste of time until the first time you skip it or forget and end up spending a long, frustrating time fighting with answers because you symbolized a clue incorrectly or left it out entirely.

Step 3: Look for links and size up the game

Now, let's take a look at the clues we've drawn to see what kinds of deductions we might make. The first thing we notice, perhaps, is that V is fixed on Monday. What else do we know about V? That M cannot be next to it. Therefore, we know that M cannot be Sunday or Tuesday because V is always on Monday. Look at the diagram below to see how we indicated this.

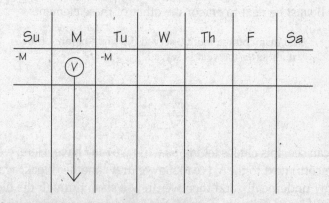

Su	M	Tu	W	Th	F	Sa
-M		-M				
	(V)					

Now, what is our next most definitive piece of information? It is the fact that L and S must always be next to each other. This is good information because there is one place that neither L nor S can go since they must be next to each other—that place is Sunday. Why? Because there's no consecutive space next to Sunday for the second letter in this block to go in—V is in Monday. Therefore, *neither* L nor S can go in Sunday.

Next, let's go to our B block. We know that one other entree (either P or T) must go next to B. Therefore, B needs a space next to it just like L and S do. Thus, B can't go in Sunday either, for the same reason that L and S can't. Now let's look at the work we did on the next page.

Su	M	Tu	W	Th	F	Sa
-M -L -S -B	(V) ↓	-M				

It looks as if Sunday is a very restricted day, right? Four of our seven letters can't go there. If you count V also (which you should), it's actually five out of seven letters that can't go in Sunday. So what can go in Sunday? Only P or T. Let's add that information to our diagram:

Pay close attention to slots that are very restricted.

Su	M	Tu	W	Th	F	Sa
-M -L -S -B P/T	(V) ↓	-M				

Clearly, we've done some good work with the left side of our diagram. We looked at each of the clues against the diagram itself, and came up with some solid restrictions to indicate on our diagram. We know that both blocks will need to go to the right of Monday. That leaves one more space to be filled after we place the blocks, which will have to be occupied by M (manicotti). Having both blocks—each with two elements—fit in five spaces leaves us with only a few possibilities. It turns out that M can be put only on one of the ends or right in the middle. So you can't place M on either Wednesday or Friday. Try it, and you'll see why.

So here's your final set of deductions:

Su	M	Tu	W	Th	F	Sa
-M -L -S -B P/T	(V)	-M	-M		-M	

We know that this might be the toughest concept we've thrown at you so far. Below is an illustration of what the possibilities are when you've got two blocks of two spaces each that need to go into a total of only five consecutive slots. Take a look at what happens:

1	2	3	4	5

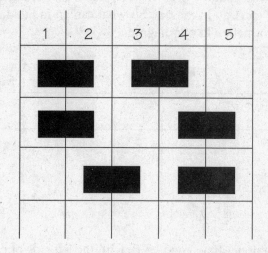

As you can see, the second and fourth spaces are always going to be needed for one half of one of the blocks. In our diagram, we're playing with five spaces—Tuesday, Wednesday, Thursday, Friday, and Saturday. Therefore, M cannot go in either the second (Wednesday) or the fourth (Friday) space because we have two blocks that we must place in those five spaces. Make sense? M is one of the most restricted elements left, so, if we can place M—which can now only go on Thursday or Saturday—we'll know exactly where our blocks can and can't go!

At this point, we've come up with all the deductions we can and have a pretty good sense of the way this game is going to work. Things will hinge on the most restricted places (like Sunday), and the placement of restricted elements (like M and the two blocks). All the information that we've put in the diagram so far will be true for the whole game, so we'll draw a line under it to separate it off and remind ourselves to pay attention to those limitations as we work each new question. We'll call this row of restrictions that apply to the whole game our *clue shelf* and keep it separate from the other information we fill in as we work the questions so we can easily refer to the conditions that are always true.

Steps 4 and 5: Evaluate the question task and apply the strategy

There are basically three types of questions that you will encounter on games. Our favorite kind—the kind you'll want to search out and do first—we'll call "if" questions. You'll be able to identify them because they start with the word *if* and ask you to find the answer choice that *must be true, must be false, could be true*, or *could be false*. They will also give you an extra piece of information that will further limit the possibilities on your diagram—for that question only, of course. The more concrete the information given by an "if" question, the easier the question will be to do.

Hunt down and do all the specific questions that have straightforward tasks FIRST.

Next come the "which" questions. Not surprisingly, these begin with the word *which* and differ from "if" questions in that they don't give you any extra limiting information. That's why we don't answer them first. If you save these more general questions until after you've done the "if" questions, you'll find that you will be able to eliminate many answer choices simply by referring back to the work that you've already done on "if" questions. How's that for efficiency?

Finally, there are the aptly named "complex" questions. Sometimes these will start with the word *suppose* and an established condition will be removed or, rarely, a new condition will be added. Talk about time consuming! Other times they will start with either *if* or *which* but will have a complicated task like figuring out which of the answer choices, if it were true, would completely determine the outcome of the game. Ugh. You'll see later why they're last, if it's not clear already.

Step 6: Use Process of Elimination

Because there are between five and seven questions for each game, Steps 4 through 6 will go hand in hand for each until it's time to move on to the next game.

You'll find that POE on games is sometimes quite straightforward and other times a more murky business, but the goal is always the same: Get to the credited response by eliminating answer choices that have a flaw. When you have a question for which the answer seems clear before you even go to the answer choices, the credited response will jump right off the page at you. With other questions, you'll find you need to check each answer choice carefully and perhaps even use work from other questions to help you eliminate. And with some particularly unwieldy questions, you may find that you need to put each answer choice through the wringer by actually working it out in the diagram. We call these time-consuming chores "plug and chug" questions.

For now, just be conscious of using POE on each answer choice, and you'll learn to recognize the various types as you practice more. The bottom line: POE works *every* time, but it should also be your last resort on most questions.

Let's answer the "if" questions in this game and see how we do.

2. If lamb is served on Saturday, which one of the following must be true?

   (A) The spaghetti is served on Thursday.
   (B) The beef is served on Tuesday.
   (C) The manicotti is served on Thursday.
   (D) The pork is served on Wednesday.
   (E) The trout is served on Sunday.

Here's How to Crack It

First, include the extra information from this question into a row of your diagram. Next, determine what other restrictions will allow you to fill in more information by looking for any overlap with your clues. Continue to include conditions that you know must happen or can't happen until you can't fill in any more information. If you find yourself in a situation where slots have been limited to only two options, it's worth filling them in. If there are more than two options, don't bother or it will get messy fast. Let's see what happens on the following page.

Su	M	Tu	W	Th	F	Sa	
-M -L -S -B P/T	(V)	-M	-M		-M		
				M	S	L	(2)

As you can see, putting L into the Saturday slot forces the S into the Friday slot because they need to be together. And because M can only go on Saturday or Thursday, we know that M is now in the Thursday slot. L in Saturday, S in Friday, and M in Thursday: These three things MUST be true. We don't know for sure where B, P, or T are, so we won't try to write down all the possible options for them. Remember that our task is to find the answer choice that *must be true,* so odds are we won't need to know anything about elements that we can't place concretely anyway. We'll just head to the answer choices and see if we can find an answer. We can—it's answer choice (C). Because we were able to fill in a fair amount of information and the question was asking for something that *must be true,* this was a pretty straightforward job of POE.

On to our next "if" question:

3. If the trout is served on Thursday, the pork must be served on
   (A) Sunday
   (B) Tuesday
   (C) Wednesday
   (D) Friday
   (E) Saturday

Here's How to Crack It

Fill in all the information you can BEFORE looking at the answer choices.

Wait! Don't erase the information from the last question. You won't need it for another "if" question, but remember, the work you do for the "if" questions will help you with POE when you get to the more general questions. Just leave that information for now, draw a line, and start another row of information. It's useful to write the number of the question next to the row that you're working on in case you need to come back to it later for some reason.

We have another "if" question, which will give us a new set of possibilities for entree orders, so we'll fill in new information for this question first and then look for any other ramifications until we've gotten all the concrete information written down on the next page.

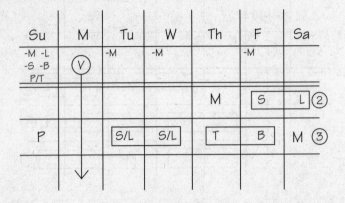

Su	M	Tu	W	Th	F	Sa	
-M -L -S -B P/T	(V)	-M	-M		-M		
				M	S	L	(2)
P		S/L	S/L	T	B	M	(3)

This question tells us to put T into Thursday. This forces M into Saturday. Putting T into Thursday also forces P into Sunday, because Sunday can be only P or T. Finally, there are only three spaces left, and only two (Tuesday and Wednesday) are consecutive. Thus, the S/L block must go into Tuesday and Wednesday. Notice that we couldn't be sure of their order, but there were only two possibilities, so it was worth writing down what we knew. We indicated the possibility with a slash. Now, we've only got B left, and the only place it can go is Friday. What's the question again? P must be where? Sunday, of course. (A) is our answer.

You might be wondering why we kept filling in information after we knew that P had to go to the Sunday slot. After all, that answered the question. Keep in mind that the information we generate here can help us with POE on later questions, and because we're in the groove, it's worth taking a few extra seconds to finish the sequence of events triggered when we started the question.

We'll skip number 4 and move on to our final "if " question:

5. If beef is served on Saturday, which one of the following must be true?

   (A) The trout is served on Friday.
   (B) The pork is served on Thursday.
   (C) The spaghetti is served on Wednesday.
   (D) The lamb is served on Tuesday.
   (E) The manicotti is served on Thursday.

Here's How to Crack It

Use the same process. Fill in the information the question gives you plus any other concrete information that you can. Here's what we've got:

Su	M	Tu	W	Th	F	Sa	
-M -L -S -B P/T	(V)	-M	-M		-M		
				M	S	L	(2)
P		S/L	S/L	T	B	M	(3)
P/T	↓	S/L	S/L	M	P/T	B	(5)

So we're told B is in Saturday. That only leaves Thursday for M, and P or T must be in the Friday slot next to B. This once again pushes the S/L block into Tuesday and Wednesday. That's all we can fill in so we'll head to the answers. We can eliminate any that *could be false*. Let's see how it works:

Choice (A) could be false because P could be in Friday. Cross it off.
Choice (B) *must* be false according to our diagram. Cross it off.
Choice (C) could be false because L could also be in Wednesday. Cross it off.
Choice (D) could be false because S could also be in Tuesday. Cross it off.
Choice (E) must be true from our diagram. Keep it.

It's much easier to get through the answer choices once you have that diagram filled in, isn't it? The investment was worth it.

We've got only two questions left now. Both of them begin with the word *which,* indicating that the questions will be general in nature. Typically, this means that you won't be able to fill in any information in your diagram prior to evaluating the answer choices. Just head to the answers and start POE.

Take a look at the following question:

1. Which one of the following is a possible menu in order from Sunday to Saturday?

    (A) pork, veal, trout, lamb, beef, spaghetti, manicotti
    (B) trout, veal, manicotti, beef, lamb, spaghetti, pork
    (C) spaghetti, veal, lamb, trout, manicotti, beef, pork
    (D) trout, veal, beef, pork, manicotti, lamb, spaghetti
    (E) manicotti, veal, beef, trout, lamb, spaghetti, pork

Here's How to Crack It

This is a special kind of "which" question. It's called a grab-a-rule question because all you have to do is apply each rule—or clue—to the answer choices and eliminate any choice that violates the rule. These tend to be straightforward, quick questions that will give you valuable insight into how a game works (if you missed anything during the deductions step).

Grab-a-rule questions: Apply each clue to each answer choice, starting with the most concrete and restrictive.

You should do grab-a-rule questions first. They sound almost too good to be true, and, as is so often the case, there's a catch: Not all games have one. But if they do, it's the first question and you should work on it right away. A hint: If you start with the most restrictive clues, you'll eliminate most efficiently. Let's go to it. We'll start with this clue:

> The veal must be served on Monday.

Drat! That doesn't get rid of any. We'll just look at the next most restrictive piece of information.

We found out from our deductions that Sunday has to have either P or T. That eliminates answer choices (C) and (E).

We also deduced that M has to be in either Thursday or Saturday. That eliminates answer choice (B).

Back to the clues from our diagram:

> The lamb must be served either the night before or the night after the spaghetti is served.

That eliminates answer choice (A).

Voila! We've crossed off four choices, so (D) is left and that's our answer.

Note: Your process here is to take the clues and apply them to the choices, *not* the other way around. Taking each choice and applying it to each of the clues is very cumbersome. It will take more time and could lead to careless errors. Trust us.

Here's our last "which" question. Go to it:

4. Which one of the following is a night on which the manicotti could be served?

   (A) Sunday
   (B) Tuesday
   (C) Wednesday
   (D) Friday
   (E) Saturday

Here's How to Crack It

Well, we deduced that M can only go in one of two places—Thursday or Saturday. Even if we hadn't come up with that deduction, we could check back to our previous work and see where M has been placed throughout the game—we'd see that Thursday and Saturday were the only possible answers. Only Saturday is listed in the choices, so (E) is our answer.

So, what did we just do? Once again, here's the step-by-step approach to all games:

Step 1:	Diagram and inventory
Step 2:	Symbolize the clues and double-check
Step 3:	Look for links and size up the game
Step 4:	Evaluate the question task
Step 5:	Apply the strategy
Step 6:	Use Process of Elimination

Games Technique: Use Good Symbolization

Good symbolization is a major step toward getting all the questions in a particular game correct. Success with symbolization comes from familiarity and practice. There are a number of common types of clues that you'll see repeatedly on the LSAT; once you become familiar with them, most of the process becomes mechanical. While you're practicing your symbolization, keep in mind the three C's: *clear*, *concise*, and *consistent*.

Clear: You want your symbols to make quick and apparent sense. If you find yourself having to interpret a clue as you use it in the game, it's not working.

Concise: Your symbols should be terse and to the point. Part of the reason for having them is to eliminate the wasted energy of reading those long-winded, confusing clues each time you refer to them in working the questions.

Consistent: As we mentioned above, you should start to recognize distinct types of LSAT clues that you'll symbolize in the same manner each time they show up in a game. But you should also be sure that your clues are consistent with one another within a game and that they are consistent with the way that you drew your diagram. They should all fit together.

Go ahead and symbolize the clues listed on the next page. First take a sheet of scratch paper and cover up the rest of the page. Move it down as you work, keeping the material covered until you get to it. Now symbolize each clue in the margin next to where it is written out on the page. Then compare your symbol with the symbol we have. We'll explain how we got to ours, and why you should be symbolizing in much the same way.

Anna sits to the east of Bob and to the west of Carol.

This is a very common type of clue. It's testing your ability to read carefully and to recognize the fact that you are being given two separate pieces of information: the relationship between A and B and the relationship between A and C. It is possible to consolidate these pieces of information into one symbol, but be careful! Make sure you are consistent throughout the game about which way is east and which way is west—under time pressure, these basic pieces of knowledge can get twisted around.

B – A – C

As you can see, we've put A in between B and C. "To the east" here means to the right, so the first thing we did was to put A to the right of B. Then, we read that Anna sits "to the west," or to the left, of Carol, so we can place A to the left of C. We didn't put this in a box because we don't know whether these people are sitting right next to one another—all we know is "to the right" and "to the left." Therefore we used a line to show that there might be one or more elements in between them or that they could end up right next to one another. We'll call these *range* clues because they tell us only the range of places that one element can occupy in relation to another element. You can think of the line as a rubber band; sometimes the elements will be pulled apart from one another and one or more other elements will be placed in between them, and other times they will pull right up next to one another.

Because we were able to link these two range clues into one larger clue, we actually know more than if we had symbolized them separately. For instance, we know that A must always be placed in between the other two elements. And we know that B must always have *at least* two other elements to its right. Whenever you have the chance to link two or more range clues together, do so.

The two philosophers never sit together.

This is very similar to a clue we had in the menu-planning game we just did. Remember the M/V antiblock? It didn't give us information about how two elements *must be* positioned with relation to each other, but rather how they *cannot be*. Here we know that there are two P's and that these two P's can never be together. It's another basic antiblock:

P/P

If the game ever gives us the placement of one of the philosophers, we know now that the other philosopher can't go immediately to the right or left of the first one. We also know that there are only two philosophers from the concrete language used in the clue. If we weren't sure how many philosphers there were in the game, we would want to be sure to note that fact in addition to our antiblock clue.

In a five-story building, J lives two floors above W.

This type of clue would be symbolized best by inserting it directly into the diagram. So for our example, we're going to draw a rough little diagram similar to what you would have already constructed had you come across this clue in an actual game.

5
4
3
2
1

We've made this diagram vertical because that makes the most sense visually. Now let's symbolize the fact that J lives two floors above W. But be careful here—if you live two floors above your friend, for instance, there is only *one* floor that actually separates you. Take a look at our symbol:

J
W

Reread each clue to see if your visual matches the exact text of the clue.

As you can see, the wording is meant to lead you astray. If you weren't vigilant and had inserted an extra floor, your game would have swiftly degenerated into confusion. Also, notice the fact that our symbol was consistent with the diagram—we used a vertical diagram, so we need a vertical symbol.

The three boys are flanked by two girls.

This clue gives you several pieces of information. First, there are exactly three boys. Second, there are at least two girls. Third, the three boys all sit together. Fourth, one girl sits on either end of the line of boys. Let's put it all together:

G B B B G

Notice that we didn't just write "3B" and "2G." Instead, we wrote three separate B's and two separate G's. That's consistent with the information the clue gives. If the clue involves five engines, for instance, draw "EEEEE" and not "5E." The former is much more visual, which is your goal. And if later you are given further characteristics about the boys and girls, such as what color hats they might be wearing, you will be able to note these characteristics as subscripts.

Hannah will not attend the dance unless David attends the dance.

Here, we have another instance of a conditional statement. Remember this from Arguments? This conditional statement doesn't have the words *if* and *then* as cues for us, but take note that the word *unless* is another cue for a conditional statement. And because it's a conditional statement, we can draw the contrapositive. Before we can flip and negate, however, we need to put the original into the same form that we used before. There's a very simple rule for how to accomplish this. Replace the word *unless* with the words *if not* and start your statement there. So for our example above, we would get the following:

If not David attends the dance, Hannah will not attend the dance.

Granted, this is a bit awkward to say, but we're just going to be using it to generate a conditional statement, and for that purpose it will work just fine. Here's what we get when we symbolize:

$$-D \rightarrow -H$$

Look familiar? Good. Now to get the contrapositive, all we have to do is flip and negate.

$$H \rightarrow D$$

So we have a nice, mechanical way to generate both the conditional statement and its contrapositive. Remember the rule, and you're all set. If you're more familiar with symbolic logic, you might be able to get to the symbols without having to use our rule, but you should still learn it. What seems like a simple task right now might feel entirely different on the day of the test. Leave nothing to chance. Here's the rule once more so you won't forget:

Replace the word unless *with the words* if not *and start your statement there.*

Make a flash card if you'd like. Just make sure you know the process for the LSAT.

A, B, and C are saxophonists; D, E, and F are percussionists.

In this case, we are given elements that fall into two categories: saxophonists and percussionists. We'll want to have a way to keep these straight as we work the game. Probably the simplest way to accomplish this is by symbolizing one group with uppercase letters and the other with lowercase letters. We'll end up with:

S: A B C
p: d e f

There are games that have more than two types of elements, or elements that can have more than one characteristic associated with them. In these cases, you'll want to use subscripts to distinguish the elements. For instance, if we had those same saxophonists and percussionists, but we were also told that A and f were leads and C and e were backups, we would need some way to keep all of this straight. Furthermore, we might have to assign these elements to either the marching band or the orchestra, the two groups available in the game. We would need to make sure that we could tell what characteristics each element had so that we could assign them accordingly. Here's how we would symbolize:

S: A_L B C_B
p: d e_B f_L

You'll have to be sure to keep things neat, but now you'll be able to work with the elements effectively.

There is at least one fire drill per week.

How would you do this one? This doesn't give us very concrete information because we still don't know exactly how many fire drills there will be each week. But it is an important piece of information because we know for sure that we have to include a fire drill in each valid arrangement for the game. It's a pretty simple piece of information, so our symbol will also be pretty simple. Don't succumb to the urge to just keep it in your head; yes, it's simple, but no, that doesn't give you license to skip the visualization. Here's a good way to symbolize it:

$$F^{1+}$$

We used the plus sign to indicate *at least*, which will remind us that we can have more than one of these, according to the rules. A corollary clue type is one that tells you that an element will be used *at most* a certain number of times; in that case we would use a minus sign as the superscript.

Here's a summary chart of how we symbolized each clue:

CLUE	SYMBOL
Anna sits to the east of Bob and to the west of Carol.	B — A — C
The two philosophers never sit together.	[P/P]
In a five-story building, J lives two floors above W.	[J] [ ] [W] (stacked boxes)
The three boys are flanked by two girls.	[GBBBG]
Hannah will not attend the dance unless David attends the dance.	–D → –H
[Contrapositive]	H → D
A, B, and C are saxophonists; D, E, and F are percussionists.	S: A B C p: d e f
There is at least one fire drill per week.	F^{1+}

Games Technique: Know When Not to Symbolize

Ideally, you will symbolize every clue. Some clues, however, have no clear and concise visual equivalent, especially negative clues that do not refer to any specific element. For example, consider the following clues:

> No more than three books of any given subject are put on the shelf.
>
> Players cannot score more than three points in the first round.

A visualization of these would end up being obtuse and potentially confusing. So we need another method. Remember that we want to keep all the information in one place and not have to refer to the written information provided. Just jot down the essence of the clue in a few words among the rest of your clues. That way you can't forget about it and you won't have to wade through the original, confusing clue. Now let's try another game.

If you can't think of a quick and simple way to symbolize a clue, just jot down the essence of it and move on.

GAME #2: TENANTS AND APARTMENTS

You will be able to use a grid diagram with many types of games. However, at times you'll manage two or more sets of elements within this grid diagram. Not to worry—it's very approachable. Take time now to master the process. You can worry about pacing later as you work through the games from the back of this book as well as from the real LSATs you'll take for practice.

> Eight tenants—J, K, L, M, N, O, P, and Q—live in a five-story building. On each floor, there is one studio apartment and one one-bedroom apartment. From the ground floor up, the floors are numbered one through five. The following is known about the tenants' living arrangements:
>
> No tenant shares an apartment with any other tenant.
> No one lives in the fifth-floor studio.
> No one lives in the third-floor one-bedroom.
> M lives in the second-floor studio.
> P lives in the fourth-floor studio.
> M and O each live on a higher floor than Q.
> K, N, and Q live in one-bedroom apartments.

1. If K lives on a lower floor than P, then who must live in the second-floor one-bedroom?

   (A) J
   (B) K
   (C) L
   (D) N
   (E) Q

2. What is the maximum number of tenants any one of whom could be the one who lives in the fifth-floor one-bedroom?

(A) 1
(B) 2
(C) 3
(D) 4
(E) 5

3. If J lives on a lower floor than L, then which of the following statements must be false?

(A) J lives in the second-floor one-bedroom.
(B) K lives in the fourth-floor one-bedroom.
(C) L lives in the third-floor studio.
(D) N lives in the fourth-floor one-bedroom.
(E) O lives in the fifth-floor one-bedroom.

4. If P lives on the floor above O, and O lives on the floor above N, then what is the maximum number of possible living arrangements for all eight tenants?

(A) 1
(B) 2
(C) 3
(D) 4
(E) 5

5. Suppose that M moves from the second-floor studio into the second-floor one-bedroom, but all the other conditions remain the same. Which of the following statements could be false?

(A) J lives on a floor below K.
(B) K lives on a floor below N.
(C) L lives on a floor below K.
(D) O lives on a floor below N.
(E) O lives on a floor below K.

Cracking Game #2

Step 1: Diagram and inventory

This looks a bit more complex than what we've seen so far. Notice here that there are more spaces (10) than elements (8). However, the clues tell us that there are two unoccupied spaces, so we will end up using all of our elements, without repeating any of them; we have another one-to-one ratio of elements to slots. In this game we have two types of apartments: studios and one-bedrooms. Here's how we drew our diagram:

	S	1B	S	1B	S	1B
5						
4						
3						
2						
1						

We have another grid here—now it's just two columns for each question.

First, we drew a vertical grid because it will mimic an apartment building. The clues include words such as *above* and *below* when referring to the relationship between the elements, so a vertical diagram will keep us organized. Second, notice the fact that we really had to make two columns in the diagram for each arrangement—a studio apartment column and a one-bedroom column. We indicated the difference between the columns by making dashed lines. We used solid lines to separate the work we do for each new question. Now let's look at the clues.

Step 2: Symbolize the clues and double-check

The first clue tells us that we'll put one element in each slot. We can jot down a note like "one per slot." The next four clues are all things we can put directly into our diagram. Here they are:

> No one lives in the fifth-floor studio.
> No one lives in the third-floor one-bedroom.
> M lives in the second-floor studio.
> P lives in the fourth-floor studio.

We'll get to these clues in a minute. The fifth clue is this:

M and O each live on a higher floor than Q.

This clue is giving us two pieces of information, that both M and O live on a higher floor than Q. Here are our symbols for this clue:

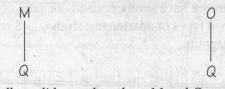

As you can see, all we did was show how M and O are both "above" Q. We used a line because we don't know how far above Q each one is. This is another range clue. Here's the sixth and final clue:

K, N, and Q live in one-bedroom apartments.

Now we know that K, N, and Q all have to be in the one-bedroom column. We made a quick notation of that:

K,N,Q = 1B

However, we'll probably wind up integrating this information directly into the diagram before we go to the questions. Now, here are the first four clues again—and then our diagram that shows how we added the information.

No one lives in the fifth-floor studio.
No one lives in the third-floor one-bedroom.
M lives in the second-floor studio.
P lives in the fourth-floor studio.

	S	1B	S	1B	S	1B	S	1B
5	X							
4	P							
3		X						
2	M							
1								

So we've put Xs through the two empty apartments and then put the P and the M directly into the diagram. Now, once we double-check, then we're ready for Step 3.

Step 3: Look for links and size up the game
As for deductions, if M lives on the second floor and must live above Q, then Q must live on the first floor. Because Q must live in a one-bedroom, Q lives in the first-floor one-bedroom. That's our first major deduction. There are several more deductions that we can make. Take a look at the diagram to see how many other deductions we were able to make. Remember also that we wanted to indicate that K, N, and Q all had to be in one-bedrooms, but because we have no way of knowing which one each will be in, we'll note the places where they *cannot* be. Here is our diagram:

	S	1B	S	1B	S	1B	S	1B
5	X							
4	P							
3	-N -K	X						
2	M							
1	-O -N -K J/L	Q						

There are only two studios that remain open. Both are limited because neither N nor K can go in them. Furthermore, O cannot go in the first-floor studio, because O must be higher than Q. Therefore, the first-floor studio is an extremely limited space, and the only remaining elements that can go in it are J or L. Because there are only two elements that can occupy the space, it's worth writing this in our diagram. If we step back and evaluate things before diving right into the questions, we'll notice that the studios are much more restricted than are the one-bedrooms. Keep this in mind as you work.

Steps 4 and 5: Evaluate the question task and apply the strategy
Remember, go for the "if" questions first and leave the "which" and other general questions for later.

Step 6: Use Process of Elimination
Here's our first "if" question.

1. If K lives on a lower floor than P, then who must live in the second-floor one-bedroom?

   (A) J
   (B) K
   (C) L
   (D) N
   (E) Q

Here's How to Crack It

This question provides us with new information about the relationship between K and P. It tells us that K must live on a lower floor than P, and there is only one open slot below P for K to fill. So take a look at our diagram:

	S	1B	S (1)	1B	S	1B	S	1B
5	X		X					
4	P		P					
3	-N -K	X		X				
2	M		M	K				
1	-O -N -K J/L	Q	J/L	Q				

That's right! K is forced into the second-floor one-bedroom, and hence it's our answer. Circle (B). Let's work on the next "if" question:

3. If J lives on a lower floor than L, then which of the following statements must be false?
   (A) J lives in the second-floor one-bedroom.
   (B) K lives in the fourth-floor one-bedroom.
   (C) L lives in the third-floor studio.
   (D) N lives in the fourth-floor one-bedroom.
   (E) O lives in the fifth-floor one-bedroom.

Here's How to Crack It

Well, this settles the question about who will occupy the first-floor studio, doesn't it? If J is lower than L, that means that J must live in the first-floor studio and L must be somewhere above the first floor. Take a look at our diagram:

	S	1B	S (1)	1B	S (3)	1B	S	1B
5	X		X		X			
4	P		P		P			
3	-N -K	X		X	-N -K	X		
2	M		M	K	M			
1	-O -N -K J/L	Q	J/L	Q	J	Q		

Our task is to find the statement that must be false. So we'll head to the answer choices and cross out any choices that can be true. You do this by reading each choice and looking at your diagram. So let's do that. (A) cannot be true because we've already definitively placed J on the first floor. So it's our answer. (B), (C), (D), and (E) can all be true because those spaces are still open on the diagram. Let's move on.

4. If P lives on the floor above O, and O lives on the floor above N, then what is the maximum number of possible living arrangements for all eight tenants?

   (A) 1
   (B) 2
   (C) 3
   (D) 4
   (E) 5

Here's How to Crack It

This question contains two very good pieces of information. Let's put the information in first and then talk about exactly what our task is.

			①		③		④	
	S	1B	S	1B	S	1B	S	1B
5	X		X		X		X	
4	P		P		P		P	
3	-N -K	X		X	-N -K	X	O	X
2	M		M	K	M		M	N
1	-o -n -K J/L	Q	J/L	Q	J	Q	J/L	Q

Keep everything neat so you can refer back to your previous work accurately and efficiently.

Good, we were able to definitively place two other elements. However, the question asks us about how many different ways the full diagram can look. The manner in which the question is phrased ("the maximum number of possible living arrangements for all eight tenants") might be confusing. If so, translate it to say something like, "How many different ways can we make the diagram work?" Then, write out the possibilities in your diagram. The only open spaces are the first-floor studio, the fourth-floor one-bedroom, and the fifth-floor one-bedroom. Additionally, the first-floor studio can only be one of two possible elements—J or L. So break it down as we do on the following page.

WHEN *J* IS IN 1S:

1S	41B	51B
J	K	L

OR

1S	41B	51B
J	L	K

WHEN *L* IS IN 1S:

1S	41B	51B
L	J	K

OR

1S	41B	51B
L	K	J

So we've got two possibilities for each of the two scenarios—when J is in the first-floor studio, and when L is in the first-floor studio. Hence, a total of four possibilities, so the answer is (D). Let's move on.

The final two questions in this game are "complex" questions. Let's leave the one that changes the rules for the end.

2. What is the maximum number of tenants any one of whom could be the one who lives in the fifth-floor one-bedroom?

(A) 1
(B) 2
(C) 3
(D) 4
(E) 5

Here's How to Crack It

This is an overly complex way of asking how many different people can be in the fifth-floor one-bedroom. You know it can't be P, M, or Q. Now check your previous work and see who we've placed there before: On question 4, we put K, J, and L there. This leaves us with O and N. Can we put them there without breaking any rules? Try, and you'll find you can. So the correct answer is (E).

Now let's knock out the last question, the "suppose" question. You can use your original diagram for this question, but you must review all the clues before you can start filling anything in. The addition of new rules can alter deductions and/or add new ones.

5. Suppose that M moves from the second-floor studio into the second-floor one-bedroom, but all the other conditions remain the same. Which of the following statements could be false?

(A) J lives on a floor below K.
(B) K lives on a floor below N.
(C) L lives on a floor below K.
(D) O lives on a floor below N.
(E) O lives on a floor below K.

Here's How to Crack It

Well, we have to shift M over to the second-floor one-bedroom. Do that, and then make sure that this doesn't screw up any of your original deductions. Does it?

			①		③		④		⑤	
	S	1B	S	1B	S	1B	S	1B	S	1B
5	X		X		X		X		X	K/N
4	P		P		P		P		P	K/N
3	-N -K	X		X	-N -K	X	O	X		X
2	M		M	K	M		M	N		M
1	-O -N -K J/L	Q	J/L	Q	J	Q	J/L	Q	J/L	Q

Fortunately, it doesn't. In fact, it further limits the diagram (as we've indicated) because now K and N have only two places to go. So now let's approach the answer choices, and we'll do that by eliminating anything that must be true to isolate the one that could be false. (A) must be true because K, N, P, and an empty apartment take up the entire fourth and fifth floors. Cross it out. (B) does not have to be true—K could also live above N. Therefore, it "could be false" and it's our answer. (C), (D), and (E) all must be true, if you feel like checking. That's another game under our belts.

GAMES TECHNIQUE: MAKING DEDUCTIONS

Two ways to make deductions: Learn and practice them.

We've worked through two games now, and hopefully you recognize how important it is to make deductions before starting to work through the questions. Think of them as unwritten clues. You can't make good deductions by glancing briefly at your diagram and clues, while hurrying to get to the questions. You have to look carefully at the diagram and your symbolizations. Some people think that making deductions is the result of some kind of epiphany, that you either see them or you don't. Actually, finding deductions is the result of a purely mechanical process. Once you understand the process and have had some time to practice it on a number of different games, you'll be able to ferret out those critical extra pieces of information that will save you valuable time down the road. Here's an overview of the process.

- First, take each symbol and apply it to the diagram. Write in any deductions. In the first game, for example, once we determined that the veal had to be served on Monday, we were able to determine that the manicotti could not be served Sunday or Tuesday because it could not be served on the day before or after the veal was served. This is how you should apply clues to a diagram and make deductions.

- Second, take each symbol and apply it to all the other symbols, looking for any overlapping elements. Combine them if it's appropriate, or write a new symbol for the deduction. Then check the diagram to see if your deduction points out any more restrictions in the diagram. For example, suppose we had a game in which we had to make two teams of four players each. Suppose we're told that A and B must be on the same team, and that B and C cannot be on the same team. Because A must always be with B, and B cannot be with C, we would then be able to deduce that A and C cannot be the same team. Combining clues with common elements often leads to deductions.
- Finally, take a step back and look at the entire diagram. Notice any spaces that are extremely "limited," meaning that they have lots of minuses in them. See if there are only one or two remaining choices for that space. Write in any deductions. Limited spaces may also lead to deductions, under other circumstances. For example, suppose you had a game in which you were dividing nine children into three groups for a boating trip. You are told that Alex and Carlos are in the same boat, and that Danielle and Eleanor are in the same boat. Because only three children can be in any given boat, our two blocks can never go together in a single boat, which would allow you to make several deductions (A cannot be with D or E, C cannot be with D or E).

These three steps should take you a couple of minutes once you get comfortable with the process. And although this process won't guarantee that you find *all* the deductions on *every* game, it is time well spent: you won't spend as much time on the questions, because you'll be able to eliminate answer choices more easily. In some cases, you'll still have some answer choices to work out, but the less you have to do, the better.

GAME #3: OFFICES AND FURNISHINGS

The first two games that we worked on used one of the most common diagrams found on the LSAT: a straight grid diagram with the core across the top or on one side to which we add rows or columns as we work the questions. But sometimes the setup will describe a spatial relationship that doesn't fit into that pattern. If that happens, just be flexible and use the information given to create a visual framework that matches the description in the setup. You'll still assign elements to places according to the rules; you'll just put them into a different structure. Remember to work on the limited space of the page—or if you're using scratch paper, mark off a quarter of a page to work on—so that you won't be in for an unpleasant surprise when you get to the real thing. We're still working on cementing the games process, so don't be concerned about time right now. Be methodical and refer to the earlier parts of the chapter as necessary. After you've finished, compare your results to ours.

There are exactly ten offices arranged on either side of a hallway. The offices with windows facing north are on one side of the hallway and are numbered 1, 2, 3, 4, and 5, respectively, from the west end of the building to the east. The offices with windows facing south are on the other side of the hallway and are numbered 6, 7, 8, 9, and 10, respectively, also from west to east. The offices on the north side are directly across from the offices on the south side, facing each other in the following pairs: 1 and 6; 2 and 7; 3 and 8; 4 and 9; 5 and 10. Each office has been furnished in exactly one of the following styles: Bauhaus, Moderne, or Pop, according to the following conditions:

None of the offices is furnished in the same style as the office that is located directly across the hallway from it.

None of the offices is furnished in the same style as any office adjacent to it.

Bauhaus furnishings are found in exactly one office on each side of the hallway.

Bauhaus furnishings are found in office number 3.

Moderne furnishings are found in office number 7.

1. Which one of the following could be an accurate list of the styles of furnishings found in offices 6, 7, 8, 9, and 10, respectively?

(A) Pop, Moderne, Pop, Moderne, Pop
(B) Pop, Moderne, Pop, Bauhaus, Moderne
(C) Bauhaus, Pop, Moderne, Pop, Moderne
(D) Bauhaus, Moderne, Pop, Moderne, Bauhaus
(E) Pop, Moderne, Bauhaus, Pop, Moderne

2. If Pop furnishings are found in exactly five of the offices along the hallway, then which one of the following statements must be true?

(A) Moderne furnishings are found in office 6.
(B) Moderne furnishings are found in office 4.
(C) Pop furnishings are found in office 5.
(D) Moderne furnishings are found in office 10.
(E) Bauhaus furnishings are found in office 9.

3. Which one of the following statements must be false?

(A) Pop furnishings are found in office 10.
(B) Pop furnishings are found in office 1.
(C) Moderne furnishings are found in office 9.
(D) Bauhaus furnishings are found in office 9.
(E) Bauhaus furnishings are found in office 10.

4. If office 4 is furnished in Pop, then each of the following statements could be false EXCEPT:

(A) Pop furnishings are found in office 10.
(B) Pop furnishings are found in office 6.
(C) Bauhaus furnishings are found in office 6.
(D) Moderne furnishings are found in office 5.
(E) Moderne furnishings are found in office 9.

5. Suppose that exactly two offices are furnished in Bauhaus, rather than just one, among the offices facing south and exactly one office is furnished in Bauhaus among the offices facing north. If all of the other conditions remain the same, then which one of the following statements must be true?

(A) Moderne furnishings are found in office 4.
(B) Moderne furnishings are found in office 10.
(C) Pop furnishings are found in office 1.
(D) Bauhaus furnishings are found in office 6.
(E) Bauhaus furnishings are found in office 9.

Cracking Game #3

Step 1: Diagram and inventory

Each of our first two games was arranged in a grid, one with one level of information and the other with two. Each had a one-to-one correspondence between elements and slots. With this game, things get a little bit more complicated. No worries, though. All we have to do is follow the process and we'll be able to approach it effectively. The setup tells us that this game has a particular spatial arrangement of the slots we'll assign elements to, but the process of assigning elements to spaces is still the same. So what will our diagram look like? Just take a cue from the setup and make it look the way it's described. We ended up with:

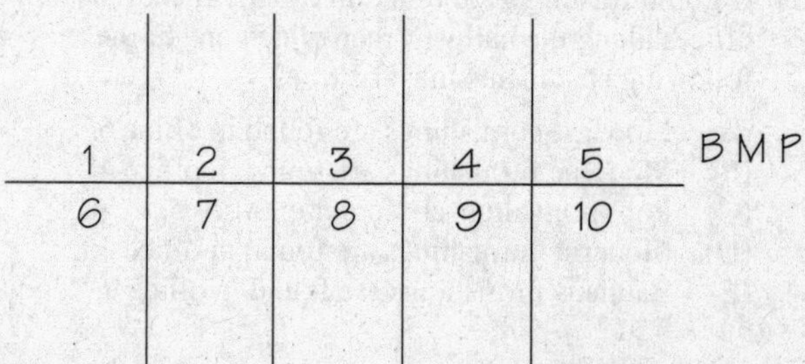

Don't forget to list the elements next to the diagram so that you'll have everything within easy reach. It's a pretty straightforward diagram. But it would be difficult to add rows in the way that we have with our previous games.

So instead, we'll use this as a template and then create another simple diagram—after all, it's only a few lines—to work each of the questions. We'll fill in the template with all of the concrete information that we have, effectively like a clue shelf. And then each of the new little diagrams that we create to work on the questions will just be a quick sketch that we can use as a framework to place our elements according to the restrictions of the question. And we still won't erase our previous work, for the same reason as before. If it's not clear, you'll see what we mean.

Notice that we only have three elements to be distributed among ten offices. That means that we'll have to repeat them. And based on how restrictive the clues are about the placement of elements of the same type in adjacent slots, we'll have to use all of the elements. Make a note of that.

Step 2: Symbolize the clues and double-check
Let's get right to it and make the restrictions visual.

> None of the offices is furnished in the same style as the office that is located directly across the hallway from it.

This tells us how elements *cannot* be arranged with respect to one another, so this is an antiblock clue, but it's broader than what we're used to. The antiblock clues we've seen so far have listed specific elements that can't be next to one another, but here it applies to all of the elements. No big deal. General clues—those that apply to all elements, all spaces, or even one entire type of element—are often the most powerful clues in a game. In this game, we only have three types of elements, so it would be easy enough to jot down the three possibilities as individual antiblocks. Because "facing" here is vertical, they would look like this:

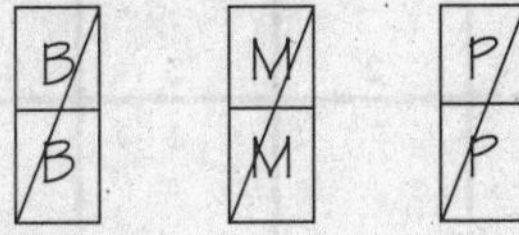

> None of the offices is furnished in the same style as any office adjacent to it.

We have another antiblock clue that applies to all of the elements. Adjacent means "right next to" so it's basically the same as our first clue, but horizontal. Like this:

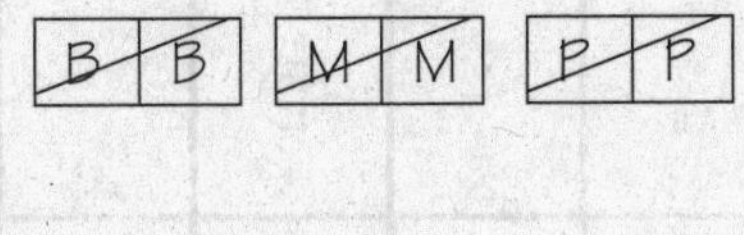

Bauhaus furnishings are found in exactly one office on each side of the hallway.

This is very specific about how many times we'll place B, but vague as to exactly where it will go within each row. So we'll jot down what we know. We'll use B exactly two times, so let's put two Bs down in our list of elements. And we'll make a note over to the side of our diagram to show that we must use B once in each row. We also know that we have eight slots to fill with M and P, so we'll have to use each more than once. Our symbol for "more than once" is a superscript 1+ next to each element in our list next to the diagram.

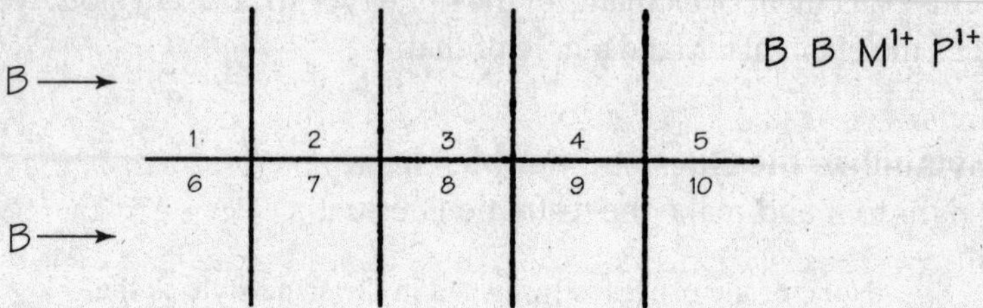

Bauhaus furnishings are found in office number 3.

Aha! More about B. This time we are able to definitively place one of the Bs, so we'll go ahead and put it right into our diagram. We'll circle it the same way we did the permanently placed element in the first game, so that we never forget to place it in the same space for each question we work through. Keep in mind that we only have one more B to use and it'll have to go in the other row.

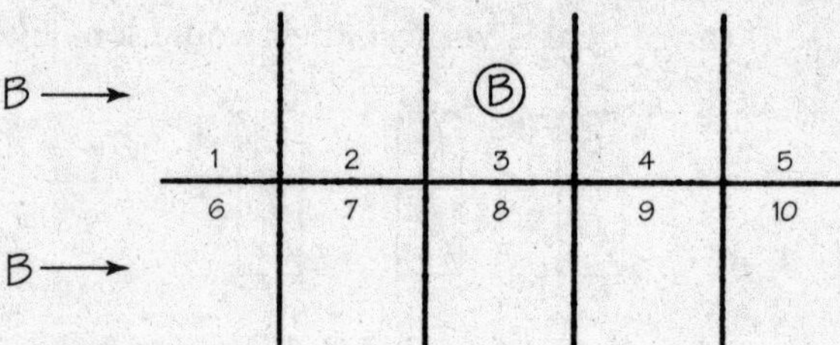

Moderne furnishings are found in office number 7.

Another wonderfully restrictive clue. We can go ahead and drop that right into the diagram as well.

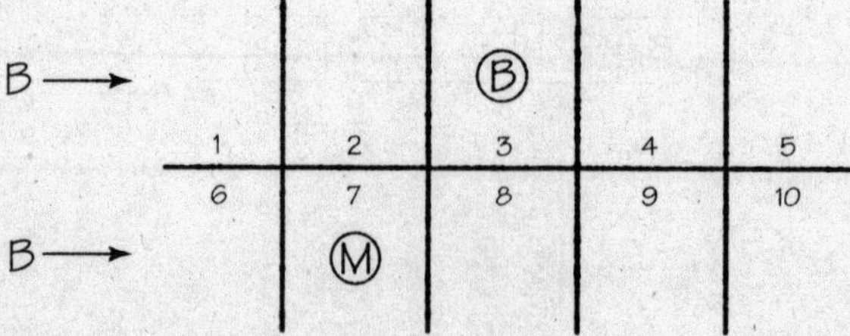

These are some pretty restrictive clues to work with. That should help to compensate for the fact that we don't have a one-to-one correspondence between elements and slots. Plus, we have only three possibilities (and in some cases fewer) for each space.

The final thing we need to do before going on to Step 3? That's right: double-check. This is especially important here because it seems we're going to be able to put together some additional information based on these fairly restrictive clues. If we don't catch any mistakes now, all our work from this point forward will be in vain.

Step 3: Look for links and size up the game

Can we come up with any deductions? Those restrictive clues should yield something because we have only three elements in any one slot. There isn't really much overlap between the clues, but we should note that two of the clues put limitations on the placement of B. Let's start by looking for any further limitations that result from having B in office 3. We know that we can't have another B across from or next to 3, so we can show that we can't have B in 8, 2, or 4.

	1	2	3	4	5
B →		−B	(B)	−B	
B →		(M)	−B		
	6	7	8	9	10

And we'll have similar results from the fact that M is placed in 7. That will eliminate the possibility of having another M in 2, 6, or 8.

	1	2	3	4	5
B →		−B −M	(B)	−B	
B →	−M	(M)	−B −M		
	6	7	8	9	10

We now have two slots that can have neither B nor M, leaving only one element to place in 2 and 8. Let's put P in both of those offices.

	1	2	3	4	5
B →		−B −M (P)	(B)	−B	
B →	−M	(M)	(P) −B −M		
	6	7	8	9	10

Placing P in 2 and 8 gives us further restrictions. After each new restriction, we can look for further impact. We can now eliminate the possibility of having P in either 1 or 9.

	1	2	3	4	5
	–P	–B –M		–B	
B ⟶		(P)	(B)		
B ⟶		(M)	(P)		
	–M		–B –M	–P	
	6	7	8	9	10

Which is the most restricted element in the top row? It's B because we can only use it once in each row. That means that we can eliminate the possibility of having another B in the top row.

	1	2	3	4	5
	–P –B	–B –M		–B	–B
B ⟶		(P)	(B)		
B ⟶		(M)	(P)		
	–M		–B –M	–P	
	6	7	8	9	10

And now that we've eliminated both P and B from being placed in office 1, the only element left to go there is M.

	1	2	3	4	5
	–P –B	–B –M		–B	–B
B ⟶	(M)	(P)	(B)		
B ⟶		(M)	(P)		
	–M		–B –M	–P	
	6	7	8	9	10

Is there anything else we know for sure? Notice that B is restricted from being in either 4 or 5, so that leaves only two elements (M or P) to go in each of those slots. And remember that we can't have the same elements in two adjacent slots. Because 4 and 5 can't be occupied by two Ms or by two Ps, we know that we'll have to have an M in one and a P in the other, right? We can't say for sure which element will be in which slot, but we can symbolize it in the same way we did before, using a slash between them.

	1	2	3	4	5
	−P −B	−B −M		−B	−B
B ⟶	(M)	(P)	(B)	M/P	P/M

	6	7	8	9	10
B ⟶		(M)	(P)		
	−M		−B −M	−P	

Anything else? Both slot 6 and slot 9 are limited to one of two elements, but we're not sure which one, and they won't have any concrete impact on each other. We've reached a point at which we can come up with a few speculative deductions. For instance, *if* B were in 6, we would know that we can't use any more Bs in the bottom row and so we'd place M in office 9. But that's a big if. Once you've gotten to the point where you can't write down any more concrete information, it's time to move on. You could spend all day running through the permutations, but that wouldn't be a good use of your limited time. The questions will give us more concrete information to work with, so let's get to them. We've got many restrictions already, so we should be able to do some efficient POE in answering the questions.

Steps 4 and 5: Evaluate the question task and apply the strategy
You know what to do—head straight for the "if" questions.

Step 6: Use Process of Elimination
Now it's time to let our investment in Step 3 pay off. Let's get right to it. Question 2 is our first "if" question:

2. If Pop furnishings are found in exactly five of the offices along the hallway, then which one of the following statements must be true?
   (A) Moderne furnishings are found in office 6.
   (B) Moderne furnishings are found in office 4.
   (C) Pop furnishings are found in office 5.
   (D) Moderne furnishings are found in office 10.
   (E) Bauhaus furnishings are found in office 9.

What's the first thing we do? Put any new information the question gives us into the diagram. Until now, we've been working in our original template. Now that we'll be filling in information that won't be true for the whole game, it's time to draw a simple diagram for each question. Just draw a basic outline and carry along the elements we placed from our template.

M	P	B	M/P	P/M
	M	P		

We'll redraw one of these for each question. We can start by filling in the new information we were given in question 2: P occupies five slots. How can we make that happen? Well, we can already see 3 Ps from our template—one in office 2, one in office 8, and one in either office 4 or 5. Where can we put the last two? We know that we can't have one in office 9, so that only leaves 6 and 10. Once we put a P in 10, we know that we can't have one in 5, so that pushes P into 4 and M into 5. Now we only have one open slot. We know we can't use P, so that leaves M or B. Can we tell which one it'll have to be? Remember that we have to use B twice, so we'll have to put B in office 9. That's it. Our diagram's all filled in. We should be able to eliminate pretty easily.

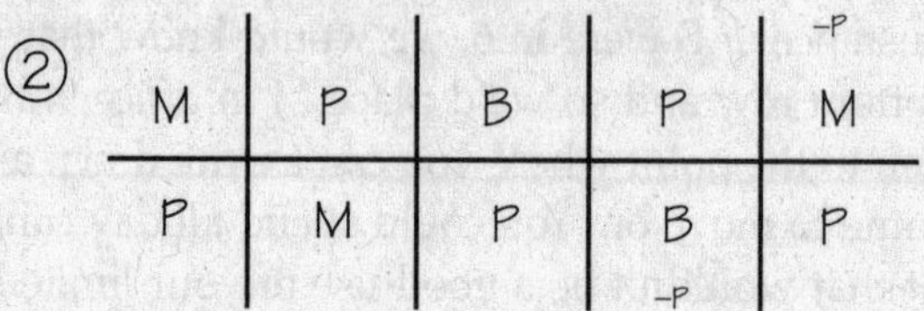

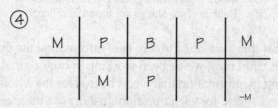

We're looking for the answer choice that *must be true*, so we'll cross off any answers that could be false, even once. That eliminates all but (E). Circle it, and move on. Our next "if" question is number 4.

4. If office 4 is furnished in Pop, then each of the following statements could be false EXCEPT:

(A) Pop furnishings are found in office 10.
(B) Pop furnishings are found in office 6.
(C) Bauhaus furnishings are found in office 6.
(D) Moderne furnishings are found in office 5.
(E) Moderne furnishings are found in office 9.

We have an EXCEPT question here, so our answer will be the one that's not like the others. But first we have to draw another sketch and fill in the information we're given in the question.

④
M P B P M
M P −M

Once we put P in 4, we know that M will have to be in 5. That means no M in 10. Can we put down anything else that we know for sure? We know that we'll have to use our second B in the bottom row, but we don't know exactly where at this point. That looks like about all we can do. Let's see what we can eliminate.

Answer choice (A) could be false because we could put B in 10. Cross it off.

Answer choice (B) could be false because we could put B in 6. Eliminate it.

Answer choice (C) could be false because we could put P in 6. Eliminate it.

Answer choice (D) has to be true from our diagram for this question. Let's keep it.

Answer choice (E) could be false because, once again, we could also fill 9 with B. Eliminate it and we're done.

We're done with all of the "if" questions, so we'll move on to "which" questions. Question 1 is a partial grab-a-rule that applies only to the bottom row. Let's see what we can do with it.

1. Which one of the following could be an accurate list of the styles of furnishings found in offices 6, 7, 8, 9, and 10, respectively?

   (A) Pop, Moderne, Pop, Moderne, Pop
   (B) Pop, Moderne, Pop, Bauhaus, Moderne
   (C) Bauhaus, Pop, Moderne, Pop, Moderne
   (D) Bauhaus, Moderne, Pop, Moderne, Bauhaus
   (E) Pop, Moderne, Bauhaus, Pop, Moderne

Remember to start with the most restricted clues and slots first.

We know from our template that slots 7 and 8 have to be occupied by M and P, respectively. That eliminates answer choices (C) and (E).

What else do we know about the bottom row? You might have spent some time trying to get rid of the remaining choices if you forgot about the restriction on B. It's a big-picture clue that's easy to lose sight of. If you find yourself struggling on a grab-a-rule question, look back to see if there are any of those big-picture clues that you forgot to apply. Let's see if we can find violations of the rule that we have to use B once—and once only—in the bottom row. That rule gets rid of (A), which has no B at all, and (D), which has two Bs. That only leaves (B), so we've got our answer. Let's move on to our next "which" question:

3. Which one of the following statements must be false?

   (A) Pop furnishings are found in office 10.
   (B) Pop furnishings are found in office 1.
   (C) Moderne furnishings are found in office 9.
   (D) Bauhaus furnishings are found in office 9.
   (E) Bauhaus furnishings are found in office 10.

Here we have to find the choice that *must be false*. You'll remember that we can eliminate any choice if it could be true, even one time. Let's see what we can do. Don't forget to use the good work you've done on the "if" questions to help with POE whenever possible.

We can use our work from question 2 to eliminate both (A) and (D). And we saw the possibility of both (C) and (E) in question 4, so we can get rid of those, too. If you were unsure about them, you could always draw another quick diagram and try them out. Answer choice (B) violates one of our deductions, so that's our answer. We have only one question left.

5. Suppose that exactly two offices are furnished in Bauhaus, rather than just one, among the offices facing south and exactly one office is furnished in Bauhaus among the offices facing north. If all of the other conditions remain the same, then which one of the following statements must be true?

(A) Moderne furnishings are found in office 4.
(B) Moderne furnishings are found in office 10.
(C) Pop furnishings are found in office 1.
(D) Bauhaus furnishings are found in office 6.
(E) Bauhaus furnishings are found in office 9.

This is one of those questions that changes one of our original conditions. It might impact our deductions, and we've had a number of them in this game, so we'll probably want to rebuild our template from scratch for this question. Yes, it's annoying, but rather than fretting, we'll just keep our pencils moving and get to it.

It turns out that because the new rule affects only the bottom row, our original deductions are still valid. The difference is that now we know that we have to place two Bs in the three remaining slots in the bottom row. Because we know that we can't have two adjacent Bs, they can't go in 9 *and* 10. So one of them will have to go in 6 and the other in either 9 or 10. We end up with something like this:

–P –B M	–M –B P	B	–B M/P	–B P/M
B –M	M	P –M –B	B/M –P	/B

Now that we've filled in everything we can, it's time to head to the answers. We're looking for the one that must be true, so if an answer choice *could be false*, even one time, we can cross it off. We found out when we were filling in the diagram that we have to have B in 6 and that's among the answers, so we've got a winner. If you'd feel more confident checking the rest of the choices, go ahead. If you're sure of your work, we're done. Just for the record, answer choices (A), (B), and (E) could be false and (C) must be false according to our diagram.

Okay, that wasn't so bad. We just followed the structure they gave us and got to work. You might think that redrawing the diagram for each question is too time consuming, but if you keep it simple you can create one quickly and then have a concrete space in which to work through the question. And you'll notice that making a new diagram for each question allowed us to use POE on the later questions quickly and painlessly. Our investment paid off.

Games Technique: Draw the Right Diagram

How can you tell when to use one of these template diagrams? The setup will let you know that you have a spatial arrangement that is not linear. Let's try it with another setup:

> Eight dishes—artichoke, beef, celery, danish, eggplant, fennel, grapes, and halibut—are being placed around a circular table.

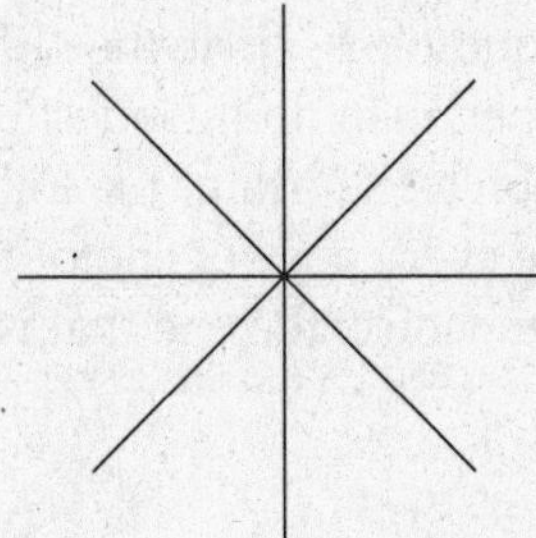

This is similar to what you just did, but here we are dealing with a circular diagram. The simplest way to deal with a circular diagram is to draw intersecting lines. Draw as many lines as you need so you have the appropriate number of spaces around the circle. Place each element at the end of a line. The basic idea is the same: Match what the setup tells you about the spatial arrangement. Remember to redraw the basic structure for each question you do. Don't erase!

Occasionally, the LSAT folks will surprise you with their generosity and will actually tell you how to draw the diagram. By all means, use their description. Copy it as many times as you need to. Draw it a bit more simply if necessary.

Games Technique: Follow This Question Strategy

Here are some guidelines for the most effective way to evaluate the answer choices when you encounter different tasks.

Make sure you've got this question strategy down COLD. Put it next to your Arguments chart on your refrigerator.

- When the task is to find the one that "must be true," you can eliminate any answer that *could be false*—even one time. First, look for the right answer that matches the deductions.
- When the task is to find the one that "must be false," you can eliminate any answer that *could be true*—even one time. Look for the right answer that contradicts a deduction.
- When the task is to find the one that "could be true," you can eliminate any answer that *must be false*—every time.
- When the task is to find the one that "could be false," you can eliminate any answer that *must be true*—every time.

- On grab-a-rule questions, use Process of Elimination. Start with the most restrictive clue and eliminate all answer choices that violate it. Do this with each clue.
- On questions that start with the word *suppose*, either a new clue is added to the original clues or one of the original clues is removed. Do these questions last because the change in the rules applies only to this question. Always remember to check to see whether any of your original deductions have changed.
- On except/cannot questions, circle the "EXCEPT/CANNOT" to help you remember, then do the question in reverse. For example, if the question asks, "All of the following could be true EXCEPT," eliminate every answer choice that could be true. Check every answer choice; the one that is not like the others is the correct answer.

GAME #4: HATS AND SCARVES

All of the games we've worked on so far have been *ordering* games. This one will be a bit different. Instead of having limitations on how the elements are arranged with respect to one another, we'll be told which elements have to be in a certain group. We'll call these *grouping* games. The order of the elements within each group won't matter. We'll just have to decide which elements make up a given group. Sometimes we'll know exactly how many elements are in each group; sometimes we won't. As you might imagine, the latter are trickier. But the process always remains the same. Let's try one.

A couple of tips before we start this game: One, reread the section on "making deductions"; two, remember what we learned about the contrapositive. Grab your pencil, and get to work.

A store is creating a window display featuring four hats and three scarves. The only hats being considered are A, B, C, D, E, and F, and the only scarves being considered are J, K, L, M, and N.

If A is displayed, then neither B nor L can be displayed.
B is displayed only if D is displayed.
C cannot be displayed unless J is displayed.
D can only be displayed if K is displayed.
If L is displayed, then M must be displayed.
F cannot be displayed unless D is not displayed.

1. Which one of the following is a possible display of hats in the window?

(A) A, B, C, F
(B) A, C, D, E
(C) A, D, E, F
(D) B, C, D, F
(E) B, C, E, F

2. If F is displayed, which one of the following must be true?

(A) A is not displayed.
(B) B is not displayed.
(C) K is not displayed.
(D) L is displayed.
(E) M is displayed.

3. If both B and E are displayed, then which one of the following CANNOT be a partial list of items displayed?

(A) C, D, E
(B) C, J, M
(C) C, D, F
(D) C, J, K
(E) D, K, M

4. Each of the following could be displayed together EXCEPT

(A) B and K
(B) B and F
(C) B and M
(D) E and F
(E) E, J, and M

5. If B is displayed, which one of the following is a list of items that could also be displayed?

(A) A, M, N
(B) C, E, F
(C) C, L, M
(D) E, F, M
(E) E, J, M

Cracking Game #4

Step 1: Diagram and inventory

Well, we've got a lot going on here—first of all, we've got two sets of elements (hats ABCDEF and scarves jklmn). Next, we know that not all of the elements will be used because only four out of the six hats are being displayed, and only three out of the five scarves are being displayed. However, we think it's important to keep track of all the elements. How would you do that? Create an "outbox" like the one on the following page.

When elements are either "in or out," or "selected or not selected," draw a two-column diagram.

IN (4+3)	OUT (2+2)
_ _ _ _ / _ _ _	_ _ / _ _

H: ABCDEF
s: jklmn

As you can see, we created an "in" column and an "out" column. We've indicated the number of hats and the number of scarves in each column. This will allow us to keep track of all the elements, so if we are given information about whether something is in or something is out, we'll be able to use it. Now let's look at the clues.

Step 2: Symbolize the clues and double-check

We've got a whole mess of conditional clues here. Remember that every time you have a conditional clue, you also can deduce the contrapositive. Symbolize the contrapositive as soon as you've symbolized the clue. Here's what we have so far:

Go slowly with "if...then" clues and making contrapositives.

CLUE	CONTRAPOSITIVE
–D → –B	B → D
–j → –C	C → j
–k → –D	D → k
l → m	–m → –l

You can save a lot of time and effort by making antiblocks.

ANTIBLOCKS

~~AB~~

~~Al~~

~~FD~~

All right. Now let's look a little more closely at these clues. Consider the first clue:

A → –B   B → –A

So if A is displayed, B cannot be displayed, and if B is displayed, A cannot be displayed. The end effect is that there is no way both A and B can be displayed at the same time. That means that this is identical to ~~AB~~ because the ~~AB~~ also tells us that A and B cannot be displayed at the same time. So rather than writing out the clue and its contrapositive, we can save a lot of time and effort by just making antiblocks whenever we have a conditional clue like this one A → –B.

Step 3: Look for links and size up the game

Did you take time to double-check before moving on to this step? Going back over how you symbolized your clues is particularly important on games such as this one where many of the clues are conditionals. If you've misrepresented even one of these, it will negate all the effort you're about to put into finding deductions. If you didn't double-check before, stop and do so now. Okay, now for the deductions. How can you make deductions with a string of "if…then" statements? By linking clues that share elements. If you see an element on one side of a conditional and the same element on the other side of another conditional, you can link them together. Do you see any two clues that can be linked? Take a look below:

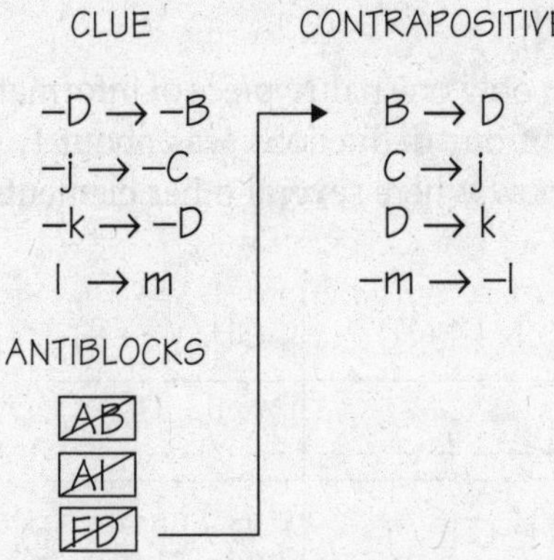

As you can see, there is one point of commonality—D is involved in both an F/D antiblock and a conditional clue. So what does that mean? Well, it means that you can make the following deduction:

F → –B

Why? Because if you have F, you cannot possibly have D since they are involved in an antiblock. You further know that without D, you cannot possibly have B. Thus, if you have F, you cannot possibly have B. Now, what have we just learned about conditional clues that are formatted like this? That they are actually antiblocks in disguise. So this clue should read:

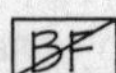

Now we have a fourth antiblock with which to work. Notice the fact that two of the elements (E and N) are not restricted at all. But if you get information about any of the other letters, you can begin to fill in pieces of your diagram. Also, a minus sign next to a letter in this game means that it's not displayed, so it goes in the "out" column.

Let's step back for a moment and see what we're going to be working with. Notice that the "out" column has fewer spaces than the "in" column. That means the "out" column is easier to fill because it's a more restricted space. And notice how much information we have from our clues about elements that cannot appear together in the "in" column.

Any time you have an antiblock, you know for certain that one of those two elements must go in the "out" column. It's possible that both will be "out"—remember, the restrictions given by the clues apply to the elements that are in the "in" column, i.e., the ones that are displayed. The restrictions do not apply to the "out" column. But if you focus on antiblocks, you will quickly be able to determine when certain elements will be in the "out" column.

Steps 4 and 5: Evaluate the question task and apply the strategy
You guessed it—go for the "if" questions first.

Step 6: Use Process of Elimination
Here is our first "if" question. Let's see what we can do with this one.

2. If F is displayed, which one of the following must be true?
   (A) A is not displayed.
   (B) B is not displayed.
   (C) K is not displayed.
   (D) L is displayed.
   (E) M is displayed.

Here's How to Crack It

We seem to have received only one paltry piece of information with this question. But remember that one of our deductions was about F, so now that we know where F is, we should know where several other elements can go:

IN (4+3)	OUT (2+2)	
_ _ _ _ /_ _ _	_ _ /_ _	
F A C E / j_ _	B D / l_	②

That little piece of information ends up making a lot happen. Once F is "in" we know that both B and D are "out." Therefore, we know the exact composition of all of the "in" hats—A, C, E, and F. Once we know that, we can also see that l must be "out" because A is "in" and that j must be "in" because C is "in." We've filled in almost the entire diagram! So what's our answer? (A) can't be true because A is "in." (B) must be true because if F is "in," B is "out." Bingo! Let's go on to the next question.

Did we go too fast for you on that one? Take a look at the diagram on the next page to see exactly how we got from start to finish.

IN (4+3)	OUT (2+2)
_ _ _ _ /_ _ _	_ _ /_ _
F	
F	BD /
FACE / j_ _	BD /
FACE / j_ _	BD /l_

Notice how it's like falling dominoes . . . and how knowing that something is "out" is just as valuable as knowing that something is "in."

Now let's work on the next question.

3. If both B and E are displayed, then which one of the following CANNOT be a partial list of items displayed?

(A) C, D, E
(B) C, J, M
(C) C, D, F
(D) C, J, K
(E) D, K, M

Here's How to Crack It

We've got two pieces of information in this question. Let's see what that gives us.

IN (4+3)	OUT (2+2)	
_ _ _ _ /_ _ _	_ _ /_ _	
FACE / j_ _	BD /l_	(2)
CDBE / jk_	FA /l_	(3)

Spending time making deductions will make answering the questions much easier.

Once again, we are able to fill in a significant amount here. Because the question tells us that four of the answer choices will work in our diagram (remember, we're looking for the one partial list that is invalid), take a look at the letters you placed in your "out" column (A, F, and l), and see if they appear in any of the choices. Choice (C) has F, doesn't it? It's our answer. Let's move on.

5. If B is displayed, which one of the following is a list of items that could also be displayed?

(A) A, M, N
(B) C, E, F
(C) C, L, M
(D) E, F, M
(E) E, J, M

Here's How to Crack It

Only one piece of information again, but that doesn't seem to be stopping us, does it?

IN (4+3)	OUT (2+2)	
_ _ _ _ / _ _ _	_ _ / _ _	
FACE / j_ _	BD /l_	(2)
CDBE / jk_	FA /l_	(3)
CDBE / jk_	FA /l_	(5)

In composition, the arrangement of the letters looks suspiciously like the arrangement in number 3, doesn't it? Only now, we're looking for the only possibility that can work. Any answer choice that contains something in the "out" column should now be crossed off. (A), (B), (C), and (D) all contain an element that has been definitively placed in the "out" column. The answer is (E).

We're in the home stretch. Let's work on the "which" questions.

The final two questions in this game are general questions. The first one is a partial possible-arrangement question. Here we're given only lists of hats that can go in the display. Remember that the hats displayed may have an impact on scarves that might prevent the display from being valid. First, attack it like a regular grab-a-rule question; if there are two or more answers remaining after you've done a round of elimination, start thinking about whether the scarves may be factoring in. A good second step on "which" questions like this one is to check prior work. Go to it!

1. Which one of the following is a possible display of hats in the window?

(A) A, B, C, F
(B) A, C, D, E
(C) A, D, E, F
(D) B, C, D, F
(E) B, C, E, F

Here's How to Crack It

Take each of the clues from your list of symbols that have to do with the hats, and apply the clue to each answer choice, eliminating any choice that violates the clue. "If A then no B" knocks out (A). "If B then D" knocks out (E). "If F then no D" knocks out (C) and (D). The answer is (B). Sweet. Here's the final question:

4. Each of the following could be displayed together EXCEPT

(A) B and K
(B) B and F
(C) B and M
(D) E and F
(E) E, J, and M

Here's How to Crack It

Well, there are several ways to approach this question. The first is to check your deductions and see if you know anything about any of these choices. In answer choice (B), we've got F and B together, which we know can't be true. If you didn't see that, you can look at your previous work to cross off answer choices you know can work. Your work from number 3 will eliminate (A); number 2 will eliminate (D). Both (C) and (E) seem possible given the work from number 3, but you can test them to be safe. If you try to make choice (B) work, you'll see that it violates a rule, so it's our answer.

Games Technique: Find the Contrapositive

We just saw the importance of being able to work with conditional clues. And we found out that once you know how to symbolize them—and their contrapositives—even a game that has a bunch of conditionals can be approachable.

You can't practice too much with "if...then" clues.

Let's take a look at how to symbolize a couple of other tricky conditional statements. We've already dealt with those that involve the word *unless*. You'll remember that when we see "unless," we substitute "if not" and start our symbol there. Now we're going to see what to do when we run across statements that include "only if." Here's an example:

> Novels will be on sale only if reference books are not on sale.

When you see the words *only if* substitute *if not*. You can rearrange the sentence to put the *if not* part first so that it reads like a regular "if...then" statement. So far, it's just like dealing with unless. But there's one more step. *You have to negate the other half of the statement*. So with our example, we would end up with:

> If not reference books are not on sale, novels will NOT be on sale.

The double negative can be a bit confusing, so we have to be careful. The first half is really: "If reference books are on sale." But once we have the statement clear we can simply symbolize the conditional and its contrapositive as we would any other conditional statement. Here's what we've got:

R → –N
N → –R

If you memorize the rule, these will become purely mechanical.

Let's look at one more interesting thing about conditionals. When you negate the part of a conditional that includes the word *and*, it becomes *or*. And when you negate the part of a conditional that includes the word *or*, it becomes *and*. Don't ask why; just learn the rule. Let's see how it works with an example:

> If A is chosen, either B or C must be chosen.

We would symbolize the statement in our usual manner, using the word *or* in our symbol:

A → B or C

The tricky part comes when we symbolize the contrapositive. Remember that "or" will become "and" once we negate it. Here's what it will look like:

–B and –C → –A

Notice that we had to negate each element as well as "or" when we symbolized. This is confusing at first, but once you practice, it will become second nature.

To recap:

When you see the words *only if*, replace them with *if not*, start your symbol there, and then negate the other half of the statement.

When you negate *and* it becomes *or*.

When you negate *or* it becomes *and*.

Below is a chart that is going to drill you on these very skills. It's a five-column chart. Column 1 has clues. Put your symbols in column 2. Put the contrapositives of the clues in column 3. Columns 4 and 5 contain our symbols and contrapositives, so cover them up with a piece of paper before you start. Once you've finished all the symbols and contrapositives, uncover our answers and see how you did.

CLUE	YOUR SYMBOL	YOUR CONTRAPOSITIVE	OUR SYMBOL	OUR CONTRAPOSITIVE
If Jack attends, Mark must attend.			J → M	–M → –J
Ann will work only if Kate works.			–K → –A	A → K
Bob cannot work unless Gary is working.			–G → –B	B → G
If Will goes to the party, Cam won't go.*			W → –C	C → –W
Doug will not drive unless May also drives.			–M → –D	D → M
If Harry is invited, both Charles and Linda must be invited.			H → C and L	–C or –L → –H

* This could be described as an antiblock [WC].

GAMES TECHNIQUE: TAKE A MOMENT TO SURVEY

Taking a moment to survey how the game is going to work is a worthwhile investment of time that many testers will skip in their rush to get to the questions. But doing this will help you get through the questions and answers much more efficiently. What exactly are you looking for? Well, we'll run through it again.

After you've marked your deductions in the diagram, look to see which elements and spaces have the most limitations. Look for the most restrictive clues and the most restricted spaces. Those are the ones that are likely to have the greatest impact on your placement of the elements for a given question.

Often, getting through a question efficiently will depend on knowing where to get started, so take a minute to acquaint yourself with the workings of the game before diving in. And once you get started, you'll find that a logical chain of events will follow.

Note that not all games will have deductions. If you've checked for overlap among the clues and between the clues and diagram and you still can't get anything concrete down, don't keep staring in the hope that something will appear. And don't get caught in the trap of listing deductions that *might* result *if* something were to happen. Once you've completed the process used to identify deductions and have taken a moment to survey how things are likely to work in the game, it's time to head to the questions.

GAME #5: THREE BUSES

Not all "grouping" type games will tell you exactly how many elements go in each of the columns, as was the case in the last game. Some games will involve the distribution of elements among various slots. You might have twelve animals to place in four cages, or ten people to place in seven houses, for instance. Your first goal is to attempt to figure out what the exact distribution is. If you can do that, the game becomes much easier. Look for information limiting the number of elements per group or distribution clues. On this game, give yourself 20 minutes or so—try figuring out the distribution for five minutes. If you get stuck, our solution is at the end!

Five girls—Fiorenza, Gladys, Helene, Jocelyn, and Kaitlin—and four boys—Abe, Bruce, Clive, and Doug—ride to school each day in three separate buses.

Abe and Fiorenza always ride together.
Gladys and Helene always ride together.
Jocelyn and Kaitlin never ride together.
Doug always rides in the bus with the fewest children.
Boys cannot outnumber girls in any bus.
The maximum number of children in any bus is four.

1. The bus in which Doug rides can hold how many children?

   (A) 1
   (B) 2
   (C) 3
   (D) 4
   (E) 5

2. Bruce can ride with each of the following EXCEPT
   (A) Abe
   (B) Clive
   (C) Doug
   (D) Fiorenza
   (E) Helene

3. If Bruce and Clive ride in the same bus, which one of the following must also be in the bus?
   (A) Abe
   (B) Fiorenza
   (C) Gladys
   (D) Jocelyn
   (E) Kaitlin

4. Which of the following could be a list of all the passengers in one bus?
   (A) Doug, Gladys
   (B) Fiorenza, Abe, Bruce
   (C) Jocelyn, Kaitlin, Clive, Bruce
   (D) Fiorenza, Gladys, Bruce, Clive
   (E) Abe, Bruce, Fiorenza, Jocelyn

5. Abe can NEVER ride with which one of the following?
   (A) Bruce
   (B) Clive
   (C) Gladys
   (D) Jocelyn
   (E) Kaitlin

6. If Bruce rides with Fiorenza, Gladys must ride with which one of the following?
   (A) Clive
   (B) Doug
   (C) Fiorenza
   (D) Jocelyn
   (E) Kaitlin

Cracking Game #5

Step 1: Diagram and inventory

So we've got a total of nine children to place in three buses. Our diagram will consist of three columns—the only thing missing will be the exact number of children to be placed in each bus. We know that we'll need to use all of the elements and that we can't have any repeats, but uncertainty about the distribution of elements might make things complicated. Our diagram and elements are on the following page. Don't forget to distinguish between the two types (girls and boys).

First draw the diagram, then worry about distribution.

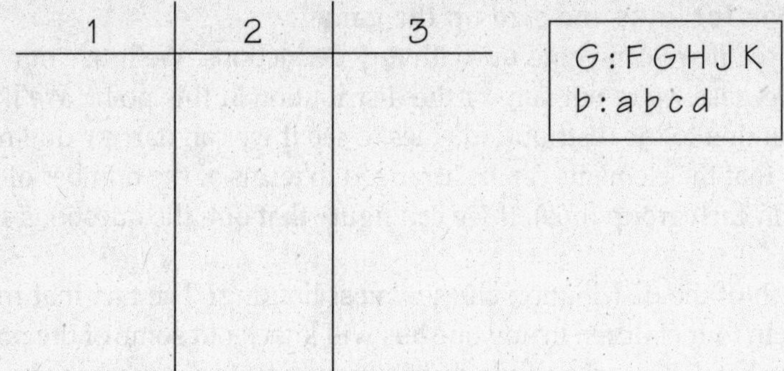

Step 2: Symbolize the clues and double-check

We've got several clues here; some should look familiar, and some will be new. You should be comfortable by now with how the blocks and antiblocks work. We'll see how the others—known as distribution clues—work as we move through the rest of this game. Distribution clues give you information about how the elements will be distributed among the slots. In some cases, they may lead to only one possible distribution, and in others, they may merely limit the options, leaving a couple of different possible distributions. Let's get to work and see how it plays out.

The first three clues are all pretty straightforward. We've already worked with similar clues and the symbols are becoming second nature. Now let's briefly symbolize our distribution clues to make sure we have a clear handle on how they work:

d = fewest

boys fewer than girls

Maximum 4 per group

We are able to symbolize the information, but it may not seem very useful at this point. Don't forget to double-check before moving on to the next step.

Step 3: Look for links and size up the game

Now let's see if we can come up with any deductions. We'll use our standard methods because we're not sure of the distribution at this point. We'll also pay special attention to the distribution clues to see if we can narrow down the possible ways that the elements can be arranged in terms of the number of elements (children) in each group (bus). If we can figure that out, the questions should be a lot easier.

Spend a few minutes trying to narrow down the possible distributions—it's worth it!

So which of the distribution clues is most limiting? The fact that there can't be more than four children in any one bus will knock out some of the possibilites right off the bat. Let's make a little distribution chart to see what the possibilities are. Remember that buses 1, 2, and 3 represent no particular buses, so it doesn't matter if the bus with four children is the first or second or third bus, or if there will even be a bus with four children. Check out our possibilities below:

1	2	3
③	③	③
④	③	②
④	④	①

As you can see above, limiting the maximum number of elements to four per group narrows the possibilities to three separate distributions: 3-3-3, 4-3-2, and 4-4-1. Let's take a look at our second distribution clue, the fact that boys cannot outnumber girls in any bus. Does this clue do anything to limit the number of distributions? It sure does. Take a look below:

1	2	3
~~3~~	~~3~~	~~3~~
④	③	②
④	④	①

If boys cannot outnumber girls in any bus, and there are four boys, that means that the 3-3-3 distribution cannot be valid for this game. Why not? Because if the distribution is 3-3-3, then in one of the buses, there must be two boys and one girl, which we can't have. Another limitation. Now what about the final clue, that Doug must ride in the bus with the fewest children? Take a look:

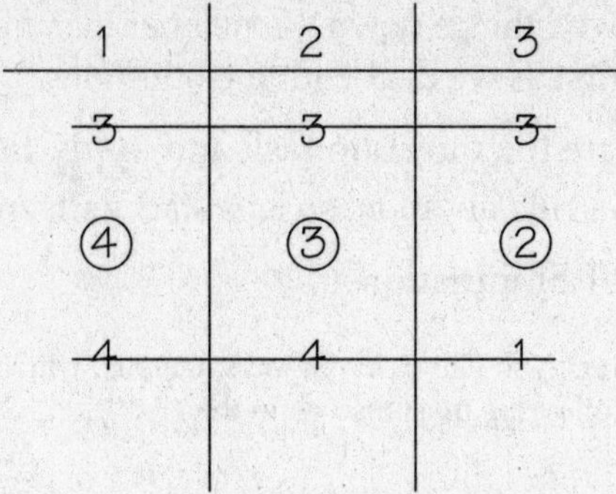

If Doug must ride in the bus with the fewest amount of children, then the 4-4-1 distribution isn't possible in this game either. Doug would have to go alone. Doug is a boy, and we know that boys cannot outnumber girls in any bus, so he can't be the only rider. Therefore, after eliminating distributions that violate the rules, we're left with a diagram that will look like this:

1 (4)	2 (3)	3 (2)
_ _ _ _	_ _ _	_ d

Because there is no information to suggest that buses 1, 2, and 3 are distinguished from one another, as we just said above, we'll put four children in bus 1, three children in bus 2, and two children in bus 3. Any other deductions? Using the diagram above, go back to your relationship clues. Is there any more overlap that provides further limitations? Check this out:

1	2	3
		-G -H -F
b b G G	b G G	J/K over G, d over b

Yes, we've spent some precious minutes figuring out all this stuff. However, we now know the exact distribution of the children, how many of each gender are in every bus, the definitive placement of one child, and several other limiting factors—such as the fact that neither the G/H block nor the a/F block can go in bus 3, leaving d to go with either J or K only.

We've really narrowed things down. Remember that we'll keep an eye on the most restricted spots first as we deal with the questions.

Steps 4 and 5: Evaluate the question task and apply the strategy

We don't have a grab-a-rule question, so let's start with any "if" questions.

Step 6: Use Process of Elimination

3. If Bruce and Clive ride in the same bus, which one of the following must also be in the bus?
   (A) Abe
   (B) Fiorenza
   (C) Gladys
   (D) Jocelyn
   (E) Kaitlin

Here's How to Crack It

Because boys cannot outnumber girls, we know where b and c have to go if they're together, right? Let's check it out:

1	2	3
_ _ _ _ b b G G	_ _ _ b G G	J/K d G b
b c G H	a F _	_ d ③

As you can see, b and c in the first slot puts the a/F block in the second slot. This then forces the G/H block into slot 1 along with b and c. Looks like (C) is our answer. Now try this one:

6. If Bruce rides with Fiorenza, Gladys must ride with which one of the following?
   (A) Clive
   (B) Doug
   (C) Fiorenza
   (D) Jocelyn
   (E) Kaitlin

Here's How to Crack It

Well, you know that a always comes with F, so you've once again got two boys (a and b) to place. Take a look at the following page.

1	2	3
_ _ _ _ b b G G	_ _ _ b G G	J/K d G b
b a F _	c G H	_ d ⑥

So we've got b, a, and F all in bus 1, which means that the G/H block must go in bus 2. A boy must also go in bus 2, and the only one left is c. It's our answer—choice (A).

Never forget that blocks are your best pieces of information—always remember to place them in the diagram.

The final four questions in this game are general. However, you were able to deduce so much that they probably won't present too much of a problem. Let's do this one first:

4. Which of the following could be a list of all the passengers in one bus?

   (A) Doug, Gladys
   (B) Fiorenza, Abe, Bruce
   (C) Jocelyn, Kaitlin, Clive, Bruce
   (D) Fiorenza, Gladys, Bruce, Clive
   (E) Abe, Bruce, Fiorenza, Jocelyn

Here's How to Crack It

This isn't quite a grab-a-rule question because it doesn't address all the elements in each answer choice. But we can probably eliminate at least a few answers by applying the clues to the answer choices and crossing off any violations. If more than one choice remains, we can see if there might be any violations in possible arrangements of the groups that are not shown in the answers, given what we know from this one group. The G/H block eliminates (A) and (D), the boys not being able to outnumber the girls eliminates (B), and the J/K antiblock eliminates (C). We're left with (E). Let's move on.

1. The bus in which Doug rides can hold how many children?

   (A) 1
   (B) 2
   (C) 3
   (D) 4
   (E) 5

Here's How to Crack It

We've answered this one already because we made the proper deductions. It's (B): two children.

2. Bruce can ride with each of the following EXCEPT
   (A) Abe
   (B) Clive
   (C) Doug
   (D) Fiorenza
   (E) Helene

Here's How to Crack It

Look at your diagram and your previous work. Is there anywhere b can't go? It can't go with d in bus 3, so (C) is our answer. Also note that you had b with a, c, F, and H in previous questions, so we can cross off (A), (B), (D), and (E). Let's finish off the last question:

5. Abe can NEVER ride with which one of the following?
   (A) Bruce
   (B) Clive
   (C) Gladys
   (D) Jocelyn
   (E) Kaitlin

Here's How to Crack It

We can approach this in several ways; using our previous work is one way. We've had a with b in the past, so (A) is gone. And because J and K are interchangeable, neither (D) nor (E) can be the answer either. That leaves us to try either c or G to see whether it's possible to group it with a. If we look at the work we did for question 6, we see that it would be possible to switch c and b, putting both a and c in the same group and allowing us to eliminate (B). Therefore our answer must be (C), Gladys, because you can't have a situation where both blocks are in the same bus. Try it if you need to, but it won't work because that leaves three boys left to place between buses 2 and 3, which we can't have. So you're done.

Games Technique: Identify the Interchangeable Elements

In the solution above, we mention that J and K are interchangeable, but what *are* interchangeable elements? Interchangeable elements are groups—usually pairs—of elements that have exactly the same restrictions (or no restrictions at all). In the game above, J and K are interchangeable because they are both girls and the only limitation on either is mutual: They cannot be in the same group. This means that unless a question gives us additional information about one or both of the elements, there is no reason why we couldn't switch J and K without affecting any other elements.

Interchangeable elements are important to identify because they often allow you to eliminate wrong answers and thus are useful for POE. As we just saw in question number 5, we were able to eliminate answers (D) and (E) because J and K are interchangeable, and therefore neither can be the answer to a question asking for something that *must be true*. In other words, if a could not ride with J, neither could he ride with K. Because it's not possible for both answers to be right, neither one can be. So make note of interchangeable elements and remember how they function.

GAMES TECHNIQUE: IDENTIFY THE DIFFICULTY OF EACH GAME

To be successful on a Games section, it is important to be able to predict the relative difficulty of the games before you get started. How can you tell? There are several things to look for *after* you've read through the setup and the clues.

Start with the relationship between the elements and the places to which they'll be assigned. In an *ordering* game, you want a one-to-one correlation between elements and slots. In a *grouping* game, by definition, there will be more than one element in each group. In this case, you want to know if there are a set number of elements per group. If there are multiple distributions, the game is more complicated than if everything is determined from the outset. Remember that having an "out" column will account for the elements that are not "in" the game, so if you know how many elements are not assigned, it becomes just like a *grouping* game with one more group.

Being able to predict the relative difficulty of games before you start working on them will have a significant impact on your games performance.

Then, you'll want to ask two important questions: Can we leave out any elements? Can there be any repeats? If the answer to either or both of those questions is yes, the game will be more complicated.

Next, you'll evaluate the clues. The more restrictive and concrete they are, the better because you'll have more limitations on the game to help in placing the elements. For instance, a clue such as:

> Wednesday must be staffed by a member of the Quality committee.

will be much more useful than a clue such as:

> The juggler will perform at least once, but no more than three times during the week.

Finally, briefly scan the questions. The more "if" questions with straightforward tasks, the better. The more complicated questions there are, the more complicated the game. And you'll definitely end up spending more time plugging away at the questions and answer choices to find the correct response.

We've presented these things to look for in order of importance; the characteristics near the top of this list are much more important predictors of a game's level of difficulty than the ones near the bottom. So a game that has great questions but allows you to use elements more than once and doesn't have a set distribution is still a bad choice to do early in the section.

The process of evaluating a game shouldn't take more than 15 or 20 seconds once you've had some practice. You'll want to spend enough time with the setup and clues so that you have a good grasp of the concepts mentioned above, but spending too much time sweating all the minor details will defeat the purpose of making you a more efficient "game player."

You should evaluate the level of difficulty even if you are planning to work through all four games. You always want to start with an easier game so that you can get into the groove. And if you get thrown by an early game, it can blow your confidence on the rest of the section and cost you points that you otherwise would have had in the bag; all the more reason to start with a more manageable game. Let's try another one.

GAME #6: BIRDS AND MAMMALS

Now we think you're ready to handle something a bit more complex. Remember that not all games will use each element only once. Sometimes you will not know how many times a given element might be used. However, your process remains exactly the same for these games as it is for all other games. Give yourself 20 minutes on this one and see how you do.

A zoomaster is deciding which birds and mammals will go in five consecutive cages, numbered 1 through 5, left to right. Each cage will contain one of three species of birds—egret, finch, or parrot—and one of three species of mammals—antelope, giraffe, or otter. The zoomaster must abide by the following conditions:

If finches are in a given cage, antelopes must also be placed in that cage.

If otters are in a given cage, egrets cannot be in that same cage.

In at least one cage, parrots and antelopes are together.

Parrots are never in consecutive cages.

If egrets and finches are both exhibited, the egrets must always be in lower-numbered cages than the finches.

The second cage contains otters.

1. Which one of the following must be true?
   - (A) Egrets are exhibited in the first cage.
   - (B) Parrots are exhibited in the second cage.
   - (C) Parrots are exhibited in the third cage.
   - (D) Antelopes are exhibited in the fourth cage.
   - (E) Antelopes are exhibited in the fifth cage.

2. Each of the following is a possible line-up of mammals in the five cages EXCEPT:
   - (A) antelope, otter, antelope, giraffe, otter
   - (B) antelope, otter, giraffe, antelope, antelope
   - (C) antelope, otter, antelope, antelope, antelope
   - (D) giraffe, otter, giraffe, giraffe, antelope
   - (E) giraffe, otter, antelope, antelope, antelope

3. Which one of the following is not possible when both egrets and finches are exhibited?
   - (A) Antelopes are exhibited in two consecutive cages.
   - (B) Finches are exhibited in two consecutive cages.
   - (C) Giraffes are not exhibited.
   - (D) Otters are exhibited in the third cage.
   - (E) Parrots are exhibited in two different cages.

4. If egrets are exhibited in the fifth cage, which one of the following must be true?
   - (A) Antelopes are exhibited in the third cage.
   - (B) Egrets are exhibited twice.
   - (C) Finches are exhibited twice.
   - (D) Giraffes are not exhibited in consecutively numbered cages.
   - (E) If giraffes are exhibited, then they are exhibited in the fifth cage.

5. If egrets are exhibited exactly twice, each of the following must be true EXCEPT:
   (A) Antelopes are exhibited in the fourth cage.
   (B) Antelopes are exhibited in the fifth cage.
   (C) Egrets and finches are exhibited in consecutively numbered cages.
   (D) If antelopes are exhibited in as many cages as possible, then they are exhibited four times.
   (E) Giraffes cannot be exhibited in consecutively numbered cages.

6. If finches are exhibited exactly twice, it is possible to determine the types of mammals and birds for how many of the ten slots?
   (A) 7
   (B) 6
   (C) 5
   (D) 4
   (E) 3

Cracking Game #6

Step 1: Diagram and inventory

Well, the diagram is pretty well laid out for you. Five cages, with a bird and a mammal in each cage. Here's what we got:

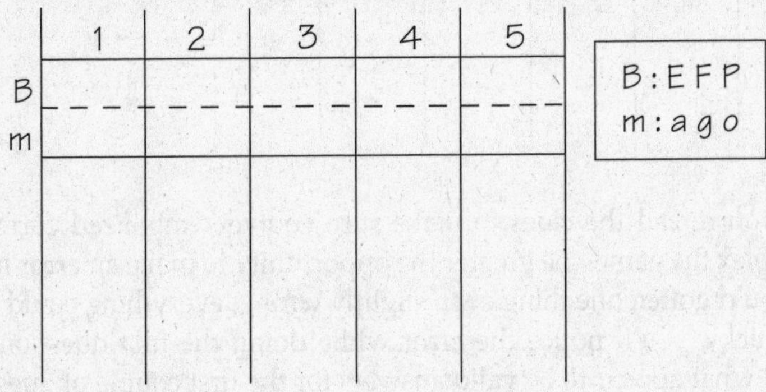

Now let's examine the clues.

Step 2: Symbolize the clues and double-check

We've got many different types of clues here. Clues 1, 2, and 5 are conditional; clue 3 is a block; clue 4 is an antiblock; and clue 6 definitively places something into our diagram. Remember when you have a conditional clue such as o → –E, it's faster to write it as an antiblock: o → –E/E → –o is better written as

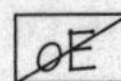

Here's what we got for the conditional clues:

F→ a   –a → –F

oE

E — F (if both)

You'll notice that our clue symbolizing egrets in lower-numbered cages is represented as a range clue with E to the left of F because lower-numbered cages are to the left of higher-numbered cages in our horizontal diagram.

Looks okay, right? Of course, we've added the contrapositives for each conditional clue. Here are the other two clues:

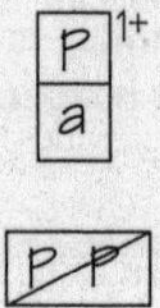

PP

There's a small wrinkle to the block: the fact that we know that there might be more than one of them. So we've added a little "+" after the block to indicate that there might be more than one. Finally, we've got a diagram that has an o placed in the mammal slot for cage 2.

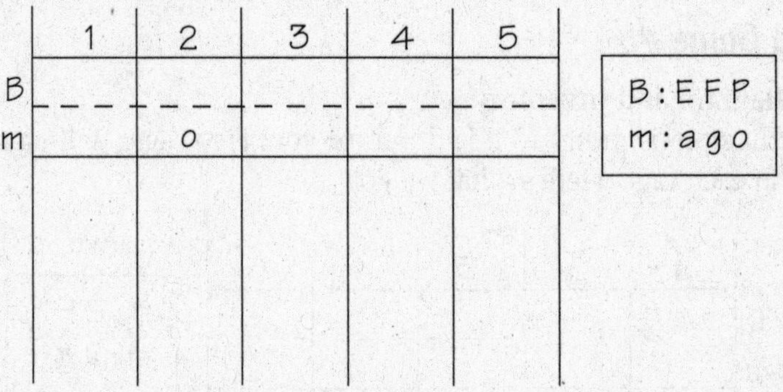

Have you reread the clues to make sure you've symbolized correctly? The more complex the game, the greater the opportunity to make an error in symbolizing. If you'd gotten one thing even slightly wrong, everything could fall apart. If you're lucky, you'll notice the error while doing the first question, but you might find what appear to be valid answers for the first couple of questions and only realize the problem when the second or third question just doesn't work. At that point, you'd have to fix the error and go back to rework those first questions. What a nightmare. Not only does it waste valuable time, but you'd also become frustrated, and that can affect your performance on the next game or the next section. Avoid this by investing the time to double-check.

Step 3: Look for links and size up the game

As for deductions, there's a major one that you can find. Start by identifying elements that aren't able to go in certain cages, and also remember that there are only three possibilities for any given slot. Start by looking at the most restricted elements or places.

Here's what we got:

P/a 1+ (slot 4 or 5)

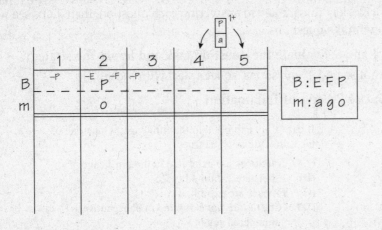

	1	2	3	4	5
B	–P	–E –F P	–P		
m		o			

B:EFP
m:ago

We were able to definitively place P along with o in cage 2 because neither F nor E can go with o—because if you have o, you can't have E, and if you have F, you need to have a with it. In fact, if you have o in a column, you'll never be able to have F with it, so we can add another deduction to our list: an F/o antiblock. Take note of the other "minuses" in the diagram—i.e., cases in which certain elements are restricted from certain slots. These will all be very helpful because then you've got at most only two different elements that can go in those slots!

Also, as a result of placing P definitively in slot 2, we know that P can be in neither slot 1 nor slot 3. That only leaves two slots for any other P to go in. And remember that we always have to place at least one P/a block. So that block will have to go in either slot 4 or slot 5, but not both. Let's make a note of that over the columns.

Now, let's consider our conditional clue about finches a little more carefully. If F is placed in a cage, a must also be placed in that cage. So suppose you have o in a cage. Could you have F? No. What about g? Again, no. So ultimately, you can also conceive of this clue as two separate antiblocks: F can be with neither g nor o because the presence of an F requires an a as well. If you look at the contrapositive of the original, you can see that –a → –F, and in this game –a is the same as either g or o. So that leads to another couple of antiblocks we'll need to keep in mind:

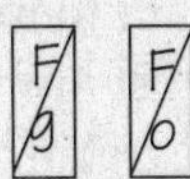

This is a way to show all of the ramifications of that clue. You might not realize this until you get into the game. No big deal; just jot it down when it becomes apparent. It makes clear just how restricted F is.

Let's step back and survey the big picture. In almost all games that contain two sets of elements, one set will be more restricted than the other. You will have more information on that set of elements, and when answering questions, that set of elements is *the* set you should focus on first. In this game, there are more restrictions and information about birds than there are about mammals.

Additionally, note the fact that you have a block you must place every time—the P/a block. Where can this block go? It can't go in cage 1, 2, or 3 anymore. Placing the P/a block is a major key to answering each question, then. Let's see what we can do with the questions.

Steps 4 and 5: Evaluate the question task and apply the strategy

We've got some "if" questions, so let's start with those.

Step 6: Use Process of Elimination

4. If egrets are exhibited in the fifth cage, which one of the following must be true?

    (A) Antelopes are exhibited in the third cage.
    (B) Egrets are exhibited twice.
    (C) Finches are exhibited twice.
    (D) Giraffes are not exhibited in consecutively numbered cages.
    (E) If giraffes are exhibited, then they are exhibited in the fifth cage.

Here's How to Crack It

Well, we've got an E in the fifth cage, so that's going to determine the placement of our P/a block. Here's what we got:

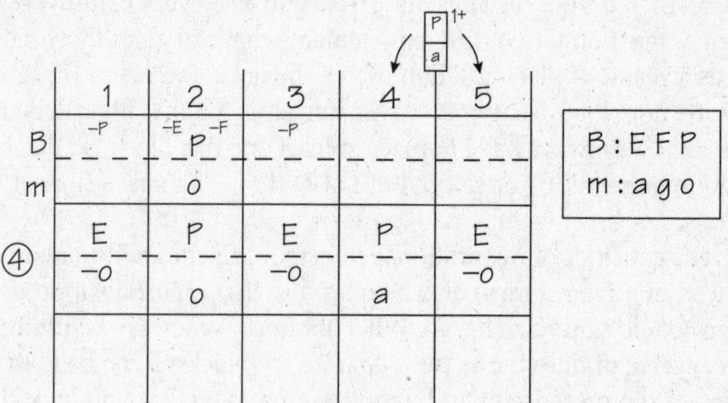

As you can see, putting E into the fifth slot forces our P/a block into cage 4. The other piece of information we want to focus on is the clue "If egrets and finches are both exhibited, the egrets must always be in lower-numbered cages than the finches." Because we've got an egret in cage 5, that means that no finches can be exhibited because if you put a finch in a lower-numbered cage than an egret, it would violate this clue. Hey, wait a minute! Can we have an arrangement with no finches? Well, you'll notice that it was never mandated by the setup that we use all the elements, so it is a possibility. Hence, we've got egrets in cages 1, 3, and 5. We've wound up filling in seven out of our ten spaces. When we check the answer choices, the only thing that must be true is (D), the fact that giraffes can't be exhibited in consecutively numbered cages because we've got an o in cage 2 and an a in cage 4. So that's our answer.

Here's the next "if" question:

5. If egrets are exhibited exactly twice, each of the following must be true EXCEPT:
   (A) Antelopes are exhibited in the fourth cage.
   (B) Antelopes are exhibited in the fifth cage.
   (C) Egrets and finches are exhibited in consecutively numbered cages.
   (D) If antelopes are exhibited in as many cages as possible, then they are exhibited four times.
   (E) Giraffes cannot be exhibited in consecutively numbered cages.

Here's How to Crack It

You now know from the question the exact number of times each type of bird is exhibited—you've probably already figured out that P is always exhibited twice because you need a P/a block and P/o is in cage 2. This question tells us that E is exhibited twice also, so you know that there is one F. And because we're using both E and F, we'll have to be sure that both Es come before the F. Here's our diagram:

	1	2	3	4	5
B	−P	−E −F P	−P		
m		o			
④	E −o	P o	E −o	P a	E −o
⑤	E −o	P o	E −o	P/F a	F/P a

P/a block (1+), can go in 4 or 5

B : E F P
m : a g o

So we've got the Es definitively in cages 1 and 3. This means that P and F must be in cages 4 and 5—you don't know exactly where each one goes. Either way, however, an a must be in both cage 4 and cage 5 because a must always go with F and we already know the other spot is our P/a block. This means that the mammal slots for cages 1 and 3 must be either giraffes or antelopes. Thus, (A), (B), (D), and (E) must all be true. Only (C) can be false, so it's our answer. Let's work on the next question.

Question number 6 also starts with the word *if*, but it's not one with a straightforward task such as finding what *must be true* or what *could be false*. It sounds as if it could be complicated, so we'll leave it for later.

Now we're on to the "which" questions. Let's take a look at number 1.

1. Which one of the following must be true?
   (A) Egrets are exhibited in the first cage.
   (B) Parrots are exhibited in the second cage.
   (C) Parrots are exhibited in the third cage.
   (D) Antelopes are exhibited in the fourth cage.
   (E) Antelopes are exhibited in the fifth cage.

Here's How to Crack It

We've done a lot of work on this game, so chances are that our previous work will allow us to eliminate some answer choices by showing us that they could be false. In the questions we've worked through so far, E was in slot 1, but that doesn't necessarily mean it *must* be true every time, so let's leave answer choice (A) in for the moment. We know for sure that (B) must be true (it's our deduction) so it's our answer. If you're confident with that, you can move on. If you'd feel better checking the last three answers, it will only take a few seconds.

2. Each of the following is a possible line-up of mammals in the five cages EXCEPT:

   (A) antelope, otter, antelope, giraffe, otter
   (B) antelope, otter, giraffe, antelope, antelope
   (C) antelope, otter, antelope, antelope, antelope
   (D) giraffe, otter, giraffe, giraffe, antelope
   (E) giraffe, otter, antelope, antelope, antelope

Here's How to Crack It

On this question, you're looking for the one line-up that can't work. You can still use the Grab-a-Rule technique of applying the clues to the answer choices, but here a violation of the rule means you want to keep the answer rather than eliminate it. Your two best clues are of course: (1) an otter must be in cage 2, and (2) there is a P/a block in either cage 4 or cage 5. The P/a block in cage 4 or cage 5 means that line-up (A) can't work because it doesn't have a in either slot 4 or slot 5, so it's our answer. Here's the next question:

3. Which one of the following is not possible when both egrets and finches are exhibited?

   (A) Antelopes are exhibited in two consecutive cages.
   (B) Finches are exhibited in two consecutive cages.
   (C) Giraffes are not exhibited.
   (D) Otters are exhibited in the third cage.
   (E) Parrots are exhibited in two different cages.

Here's How to Crack It

We're asked to find the one that's not possible, so really our task is to find the one that *must be false*. We've learned that we'll eliminate any answer that could be true. Take a look at previous scenarios in which you've had both egrets and finches exhibited. Then, run through the answer choices and see if you've already drawn any of them. You've had the possibility of (A), (C), and (E) in question 5. So now we have to try the last two. Let's see if we can make (B) work.

If we have F in two consecutive slots, they would have to be slots 3 and 4, forcing the P/a block into slot 5. Because we have to include E according to the question, we'll have to put it in slot 1. We can make it work once, so we can cross out (B). We know that P can't be in slot 3, so that leaves either E or F. If we have E in 3, we know that we can't use o. Likewise, if we have F in 3, we know that we must use a—which is the same as saying that we can't use o. So it looks as if we can't use o in 3 no matter what. That's another deduction that we can put in our clue shelf. And we can circle (D). Nice work. Only one more question.

6. If finches are exhibited exactly twice, it is possible to determine the types of mammals and birds for how many of the ten slots?

(A) 7
(B) 6
(C) 5
(D) 4
(E) 3

Here's How to Crack It

As with the last question, the information provided tells us the exact number of each type of bird. Because we always have two of P, and now we have two of F, we've got one E. That E must be in the first cage because it has to go in a lower-numbered cage than any and all Fs. So here's our diagram:

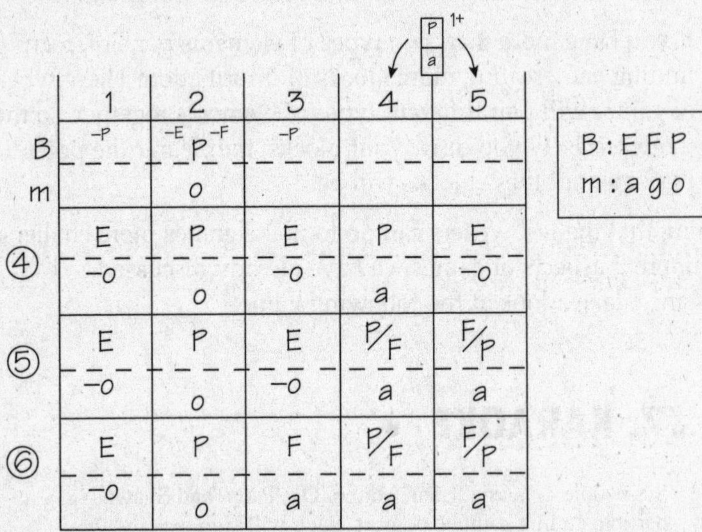

Fill in everything you can, then head to the answer choices.

We've wound up being able to definitively place only three birds, but because cages 4 and 5 contain either an F or a P, we know that the mammal exhibited must be an a. So we've got four mammals definitively placed as well, giving us seven total. Our answer here is (A).

Games Technique: Be Flexibe in Your Approach

As you can see, the last game required a lot of flexibility. It had several types of clues, required that you keep track of ten slots, and didn't have a fixed number of each type of element. The key thing to remember, however, is that the process in approaching this game is exactly the same process as in every other game. Here's a brief run-down of some LSAT curve-balls, and how to handle them:

- If you have many more elements than spaces, focus on distribution. Chances are you'll be given distribution clues that may determine exactly how many elements will go in each space. This will make the game much easier because the number of possibilities will be greatly reduced.

- If you don't know the exact number of all types of elements, focus on making deductions and filling in slots. Typically, these types of games will provide you with spaces that can have only one of two or three types of elements anyway, so the number of possibilities for any one slot will be quite low. The more slots you're able to either definitively fill in or reduce to only one of two choices, the easier the game will be.
- If you have all conditional clues and no definitive information, focus on making sure you've diagrammed everything correctly and have gotten all the contrapositives possible. Then, look to link these conditional clues to see if you can make any deductions. Many times the questions will be mainly "if" questions, which will provide you with more concrete information.
- If you have more than two types of elements per slot, focus on finding and creating more blocks of information. These types of games will pair different types of elements together, so the more precisely you draw your blocks, the clearer the potential placement of these blocks will be.

One thing that the test writers can do to make games more challenging is to combine different aspects of games we have already discussed.

For instance, take a look at the following game:

GAME #7: KARAOKE

Six people—Kassia, Lani, Marco, Ox, Patty, and Shawn—participate in a karaoke contest. Each will sing exactly one song in one of two styles—pop or country. If more than one of the six people sings a song in one style, then the order in which they sing will be determined from first to last, with no two people singing at the same time. The following conditions must apply:

Ox sings a pop song.

Lani sings a country song.

No country singer sings before Lani.

If Marco sings a country song, then Patty and Shawn sing country songs, with Patty singing after Marco but before Shawn.

If Marco sings a pop song, then Shawn sings a pop song, with Shawn singing after Ox but before Marco.

If Patty sings a pop song, then so does Kassia, with Ox singing after Kassia but before Patty.

1. Which one of the following could be true?

(A) Marco sings a pop song and Shawn sings a country song.
(B) Patty sings a pop song and Kassia sings a country song.
(C) Kassia sings a pop song and Patty sings a country song.
(D) Patty and Ox sing pop songs, with Patty singing before Ox.
(E) Marco and Shawn sing pop songs, with Marco singing before Shawn.

2. Each of the following could be the last pop singer EXCEPT:

(A) Shawn
(B) Kassia
(C) Ox
(D) Patty
(E) Marco

3. Which one of the following could be a complete and accurate list of the people who sing pop songs, listed in singing order from first to last?

(A) Shawn, Patty, Ox
(B) Ox, Patty, Kassia
(C) Shawn, Ox, Marco
(D) Ox, Shawn, Kassia, Marco
(E) Patty, Marco, Shawn, Kassia

4. If Shawn sings a country song, then each of the following are pairs of people who must sing in the same style as each other EXCEPT:

(A) Patty and Marco
(B) Patty and Shawn
(C) Kassia and Marco
(D) Patty and Lani
(E) Marco and Shawn

5. If Ox is the first pop singer, then which of the following must be true?

(A) Ox and Marco sing in the same style as each other.
(B) Patty and Lani sing in the same style as each other.
(C) Patty and Ox sing in the same style as each other.
(D) Kassia and Lani do not sing in the same style as each other.
(E) Kassia and Patty do not sing in the same style as each other.

6. Suppose that the condition is added that Shawn and Patty do not sing in the same style as each other. If all the other conditions remain in effect, then each of the following could be true EXCEPT:
   (A) Marco and Kassia sing in the same style as each other.
   (B) Patty and Kassia sing in the same style as each other.
   (C) Patty and Marco sing in the same style as each other.
   (D) Kassia and Patty do not sing in the same style as each other.
   (E) Marco and Kassia do not sing in the same style as each other.

There are many ideas we're familiar with here, but they're all jumbled together in a way we haven't seen before. We call these *hybrid games*, and chances are good that you'll see some new combination of ideas on your actual LSAT.

This game, for example, is an in/out type, because each person sings either country or pop, but not both, and consequently you know that each element will be used exactly once. But there's a twist: Each group is ordered from first to last, and we don't know how many people will be singing in each group. Furthermore, many of the clues are conditionals, but not all, and they're complicated because they involve ordering as well as grouping.

As we mentioned earlier, the key is to stick to your basic steps but remain flexible.

Cracking Game #7

Step 1: Diagram and inventory

As we mentioned earlier, this is a grouping game in which each element is either a pop singer or a country singer. Here's what we got:

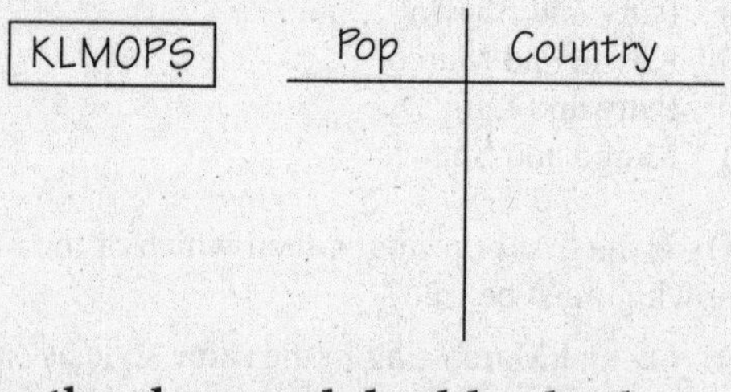

KLMOPS

Pop	Country

Step 2: Symbolize the clues and double-check

This is where some flexibility is required. The first two clues are very straightforward. The third one is harder because we don't know how many other people, if any, will sing country songs. No matter what, however, Lani will come first.

So far, we have this:

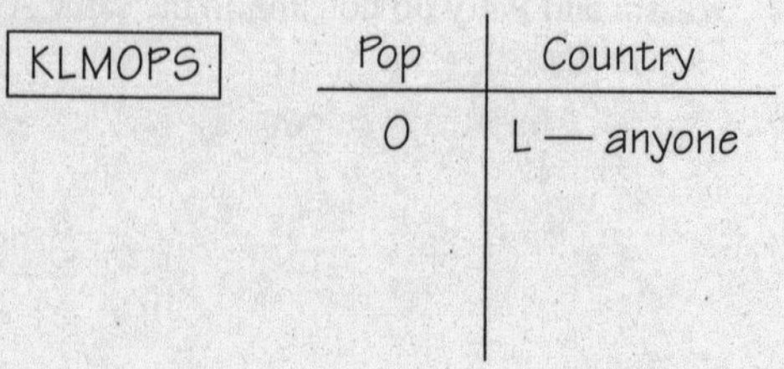

KLMOPS

Pop	Country
O	L — anyone

We've got two elements definitively placed, and notice we used a range clue to show that Lani sings first in the country group. But, the other clues are even stranger. If M sings country, then the order has to be M-P-S. Okay. But how would you diagram the contrapositive? If the country order isn't M-P-S, then M doesn't sing country (and must therefore sing pop). Is there an easy way to diagram that? Not really.

But wait—remember that although order is important, it's not the only thing going on here. This is ordering within an in/out grouping. The other people (P and S) have to be on the country side before they can be placed in order. So a more useful way to think of the contrapositive in this case is to say that if P doesn't sing country, then M can't sing country, and that if S doesn't sing country, then M can't sing country.

Because it's more useful to state these positively, we should say that if P sings pop then M sings pop, and if S sings pop, then M sings pop. Because there are only two groups, if you're not in one, you're automatically in the other.

It's also more useful to write these on the sides of the diagram that they correspond to. So now we have:

KLMOPS

Pop	Country
O	L — anyone
S → M	M → M—P—S
P → M	

If we follow the same logic for the last two clues, we end up with the following:

KLMOPS

Pop	Country
O	L — anyone
S → M	M → M—P—S
P → M	S → M
M → O—S—M	K → P
P → K—O—P	

Notice that we don't end up with clues that start with "If O sings country" because that can never happen.

Carefully reread the clues and make sure that you've written the contrapositives correctly. This is a complicated game, so there are many things to double-check.

Step 3: Look for links and size up the game

There aren't many useful individual deductions to be made here. There are many places you could connect conditional statements, but that's not terribly useful because you'll be able to do that easily if the need arises.

But don't forget to look at the big picture. It may have occurred to you that although there are six elements, two are already fixed, and it may also have occurred to you that we know a lot of information as soon as we find out where M belongs. In a situation like this, where there are a small number of free elements and a large number of restrictive clues centering around one element in particular, it's worth considering just how many different situations could arise.

In this case, we know that O and L are already placed. Then, because each element has to appear somewhere, we know that there are only two ways this can go: Either M sings country, or M sings pop. Take these one at a time.

If M sings country, then he takes P and S along with him, in that order, and we already know that L belongs there (and must sing first). O is on the other side, and apparently K could sing either style, anytime, except for being the first country singer (that spot is already taken by L). We can collect all that information as follows:

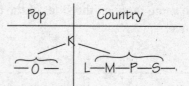

Pop	Country
K (either side)	
—O—	L—M—P—S—

Now, let's look at the other possibility. What if M sings pop? That means O, S, and M all sing pop, in that order, and we already knew that L sings country. Hmm. That leaves two floaters in this case, P and K. We could leave it like this:

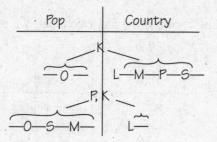

Pop	Country
K (either side)	
—O—	L—M—P—S—
P, K (either side)	
—O—S—M—	L—

But that's not really the whole story. We know a whole lot more if we know where P is, and, of course, P must be either a pop singer or a country singer. So let's try both of those.

If P sings pop, then it's K-O-P in that order, and O-S-M in order at the same time. So K and O must be the first two singers, and P can be wherever it likes with respect to S-M. L, of course, is by itself on the other side.

If P sings country, then it must come after L, and remember O-S-M are all still on the other side (because we already considered the case where M sings country). K, then, is unrestricted (except it couldn't be the first country singer, as usual).

We can encapsulate this as follows:

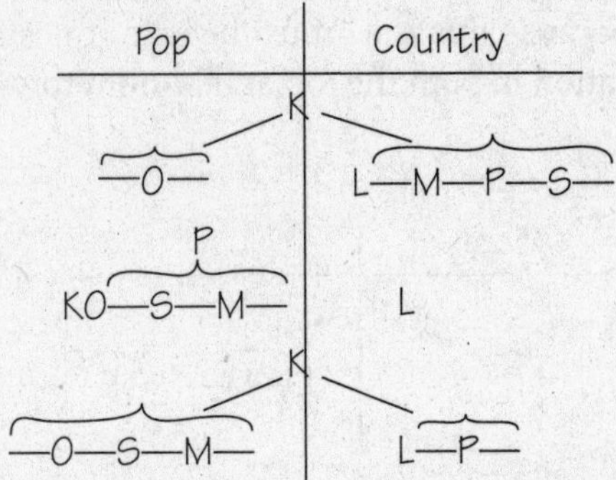

That's not bad. Except for K floating a little bit, there are really only three basic scenarios that can occur here. This is a valuable time-saver, as long as you're dealing with a game that has a small number of very restricted elements. You won't be able to approach most games with this technique (imagine trying to list out all the possibilities on some of the other games in this chapter!), but it makes your life easier when you can because the questions go much faster.

Let's try it.

Steps 4 and 5: Evaluate the question task and apply the strategy

The first "if' question is number 4, so go to it.

Step 6: Use Process of Elimination

4. If Shawn sings a country song, then each of the following are pairs of people who must sing in the same style as each other EXCEPT:

(A) Patty and Marco
(B) Patty and Shawn
(C) Kassia and Marco
(D) Patty and Lani
(E) Marco and Shawn

Here's How to Crack It

Compare the information given in the question to our diagram. Only the first row of our diagram has S on the country side, and everyone but O and K must sing country in that row. So the right answer must involve either O or K and one of the other four. If you look at the answer choices, you'll see that only (C) fulfills that requirement.

Let's try number 5 (the next "if" question):

5. If Ox is the first pop singer, then which of the following must be true?

(A) Ox and Marco sing in the same style as each other.
(B) Patty and Lani sing in the same style as each other.
(C) Patty and Ox sing in the same style as each other.
(D) Kassia and Lani do not sing in the same style as each other.
(E) Kassia and Patty do not sing in the same style as each other.

Here's How to Crack It

There are two rows in our diagram where O could be the first pop singer: the top and the bottom. Because this is a "must be true" question, the right answer has to fit with the situation in both the top and bottom rows. Here's the diagram again:

Pop	Country
K	
—O—	L—M—P—S—
P	
KO—S—M—	L
K	
—O—S—M—	L—P—

Let's compare the answer choices to the diagram. In (A), O and M are together in the bottom row but not the top row. Cross it off. Now compare (B) to the diagram. Yes, P and L are country singers in both rows. This is the right answer.

Moving right along to question 1:

1. Which one of the following could be true?
   - (A) Marco sings a pop song and Shawn sings a country song.
   - (B) Patty sings a pop song and Kassia sings a country song.
   - (C) Kassia sings a pop song and Patty sings a country song.
   - (D) Patty and Ox sing pop songs, with Patty singing before Ox.
   - (E) Marco and Shawn sing pop songs, with Marco singing before Shawn.

Here's How to Crack It

This is a "could be true" question, so we just need to find one example in any of the three rows.

What about (A)? No. M and S are always together. Choice (B)? Again, no because P sings pop only in the second row, and K is there, too. Aha! Look at (C)—yes, this could happen in either the first or third rows. That's the answer.

On to question 2:

2. Each of the following could be the last pop singer EXCEPT:
   - (A) Shawn
   - (B) Kassia
   - (C) Ox
   - (D) Patty
   - (E) Marco

Here's How to Crack It

Try these one at a time. The one that can't be the last pop singer is the right answer.

Look at (A). S can't be the last pop singer because in both situations where S sings pop (rows two and three), M (at least) must follow. This is the right answer.

Question 3 is next:

3. Which one of the following could be a complete and accurate list of the people who sing pop songs, listed in singing order from first to last?

   (A) Shawn, Patty, Ox
   (B) Ox, Patty, Kassia
   (C) Shawn, Ox, Marco
   (D) Ox, Shawn, Kassia, Marco
   (E) Patty, Marco, Shawn, Kassia

Here's How to Crack It

This is another "could be" question, so we're just looking for one match.

On to choice (A). Nope. There is no row that has only S, P, and O on the pop side. There is also not a row that has only O, P, and K on the pop side, so cross off (B). O is before S in the third row (the only one that has just O, S, and M), so (C) is also out. Choice (D)? Yes. In the bottom row, you could have exactly O, S, K, and M in that order. This is the right answer.

And finally, go to question 6:

6. Suppose that the condition is added that Shawn and Patty do not sing in the same style as each other. If all the other conditions remain in effect, then each of the following could be true EXCEPT:

   (A) Marco and Kassia sing in the same style as each other.
   (B) Patty and Kassia sing in the same style as each other.
   (C) Patty and Marco sing in the same style as each other.
   (D) Kassia and Patty do not sing in the same style as each other.
   (E) Marco and Kassia do not sing in the same style as each other.

Here's How to Crack It

This is actually very helpful because all it says is that we don't need to pay attention to our first two rows any more. The only row we're concerned with is the last one, and we're looking for an answer choice that can't be true.

Let's look at (A): This could be true. K can be on either side. (B) could be true for the same reason. But (C)? No. They're on opposite sides. This is the right answer.

Ready for the last game? Here it is:

GAME #8: COOKING CONTEST

Some games, such as the game you're about to try, don't require one of our standard diagrams in which you fill in a different set of information for each possible arrangement of elements. What you'll see is a set of rules (usually two or three) for either mixing, combining, or switching elements from one position to another. Your goal here is to go slowly, making sure you understand the rules given. You can still use your pencil by drawing the "movements" the rules denote to make sure you can see what's going on. And you'll want to draw out what happens with the elements over the course of each question. Keep it visual even when it doesn't fit the most common models.

Billy, Carly, Debbie, and Ethan are competing in a cooking contest. In each round of the contest, different dishes are prepared. A contestant is eliminated the first time he or she fails to prepare a dish properly. The contestants will be reordered between rounds according to one of the following rules:

Rule X: Whoever was in third place moves in front of the contestant who was previously in second place.

Rule Y: Whoever was in third place moves in front of the contestant who was previously in first place.

Rule Z: Whoever was in last place moves into the first place position.

If reordering involves a place where a contestant has been eliminated, that reordering cannot occur.

If none of the reorderings can occur, the contestants will remain in the same order as they were in the preceding round.

1. If the order in one round is Ethan, Billy, Carly, Debbie, and if Carly alone is eliminated in that round, which one of the following must be the order of the contestants for the next round?
   (A) Billy, Debbie, Ethan
   (B) Billy, Ethan, Debbie
   (C) Debbie, Billy, Ethan
   (D) Debbie, Ethan, Billy
   (E) Ethan, Billy, Debbie

2. If the order in one round is Carly, Billy, Debbie, Ethan, and if no one is eliminated in that round, it must be true that in the next round
   (A) Billy is third
   (B) Carly is second
   (C) Debbie is first
   (D) Ethan is first
   (E) Ethan is fourth

3. If the order in a round is Billy, Debbie, Ethan, Carly, and no one is eliminated, which one of the following could be the order in the next round?

(A) Billy, Carly, Ethan, Debbie
(B) Carly, Billy, Ethan, Debbie
(C) Carly, Ethan, Billy, Debbie
(D) Debbie, Billy, Ethan, Carly
(E) Ethan, Billy, Debbie, Carly

4. If two rounds go by with no eliminations, and if the order of contestants in the third round is the same as it was in the first round, which one of the following represents the reorderings taking place so far?

(A) X, followed by Y
(B) X, followed by X
(C) Y, followed by X
(D) Z, followed by Y
(E) Z, followed by Z

Cracking Game #8

Step 1: Diagram and inventory

We don't really have a diagram here, so all we should do is note the "contestants"—B, C, D, and E. Let's see what the rules are.

Step 2: Symbolize the clues and double-check

We can draw the three rules to see who goes where after a "round." Take a look at the diagram below:

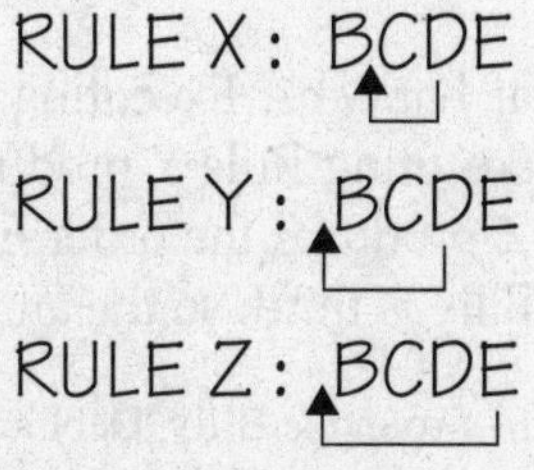

RULE X : BCDE

RULE Y : BCDE

RULE Z : BCDE

The final two clues talk about whether a reordering can occur based on the number of contestants left. Make sure you understand what this means before going to the questions.

Step 3: Look for links and size up the game

Have you symbolized the rules correctly? Good. You want to look for questions that will tell you definitively whether someone has been eliminated and what the exact positions of the contestants are. That way, you'll be able to properly manipulate the rules and the contestants.

Steps 4 and 5: Evaluate the question task and apply the strategy

Fortunately there are only four questions and they are all "if" questions. Let's see how you do.

Step 6: Use Process of Elimination

1. If the order in one round is Ethan, Billy, Carly, Debbie, and if Carly alone is eliminated in that round, which one of the following must be the order of the contestants for the next round?

(A) Billy, Debbie, Ethan
(B) Billy, Ethan, Debbie
(C) Debbie, Billy, Ethan
(D) Debbie, Ethan, Billy
(E) Ethan, Billy, Debbie

Here's How to Crack It

If Carly is eliminated, and she was in the third position, no reordering that involves a contestant in the third position can take place because all we have left is EBD. That means no Rule X and no Rule Y. So, we execute Rule Z, which puts our last contestant, Debbie, into the first position. Ethan and Billy don't move. The new order is Debbie, Ethan, Billy, or choice (D).

2. If the order in one round is Carly, Billy, Debbie, Ethan, and if no one is eliminated in that round, it must be true that in the next round

(A) Billy is third
(B) Carly is second
(C) Debbie is first
(D) Ethan is first
(E) Ethan is fourth

Here's How to Crack It

Try each move and see what happens. Executing Rule X produces the order Carly, Debbie, Billy, Ethan. Executing Rule Y produces the order Debbie, Carly, Billy, Ethan. Executing Rule Z produces the order Ethan, Carly, Billy, Debbie. In all three of those situations, Billy is third, so the answer is (A).

3. If the order in a round is Billy, Debbie, Ethan, Carly, and no one is eliminated, which one of the following could be the order in the next round?

(A) Billy, Carly, Ethan, Debbie
(B) Carly, Billy, Ethan, Debbie
(C) Carly, Ethan, Billy, Debbie
(D) Debbie, Billy, Ethan, Carly
(E) Ethan, Billy, Debbie, Carly

Here's How to Crack It

Try each move and see what happens. Executing Rule X produces the order Billy, Ethan, Debbie, Carly. There is no answer choice with that order. Executing Rule Y produces the order Ethan, Billy, Debbie, Carly, which appears in choice (E). That's our answer.

4. If two rounds go by with no eliminations, and if the order of contestants in the third round is the same as it was in the first round, which one of the following represents the reorderings taking place so far?

(A) X, followed by Y
(B) X, followed by X
(C) Y, followed by X
(D) Z, followed by Y
(E) Z, followed by Z

Here's How to Crack It

Start with a random order: Billy, Carly, Debbie, Ethan. Now try the answers. We have to make sure that we end up with the same order in the third round that we have in the first round. Choice (A) suggests X, then Y. So if we started with B, C, D, E, Rule X produces B, D, C, E. Then execute Rule Y. That produces C, B, D, E. We do not have the same order in the third round as we did in the first round, do we? On to choice (B). If we started with B, C, D, E, Rule X produces B, D, C, E. Then execute Rule X again. That produces B, C, D, E. We have the same order in the third round as we did in the first round. (B) is our answer.

Why do we leave games like this until last in the section? They can often be complicated and time-consuming because we can't really make any deductions before the game. In all the other games, there is a system: a diagram, clues, deductions. The worst thing about these games is that you usually have to test the answer choices, which is the biggest time-waster of all.

Games Technique: Organize the Section in Order

We talked about how to predict the relative difficulty of the games earlier in this chapter. Now let's make sure we're clear on how to put that knowledge to use.

Approaching the games in a "workable" order is the most powerful tool you have for doing well on the section. Before you start working through any games, you should take a couple of minutes to look through all four games and evaluate them for difficulty. You should make a note on each game as to whether it's a game you'd like to work on now, later, or never. If you get to all four games, the "never" game will be the one you do last. The LSAT rewards confidence, and if you choose your first game well, you'll come away from it warmed up for the later games and fully confident that you'll be able to handle them successfully, too. And leaving the worst game for the end will ensure that you'll spend your time working through the questions that you'll best be able to answer; this will allow you to get as many points in those 35 minutes as you can.

Games Technique: Practice on Your Own

- Do everything in pencil, and don't erase your work.
- Work and write small—you will not be given much space to draw your diagram.
- If a particular symbol isn't working, or is even causing mistakes, stop using it. Try something else.

- Do games over and over. If you had trouble with one, go back to it later, and try it again until you get it.
- Practice games only when you are able to give them your full attention.
- *Very important:* Rework all the games you do (including the games in this chapter) at least twice.
- Always keep in mind which games you're able to do most quickly. Look for those games and do those first on the real LSAT.

SUMMARY

Here's the step-by-step approach to ALL games:

Step 1: Diagram and inventory

Step 2: Symbolize the clues and double-check

Step 3: Look for links and size up the game

Step 4: Evaluate the question task

Step 5: Apply the strategy

Step 6: Use Process of Elimination

On the following page is a summary chart of all the games you did in this chapter. The games are organized by task and broken down to show the variations each displayed within that task. Although every once in a while, LSAC may give you a straightforward game that's purely about one simple task with no caveats, that's particularly rare. You should expect to see games that are more layered, that make use of several different ideas on top of whichever basic task it asks of you, and that employ several different types of clues.

As you can see from the chart, clue type isn't restricted to any particular sort of game. To evaluate a game's difficulty accurately, you want to look at the sum of the parts—the diagram, the relationship between the elements and the diagram, and the nature of the clues. By recognizing the things that add to a game's difficulty, you can better assess when (or if) to attempt a certain game.

Use this chart to recall which games were more difficult for you and to determine what aspects of the games were behind those difficulties. Compare the games you do from the real LSATs to this chart to look for similarities. Ideally, when you're taking the real test, you want to be able to recognize those components of a game that are familiar so that you can recall what will be necessary to work on the game efficiently. Once you've focused on that, it will be easier to see how the seemingly new or different aspects of a game affect the way it operates.

Ordering Games

Variation	Inventory	Clue Types
Game #1: Days and Entrees	One-to-one correspondence, grid diagram	Blocks, antiblocks, fixed element
Game #2: Tenants and Apartments	Two-tiered vertical grid diagram, one-to-one correspondence after accounting for empty spaces	Fixed elements, range clues, restricted elements
Game #3: Office and Furnishings	Elements used more than once, spatially oriented diagram, template approach/ redraw simpler version of diagram for each specific question	Antiblocks, fixed elements, restricted elements
Game #6: Birds and Mammals	Two-tiered diagram, elements used more than once, not all elements used	Blocks, antiblocks, conditionals, range clue, fixed element

Grouping Games

Variation	Inventory	Clue Types
Game #4: Hats and scarves	Two columns—"in" and "out" groups, specified how many of each type of element were to be selected	All conditional clues
Game #5: Three Buses	Three groups with unspecified number in each, more elements than columns, distribution based on both number and type of element	Blocks, antiblocks, distribution clues
Game #7: Karaoke	Two groups, ordering within each group (more of a hybrid game), all elements used, so if not in one group must be in the other one	Conditional clues, conditional clues combined with range clues

Other Games

Variation	Inventory	Clue Types
Game #8: Cooking Contest	No standard diagram, must manipulate elements as dictated by question (also known as "switch and mutate"), resulting in a lot of trial and error	Series of rules to play the game by, a couple of clues that don't readily lend themselves to symbolization

APPLY WHAT YOU'VE LEARNED

Now it's time to put everything you've learned in this chapter to work on the following three games. The goal of this drill is to see how well you've mastered the six steps and how accurately you can work, not to see how fast you can get through these games. Remember, if you finish a section but acquire only half the number of points, you may as well have done only two games. So, work carefully and thoroughly on these until you're sure you have them right.

If you want, you can measure the time it takes you to do each game. By measure, we mean set your timer to count up, and then turn it away so that you can't see the clock as you work the game. Put the timer in a drawer or in another room if necessary. When you're done, stop the clock and note how long it took you to complete the game and then see how accurate you were. This will help you figure out approximately how long it takes you to do a game accurately, and by extension, how many games you can reasonably expect to get through on a given section. Take note, too, of the difficulty level of each game—if you found a game particularly challenging, it's only natural that it would have taken longer to work on.

GAMES PRACTICE DRILL

GAME 1

In one day, a software maker updates exactly six files—G, H, J, K, L, and M—one at a time, not necessarily in that order. Each updated file is assigned a priority for distribution to users of the software. One of these files receives top priority, two of them receive standard priority, and the rest receive rush priority. The order in which the software maker updates the files and the priorities they receive are subject to the following conditions:

No two files that are updated consecutively receive the same priority.

File H is updated later than is the file that receives top priority but earlier than file K, which receives rush priority.

Files G and M are not updated consecutively.

File G receives top priority, and file H receives standard priority.

The fourth file updated receives rush priority.

1. Which one of the following must be true of the order in which the files are updated?

    (A) File G is updated later than is file H.
    (B) File H is updated later than is file J.
    (C) File K is updated later than is file G.
    (D) File K is updated later than is file M.
    (E) File M is updated later than is file G.

2. If M is the third file updated, then each of the following must be true EXCEPT:

    (A) G is the first file updated.
    (B) H is the fifth file updated.
    (C) L is the second file updated.
    (D) The third file updated receives standard priority.
    (E) The sixth file updated receives rush priority.

3. Which one of the following must be false?

    (A) G is the third file updated.
    (B) H is the third file updated.
    (C) J is the fifth file updated.
    (D) L is the third file updated.
    (E) M is the second file updated.

4. If the file that receives top priority is updated immediately before a file that receives standard priority, then it CANNOT be true that

    (A) G is the second file updated
    (B) H is the fifth file updated
    (C) J is the first file updated
    (D) K is the fourth file updated
    (E) M is the third file updated

5. If file J is updated immediately before file L is updated, then which one of the following must be true?

    (A) G is the third file updated.
    (B) J is the second file updated.
    (C) K is the fourth file updated.
    (D) L is the sixth file updated.
    (E) M is the second file updated.

6. Each of the following could be false EXCEPT:

    (A) Either the first or the second file updated receives rush priority.
    (B) Either the first or the second file updated receives standard priority.
    (C) Either the second or the third file updated receives standard priority.
    (D) Either the second or the third file updated receives top priority.
    (E) Either the fifth or the sixth file updated receives top priority.

Answers for Game 1

1. C
2. C
3. E
4. E
5. B
6. A

Explanations for Game 1

Diagram and take inventory

The task in this game is to order the software updates from 1 to 6 and determine what priority each update is given. We'll use a standard two-tier diagram for this, with 1 to 6 as the core of the diagram, the updates in the top row, and the priorities in the bottom row. Here's what it looks like.

GHJKLM
tssrrr

1	2	3	4	5	6

Symbolize the clues and double-check

Clue 1 is a global rule, which we can symbolize this way.

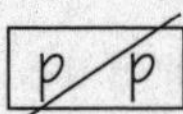

Clue 2 is the sort of clue we expect to see in an ordering game. We note that clue 4 gives us further information about G and H, which are also mentioned in this clue. We'll combine all this information in a single symbol.

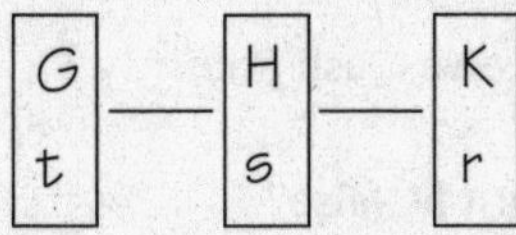

Clue 3 is an antiblock.

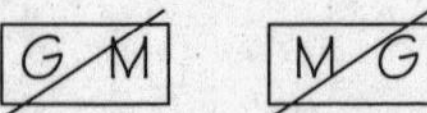

Clue 5 can be represented directly in our diagram.

Look for links and size up the game

We've already done some linking by making a combined symbol for clues 2 and 4 above. There are a few other things we can deduce here: Because the fourth update is rush priority, and we can't have consecutive files with the same priority, we know that the third and fifth files can't have rush priority. There are two other rush-priority files to place and only three spaces left they can occupy. Because two of these are the first and second spaces, one of the rush-priority files has to be last; the other one will be either first or second.

Now look at our large combined symbol. G has to have at least two other files after it, and it must be the top-priority update, so the absolute latest it could be updated is third. In particular, then, this means that the fifth file to be updated not only can't be rush priority, but it can't be top priority either. The only option remaining is for it to be standard priority. This large clue also allows us to restrict the placement of files G, H, and K somewhat: We've already seen that G can't be later than third; H can't be first because G has to be before it, and it also can't be fourth or sixth because of its priority; finally, K can't be first or second because of other files that must go before it, and it can't be third or fifth because of its priority, which leaves fourth or sixth as the only two possible locations for it.

Here's our final full diagram.

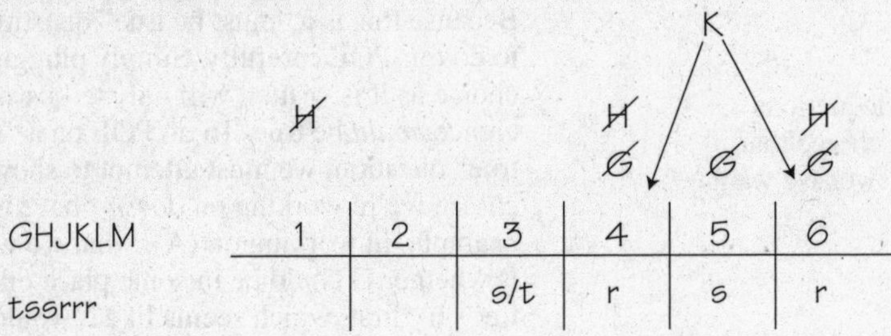

Questions

We'll work the specific questions on a first pass, then the general questions on a second.

2. **C** Specific

M is third.

M third means that G can't be second. Because G can only be first, second, or third, we conclude that G must be first. This forces the second file to have rush priority and the third to have standard priority. Given these facts, we see that H must be the fifth file updated because that is the only standard-priority position left. H fifth means that K must be sixth. The only remaining elements are J and L, which we see are both unrestricted, and therefore identical: They can go in the remaining spaces—second and fourth—in either order.

Here's the diagram we've just come up with.

1	2	3	4	5	6
G	J/L	M	L/J	H	K
t	r	s	r	s	r

Choices (A), (B), (D), and (E) are all deductions we've made in our diagram. (C) is the choice that doesn't have to be true, and it's the answer we want.

4. **E** Specific

We're given a new block—ts—to add to our diagram.

We already know that G, the top-priority file, can only be first, second, or third, so let's focus on where we can put it. Clearly third is out—the fourth file has to be a rush-priority file. Second looks okay. First may look all right at a glance, but remember that either the first or second file must be a rush-priority file, and putting G in first would occupy both of them, forcing us to put two rush-priority files next to each other. So G must be the second file updated. This makes the second file top-priority, the third file standard-priority, and the first file rush-priority. We can also conclude from G's placement that M cannot be first or third. It appears that there is still enough room to put K in either of its possible spots, so there isn't anything more definite that we can conclude here.

This is the diagram we're working with.

~~M~~ 1	2	~~M~~ 3	4	5	6
	G				
r	t	s	r	s	r

(A) not only can be true, it has to be. (B), (C), and (D) are all possibilities that aren't excluded by our diagram. (E), however, is excluded by our diagram, and it's the choice we want.

5. **B** Specific

This question gives us a new block—JL—to work with.

Unfortunately, it isn't immediately clear how this block fits into our diagram or what other deductions it leads to. The best strategy in this case is to work the choices one at a time.

Because this is a "must be true" question, we have to do our POE carefully. Simply plugging in the choice as it is written will only tell us whether that choice *could* be true. To do POE on a "must be true" question, we must attempt to show that the choice we're working on *doesn't* have to be true. For example, in working on (A), what we want to check is whether G could be in some place other than third. Let's try first, which seems like it would be pretty easy to do; here's a diagram that demonstrates G can, in fact, be first while still keeping our JL block intact.

1	2	3	4	5	6
G	J	L	M	H	K
t	r	s	r	s	r

Because G evidently doesn't have to be third, this diagram eliminates choice (A). Happily, this diagram also shows that K doesn't have to be fourth—eliminate (C); that L doesn't have to be sixth—eliminate (D); and that M doesn't have to be second—eliminate (E). The only remaining choice is (B), which is the choice we should select.

1. **C** General

We're looking for something that has to be true in all cases.

A quick scan of the choices shows that (C) is one of our initial deductions, and it's the choice we should select.

3. **E** General

We're looking for something that can't be true.

A quick scan of the choices may get us to the answer immediately. If so, great! If not, there are still plenty of other things we can try. Prior work can sometimes be helpful in these cases because it's possible that we've already generated an example of one or more of these answer choices. In this case, the only choice we've seen before is (D)—in our example in question 5 above.

At this point, we try the choices one at a time. (A) can be done; here's an example that demonstrates it; we've left open the fact that r and s can switch between the first and second spaces, and we've also left open the fact that J and L can be switched between second and fourth. Hopefully, some of these possibilities can help us with later answer choices or questions.

1	2	3	4	5	6
M	J/L	G	L/J	H	K
r/s	s/r	t	r	s	r

We try (B) and find that it, too, can be done. As before, we leave open the positions of our identical elements J and L.

1	2	3	4	5	6
J/L	G	H	K	L/J	M
r/s	s/r	t	r	s	r

A little foresight in generating this example allows us to use it to verify (C) as well. At this point, (E) is the only remaining choice. You may have noticed on your initial pass that putting M second would prevent us from putting G either first or third, and so because G can only be first, second, or third, M can never be second. However you get there, we see that (E) is the choice we have to pick here.

6. **A** General

We're asked to find the answer that can't be false—in other words, the one that must be true. (A) is one of our initial deductions, and it's the choice we should pick here.

Lest you wonder, at this point we've generated counterexamples to all of the other choices here in our prior work. Our work from question 2 shows that (B) can be false; our work from question 3 choice (A) shows that (C) can be false; our work from question 5 shows that (D) can be false; and every example we've generated shows that (E) can be false—in fact, it can never be true.

GAME 2

A company's board of directors consists of exactly seven members: three founding members—Garcia, Hayes, and Jackson—and four recent members—Stone, Tan, Uqbar, and Vellini. The board evaluates three proposals—K, M, and O—with three board members evaluating K, four board members evaluating M, and four board members evaluating O. Each board member evaluates either one or two of the proposals, and each proposal is evaluated by at least one founding member. The assignment of proposals to board members is subject to the following restrictions:

Exactly twice as many founding members evaluate M as evaluate O.

If exactly two founding members evaluate K, then Garcia does not evaluate any proposal that is evaluated by either Hayes or Jackson.

If Stone evaluates a proposal, then Uqbar does not also evaluate that proposal.

Any proposal evaluated by Tan must also be evaluated by Garcia.

1. Which one of the following could be a complete and accurate list of the board members who evaluate proposal K?
   (A) Garcia, Hayes, Jackson
   (B) Garcia, Jackson, Tan
   (C) Hayes, Jackson, Tan
   (D) Hayes, Jackson, Vellini
   (E) Hayes, Stone, Uqbar

2. If Vellini does not evaluate proposal M, then which one of the following must be true?
   (A) Garcia evaluates exactly one proposal.
   (B) Hayes evaluates exactly two proposals.
   (C) Jackson evaluates exactly one proposal.
   (D) Stone evaluates exactly two proposals.
   (E) Vellini evaluates exactly one proposal.

3. Which one of the following statements must be true?
   (A) Garcia evaluates proposal M.
   (B) Jackson evaluates proposal K.
   (C) Tan evaluates proposal M.
   (D) Uqbar evaluates proposal M.
   (E) Vellini evaluates proposal O.

4. If Garcia evaluates at least one proposal that is evaluated by Jackson but does not evaluate any proposal that is evaluated by Hayes, then how many different assignments of proposals to board members are possible?
   (A) three
   (B) four
   (C) five
   (D) six
   (E) seven

5. If Jackson evaluates proposal K but does not evaluate any other proposal, then which one of the following could be true?
   (A) Garcia evaluates exactly one proposal.
   (B) Hayes evaluates exactly two proposals.
   (C) Stone evaluates exactly one proposal.
   (D) Tan evaluates exactly one proposal.
   (E) Vellini evaluates exactly one proposal.

6. Which one of the following CANNOT be true?
   (A) Both Garcia and Hayes evaluate proposal M.
   (B) Both Garcia and Stone evaluate proposal O.
   (C) Both Garcia and Uqbar evaluate proposal K.
   (D) Both Hayes and Jackson evaluate proposal M.
   (E) Both Tan and Vellini evaluate proposal M.

Answers for Game 2

1. A
2. C
3. E
4. D
5. C
6. E

Explanations for Game 2

Diagram and inventory

The task in this game is to place the seven board members into three groups—K (3 elements), M (4 elements), and O (4 elements). We should make sure to include the sizes of the groups in our initial diagram. There are two types of elements, so we'll use uppercase for the founding members and lowercase for the recent members. We also should indicate the rules for using the elements here: Because we have eleven spaces but only seven elements, multiple uses of some elements will be necessary. We are told, however, that no element can be in all three groups. A quick summary—"1 or 2 uses of each"—gets all this information across nicely. Finally, we are told that at least one founding member is in each group, so we can reserve spaces for them to start with. Here's our initial diagram.

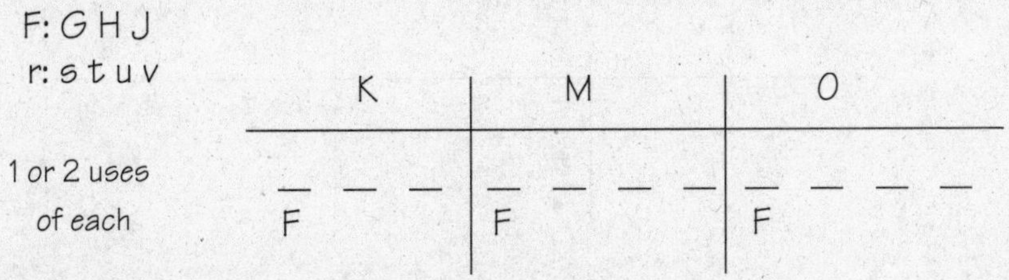

F: G H J
r: s t u v

1 or 2 uses of each

K	M	O
F _ _	F _ _ _	F _ _ _

Symbolize the clues and double-check

Clue 1 may be a little difficult to symbolize clearly, but what it means is relatively easy to see. Because we have at least 1 founding member in group O, we must have at least two founding members in group M. Moreover, because there are only three founding members in the game, this is the only combination that satisfies the clue. Thus O consists of one founding member and three recent members, and M consists of two founding members and two recent members. This is pretty easy to reflect in our diagram.

Clue 2 is conditional. Here's a symbol for it and its contrapositive.

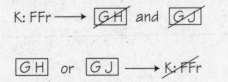

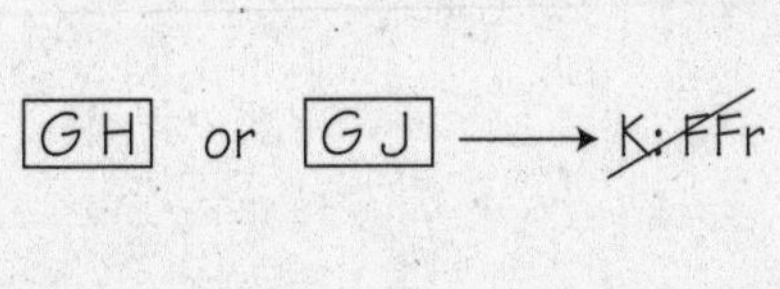

K: FFr ⟶ ~~[GH]~~ and ~~[GJ]~~

[GH] or [GJ] ⟶ ~~K: FFr~~

Clue 3 sounds like a conditional, but further examination shows it can be symbolized more easily. Because having either s or u in a group prevents us from putting the other in the same group, this is simply an antiblock, which we symbolize this way.

[su] (crossed out)

Clue 4 truly is a conditional. Having t in a group forces us to have G, but not, it's worth noting, vice-versa. This clue also has a contrapositive, so we'll use this symbol.

t ⟶ [Gt]

G̸ ⟶ t̸

Look for links and size up the game

We've already done some linking by figuring out what clue 1 means for the makeup of groups M and O, but there's a little more we can do here. Look at group O, which must contain three recent members. Because s and u can't be in the same group as one another, we know that the three recent members here must be t, v, and one of s or u; because t is in the group, then G must be as well. We know, basically, the makeup of group O to start with. Beyond that, it's difficult to predict what the most important factors in working this game will be. Here's our final diagram.

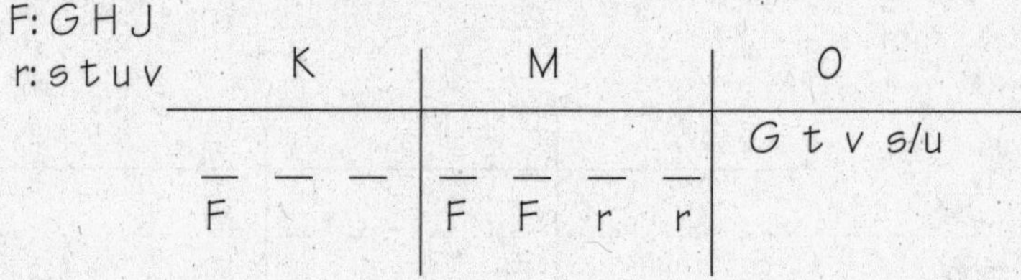

Questions

We'll work the specific questions on a first pass, then the general and complex questions on a second.

2. **C** Specific

v is not in group M.

If v is not in group M, then t must be; otherwise, we would be forced to put s and u in the same group. Thus the recent members in group M are t and one of either s or u, and because t is in this group, then G must be as well. Either J or H is the remaining founding member in this group.

Consider what this means for group K. Either J or H is in group M with G, so we can't have exactly two founding members in group K. We also can't have three founding members in group K because that would put G in all three groups. So group K includes one founding member and two recent members, and the founding member is the other of H or J who wasn't used in group M; everyone, after all, has to be in at least one of the groups.

Who are the recent members in group K? It can't be t because G isn't there, and also putting t in group K would have that element in all three groups. Because s and u can't be together, we must put v in group K and fill the remaining space with one of s or u. We aren't sure which exact groups s and u are in, but we know that one of them fills two of the spaces reserved for them and the other fills one. Here's the full diagram.

K	M	O
H/J v s/u	J/H G t s/u	G t v s/u

The choice here that must be true is (C). (D) could be true, but s may be in either one or two of our groups; none of the rest of the choices could ever be true.

5. **C** Specific

J is in group K but in no other groups.

This tells us right away that G and H are the founding members in group M. Because G and H are together, we can't have two founding members in group K; also, we can't have three founding members in that group because that would put G in all three groups. So group K includes J and two recent members.

Who are the recent members in group K? They can't include t because G isn't in this group; to prevent s and u from being together, we'll have to use v and one of s or u. Now consider group M: We have two recent members to place there; v is in two of the groups already, so we can't include it. Again, because s and u can't be together, we'll have to choose t and one of s or u. Our diagram is filled out; here's what it looks like.

K	M	O
J v s/u	H G t s/u	G t v s/u

The choice here that could be true is (C). All of the rest are contradicted by our deductions.

1. **A** General

Which could be a listing of the members of group K?

The first strategy to try here is to eliminate choices that blatantly violate rules. Choice (B) violates clue 2: It has two founding members in group K but shows G and J together. Choice (E) violates clue 3: It has s and u in the same group. Choice (C) violates clue 4: It has t in a group without G. That leaves only (A) and (D) to consider.

The best thing to do at this stage is try choice (A), which we find can actually work. Here's how.

K	M	O
G H J	H J v u/s	G t v s/u

As to why (D) doesn't work, that's a little more difficult to see (remember, if you've figured out that (A) works, then you shouldn't waste time checking (D)—trust your work). (D) shows two founding members in group K, which means that G can never be with either H or J; that means the two founding members in group M must be H and J. But consider who the recent members in that group must be: It can't be t because G isn't there; it can't be v either because that would put v in all three groups. Choice (D) forces us to put s and u together in group M, which isn't allowed.

However you get there, (A) is the choice we want on this question.

3. **E** General

What must always be true?

On a game where we have initial deductions, it's a fair bet that a question like this will involve one of them. Sure enough, we see on a quick scan that (E) is one of the things we found to start with.

You can also eliminate on a question like this by looking at prior work. (A) doesn't have to be true; we saw a counterexample in our work for question 1 choice (A) above; that counterexample also allows us to eliminate choice (C). We saw a counterexample for choice (B) in our work for question 2, and we've seen numerous potential counterexamples for (D).

Whichever way you go, we have to pick (E) on this one.

4. **D** Complex

G appears at least once with J but doesn't appear with H.

We classified this one as complex because of its task: Count-the-ways questions are often time-consuming, but they may be a little easier once you're familiar with the game.

The fact that G and J are together means we can't have two founding members in group K. The fact that G doesn't appear with H means we can't have three founding members in that group, either. In other words, we have one founding member and two recent members in group K, which leaves group M as the only place where G and J can appear together. H, then, must be the founding member in group K.

Who are the recent members in group K? They can't include t because G isn't there, so to prevent s and u from appearing together, we have to choose v and one of s or u. Now take a look at group M, which also needs two recent members; v is already in two groups, so the recent members here have to be t and one of s or u again. Here's the full diagram, which may look a little familiar from some previous questions.

K	M	O
H v s/u	J G t s/u	G t v s/u

All that's left is to count how many possibilities this represents. There are two basic cases: Either we have two s's and one u or two u's and one s. Nothing constrains us when it comes to choosing which groups these elements appear in, so we just have to make sure we count correctly: If we have two s's and one u, then all we're basically doing is choosing which one of the three groups the u will go in. That's three possibilities. We see that the same situation arises when we have two u's and one s, which gives us three more possibilities.

That's a grand total of six possibilities, which is answer choice (D).

6. **E** General

What can't be true?

Prior work may be helpful on this one. Our work for question 2 includes examples of (A) and (B), both of which we can eliminate off the top. We saw an example of (D) in our work for question 1 choice (A). That leaves (C) and (E) as possibilities. If we try (C), we'll find that it works.

K	M	O
G t u	J H v s	G t v u

The only remaining choice is (E), and we should choose it at this stage. In case you're curious, the reason why (E) can't work is a little complicated. If t and v are in group M, then G must be in group M as well, leaving either J or H to fill out the group as its remaining founding member. Think about what that means for group K: Because G, t, and v are all in two groups already, none of them are available for use in group K, which means among other things that we can't have all three founding members in group K. Because G is already in group M with one of J or H, we can't have two founding members in group K. That means group K includes one founding member and two recent members, but the only two recent members available to put in group K are s and u, which can't go together. No matter how you slice it, the answer here has to be (E).

GAME 3

The four participants in a chess tournament will be selected from a group of six players—S, T, V, W, X, and Z. The participants will be seeded in rank order from first through fourth, with first considered the highest seed and fourth considered the lowest seed. The seeding of the tournament is made according to the following considerations:

Player V cannot be seeded lower than any of players S, T, or X.

Player T cannot be seeded lower than either of players S or X.

Player X cannot be seeded lower than player S.

If player W participates in the tournament, then player X must be the tournament's second seed.

If player Z participates in the tournament, then player T also participates, with player Z seeded higher than player T.

1. Which one of the following could be a complete and accurate list of the players participating in the tournament and their seeds?

(A) first: V; second: T; third: X; fourth: W
(B) first: V; second: X; third: Z; fourth: W
(C) first: V; second: Z; third: T; fourth: S
(D) first: Z; second: T; third: V; fourth: S
(E) first: Z; second: X; third: W; fourth: T

2. Which one of the following is a complete and accurate list of the players, any one of whom could be seeded first?

(A) V, Z
(B) T, V, Z
(C) V, W, Z
(D) T, V, X, Z
(E) V, W, X, Z

3. If T is the second-seeded player in the tournament, then which one of the following could be true?

(A) W is the third-seeded player in the tournament.
(B) X is the fourth-seeded player in the tournament.
(C) S does not participate in the tournament.
(D) X does not participate in the tournament.
(E) Z does not participate in the tournament.

4. Which one of the following is a pair of players, at least one of whom must participate in the tournament?

(A) S and W
(B) T and Z
(C) V and W
(D) X and W
(E) X and Z

5. If X participates in the tournament but S does not, then which one of the following must be true?

(A) T is the third-seeded player.
(B) V is the first-seeded player.
(C) W is the third-seeded player.
(D) X is the third-seeded player.
(E) Z is the first-seeded player.

6. Suppose that instead of including four participants from among the six players, the tournament instead includes five participants, seeded in rank order from first through fifth. If all the other original conditions remain in effect, then each of the following is a player who must participate in the tournament EXCEPT:

(A) S
(B) T
(C) V
(D) W
(E) Z

ANSWERS FOR GAME 3

1. C
2. B
3. E
4. E
5. A
6. D

EXPLANATIONS FOR GAME 3

Diagram and inventory

The task in this game is to order four of the six chess players from first through fourth, with the other two being "out." We'll use a standard ordering diagram with two spaces in an "out" column.

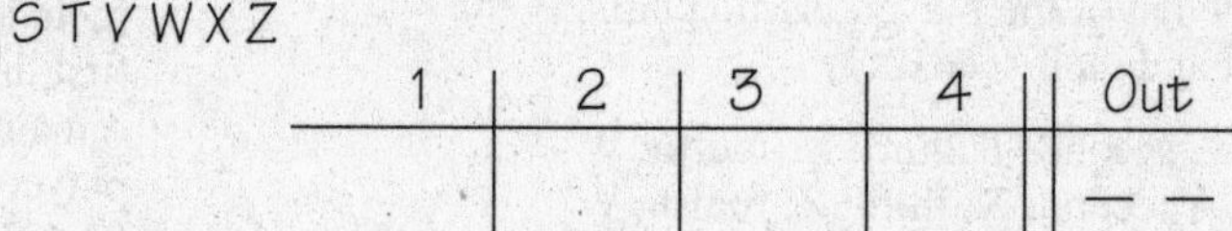

Symbolize the clues and double-check

Clues 1, 2, and 3 are a little difficult to interpret and symbolize until you look at them together. Because there's no assurance that all of the four elements mentioned in these clues are in, these clues are less straightforward than we'd like, but what they add up to is that whichever of these elements are in have to go in the order V, T, X, S, with other elements possibly thrown in. For the sake of clarity, we'll symbolize these three clues together this way.

V—T—X—S

We need to understand that this clue doesn't guarantee us that any particular ones of these elements are in—only that the ones that are must occur in this order.

Clue 4 is a fairly straightforward conditional.

$W \longrightarrow X_2$

$\not{X}_2 \longrightarrow \not{W}$

Clue 5 is a little more complicated. When Z is in, T is also in, with Z before T; the most useful contrapositive of this would be that if T is out, then Z must also be out, although there are other circumstances in which we might be able to deduce that Z is out (for instance, if T is the first seed). Here's the simplest and most useful symbol we can come up with for now.

Z ⟶ Z — T (both in)

~~T~~ ⟶ ~~Z~~

Look for links and size up the game

It's difficult to make definite deductions at this stage, although there do turn out to be at least a few. Because they depend on thinking about several "what-if" scenarios, however, we'll move to the questions under the assumption that we don't have these deductions in hand. The one thing we can see right away that we'll need to look out for in working the questions is when we've filled up our "out" column; once the four players participating are set, our ordering clues should provide us some very good guidance on how players have to be seeded.

Questions

We'll work the grab-a-rule question first, then the specific questions on a first pass, then the general and complex questions on our second pass.

1. **C** Grab-a-rule

Always a nice way to start out a game. Our composite ordering symbol (clues 1 through 3 combined) gets rid of choice (D), which violates clue 1, and choice (E), which violates clue 2. Clue 4 gets rid of choice (A), which has W in but X not second. Clue 5 gets rid of choice (B), which has Z in but T out. That leaves us with the answer, (C).

3. **E** Specific

T is seeded second.

T second tells us that X can't be second, so W must be out. It also leaves only one slot with a higher seed than T; although this space could be occupied by either V or Z, because there's only one available, we know that the other of Z or V has to go out. That leaves our remaining elements—X and S—to receive the third and fourth seeds, respectively. Here's the diagram.

1	2	3	4	Out
V/Z	T	X	S	W Z/V

The only choice that could be true, given the information in our diagram, is (E), and that's the choice we want.

5. **A** Specific:

X is in; S is out.

The main deduction here is pretty tough; it depends on looking at what happens if we put W in. W in would force X to go in second, which would leave only one space open in front of it. V and T can only be ranked above X, so one of them would have to receive the first seed, and the other would have to go out, filling that area of our diagram. But then what about Z? Putting it in forces us to use T, but then both Z and T would have to be seeded higher than X, and there simply isn't room for them both. The upshot of all of this is that there's no way, in this case, that we can put W in.

Once you've got that deduction, the rest is pretty easy. With S and W both out, we're left with V, Z, T, and X in. V and Z go in higher seeds than T, and X has to go in a lower seed than T, leaving V and Z to occupy the first and second seeds in either order, T in the third seed, and X in the fourth seed. Here's the diagram.

1	2	3	4	Out
V/Z	Z/V	T	X	S W

The one that has to be true here is (A), the choice we want.

2. **B** General

Complete and accurate list of players who could be first.

It's a judgment call as to whether you want to work this one before or after question 4, but we'll go ahead and do it at this point in the order.

We've already seen examples in which V and Z are first; unfortunately, all of the choices include both of these elements. The first thing to try is looking for differences: T seems like a key one because there's a 2/3 split of choices that involve it. We check to see whether T can be first. T first forces both V and Z out because there's no higher seed available. That means that we're left with X, S, and W to go in with T. W in forces X into the second seed, but there's no problem with that: S and W can go in the third and fourth seeds in either order. Here's the diagram.

1	2	3	4	Out
T	X	S/W	W/S	V Z

Because we now know that T can be first, we eliminate (A), (C), and (E). The only difference between our remaining answer choices is X, so we consider what happens when we try to put X first. X first forces both V and T out because there's no higher seed available, and that fills our "out" column. But T out forces us to put Z out as well, and there isn't enough space in the "out" column to accommodate it. So there's no way we can have X first.

That leaves us with (B) as the answer to pick here.

4. **E** General

A pair of elements, at least one of which must be in.

This amounts to asking us to find the choice that lists a pair of elements that can't both be out. A quick scan may allow you to see the answer, and if so, that's great. Otherwise, prior work is a good place to start. We've seen S and W out together in question 5, so we can eliminate (A). We've seen V and W out together in question 3, so we can eliminate (C). We haven't seen relevant examples of any of the other cases, so now we have to do a little work.

To check (B), we try to put T and Z both out. That leaves us with S, V, W, and X all in. W in means X must be second; V, then, has to go in front of it in first. That leaves S and W to go in either order in third and fourth. Here's the diagram.

1	2	3	4	Out
V	X	S/W	W/S	T Z

That eliminates (B), but we're not there yet. To check (D), we try to put X and W both out. That leaves us with S, T, V, and Z all in. V and Z both have to be seeded higher than T, and S must be seeded lower. So T is the third seed, S is the fourth seed, and V and Z are the first and second seeds in either order. Here's the diagram.

1	2	3	4	Out
V/Z	Z/V	T	S	W X

That eliminates (D), leaving us with (E) as the only remaining answer. We should definitely pick it at this stage; no need to spend time trying it out as well.

In case you're curious, a moment's inspection shows why we can't have both X and Z out. X out forces W out, but there's no room for it in the out column. (E) is definitely the right answer here.

6. **D** Complex

Rule-changer.

Beware! Whenever you see a question like this on a game, always work it last. Because any example you generate here won't follow all the rules of the game, you don't want to put yourself in the position of, perhaps, accidentally using this work on a general question. Also, rule-changer questions can be much more difficult and time-consuming than the other questions in a game, although this isn't always the case.

This one isn't too awful, despite how it looks. Now we're picking five players, not four, which means we have only one space available in the "out" column. The question asks us to find the element that doesn't have to be in. From the contrapositives of our conditional clues, we know that X and T must be included because each of these elements, if it's out, brings another element out with it. Only T, sadly, is among our answer choices.

The next thing to do is to work on (A) by seeing what happens when we put S out. That forces us to put T, V, W, X, and Z all in. The key here is that having W in still forces X to be the second seed. There are three elements—V, Z, and T—that would all have to be seeded higher than X, and only one space to put them in. So not only is (A) not our answer (there's no way we could put S out, so it has to be in), but we've got a pretty good idea of what's going on in this new situation.

Any time we put W in, we're going to be forced to put X second, but because three elements have to appear in front of X, and we only have room to put one ahead of X and one out, there's no way we'll be able to make it work. In other words, any time we put W in, we encounter a problem. That means W has to be out, and we need look no further than (D) to find the answer we want for this question.

4

Reading Comprehension

WHAT IS READING COMPREHENSION?

The Reading Comprehension section, as you might suspect, consists of long, fairly complex passages, each accompanied by a series of questions about that passage. The passages span quite a wide range in subject matter, but typically there's one from each of the following areas: arts/humanities, social sciences, physical sciences, and law. You do not need any prior knowledge of any of these areas to be able to answer the questions.

You may be wondering where these passages come from. Does LSAC write them, or did they come from some other published source? The answer is: a little bit of both. Many times, the LSAT writers will take material from a book or journal and then "adapt" it to make it suitable for testing purposes. What does "adapt" mean? Because you're not supposed to need outside information to be able to understand the passage, the test writers must remove any material that would require a deeper understanding of the subject beyond the limits of the passage. As they edit out these references, however, much of the transitional material that made the passage readable in the first place is taken out as well. What they're left with is a pretty dense passage, chock full of details, with choppy or sometimes even nonexistent transitions from one subject to the next. That sounds exactly like an LSAT passage.

WHAT DOES THIS SECTION TEST?

More than anything, Reading Comprehension tests your ability to answer questions about the author's main idea and find specific details scattered throughout the passage. Because the passages are presented in such a way as to hinder comprehension, this section also tests your ability to manage these tasks efficiently in a short period of time.

WHY IS THIS SECTION ON THE LSAT?

Reading Comprehension is on the LSAT to test your ability to read carefully and manage large amounts of information in a short period of time. This section also tests your ability to answer questions about a passage without bringing in any information from outside the passage.

THE SECTION ITSELF

The Reading Comprehension section contains four passages, and each passage has five to eight questions attached to it, for a total of 26 to 28 questions. The passages are all typically between 55 and 65 lines.

Before we begin, take a moment to read the instructions to this section:

> Directions: Each passage in this section is followed by a group of questions to be answered on the basis of what is stated or implied in the passage. For some questions, more than one of the choices could conceivably answer the question. However, you are to choose the best answer, that is, the response that most accurately and completely answers the question, and blacken the corresponding space on your answer sheet.

These are the directions that will appear on your LSAT. As usual on the LSAT, the official directions provide very little help. Review them now. They will not change. Don't waste time reading them in the test room.

Reading Comprehension: General Strategies

The following text is a list of general strategies that you should use when you are working on the Reading Comprehension section. Make sure you take these strategies seriously.

Take your time

If you rush through the Reading Comprehension section of the LSAT, you're going to make several mistakes. The questions and answer choices are just as difficult as they are in the Arguments section, and you've got more of them, too. So if you've been getting to all four reading comprehension passages, but you're only getting 60 percent of the questions correct, slow down! Try working on only three passages and see how your accuracy will increase. If you're getting more right than not, however, then you need to get to all four.

Your mantra: *I will slow down and focus on getting the questions I work on right, even if that means not getting to all the questions. I will increase my accuracy and thereby increase my score.*

Pick your passages

As in Games, you don't want to open up the Reading Comprehension section and just start doing the first passage. Look at all four passages—see which one or ones look easier to you, and start there. There are several criteria—organization of the passage, subject matter of the passage, number of questions, types of questions, length of the questions and answer choices, and so on. We'll talk more about how to choose reading comprehension passages, but the point is to find the passages that you think you'll be more effective on and do those first.

Your mantra: *I will evaluate the Reading Comprehension section and put the passages in my own order.*

Transfer your answers after each passage

Work on *all* the questions on a particular passage and then transfer your answers to the answer sheet. You need a few seconds to regroup after each passage, and transferring your answers allows your brain to do something mindless for a few seconds. When you're down to five minutes, make sure you've filled in an answer for every single question. Then, go back and work on remaining questions you have time for, changing bubbles one at a time as you go. That way, if time is mistakenly called early, you've got an answer for every single question.

Your mantra: *I will transfer my answers in groups after each passage until five minutes are left.*

Breathe

After you've completed each passage, take a ten-second break to take three deep breaths. Transfer your answers from that passage, and then start another passage. You've cleared your mind, and you're ready to push on.

Your mantra: *I will use ten seconds after each passage I complete to take some deep breaths.*

Your Mantras and You

Here they are again:

> *I will slow down and focus on getting the questions I work on right, even if that means not getting to all the questions. I will increase my accuracy and thereby increase my score.*
>
> *I will evaluate the Reading Comprehension section and put the passages in my own order.*
>
> *I will transfer my answers in groups after each passage until five minutes are left.*
>
> *I will use ten seconds after each passage I complete to take some deep breaths.*

Reading Comprehension: A Step-by-Step Process

We're about to give you a four-step process that will help you with the Reading Comprehension section of the LSAT. Whenever you do a passage, follow these steps exactly. This process is designed to help you read the passage actively, searching for what you'll need to answer the questions. That's the key to working efficiently and effectively through this section of the LSAT.

Step 1: Analyze the passage

LSAT passages are unlike probably anything else you've ever read, either for school, work, or personal enjoyment. Because of this, you need to develop a method of reading that will suit both the passage and the purpose of the section, which is not about reading but about answering questions. If you read the passage the way you normally might, you'd probably focus on the ideas you think are significant or perhaps interesting. The problem with this approach is that what determines whether information is important is whether it will show up in a question or answer choice. Plus, the passages are often so dense that they're very difficult to read, not to mention at times deadly boring. Remember, that's the test writers' intent: to make your eyes start to glaze over, forcing you to reread a single sentence multiple times, thereby wasting time, or to force you to reread the passage several times later on, looking for something in an answer choice. You need to have an effective reading strategy to combat these issues.

So what should you do? You do want to read the passage, not just skim it, but when you read you need to focus on finding the passage's thesis, key ideas, and structure. Don't worry about the details at this point. By doing this, you will avoid getting bogged down in the passage's details, but you'll also make it possible to find those details later on should you need to. This will also save time—if there's a complicated process described, it's more important at this stage to know what's being described and where in the passage it's located than to fully understand the description that's given. If you are asked about it later, that's when you'll spend the time to really understand that information.

How you mark up the passage during this time is also crucial. You should be making notes next to each paragraph about what you'll find there, bracketing sentences that express the author's thesis or key ideas of the passage, and circling key transitional words. What you shouldn't be doing is underlining. Why not? When you underline text, all you've indicated to yourself is that there's important stuff there, but not what the ideas themselves are. Imagine that you've done that for several places in a passage. Each time you go to a new question, you'll have to look at each underlined area to remind yourself of what's there to figure out which underlined section might be relevant to the question. On a timed test, this is inefficient. Margin notes, brackets, circles—these will serve the same purpose as underlining, but they will also be much easier for your eye to see, thereby saving time. Essentially, by annotating in this way, you're creating a *visual map* of the passage to help you locate information quickly and easily. How much you put into the map will be up to you, based on how challenging the passage itself is.

Aside from the author's thesis, which you should always try to find and then make note of (often it can be found in the first paragraph or at the end of the passage), what other key ideas should you be looking for? Many LSAT passages contain multiple points of view. You should be keeping track of when the point of view shifts, generally by circling whatever indicator word announces this change (e.g., "however," "on the other hand," "contrary to," etc.) and making a note in the margin as to which perspective is now being discussed. Also pay attention to shifts in the author's own argument: It's common for an author to describe a theory in detail only to discount it in the next sentence. Think about the author's tone. Does he or she seem to favor or criticize something in the passage, or is he or she completely impartial? Put + or – signs in the margin next to the places where the author's tone comes across so you can find it later. Does the passage contain a sequence of events? Circle words such as *first*, *next*, and *final*, to help you keep track of that sequence.

By the time you've finished working on the passage, you should be able to state the author's main idea and describe the overall structure of the passage. If you are able to extract this much from your initial reading of the passage, you will be well equipped to deal with the questions that follow.

Step 2: Evaluate the question task

As we saw with both arguments and games, understanding what the question is asking is crucial to getting the question right. The LSAT writers are very skilled at finding complicated ways to ask you otherwise straightforward questions. Always take a moment to rephrase the question in your own words.

Another important aspect of successfully working a reading comprehension passage is to approach the questions on your own terms. Just as we saw with games, the order in which the questions are presented may not be the best order in which to answer them. LSAT reading comprehension questions fall into three basic categories: specific, general, and complex. We'll talk more about what each of these categories includes a little further on in this chapter. For the purposes of ordering the questions, however, we generally recommend that you begin with specific questions and then move on to the general ones, saving the complex ones for last. Some test takers find that once they've stated the main idea for themselves after working on the passage, they can readily attempt the general questions and then do the specific ones. This is also fine, as long as you leave the complex questions for last. If you find that you tend to miss many of the general questions, however, go back to doing them in the order we suggest.

Specific questions ask you to find certain information in the passage, and they may ask you either for that information directly or why the author chose to include it. They may ask about the function of a particular part of a passage. They may have line references but often do not, which is why it's necessary to map the passage well in Step 1. The basic premise behind a specific question, however, is that the information will be found directly in the passage.

General questions, on the other hand, require you to take the entire passage into account. These will ask for the author's main idea (what the author wants to get across), the author's primary purpose (why the author is writing), the author's tone (how the author feels about the subject at hand), or the overall structure or organization of the passage (how the passage is constructed or moves from topic to topic).

Finally, complex questions will ask you to take something from the passage, be it a specific piece of information or the author's main idea, and apply it to something not included in the passage. They may ask you to weaken or strengthen a claim or to find a situation analogous to something in the passage. What defines these questions, however, is the fact that they require you to take one step away from the passage when working with the answer choices, and the choices will often deal with new information not mentioned in the passage. For this reason, you want to save these for last.

Step 3: Apply the strategy

For each of the different question types, you'll have a specific approach to follow. Regardless of question type, you'll always want to go back to the passage to find whatever information the question asks about. Remember, the LSAT is basically like an open-book test, and therefore you shouldn't rely on your memory of the passage when answering the questions (if you do, the test writers have made sure that you'll see a wrong answer you'll like). This test is mentally exhausting enough already. What if you have reading comprehension as section 5 on the test? How will your brain feel at that point? Pretty tired, we're guessing. So always go back to the passage to see what was said.

Once you've done that, try to get a sense of what the answer choice needs to talk about or accomplish to answer the question. Just as with arguments, you'll be much better off if you have a sense of what you need before you begin reading through the answer choices. And if you get a question that doesn't give you any leads in the question stem, you'll have to go back to the passage to check out each answer choice instead, which is one more reason to have a solid map of the passage from Step 1.

Step 4: Use Process of Elimination

As usual, this is the final step in our strategy. You want to compare what you said the answer needed to do in Step 3 with the choices you're given. Your goal is to eliminate things that are definitely wrong, meaning that you can pinpoint something in the choice that makes it wrong. "It sounds bad" is never a valid reason to cross off an answer choice—the choices are designed to be unappealing. Cross off answers that don't match what you came up with or that aren't supported by information in the passage. Also beware of information that's in the passage but has no relevance to the question being asked. We'll talk at greater length about POE later on in this chapter.

What you should definitely keep in mind as you go through answer choices, however, is that the one that has nothing wrong with it is the one you're looking for, whether or not it's phrased in a way that matches what you said you were looking for. We're not looking for the best-phrased answer choice; we're looking for one that does what we need it to do without having anything wrong with it. Whether we think the credited response is worded badly is beside the point.

Let's Do a Reading Comprehension Passage

Okay, those are the steps. Now let's see how they work on a real reading comprehension passage. Try to complete all of this in about 15 minutes—don't worry if it takes you longer than that, however. With practice, you can get your speed down to 12 or even 9 minutes (i.e., three or four passages completed).

After the passage, we'll give you some extra techniques for attacking this section of the LSAT, just as we did in the Arguments and Games chapters.

READING COMPREHENSION PASSAGE: *CELEBRITY LAW*

Recently, the right of public personalities to direct and profit from all commercial exploitations of their fame has gained widespread acceptance. Recognition of this "right of publicity," however, has raised difficult questions concerning the proper scope and duration of the right as well as its relationship to free speech and free trade interests. Often, the "type" of personality, be it an entertainer, politician, or athlete, also weighs on this decision-making process.

The right of publicity protects economic interests of celebrities in their own fame by allowing them to control and profit from the publicity values that they have created. Before courts recognized this right, celebrities' primary protection against the unauthorized commercial appropriation of their names or likenesses was a suit for invasion of privacy. Privacy law, however, proved to be an inadequate response to the legal questions presented by celebrities seeking to protect their economic interest in fame. Whereas privacy law protects a person's right to be left alone, publicity law proceeds from antithetical assumptions. Celebrities do not object to public attention—they thrive on it. However, they seek to benefit from any commercial use of their popularity.

A celebrity's public image has many aspects, each of which may be appropriated for a variety of purposes. Plaintiffs have sought to protect various attributes including name, likeness, a particular routine or act, characters made famous by their celebrity, unique style, and biographical information. In deciding whether the right of publicity applies to a particular attribute, courts consider underlying legal and policy goals.

Two goals support recognition of the right of publicity: the promotion of creative endeavor and the prevention of unjust enrichment through the theft of goodwill. Courts determine the scope of publicity rights by balancing these policies against countervailing First Amendment and free trade interests. Recognizing a celebrity's ability to control the exercise of some personal attribute may limit the "speech" of would-be appropriators and give the celebrity a commercial monopoly. Thus, the value of promoting creativity and preventing unjust enrichment must outweigh negative constitutional and commercial repercussions before courts extend the right of publicity to any particular attribute.

The value of a publicity right in a particular attribute depends, in large part, on the length of time such a right is recognized and protected by the law. Courts disagree on whether publicity rights survive the death of their creators. Some courts advocate unconditional devisability. They emphasize that the ability to control exploitation of fame is a property right, carrying all the characteristics of the title. Other courts conclude that the right of publicity terminates at the celebrity's death. These courts fear that recognizing postmortem publicity rights would negatively affect free speech and free trade.

The right of publicity, especially in the cases of well-known politicians and statesmen, often conflicts with First Amendment interests and thus should be defined with care and precision.

1. Which of the following statements best summarizes the above passage?

(A) An assessment of privacy law reveals that publicity law is a more appropriate legal remedy for public personalities.

(B) The promotion of creative endeavor justifies the legal recognition of the right of publicity.

(C) The courts, rather than the celebrities themselves, must determine the relative importance of commercial and constitutional concerns.

(D) The legal issues regarding the right to publicity are complex and have yet to be fully resolved.

(E) Widely accepted approaches to deciding publicity law cases conflict with First Amendment interests.

2. According to the passage, the judicial response to "right of publicity" questions has been

(A) theoretical
(B) inconclusive
(C) creative
(D) disdainful
(E) widely respected

3. It can be inferred from the passage that a characteristic of "devisability" (line 68) is the ability to be

(A) commercially appropriated with the author's permission
(B) divided into more than one legal entity
(C) assigned by a will
(D) recognized as a commercial monopoly
(E) structured in several equal branches

4. Which one of the following can be inferred from the information in the passage?

(A) First Amendment ramifications of extending the right of publicity to politicians should be analyzed.
(B) There is rarely any provable nexus between exploitation during life and career incentive.
(C) Celebrities invest substantial time and money to achieve uncertain success and are thus entitled to whatever value accrues from these efforts.
(D) Concerns regarding unjust enrichment from biographical data outweigh the right to disseminate information under the First Amendment.
(E) It is in the public interest to reward successful entertainers for their efforts and thereby encourage artists to devote their lives to creative endeavors.

5. According to the passage, privacy laws are inadequate as legal remedies for celebrities because

(A) public personalities have no redress for unauthorized commercial appropriation of their images
(B) private individuals waive privacy rights by becoming public figures
(C) stars wish to be protected from the public only when they are not successful
(D) the laws do not address the financial issues inherent in a public figure's fame
(E) celebrities have a responsibility to the public to share their created personae and not avoid public attention

6. Which one of the following situations would most reasonably call upon the "right of publicity" as discussed in the passage?

(A) A novelist objects to the unauthorized reprinting of a portion of his book in a student's paper.
(B) An athlete plans to design and market, but not promote, a line of sportswear.
(C) The well-known "catch-phrase" of a local talk-show host is used as part of an ad campaign for a supermarket.
(D) The president of a small company bequeaths his business to an employee but his family contests the will.
(E) The work of a celebrated screen actor is re-edited after the actor's death.

Step 1: Analyze the passage
Below is a list of what each paragraph of the passage told us, and what we felt was important in it. Then we'll show you what we thought were the main idea and structure of the passage as a whole. Here we go:

Paragraph 1: Introduction of the concept of "right of publicity" and its problems.

Paragraph 2: Why right of publicity was needed: Privacy laws didn't do the job.

Paragraph 3: What the right of publicity seeks to protect.

Paragraph 4: Pros and cons of the right of publicity.

Paragraph 5: How long does right of publicity apply: differing judicial perspectives.

Paragraph 6: Right of publicity and politicians: often a problem.

Break up the passage into smaller chunks of information—remember, it's easier to process a little at a time and then put it all together.

As you can see, we've retained very little information here; all we've done is created an outline of what each paragraph contributes to the passage as a whole. From this outline, however, we should be able to come up with the main idea of the passage and describe its structure as a whole. You should always be able to state both the main idea and structure of a passage after you're finished reading it.

Main idea: *Something about the origins of "right of publicity," and how there are disagreements about how and when this right applies.*

Structure: *The concept of right of publicity is introduced, its origins are discussed, and several situations to which it applies are described.*

That's it. We'll save a more in-depth analysis of this for when we come up with our answers to the questions. And now that we know where the information is in the passage, we should be able to do that with efficiency. Let's go to Step 2.

Step 2: Evaluate the question task
For each question, we'll need to state what the question is asking for in our own words. We'll do this as we go through each question; for now, though, let's set up the question order based on question type. Questions 2, 3, and 5 are specific, so you should answer those first; questions 1 and 4 are general; and question 6 is complex, so that one should definitely be saved for the end. You may have chosen to do questions 1 and 4 earlier on; whether or not you got them correct will help you determine what strategy you should use in the future. To make it simple for now, though, we'll go through the questions in the order in which they appeared.

Steps 3 and 4: Apply the strategy and use process of elimination
We'll go through each of these steps for each question individually. Our approach to answering the question in our own words and our use of POE will vary with each question. Let's get started.

1. Which of the following statements best summarizes the above passage?

(A) An assessment of privacy law reveals that publicity law is a more appropriate legal remedy for public personalities.
(B) The promotion of creative endeavor justifies the legal recognition of the right of publicity.
(C) The courts, rather than the celebrities themselves, must determine the relative importance of commercial and constitutional concerns.
(D) The legal issues regarding the right to publicity are complex and have yet to be fully resolved.
(E) Widely accepted approaches to de iding publicity law cases conflict with F rst Amendment interests.

This is a main idea question, so we'll want to remind ourselves of what we said the author's main point was. We said that the right of publicity is a relatively recent development and that all its ramifications have yet to be fully worked out. We'll want to match this against the answer choices.

(A) is too specific. Privacy law is mentioned only briefly in the second paragraph. (B) is also too narrow; the promotion of creative endeavor is mentioned only in the fourth paragraph. Although (C) is probably true, the passage is not about who must determine the relative importance of these concerns—it's about right of publicity. (D) looks pretty good; it mentions right of publicity, and the lack of complete resolution. (E) is just plain wrong; according to the passage, there are no widely accepted approaches to right of publicity.

2. According to the passage, the judicial response to "right of publicity" questions has been

(A) theoretical
(B) inconclusive
(C) creative
(D) disdainful
(E) widely respected

This is a specific question; we're asked to characterize the judicial response to questions concerning the right of publicity. We should be able to find this somewhere in the passage. A quick look at our map from before indicates that there's a discussion of judicial perspectives on this in the fifth paragraph. Rereading that paragraph, we learn that there are differing opinions on at least one aspect of the right of publicity. Our answer to this question, then, would be something such as "lacking consensus." When we compare our answer to the answer choices, choice (B), "inconclusive," is the only one that comes close.

3. It can be inferred from the passage that a characteristic of "devisability" (line 68) is the ability to be

(A) commercially appropriated with the author's permission
(B) divided into more than one legal entity
(C) assigned by a will
(D) recognized as a commercial monopoly
(E) structured in several equal branches

This is a specific question; we're asked to figure out what the concept of "divisability" might mean. Notice that this question began with the phrase "It can be inferred from the passage that." Regarding inference questions in Chapter 2 on Arguments, you'll remember that we said that "infer" means "paraphrase"—you have to be able to prove your answer based on the information presented in the passage. The same holds true here. You should never try to make real-life inferences on LSAT reading comprehension questions; that is, you should never try to extrapolate or make use of any outside knowledge you might have on a given subject. If it helps, just cross those words off and read the question as beginning "A characteristic of...."

We've also been given a line reference, so that helps us locate the information in the passage. Don't fall into the trap, however, of only reading that one line in the passage. Make sure to go back and read the paragraph it's located in because context will be crucial to determining the answer. In this case, all we know is that it relates to the issue of whether right of publicity ends with a celebrity's death or whether it continues, as would a property right. That may not be much information, but it's a start. Now let's look at the answers.

(A) mentions cases in which permission *has* been obtained from the author—this is not discussed anywhere in the passage. (B) talks about division into more than one entity, which is also something not discussed in the passage. (C) talks about wills, so it might work because wills have something to do with death. (D) brings up the concept of a commercial monopoly, which is used in a different context in the passage. (E) is out of scope—structuring something in branches is never mentioned. So we're going to have to pick (D).

4. Which one of the following can be inferred from the information in the passage?

(A) First Amendment ramifications of extending the right of publicity to politicians should be analyzed.
(B) There is rarely any provable nexus between exploitation during life and career incentive.
(C) Celebrities invest substantial time and money to achieve uncertain success and are thus entitled to whatever value accrues from these efforts.
(D) Concerns regarding unjust enrichment from biographical data outweigh the right to disseminate information under the First Amendment.
(E) It is in the public interest to reward successful entertainers for their efforts and thereby encourage artists to devote their lives to creative endeavors.

This time we have a question that asks for what we know to be true based on the passage, and as we saw above, "infer" means "paraphrase." One of these choices we must be able to prove from information in the passage. Unfortunately, there's nothing in the question stem to lead us to a particular place in the passage as a starting point. And from the question stem alone, we don't even know whether we'll be looking for an answer that addresses the passage as a whole or only one part of the passage. We do know that we're going to have to check each answer choice against what was said in the passage, and this is where our map will be a real time-saver. Use POE to eliminate anything we can't find in the passage. No mention is made of exploitation versus career incentive (B), the time and money needed to achieve celebrity status (C), enrichment from biographical data (D), or what is in the public interest (E). So (A) must be the right answer, and this answer is, incidentally, clearly supported by the final paragraph of the passage.

5. According to the passage, privacy laws are inadequate as legal remedies for celebrities because

(A) public personalities have no redress for unauthorized commercial appropriation of their images
(B) private individuals waive privacy rights by becoming public figures
(C) stars wish to be protected from the public only when they are not successful
(D) the laws do not address the financial issues inherent in a public figure's fame
(E) celebrities have a responsibility to the public to share their created personae and not avoid public attention

This is a specific question; we are asked why privacy laws don't adequately take care of celebrities' legal needs. If we look at our map, we see that this issue is addressed in the second paragraph. Upon rereading it, we learn that privacy laws weren't fully equipped to deal with the economic aspects of fame. We want an answer that talks about the financial side of things.

(A) is a trap answer—check back against the passage and you'll see why. Lines 17 to 21 discuss this very concept, yet it's stated that privacy law in fact provided some means of protection against this problem. Plus, there's no mention made here of monetary issues. Cross it off. (B) also omits any mention of economic matters, so it's gone as well. (C) is not relevant because right of publicity has to do with financial protection, not protection from the public. (D) looks like a solid answer; it covers the whole scope of financial issues relevant to right of publicity. (E) is not relevant; once again, the issue at hand is why we need "right of publicity" laws, not whether celebrities actually have a right to privacy.

6. Which one of the following situations would most reasonably call upon the "right of publicity" as discussed in the passage?

(A) A novelist objects to the unauthorized reprinting of a portion of his book in a student's paper.
(B) An athlete plans to design and market, but not promote, a line of sportswear.
(C) The well-known "catch-phrase" of a local talk-show host is used as part of an ad campaign for a supermarket.
(D) The president of a small company bequeaths his business to an employee but his family contests the will.
(E) The work of a celebrated screen actor is re-edited after the actor's death.

This is a complex question; we are asked to take the concept of "right of publicity" and apply it to a situation that is outside the scope of the passage. As with any complex question, however, we'll still need to go back to the passage to figure out what we need to compare the answer choices to. In this case, we need a solid definition of what the right of publicity covers. Once more, we look to our map. The third paragraph discusses what the right of publicity is meant to protect, so we should look there. We also know, from our previous question, that what's underlying this right is the desire for financial protection.

(A) is not appropriate because the student is not writing the paper for financial gain. (B) is not appropriate because the athlete has a right to his or her own fame. (C) looks good—the supermarket is making commercial use of the talk-show host's celebrity image. (D) has nothing to do with fame, and (E) is not a clear issue because we do not know who is doing the re-editing and whether they have the right to do it.

So, that's that. Now that you know the basic approach, you just need to practice, practice, practice. But first, a few more words of advice.

Reading Comprehension Technique: Reading the Questions First

Some test takers find that it helps them to read through the questions first before beginning to read the passage. Although we don't consider it necessary to an effective reading comprehension strategy, it can certainly be useful as a sort of Step 0, a prelude to Step 1.

What does previewing the questions entail? You quickly look through the questions to see what subject matter or themes show up with the greatest frequency, perhaps circling the specific questions that you think you'd like to start with once you've finished working on the passage. One advantage to doing this is that it gives you a bit more guidance as to what might be important to focus on while reading the passage; you may be able to note exactly where the answers to certain questions are as you map the passage. It also provides a bit more familiarity when reading, especially if the subject matter itself appears foreign.

If you're not sure whether this will help you, try out our four-step strategy with and without previewing the questions on a few passages each. See which one helps you to be more accurate—that's the strategy you ultimately want to adopt, even if it feels a bit strange at first.

A few things to keep in mind when reading the question first—it shouldn't take you more than 30 seconds' worth of time. If you do this on all four passages, that would be two full minutes devoted to just that step, before you even begin reading anything in the passages. So for it to be effective and efficient, you have to be able to get what you need from the questions quickly. Also, don't allow your reading the questions first to justify stopping midway through the passage to answer a question. Although you may have found an answer to one question, recall that at least a couple of questions, if not more, will depend on your understanding of the author's main idea. If you stop to answer a question in the middle of the process of working the passage, it will be more difficult to get a clear sense of what the author's larger point is.

Reading Comprehension Technique: Question Types

Reading comprehension questions fall into three basic categories: specific, general, and complex. These categories are based on what type of information you'll need to answer the question and how you'll be asked to apply that information. Let's take a closer look.

Specific questions

These questions ask you about information that will be found directly in the passage, usually in only one part of the passage. There are several varieties that you might see.

- Retrieval questions: These will ask you to locate information in the passage and match it to one of the answer choices. Your focus will be on what is said about a particular matter.

- Purpose questions: These will ask about the author's reason for including specific facts. Your focus will be on why it is mentioned as opposed to what is said.
- Infer/Imply/Suggest questions: Treat these as you would a retrieval or purpose question. Find the information and paraphrase it, but don't extrapolate. These can also be more general in scope, depending on the answer choices. But you should always be able to put your finger on the place in the passage that supports your answer.
- Tone/Attitude questions: These questions will ask how the author feels about a particular idea or concept in the passage. The author's attitude here may differ from the overall tone of the passage.
- Organization/Structure questions: These will ask how a particular part of the passage functions in relation to another part or to the passage as a whole.

General questions

These questions will ask about the passage as a whole. As with specific questions, there are several types that may appear.

- Main Idea questions: Very often, a main idea question may be the first question you'll see. You're looking to state the general point of the passage or the author's thesis.
- Primary Purpose questions: These are similar to main idea questions, but for these you'll focus on what the author wants to accomplish by writing the passage (*why* he or she is writing) instead of on what the author actually says.
- Tone/Attitude questions: In this case, you'll be asked for the overall tone of the passage.
- Organization/Structure: These will focus on the passage's overall structure and how the passage moves from one topic to the next.

Complex questions

These questions require a couple of steps and thus are more involved than either general or specific questions. They will usually ask you to take information from the passage and then apply it to situations or ideas not discussed in the passage. Unlike specific and general questions, you will have to take a step away from the passage when approaching these questions, although not a very big one.

- Weaken questions: These will ask you to attack a claim or idea expressed in the passage. Do not treat these like weaken arguments, however. There's no need to look for assumptions, only the information you're asked to weaken. The answer choices will likely bring in new information not found in the passage.

- Strengthen questions: These will ask you to further support a claim or idea expressed in the passage. Do not treat these like strengthen arguments, however. There's no need to look for assumptions, only the information you're asked to strengthen. The answer choices will likely bring in new information not found in the passage.
- Analogy questions: These will ask you to focus on a particular idea or situation from the passage and then find a similar instance in the answer choices. As with weaken and strengthen questions, the answer choices will likely contain new ideas not discussed in the passage.

Occasionally, you'll also come across some miscellaneous questions that don't easily fit into any of the categories we've mentioned here. There's no reason to panic, however. Just put a little more effort into Step 2 on those—take the time to figure out what the question is asking and restate it in your own words before moving on.

Reading Comprehension Technique: Process of Elimination

As you can see from the previous passage, coming up with your own answers helped you on many of the questions. You will still have to use Process of Elimination, however, in many instances. Just like in arguments, you can use several Process of Elimination techniques when working on reading comprehension passages. The most important ones are described below.

Wrong part of the passage

As we mentioned earlier in the chapter, many of the wrong answer choices do contain content consistent with the passage. The problem is that this information is from a different part of the passage. For instance, if a passage is describing the properties of three different kinds of acids, and a question asks about the properties of the second acid, many of the wrong choices will be properties of the first and third acids. As long as you focus on the information about the second acid only, you'll be able to eliminate any choices that talk about the first and third acids.

Extreme language

Here's a familiar technique from arguments. And as we mentioned in the arguments chapter, extreme language is usually very difficult to prove, so it's rarely contained in correct answers. Because LSAT authors can have some strong opinions from time to time, however, you shouldn't simply eliminate choices with extreme language without checking that language against what was said in the passage. Think of extreme language as a red flag. When you see it, you should automatically look back to the passage to see whether you can prove that the author really did use such extreme language. If not, then you can eliminate the answer choice.

Too narrow or too broad

Main idea and primary purpose questions often have wrong answers that are either too narrow or too broad. Remember that the main idea or primary purpose should encompass the entire passage but not more or less than that. You'll see many wrong answers that either mention something true that was contained in only a part of the passage or was accomplished in only a single paragraph, or others that would include not only the main topic of the passage, but also much more beyond that (for instance, the passage discusses dolphins, but the answer choice talks about all marine life forms).

Partially wrong

This is a popular type of wrong answer on LSAT reading comprehension. Your goal is to seek out and eliminate answer choices that contain anything at all that might make them wrong, so no matter how good a choice may start out, if you see anything amiss, you have to get rid of the answer. Very often, a single word may be the cause of the problem (for example, use of the word *not* to create a contradiction). In addition, it's possible that the problem with the answer choice may show up later in the choice—the test writers are hoping to lull test takers into a false sense of security. For this reason, it is imperative that you read each answer choice thoroughly and carefully all the way to its end.

Not supported by the passage

As we've said many times, you must be able to prove your answer with information from the passage. Any answer choice that can't be proven in this way can't be right, even if you know it to be true from outside knowledge of a subject. Don't invent a connection between an answer choice and the passage if you can't find one already present.

Reading Comprehension Technique: Passage Selection

There are many things to consider when choosing which passages to attempt on a section, but the main thing that should guide you is the number of passages you'll be doing on a given section. (For more information on figuring that out, see Chapter 6 in this book.)

If you're able to do all four passages, you may not want to invest much time at first in ranking them all; instead, you'll want to work whichever ones seem approachable to you as you turn to them. If, however, something seems extremely difficult, then skip over that passage and come back to it. For those test takers attempting two or three passages, it's important to be able to identify which one or ones will be the least efficient use of your time. Those are the passages you'll either end up skipping altogether and picking your letter of the day for or doing as your last-choice passage near the end of the section. However, don't spend more than two minutes maximum on ranking the passages.

What are the ingredients that will help you to determine a passage's difficulty? There are several, and what some people tend to focus on the most—subject matter—isn't as important as you might think. Given that you're planning to apply to law school, a passage on some law-related theme might be of greater interest, but that doesn't necessarily mean it will be easier to read. It's possible that it might be written in a very abstract manner, making it difficult to process.

Likewise, a science passage might not be familiar territory, but the questions could be more specific and therefore easier to approach.

Some students also think that the number of questions a passage has should determine when they attempt it. But if a really difficult passage has a large number of questions, that doesn't mean it will be any easier to get those questions right. In fact, you could end up sacrificing more time on that passage, causing you not to attempt an easier one with fewer questions, and still end up missing half of them. It's always preferable to get all the points you're most assured of first, and then to spend the rest of your time on the more difficult questions. If you're going to run out of time on a section, it should always be while you're in the middle of the more challenging questions. If two passages appear to be of equal difficulty, however, feel free to go for the one with more questions.

Here's what to look for when assessing a passage.

- Level of language and complexity: Passages that have clear, straightforward language and only one point of view will be easier to work than those that contain multiple perspectives and abstract ideas.
- Passage and sentence structure: Long, convoluted sentences don't bode well for a passage. Nor do long paragraphs that lack clear transitions or topic sentences but are jammed with information or several different ideas. Shorter paragraphs that address a single concept and flow clearly from one idea to the next are what you want.
- Questions and answer choices: Look at the wording of the questions and answer choices. How many complex questions are there? How many specific questions, and will it be easy to find the information in the passage or will you have to work from the answer choices? How long are the answer choices and are they written in a straightforward manner?

As you can see, there's no one thing that outweighs all the rest, except perhaps reading the first couple of sentences of a passage and having no clue as to what's being said. As you work through passages both in this book and in the real LSATs you've ordered, note your impression of a passage's difficulty at the top of the page before you begin it. Afterwards, check that impression against the reality of the passage—was your assessment correct? In this way, you'll begin to develop your instincts as to which passages you should attempt and which you should avoid.

SUMMARY

Here's our step-by-step approach to the Reading Comprehension section:

Step 1: Analyze the passage

Step 2: Evaluate the question task

Step 3: Apply the strategy

Step 4: Use Process of Elimination

APPLY WHAT YOU'VE LEARNED

Now it's time to put everything you've learned in this chapter to work on the following two reading comprehension passages. The goal of this drill is to see how well you've mastered the four steps and how accurately you can work, not to see how fast you can get through these passages. Remember, if you finish a section but acquire only half the number of points, you may as well have done only two passages. So, work carefully and thoroughly on these until you're sure you have them right.

If you want, you can measure the time it takes you to do each passage. By measure, we mean set your timer to count up, and then turn it away so that you can't see the clock as you work on the passage. Put the timer in a drawer or in another room if necessary. When you're done, stop the clock and note how long it took you to complete the passage and then see how accurate you were. This will help you figure out approximately how long it takes you to do a passage accurately, and by extension, how many passages you can reasonably expect to get through on a given section. Also take note of the difficulty level of each passage—if you found a passage particularly challenging, it's only natural that it would have taken longer to work on.

READING COMPREHENSION PRACTICE DRILL

Passage 1

Concern about the effects of global warming has fostered renewed interest in the Earth's recurrent ice ages. Odd as it may seem to examine the possible consequences of rising global temperatures by studying past cold epochs, an understanding of long-term patterns in the Earth's climate seems likely to provide key insights into a question of widespread current interest.

The Earth's climate is a dynamic system influenced by many interrelated factors. Most scientists agree that three of these predominate: the amount of energy received from solar radiation, the presence of greenhouse gases such as carbon dioxide in the atmosphere, and the location of Earth's major land masses. Other factors such as cloud cover, precipitation, and volcanic activity also have significant influences on global climate because they all play major roles in the planet's water cycle and carbon cycle, both of which are instrumental in regulating Earth's surface temperature.

With all of these factors at play, what seems most surprising is that Earth's global climate follows a relatively regular cyclic pattern. Cold periods called ice ages recur roughly every hundred thousand years, punctuated by brief interglacial periods that are warmer. The current interglacial period has lasted for approximately ten thousand years so far, during which all of recorded human history has taken place. The regularity and suddenness of these changes led Milutin Milankovitch in the early twentieth century to attribute them to predictable variations in the Earth's orbit, which determines the amount and distribution of solar radiation the planet receives.

Although most scientists today agree that the Milankovitch hypothesis provides at least a partial explanation of the recurrent pattern, problems with its predictions have led scientists to look elsewhere for a fuller explanation. Orbital patterns that by right should have the strongest effects on Earth's climate have been shown to have influenced it hardly at all in recent millennia. Everything from the rotation of hotspots within the Earth's interior to sunspots to the orbit of Earth's solar system around the center of the Milky Way galaxy has been advanced as an explanation of the cycle, but the most widely accepted current theories focus on the level of carbon dioxide in the atmosphere, either as a precipitating factor in causation of ice ages or as a determining factor in an ice age's severity.

If they are correct, these current theories offer an alarming perspective on the effects of industrial use of fossil fuels by humans, which has increased atmospheric levels of carbon dioxide. Although on a geologic scale, the redistribution of carbon from the Earth's crust to its atmosphere may seem slight, there is evidence that shifts of roughly similar size due to chemical weathering during the uplift of the Himalayan massif may have helped precipitate the last ice age and led to its remarkable severity. If decreases in atmospheric carbon dioxide on this scale can cause such radical climate change, there is reason to believe that similar increases may have effects of corresponding severity, and that like ice ages, their onset may be sudden and their effects global and long-lasting.

1. The primary purpose of the passage is to
   - (A) identify the likely causes of past ice ages and predict the occurrence of the next ice age
   - (B) describe efforts to understand the causes of ice ages and indicate what they suggest about the current global warming
   - (C) assess the effectiveness of Milankovitch's hypothesis at explaining past climate change and propose an alternative theory
   - (D) inventory the damage already caused by global warming and project the likely long-term consequences of this damage
   - (E) present the geological evidence indicating that Earth's past included both cold epochs and shorter interglacial periods

2. Which one of the following statements best expresses the main idea of the passage?
   - (A) Currently accepted theories attributing the incidence of ice ages to fluctuations in atmospheric carbon dioxide levels provide a fuller explanation of these phenomena than the orbital hypothesis advanced by Milankovitch.
   - (B) Currently accepted theories that describe the role of shifts in carbon distribution between the Earth's crust and its atmosphere in past climate change suggest that global warming caused by human use of fossil fuels may have serious and long-lasting effects.
   - (C) Milankovitch's hypothesis attributing the cyclical recurrence of ice ages to changes in the Earth's orbit indicates that it is possible to predict how much longer the current interglacial period will last and demonstrate that steps must be taken now to mitigate the effects of those changes.
   - (D) Climate scientists have concluded that popular fears about the possible effects of the industrial use of fossil fuels are exaggerated because factors unrelated to human activity have led to similarly radical climate change in the past.
   - (E) Climate scientists have recently recognized that the factors of land distribution, volcanic activity, and global precipitation, although they have some effects on global climate, are themselves the product of more fundamental changes in the Earth's orbit and atmosphere.

3. Which one of the following, if true, would provide the strongest support for the view of Earth's climate described in lines 8–9?
   (A) The temperature in localized areas of the Earth's surface is correlated most strongly with the amount of solar radiation received in those areas.
   (B) Fluctuations in atmospheric carbon dioxide levels on Earth appear to be primarily random and cannot be fully explained by any other factor.
   (C) No existing scientific theory can explain how the orbit of the Earth's solar system around the center of the Milky Way galaxy might affect Earth's climate.
   (D) Snow that does not melt during an unusually cold summer reflects solar radiation back into space, leading to even colder temperatures and even more snow accumulation in future years.
   (E) Volcanic activity acts to increase global temperatures by increasing atmospheric carbon dioxide but also acts to lower global temperatures by contributing to greater cloud cover and precipitation.

4. As they are described in the passage, current theories attributing climate change to shifts in atmospheric levels of carbon dioxide most directly explain which one of the following phenomena?
   (A) variations in the Earth's orbit
   (B) the sudden onset of past ice ages
   (C) the uplift of the Himalayan massif
   (D) the arrangement of land masses on Earth's surface
   (E) the severity of the last ice age

5. Which one of the following, if known, would provide the strongest further evidence against the Milankovitch hypothesis as it is described in the passage?
   (A) Variations in the Earth's orbit cannot influence the rotation of hotspots within the Earth's interior.
   (B) The amount of solar radiation received by Earth's oceans is a main determining factor in the level of atmospheric carbon dioxide.
   (C) Several past climate changes predicted by the hypothesis are known to have occurred shortly before the orbital variations purported to have caused them.
   (D) Although glacial periods recur regularly, the length of interglacial periods in recent millennia has varied from two thousand to twenty thousand years.
   (E) One orbital pattern identified by the hypothesis coincides almost perfectly with the onset of ice ages throughout Earth's geological history.

6. It can be inferred from the author's statements that each of the following influence atmospheric levels of carbon dioxide EXCEPT:
   (A) changes in Earth's land masses
   (B) volcanic activity
   (C) sunspots
   (D) the actions of organisms on the Earth's surface
   (E) global precipitation levels

7. Which one of the following best describes the organization of the passage?
   (A) A hypothesis is presented and defended with supporting examples.
   (B) A widely accepted current explanation of a past phenomenon is described and its future implications are suggested.
   (C) A claim about a widely accepted hypothesis to explain a long-standing mystery is presented but ultimately rejected.
   (D) Opposing views of a controversial subject are presented, assessed, and then reconciled.
   (E) Two current theories of a past phenomenon are evaluated in light of new information relevant to that phenomenon.

ANSWERS FOR PASSAGE 1

1. B
2. B
3. D
4. E
5. C
6. C
7. B

EXPLANATIONS FOR PASSAGE 1

Analyze the passage

The main point of this natural science passage is that recent theories advanced to explain Earth's ice ages have ominous things to say about the possible consequences of human industrial use of fossil fuels. The first paragraph describes why understanding ice ages may be important to studying the effects of global warming and human roles in causing it. The second paragraph describes the complexity of the climate system, outlining the many factors that are involved. The third paragraph indicates the regularity of past climate change and introduces the Milankovitch hypothesis, which says that changes in Earth's orbit are responsible for these changes. The fourth paragraph indicates why most believe that the Milankovitch hypothesis is incomplete, and it says that currently accepted theories emphasize the role that atmospheric carbon dioxide plays in climate change. The last paragraph ties these theories to the likely effect of fossil fuels, pointing out that decreases in carbon dioxide have led in the past to severe changes, and that this may mean that increases of similar size may have similarly drastic effects.

Questions

Although you might have chosen to leave some of these questions for a second pass, here we address them in the order in which they appear.

1. **B** General: primary purpose. The passage describes scientific efforts to understand ice ages and possible consequences of this work for the question of global warming.

Eliminate (A) because it concerns the prediction of when the next ice age will arrive, which is not a primary interest of the passage.

Eliminate (C) because it focuses too narrowly on the Milankovitch hypothesis and its potential alternatives.

Eliminate (D) because it focuses too narrowly on global warming; it needs to mention something relating to ice ages.

Eliminate (E) because it focuses on what evidence there is for past ice ages, which isn't really even mentioned in the passage.

(B) is the best choice here because it includes both ice ages and global warming and properly describes the passage's association between them.

2. **B** General: main idea. Efforts to understand the occurrence of ice ages have led to theories with ominous implications for the human use of fossil fuels and the current problem of global warming.

Eliminate (A) because it focuses completely on the question of which theory to explain ice ages is right without any mention at all of their implications for the global warming issue.

Eliminate (C) because it focuses completely on Milankovitch's theory and brings in the question of preventing the next ice age, which is not mentioned in the passage at all.

Eliminate (D) because it characterizes concern about fossil fuel use as "exaggerated," which is not consistent with the passage material.

Eliminate (E) because it focuses too narrowly on the factors affecting climate change and has nothing to do with fossil fuels or global warming.

(B) is worded a little oddly, but it works. The passage indicates that "shifts in carbon distribution" involve changes to the atmosphere's carbon dioxide levels, and although this choice doesn't mention ice ages by name, it does talk about "past climate change," which is a decent paraphrase. Its focus on what this scientific work means for global warming and fossil fuel use makes it the best of the choices we have.

3. **D** Complex: strengthen the statement that "The Earth's climate is a dynamic system influenced by many interrelated factors." We want a choice that illustrates this idea.

Eliminate (A) because it identifies one primary factor rather than the dynamic and interrelated operation of factors.

Eliminate (B) because it is not consistent with the claim. Being "random" isn't the same as being "dynamic."

Eliminate (C) because it is far off the reference. This doesn't seem to lend any support to the dynamic, interrelated nature of the climate.

Eliminate (E) because, although it does talk about interrelated factors, it isn't clear what real "influence" this describes. It seems to be saying that volcanic activity is basically a nonissue for climate, with competing factors canceling one another out. If anything, this would be evidence against the claim that volcanic activity changes climate at all.

(D) is the best of this group. It describes an interrelationship of snowfall, solar radiation, and temperature that shows how these factors work on one another to influence climate.

4. **E** Specific: which specific thing do the theories focusing on carbon dioxide most directly explain? A search of the passage only really turns up one key piece of evidence in favor of these theories: the chemical weathering that led to the unusual severity of the last ice age.

Eliminate (A); this one has to do with the Milankovitch hypothesis.

Eliminate (B); this feature is more explicitly tied to the Milankovitch hypothesis, and we aren't told how the carbon-dioxide theories explain it.

Eliminate (C); although this is mentioned in connection with the chemical weathering argument, this is something the carbon-dioxide theories use, not something they purport to explain.

Eliminate (D); like (C), this may be a cause taken into account in the carbon-dioxide theories, but it isn't something those theories attempt to explain.

(E) is the best answer here. It comes pretty directly from the last paragraph of the passage.

5. **C** Complex: weaken the Milankovitch hypothesis. Milankovitch is the one who said that changes in the Earth's orbit lead to changes in the amount of solar radiation the Earth receives, which in turn leads to climate change. We're looking for something that works against that cause-and-effect chain.

Eliminate (A). The Milankovitch hypothesis does not attempt to explain the rotation of hotspots in the Earth's interior; that's an alternative hypothesis that has been advanced to explain climate change.

Eliminate (B). Although this has to do with carbon dioxide, if anything it strengthens the Milankovitch theory against the carbon-dioxide theories by showing that orbit variations are ultimately responsible for changes in the Earth's atmospheric carbon dioxide.

Eliminate (D). The Milankovitch hypothesis doesn't purport to explain the length of interglacial periods, as far as we know.

Eliminate (E). This would definitely help the Milankovitch hypothesis.

(C) is the best choice here. If some of the changes that the hypothesis attributes to orbital variations started before the orbital variations took place, this would definitely call the causal role of orbital variations into question.

6. **C** Specific: which can influence atmospheric carbon dioxide levels? We'll need to search for each of these; we'll be able to tie four of them to carbon dioxide levels. The fifth is our answer.

There is passage support for (A). In the last paragraph, "chemical weathering during the uplift of the Himalayan massif" is associated with decreases in carbon dioxide levels in the atmosphere.

There is passage support for (B). In the second paragraph, volcanic activity is described as playing a "major" role in "the planet's…carbon cycle." It takes a step of reasoning, but because the distribution of carbon "between the Earth's crust…[and] its atmosphere" is treated as being intimately related to atmospheric carbon dioxide levels, this is a warranted paraphrase of passage material.

There is passage support for (D). Because humans are organisms on the Earth's surface, the increase in carbon dioxide levels caused by burning fossil fuels definitely qualifies.

There is passage support for (E). Like volcanic activity, global precipitation is identified as being involved in the "carbon cycle," which evidently involves atmospheric carbon dioxide somewhere along the way.

(C) is the only one that can't be even remotely related to carbon dioxide. Sunspots are mentioned in connection with alternative theories to explain climate change.

7. **B** General: structure of the passage. We want something that corresponds as closely as possible to our paragraph-by-paragraph summary of the passage.

Eliminate (A). This passage is not concerned with defending a single hypothesis.

Eliminate (C). You might say that the passage rejects the Milankovitch hypothesis, although it isn't a wholesale rejection, but it's difficult to see the entire passage as rejecting a claim about that hypothesis, and the passage really is more interested in the carbon-dioxide hypothesis, for which it seems to have at least some sympathy.

Eliminate (D). The passage doesn't really reconcile the various theories mentioned.

Eliminate (E). There isn't really new information presented in the passage.

(B) is the best choice we have. It would be nice if this choice made some mention of some theories other than the carbon-dioxide theories (the "widely accepted current explanation"), but this is the only choice that includes "future implications," which is the real thrust of the passage.

Passage 2

The English poet Richard Crashaw has long been considered an eccentric minor figure among the early seventeenth-century poets whom Dr. Johnson first characterized as "Metaphysical." In examining the poetry of those turbulent times, it is easy to understand why Donne and Herbert receive the greater share of traditional scholarship's attention: Issuing from an era when the cause of Protestantism in England became so radical that it led to the execution of King Charles I, an extended civil war, and the severe Interregnum under Oliver Cromwell, the seemingly uncomplicated devotional character of Herbert's poetry and of Donne's sermons and later sonnets lent the times an almost placid historical gloss. The intellectual inventiveness and lyric beauty of Donne and Herbert serve, as they did at the time of their writing, to convey a settled sense of orthodoxy to those most interested in finding it.

Crashaw's poetry, by contrast, seems tortured—either embarrassingly unaware of itself or actively subversive. Certainly by the standards of his day, Crashaw was a heretic: In an era when even the Anglican church was thought by many to retain too many trappings of the decadent Roman Catholic tradition, Crashaw broke with his society and his ardently Protestant father by converting to Roman Catholicism, a choice that forced him to live much of his life penniless in exile. The conflicts in which Crashaw was enmeshed manifest themselves in his poetry, which abounds with images that strike a contemporary sensibility as violent, strange, and in some cases bordering on pornographic. The energy expended by traditional scholarship to laud these strange moments as mystical, or else excuse them as manifestations of Crashaw's excessive love for rhetorical inventiveness, seems to reflect not merely a failure of interpretation, but an active determination not to interpret the poems in ways that disturb traditional views of the period but nevertheless seem patently obvious.

This failure of traditional readings of the so-called Metaphysical poets is not unique to Crashaw's work. Donne's early poetry reflects a worldliness and flirtatiousness that seems all the more surprising in light of the graceful piety of his later work; Herbert's famous image of being bound by the shackle of his faith cannot be obliterated by rhetoric and rationalization, no matter how dexterous. The tension played out in these poems is internal and intellectual, but at the time of their writing it was also profoundly political: how the human faculty of reason, an emergent interest in Renaissance England, can mediate in the traditional conflict between desire and Christian orthodoxy, and whether it can possibly tame both. It is in Crashaw's work that this tension is tuned to its highest—some might say most hysterical—pitch, and it is in critical interpretations of his work that we most distinctly see the failure of traditional scholarship to comprehend the era in which he wrote.

1. The passage suggests that the author would be most likely to agree with which one of the following statements?

(A) Traditional readings of much English poetry of the early seventeenth century overemphasize its orthodox devotional character while neglecting the tension and turmoil it reflects.
(B) Seventeenth-century poetry is noteworthy more for its intellectual inventiveness than it is for its lyric beauty.
(C) Seventeenth-century poets such as Donne and Herbert are worthy of study because they were able to provide a placid historical gloss of the turbulent times in which they wrote.
(D) The tortured quality of Crashaw's poetry and the surprise contemporary readers may feel in encountering some of his imagery were intended by Crashaw to express his mystical beliefs.
(E) The emergence of interest in the human faculty of reason in Renaissance England is responsible for the increasingly radical nature of Protestantism during that time.

2. The author suggests that the poetry of Richard Crashaw

(A) is superior to the poetry of Donne and Herbert
(B) reflects an obsession with the strictures of Christian orthodoxy
(C) was intended to convey heretical beliefs
(D) has been routinely misinterpreted by traditional scholars
(E) is characterized by an excessive love for rhetorical inventiveness

3. According to the author, traditional scholarship fails to comprehend that the poetry of early seventeenth-century England

(A) is in part a reflection of the era in which it was written
(B) represents a radical departure from earlier English poetry
(C) reflects a serious interest in reason as well as Christian orthodoxy
(D) is noteworthy only because of the work of Richard Crashaw
(E) served as a form of political protest

4. The phrase "either embarrassingly unaware of itself or actively subversive" (lines 17–18) is used in the passage to indicate which one of the following about Richard Crashaw's poetry?

(A) its similarity to early works of Donne and Herbert
(B) its mystical and unorthodox qualities
(C) its uneven and maladroit use of imagery
(D) its difference from conventional devotional poetry
(E) its intention to confuse and distort

5. Which one of the following most accurately describes the organization of the passage?

(A) description of a particular scholarly shortcoming; discussion of possible courses of action that could be taken to remedy that shortcoming; extension of these courses of action to other similar cases; assertion that these courses of action are unlikely to be taken seriously
(B) description of a particular historical era and scholarly treatment of some literature of that era; discussion of the inadequacy of that scholarly treatment in one particular case; assertion that the inadequacy is not limited to that case; explanation of the reason for and the meaning of this inadequacy
(C) description of a historical era and scholarly interpretations of it; discussion of the ways in which this interpretation neglect a key development of the era; illustration of the consequences of this neglect in a particular case; explanation of the ways scholarly errors undercut all cases of this kind
(D) summary of the conventional view of a controversial time; discussion of a new view that contradicts the conventional view; application of the new view to a particularly troublesome instance during the time in question; rejection of the conventional view in favor of the new view
(E) summary of two conflicting scholarly approaches to a literary problem; evaluation of the merits of the two approaches separately; application of these approaches to a particular historical case; assertion that both approaches must be used to ensure a complete understanding of all such cases

6. It can be inferred from the passage that the author interprets the famous image described in line 42 to indicate

(A) that Herbert's attitude toward Christian orthodoxy is not as simple as it is interpreted to be in traditional readings
(B) that Herbert's poetry contains a veiled critique of the increasing Protestant radicalism of his time
(C) that Herbert's desire to employ the human faculty of reason is constrained by Christian orthodoxy
(D) that the turmoil of Herbert's times led him to employ inventive rhetoric that undermines the stated purpose of his poetry
(E) that the conflict between desire and Christian orthodoxy led him to question the worth of human reason in mediating between them

7. The author's position in lines 29–36 would be most weakened if which one of the following were true?

(A) Traditional views of the period do not consider the possibility that Crashaw could have intentionally employed imagery and language in his poetry that would have been interpreted as shocking or sexually suggestive at the time he wrote.
(B) None of Crashaw's other writings indicate an interest in the faculty of human reason except insofar as that faculty could be exercised in accordance with the dictates of Christian orthodoxy.
(C) Although John Donne's early poetry is sexually suggestive, his later poetry and sonnets indicate that Donne regretted the excesses of his youth and fully accepted the strictures of orthodox Christianity.
(D) The images in Crashaw's poetry that seem subversive to current-day readers employ words that have taken on violent or sexually suggestive connotations that these words did not have at the time when Crashaw wrote.
(E) Although Crashaw was forced into exile by his conversion to Roman Catholicism, both Donne and Herbert were considered models of piety in their time, and they were popular both before and during the Interregnum.

ANSWERS FOR PASSAGE 2

1. A
2. D
3. C
4. D
5. B
6. A
7. D

EXPLANATIONS FOR PASSAGE 2

Analyze the passage

The main point of this humanities passage is that the poetry of English writer Richard Crashaw provides a particularly useful example both of the interests and conflicts of the time in which he wrote and of the routine misunderstandings of that period by traditional scholarship. The first paragraph introduces Crashaw in comparison to the better-known poets of his period and indicates how tense those times were, and it also suggests why scholars have paid more attention to the other poets. The second paragraph describes what makes Crashaw's poetry and life unusual and points to serious shortcomings in traditional approaches to his poetry. The third paragraph indicates that these shortcomings are also present in traditional approaches to the more famous poets of the period and identifies what traditional scholars fail to understand about the period.

Questions

Although you might have chosen to leave some of these questions for a second pass, here we address them in the order in which they appear.

1. **A** Specific (most probably): with which statement would the author agree? Whichever one we pick, we should be able to find passage support for it.

Eliminate (B). Although both are identified as characteristics of the poetry of Donne and Herbert, no preference for one characteristic over the other is expressed. It would be too much of a stretch to say that the author's interest in the poetry as portraying human reason indicates a preference because the ideas of desire and religious orthodoxy are also identified as being very important to the poems.

Eliminate (C). This is identified as the reason traditional scholarship prefers seventeenth-century poets such as Donne and Herbert, but this is not something with which the author agrees.

Eliminate (D). For one thing, *mystical* is a word used by traditional scholars, not our author, to describe Crashaw's strange imagery; for another, we know nothing really about Crashaw's intentions.

Eliminate (E). This claim ties together two statements made in the passage about the historical period, and although they're both supported, we don't know that there's a causal link here.

(A) is consistent with the author's viewpoint. The first paragraph indicates that traditional scholarship has focused on Donne's and Herbert's works because of the "placid historical gloss" and "settled sense of orthodoxy" they provide, placing too little emphasis on how they reflect their "turbulent times."

2. **D** Specific: what is true of Crashaw's poetry? Again, we're looking for the statement with the most direct passage support.

Eliminate (A). Although the author finds Crashaw's poetry interesting, it isn't clear that the author considers it "superior."

Eliminate (B). *Obsession* is too strong a word to be justified by the passage text.

Eliminate (C). Although Crashaw is identified as being a heretic by the standards of his day, there is no evidence that his intention in writing poetry was to convey heretical beliefs.

Eliminate (E). This is something that traditional scholars say about Crashaw, but it isn't clear that the author agrees with them that his poetry is "excessive."

(D) is by far the safest answer here. This is a straight paraphrase of one of the passage's central claims.

3. **C** Specific: what does traditional scholarship fail to comprehend about poetry of the era? This is most likely a reference to the material in the final paragraph, where the author claims that traditional scholars fail to emphasize properly the tension between desire and religion mediated by reason.

Eliminate (A), although it's tricky. The substance of the author's objection isn't that scholars fail to understand the link between the poetry and the times; it's that they misunderstand the nature of each of them.

Eliminate (B). The passage does seem to think that the poetry is noteworthy and somehow new, but to say it's a "radical departure" is almost certainly too strong a characterization of the passage's statements.

Eliminate (D). This is an overstatement of the passage's interest in Crashaw.

Eliminate (E). Although the passage does say that the ideas behind this poetry were political in the time they were written, to say that they were written as a form of protest is too strong an interpretation of that fact.

(C) is the safest answer here. It mentions reason and religion, and it does outline what the author seems to feel is the most serious shortcoming of traditional criticism.

4. **D** Specific: which is the best paraphrase of the meaning or purpose of the cited text in reference to Crashaw's poetry? This follows the passage's description of its "tortured" quality, and also seems to refer to the strange imagery mentioned later in the same paragraph.

Eliminate (A). Similarity between Crashaw and the other poets is not brought up until later, and certainly the phrase in question doesn't seek to highlight any such similarity.

Eliminate (B). This choice isn't completely awful, but because it uses the terms that are associated, in the passage, with the same critics the author thinks are misguided, we'd like to have something that's a bit closer to the author's own opinion here.

Eliminate (C). The negative connotations of "uneven and maladroit" are not consistent with the author's attitude toward Crashaw's poetry.

Eliminate (E). There is no statement here that the poetry was ever intended to confuse or distort.

(D) is a safe choice here. It seems a bit mild, given the text in question, but the purpose of this statement is to describe how Crashaw's poetry is different from the poetry usually referred to by traditional scholars.

5. **B** General: structure of the passage. We'll use our paragraph-by-paragraph summary to pick the answer that most closely matches the passage.

Probably the clearest reason to eliminate (A) is its identification of an "assertion that these courses of action are unlikely to be taken seriously." No such statement is included in the passage.

Probably the clearest reason to eliminate (C) is its identification of the primary topic of this passage as a "historical era." The times are certainly crucial to the passage, but this downplays the poetry of the time far too much to be a good description of the passage.

Probably the clearest reason to eliminate (D) is similar to the one used above in (C). Again, this choice focuses on the time without giving proper emphasis to the poetry of that time.

Probably the clearest reason to eliminate (E) is its identification of an "assertion that both approaches must be used to ensure a complete understanding of all such cases." The passage argues vehemently against one of the approaches discussed in the passage.

(B) is the closest choice to be found. It mentions the times, the poetry, and the scholarly treatment of it, and it generally matches the flow of the passage topic by topic.

6. **A** Specific: the meaning of the shackle image in the last paragraph. This is used as an example of an indication from Herbert's poetry that conventional readings of it as orthodox are a bit too reductive.

Eliminate (B) because the passage doesn't go so far as to say that Herbert's image is a political critique. It might conceivably be seen that way, but the passage doesn't actually say so.

Eliminate (C) because this reads a bit too much of the later statements into this particular image. It seems just as likely, if not more so, that the more properly applicable material from this later statement is desire, not reason.

Eliminate (D) because it relies on Herbert's "stated purpose," which is never mentioned in the passage, and because "inventive rhetoric" is attributed to Crashaw and perhaps to traditional scholars at various points in the passage, but not directly to Herbert.

Eliminate (E) because it reads far too much into the text here. These things are mentioned in the same paragraph as the cited text, but we can't say that the passage supports any statement this specific or elaborate about Herbert.

(A) is a good answer because it is fairly nonspecific—a virtue because the meaning of the image in the passage is not explained very fully—and because it is consistent with the author's main point throughout the passage.

7. **D** Complex: weaken the cited statement. The statement in question claims that the failure of traditional scholars to interpret some of the more provocative statements in Crashaw's poetry in ways that "seem patently obvious" is an example of critics letting their preconceived ideas distort their readings. We want something that indicates these readings might not be so bad.

Eliminate (A) because it seems to strengthen the passage statement, not weaken it. This is certainly a statement about the scholars in question with which the author would agree.

Eliminate (B) because it relates to statements made in the third paragraph, not here.

Eliminate (C) because it concerns Donne, not Crashaw. This isn't specifically focused on the statement cited in the question.

Eliminate (E) because it is primarily focused on Donne and Herbert, who aren't clearly related to the question here.

(D) is a good answer because it attacks the linchpin of the author's interpretation of these moments in Crashaw. Although the readings supported by the author are said to be "patently obvious," they might not be correct if their subversive character is attributable to changes in the language since Crashaw wrote his poetry.

The Writing Sample

The Writing Sample is a 35-minute ungraded essay whose topic is assigned. Your essay is supposed to be an argument supporting either of two given positions. You'll receive a booklet containing both the topic and the space in which to write your essay. You will also receive scratch paper.

Before we begin, take a moment to read the instructions to this section:

Don't devote too much study time to the writing sample.

General Directions: You are to complete the brief writing exercise on the topic inside. You will have 35 minutes in which to plan and write the exercise. Read the topic carefully. You will probably find it best to spend a few minutes considering the topic and organizing your thoughts before you begin writing. **Do not write on a topic other than the one specified. Writing on a topic of your own choice is not acceptable.**

There is no "right" or "wrong" position on the writing sample topic. Law schools are interested in how skillfully you support the position you take and how clearly you express that position. How well you write is much more important than what you write. No special knowledge is required or expected. Law schools are interested in organization, vocabulary, and writing mechanics. They understand the short time available to you and the pressure under which you are writing.

Confine your writing to the lined area following the writing sample topic. You will find that you have enough space in this booklet if you plan your writing carefully, write on every line, avoid wide margins, and keep your handwriting a reasonable size. Be sure your writing is legible.

Scratch paper is provided for use during the writing sample portion of the test only. Scratch paper cannot be used in other sections of the LSAT.

The writing sample is photocopied and sent to law schools to which you direct your LSAT score. A pen will be provided at the test center, which must be used (for the writing sample only) to ensure a photocopy of high quality.

As of June 2005, LSAC announced that students would receive one of two different essay topics. The traditional essay topic that has been given is what's discussed in this book; for more information on the new topics, go to www.lsac.org.

THE WRITING TOPIC

Inside the booklet you'll find the assigned topic and two blank pages on which to write your essay. You'll also get scratch paper on which to organize your essay. The assigned topics are innocuous. Expect a topic something like this:

Karen Stratton is looking into buying a property with the plan to turn it into an animal-supply store. Write an essay in support of one of two proposed properties, the cost of which would be almost exactly the same, keeping in mind Karen's needs:

- Karen needs to establish a market and begin making back her investment rather quickly because she will put most of her money into buying the property.
- Karen wants her store to be different and memorable, so she can cultivate a loyal clientele.

Fill up the page when writing your LSAT essay.

Property One is a storefront in the middle of the main drag of the bustling downtown area. The outside of the storefront looks like the fronts of most of the other stores on the block. The central location would make shopping there convenient for people who work in the downtown area, and it is accessible by all forms of public transportation.

Property Two is an old, renovated Victorian house on the outskirts of town. The design of the house is unique. It is six miles from the nearest public transport, making it accessible only by car and cab. It is closer to the farm country and has space for a garden, which Karen can use to grow organic products for her store.

How Much Will My Essay Affect My LSAT Score?

Not one bit.

Only four sections contribute to your LSAT score: one Games section, two Arguments sections, and one Reading Comprehension section. An unmarked photocopy of your essay will be sent to the law schools to which you apply.

Who Will Read My Essay?

Possibly no one.

How well or poorly you do on the Writing Sample will almost certainly not affect your admissions chances.

Then Why Do Law Schools Require It?

Law schools feel guilty about not being interested in anything about you other than your grades and LSAT scores. Knowing that you have spent 30 minutes writing an essay for them makes them feel better about having no interest in reading what you have written.

Future Changes?

Always be sure to check the LSAC website at www.lsac.org for any updates to the test.

If the Writing Sample Is So Unimportant, Why Discuss It?

Just for your own peace of mind. Once you have the rest of the test under control, look over the rest of this chapter. If you are short on time, you'd be better off practicing arguments.

There's also the possibility that an admissions officer will accidentally pass his or her eyes over what you have written. If your essay is ungrammatical, riddled with misspellings, off the topic, and wildly disorganized, the admissions officer may think less of you.

So we're going to assume that the Writing Sample counts a little bit. You should assume the same thing, but don't lose sleep over it. No one ever got into law school because of the LSAT Writing Sample, and it's doubtful that anyone ever got rejected because of it. Besides, good writing requires surprisingly few rules, and the rules we'll review will help your writing in general.

What Are They Looking For?

The general directions to the Writing Sample mention that law schools are interested in three things: essay organization, vocabulary, and writing mechanics. Presumably, writing mechanics covers grammar and style.

What they're *really* looking for

Researchers at the Educational Testing Service (the folks responsible for the SAT and the GRE, among other tests) once did a study of essay-grading behavior. They wanted to find out what their graders really responded to when they marked papers, and which essay characteristics correlated most strongly with good scores.

The researchers discovered that the most important characteristic, other than "overall organization," is "essay length." Also highly correlated with good essay scores are the number of paragraphs, average sentence length, and average word length. The bottom line? *Students who filled in all the lines, indented frequently, and used big words earned higher scores than students who didn't.*

We will discuss these points in more detail later. Because organization is the most important characteristic, let's start with that.

ESSAY ORGANIZATION

Indent fully to set off each paragraph clearly.

Your essay should contain five paragraphs (remember high school?). In the first, you state your opinion. In the last, you restate your opinion, and the three middle paragraphs form the body of your argument.

State your actual argument in three paragraphs. Three paragraphs demonstrate that your argument is concise as well as organized. Of course, if you find that one of your major ideas has secondary ideas, you may have to subdivide one of the middle paragraphs.

So your essay should consist of an introductory paragraph, a conclusion paragraph, and three main paragraphs for your argument. The more you stick with a formula outline, the less thinking you'll have to do when you actually write.

What Am I Trying to Do?

You're trying to persuade your reader that one of two given alternatives is better. You cannot *prove* that one side is better; you can only make a case that it is. The test writers deliberately come up with boringly balanced alternatives so that you can argue for either one of them.

So choose a side and justify your choice.

Picking Sides

The directions emphasize that neither alternative is "correct." It doesn't matter which side you choose. Pick the alternative that gives you more to work with.

When choosing a side to write about, list pros and cons.

Another way to decide is to compile a little list of the pros and cons on your scratch paper. Then simply pick the alternative whose list of pros is longer. Let's see how you'd do this with the sample topic we've given you.

First, list each alternative (Property One, Property Two) as a heading. Underneath each heading draw two columns, one for the pros and one for the cons. Spend the first couple of minutes brainstorming the advantages and disadvantages of each choice. The key to brainstorming is *quantity,* not quality. You can select and discard points later.

Having brainstormed for pros and cons, select the ones you intend to keep and arrange them in order of importance, from *least* to *most* important.

For the purposes of this chapter, let's assume that we intend to give the nod to Property Two.

Don't forget the cons

Some students believe that if you're trying to make a case for something, you should bring up the advantages only. This is wrong.

To persuade readers that Property Two is the better choice, you must show that you have considered every argument that could be made for Property One, and found each one unconvincing.

Your argument, in other words, must show that you have weighed the pros and cons of *both* sides. The more forceful the objections you counter, the more compelling your position becomes.

Evaluating the pros and cons: the criteria

As you think of pros and cons for each position, keep in mind the given criteria. Here you have two considerations—getting money back and establishing a unique business. You must build your essay around these criteria, so don't ignore them. They give you the structure to follow.

The criteria may not be compatible. If so, weigh the pros and cons in light of this situation. In our example, an innovative-looking store might not attract other people. You may want to rank the two criteria in terms of importance. Perhaps getting money back is more important than establishing a unique business. Perhaps not. Decide which consideration is more important. If you cannot decide, state so explicitly.

Can I Raise Other Issues?

You *must* weigh the two stated considerations, but nothing prevents you from introducing additional considerations.

You need not raise additional considerations, but if one occurs to you, and you have the time, mention it in passing. If none occurs to you, mention in the conclusion that you have evaluated the two options in view of the two stated considerations only, acknowledging that other considerations may be important.

Property One Versus Property Two: Brainstorming the Pros and Cons

Remember: Brainstorm first. You will have blank space in your test booklet to jot down your ideas before you dive into writing the essay. Next, select the issues you intend to raise. Then rank the final issues, beginning with the least important.

To organize your brainstorming, use a rough chart like this one:

	Quick money	Unique business	Other factors
Property One	possible; central location good for exposure and quick purchases	looks like every other store front	size? use of space and light?
Property Two	possible, but it might take a while. Harder to get to, but could be a "specialty" shop	probably; unique-looking store, customers would have to be loyal because it's farther away	size? use of space and light?

Beginning Your Essay: Restating the Problem

Having brainstormed the pros and cons of each choice in light of the considerations, you are ready to start writing your essay.

Your first paragraph should do little more than state your argument. Try not to use a tedious grade school opening such as, "The purpose of the essay I am about to write is to . . ."

There are several more interesting ways to introduce an argument. Which one you choose will influence how you organize the rest of your essay. Keep this in mind as you sketch your outline. We'll tell you more about this as we go along.

One possibility for an opening is simply to restate concisely the problem you are to address. Here's an example:

Karen Stratton needs to buy a property for her animal-supply business.
She must turn a profit quickly, but wants to establish a unique business.
The two properties both have positive and negative aspects. We must
weigh their respective strengths and weaknesses in light of Karen's needs.

This type of introduction sets up the conflict rather than immediately taking a side. The second, third, and fourth paragraphs are then devoted to weighing the specific advantages and disadvantages of each candidate. The author's preference isn't stated explicitly until the final paragraph, although a clear case for one should emerge as the essay progresses.

An essay such as this is really just an organized written version of the mental processes you went through in deciding which candidate to choose. In the first paragraph you say, in effect, "Here are the problems, the choices, and my decision." In the second, third, and fourth paragraphs you say, "Here are the pros and cons I weighed." In the fifth and final paragraph you say, "So you can see why I decided as I did."

Your hope is that the reader, by following your reasoning step by step, will decide the same thing. The great advantage of this kind of organization is that it *does* follow your mental processes. That makes it a natural and relatively easy method.

BEGINNING YOUR ESSAY: PUTTING YOUR CARDS ON THE TABLE

It's also possible to write an essay in which you begin by announcing your decision. You state your preference in the first paragraph, back it up in the middle paragraphs, and then restate your preference with a concluding flourish in the final paragraph.

Here's an example of such an opening paragraph:

> Property One is a centrally located storefront in a busy downtown area, which would probably bring in a lot of quick business. However, it looks like every other storefront, so it wouldn't stand out. Property Two, by contrast, would afford Karen Stratton an opportunity to create a unique-looking store that could be treated as a specialty shop that people would be willing to travel to. I believe that Karen should buy Property Two for her animal-supply store because it suits her needs.

By introducing your argument in this way, you leave yourself with a great deal of latitude for handling the succeeding paragraphs. For example, you might use the second paragraph to discuss both candidates in light of the first consideration, the third paragraph to discuss both candidates in light of the second consideration, the fourth paragraph to weigh the considerations themselves, and the fifth and final paragraph to summarize your argument and restate your preference.

THE BODY OF YOUR ARGUMENT

We've discussed the introductory and concluding paragraphs. Depending on your preference, and depending on the essay topic you actually confront, we recommend three variations for the middle paragraphs.

Variation 1

Paragraph 2:	Both sides in light of the first consideration
Paragraph 3:	Both sides in light of the second consideration
Paragraph 4:	Weighing the two considerations (and other considerations?)

Variation 2

Paragraph 2:	Everything that can be said about Property One
Paragraph 3:	Everything that can be said about Property Two
Paragraph 4:	A sentence or two for Property One, followed by three or four sentences for Property Two

Variation 3

Paragraph 2:	A sentence or two for Property One, followed by three or four sentences for Property Two
Paragraph 3:	A sentence or two for Property One, followed by three or four sentences for Property Two
Paragraph 4:	A sentence or two for Property One, followed by three or four sentences for Property Two

Again, if necessary, you can divide any one of the three middle paragraphs into two paragraphs.

All three variations do the job. Choose a variation you feel comfortable with and memorize it. The less thinking you have to do on the actual exam, the better.

The Princeton Review Thesaurus of Pretty Impressive Words

The following list of words is not meant to be complete, nor is it in any particular order. Synonyms or related concepts are grouped where appropriate.

- example, instance, precedent, paradigm, archetype
- illustrate, demonstrate, highlight, acknowledge, exemplify, embody
- support, endorse, advocate, maintain, contend, espouse, champion
- supporter, proponent, advocate, adherent
- dispute, dismiss, outweigh, rebut, refute

- propose, advance, submit, marshal, adduce
- premise, principle, presumption, assumption, proposition
- advantages, merits, benefits
- inherent, intrinsic, pertinent
- indisputable, incontrovertible, inarguable, unassailable, irrefutable, undeniable, unimpeachable
- unconvincing, inconclusive, dubious, specious
- compelling, cogent, persuasive
- empirical, hypothetical, theoretical

Only use ten-dollar words if you can use and spell them correctly.

A note on diction

Make sure you don't spoil your display of verbal virtuosity by misusing or misspelling these or any other ten-dollar words. Also, get your idioms straight.

A final note on a common diction error. If, as in our writing sample, your choice involves only two options, *former* refers to the first and *latter* refers to the second. You cannot use these words to refer to more than two options.

Another common diction error occurs when comparing two or more things. The first option is *better* than the second, but it is not the *best*, which is used when discussing three or more options.

Rules to Write By

1. Write as if you were actually making the recommendation.
2. Write naturally, but don't use abbreviations or contractions.
3. Make sure your position is clear.
4. Write as neatly as possible.
5. Indent your paragraphs.
6. Don't use first person. The assignment is formal enough that it isn't appropriate here. The objective isn't to state what "I think," but to argue in favor of one option or the other. Personal experience is not relevant.

One Final Reminder

Write legibly! If you can't, at least print.

A SAMPLE ESSAY

Karen Stratton is looking for a property to buy for her animal-supply store, and has narrowed her search to two. Property One is centrally located and would allow Karen to make money quickly. Property Two is not centrally located, but would allow Karen to cultivate a special business. In view of those considerations, she should buy Property Two

Property One would certainly be convenient for shoppers. It is also accessible by all forms of public transportation, making it even easier to get to. Karen could certainly make back some money quickly by the location alone. But her store would not be unique; it would look like every other store in the area. People wouldn't be going there for any reason but its location, which means they might not be loyal customers. Also, being in the downtown area, the store might not be big enough for Karen to feature all of the items that would make her store unique, and the outside would not suggest uniqueness either.

Property Two, on the other hand, is certainly unique-looking. It's true that people would have to travel to get there, but Karen could make it into a specialty shop, by growing her own products in the garden, for example, and would make her store worth the trip. These types of stores inspire loyalty for customers looking for hard-to-find items, and though Karen might not make back her investment right away, she would over time. Her store could also serve the farm community, whose residents might not want to travel downtown.

Another thing Property Two has in its favor is that it is probably bigger than Property One, or if not, it at least would afford Karen creative ways to use space and natural light that a downtown storefront would not. If Karen can afford to be a little patient money-wise, she could end up with a memorable, unique, lucrative business for herself.

Both properties have strengths and deficiencies as far as meeting Karen's needs. Karen should buy Property Two for her animal-supply store because its strengths outweigh its deficiencies.

Putting It All Together

Well, you've worked through five pretty arduous chapters of *Cracking the LSAT.* How should you feel? Answer: CONFIDENT. Why? Because you've been given a specific process for each section of the LSAT. You've got a good game plan—and the team with the good game plan usually wins the game. So here's a quick review of your game plan for each section of the exam.

ARGUMENTS

Step 1 Evaluate the question task

Step 2: Analyze the argument

Step 3: Apply the strategy

Step 4: Use Process of Elimination

Pretty simple, right? Well, many people begin to get anxious and they tend to skip Step 3. They want to get right to the answer choices so they can start getting confused and frustrated. However, Step 3 is the most important step in this process. If you come up with your own ideas about what should be the right answer before looking at any of the choices, you'll be misled less often by those appealing but wrong answer choices.

GAMES

You should have these steps down cold by now.

Step 1: Diagram and inventory

Step 2: Symbolize the clues and double-check

Step 3: Look for links and size up the game

Step 4: Evaluate the question task

Step 5: Apply the strategy

Step 6: Use Process of Elimination

As in arguments, many students tend to skip an essential step in the games process. That step is Step 3 (again). Students usually see how necessary it is to draw a diagram and symbolize the clues, but then they get nervous that they've spent so much time drawing and symbolizing that they go straight to the questions. However, looking at the diagram and the symbols you've drawn for 30 seconds before going to the questions will invariably make the game easier—any deduction you make will actually save you time by making you more efficient in answering the questions.

READING COMPREHENSION

Step 1: Analyze the passage

Step 2: Evaluate the question task

Step 3: Apply the strategy

Step 4: Use Process of Elimination

Well, here we've once again highlighted Step 3 because it's the most important step and it's the one students tend to skip. Again, nervousness about time is the culprit. But as you learned in the reading comprehension chapter, pinpointing the correct answer choice becomes much easier when you've already got an idea of what you should be looking for. Don't wait for the answer choices to confuse you—approach the test questions by being ready for them as much as possible.

PACING

Believe it or not, even after you've aced the techniques and you're raking in the points like never before, there's still more you can do to improve your score.

The speed at which you work through the test makes a huge difference in how many points you get. How does this happen? It all boils down to this: The faster you work, the more likely it is that you're going to make careless errors. You've probably seen it more times than you'd like to admit. Maybe you bubbled in the wrong answer choice, or you crossed out the right answer instead of the one you wanted to eliminate, or you simply overlooked some key fact that was right there all along. But all of these mistakes are preventable!

Your mantra: *If you want to get more points, stay focused and directed, but don't rush.*

Remember that the test is *designed* so that the vast majority of testers won't be able to answer all the questions. Fight the urge to rush. Use all the knowledge you've gained during your preparation for the test to make good choices about which questions to work on and which questions to skip. But also, don't second-guess yourself; some questions on the test are really easy. Slow down for the tougher situations when you're only able to narrow down the answer choices to two or three, but move quickly and confidently when you predict the answer and find it in the answer choices. Depending on your most effective pace, you may find that your best results come from skipping an entire game. Or, you may find that you only need to leave off a couple of the trickiest arguments to maximize your effectiveness on the rest. Wherever you fall on the continuum, you'll still get some extra points by using your "letter of the day" to guess on any questions on which you don't work.

Take full advantage of the opportunity to work through each section in the order that's most suited to your own strengths. Each question is worth one raw point, so spend your time on the ones that will net you the most gain.

And one final note on pacing: Many test takers develop an effective method only to fall prey to the anxiety invoked by the intimidating environment on test day. Once you've learned and practiced the methods, don't abandon them on the real LSAT. Sure, you'll be stressed and worried about your score. But don't rush. Be flexible. You are armed with a strategy that you've proven to be successful through all your practice. You know what to do. If you find yourself feeling overwhelmed, take a deep breath and remember your mantras. Focus on the process for solving whatever type of question you're working on, and don't stray from the techniques you've mastered. The process is always there to fall back on. Concentrate and take it one step at a time.

Here's a chart to help you assess your performance on the practice tests.

This is a general chart. Don't worry about being so exact here.

Pacing Yourself			
If you received . . .	**Your first goal is . . .**	**Your intermediate goal is . . .**	**Your final goal is . . .**
25–45% correct on Arguments	Work 12–15 arguments and try to get 10–12 right in 35 minutes	Work 15–18 arguments and try to get 12–15 right in 35 minutes	Work 18–21 arguments and try to get 15–18 right in 35 minutes
45–65% correct on Arguments	Work 15–18 arguments and try to get 12–15 right in 35 minutes	Work 18–21 arguments and try to get 15–18 right in 35 minutes	Work 21–24 arguments and try to get 18–21 right in 35 minutes
65–85% correct on Arguments	Work 18–21 arguments and try to get 15–18 right in 35 minutes	Work 21–24 arguments and try to get 18–21 right in 35 minutes	Work all the arguments and try to get 20–23 right in 35 minutes
25–45% correct on Games	Do two games correctly in 35 minutes	Get through two full games and halfway through a third one in 35 minutes	Do three games correctly in 35 minutes
45–65% correct on Games	Do two games correctly in 35 minutes	Get through three complete games in 35 minutes, missing only one or two questions	Get through three full games and half of a fourth game in 35 minutes
65–85% correct on Games	Get through two full games and half of a third game in 35 minutes	Do three complete games in 35 minutes and get halfway through the fourth game	Get through the entire section missing only a few questions in 35 minutes
20–40% correct on Reading Comprehension	Do two reading comprehension passages in 35 minutes, trying to miss only one question per passage	Do two full reading comprehension passages and get halfway through a third passage in 35 minutes	Do three full reading comprehension passages in 35 minutes
40–60% correct on Reading Comprehension	Do two full reading comprehension passages and get halfway through a third passage in 35 minutes	Do three full reading comprehension passages in 35 minutes	Do three full reading comprehension passages and get halfway through the fourth passage in 35 minutes
60–80% correct on Reading Comprehension	Do three reading comprehension passages in 35 minutes, trying to miss only one question per passage	Do three full reading comprehension passages and get halfway through the fourth passage in 35 minutes	Do four full reading comprehension passages in 35 minutes

EVALUATING YOUR PERFORMANCE

One of the most important things you can do to continue to improve your score is to analyze the work you do, to better gauge both the areas in which you're making errors and the amount of time you need to spend on a given question or group of questions to ensure a high level of accuracy. Here we'll discuss several ways to accomplish this.

As we recommended for the practice drills that accompanied each of the chapters on arguments, games, and reading comprehension, it's a good idea to measure how long it takes you to do a game or passage or set of arguments accurately. There's no point rushing to get to questions (and wasting brain power) if you're not going to give yourself the opportunity to get those questions right. Remember, your score is based on how many questions you answer correctly, not how many questions you actually get to attempt (and of course you're bubbling in answers for those you don't attempt). So by measuring how long it takes, on average, to work accurately through a game, passage, or group of, say, eight arguments, you can build realistic expectations of how much you'll be able to do on a given timed section. This is important because it can help you set reachable goals for each area of the LSAT—for example, you can't expect to get to all four games if you generally need to spend 15 minutes on just one of them.

To measure your work time, set your timer to count up, not down, and then don't look at it while you're working. Put it face down, in a drawer, or even in another room if necessary. When you've finished working and are certain of your answers, stop the clock and note the time elapsed. Then check your answers to see how accurate you were. If you missed two or three, you may be working a little too fast; if you missed half or more, you're definitely going too quickly. If, however, you got almost all of them correct, then you can start to think about where you might be able to speed up. Did you linger at an answer choice to convince yourself that it was really right, although you knew the other four choices were unequivocally wrong? Did you try to disprove all the choices in a games question although you already had the answer in your diagram? As you continue to work questions, you'll eventually find that you hit your optimal speed for each section—if you go any slower, you won't get to the number of questions you know you need to to reach your goal, but if you work any faster, your careless errors will start to increase.

Once you have an idea of how many questions you can reasonably expect to get to, you can start to figure out how you're going to get the score you want. Let's say you're aiming for a 160. You'd need approximately 75 correct answers to achieve that score. (You should use the conversion chart from the most recent LSAT you've ordered when making these estimates.) Perhaps reading comprehension is one of your strengths, so you can count on 23 out of 27 questions. Or maybe you average about 18 correct on an arguments section. That leaves 16 points that you'll need to pick up in the Games section. Are you stronger in games? Then your goal might be 20 points from games and only 21 points from reading comprehension, with an arguments goal of 17 points per section. Is your goal a 150? That's about 56 questions. How you break that down will be up to you, based on your own strengths and weaknesses.

Part of the reason for breaking the test down into section goals is to make it more manageable. Say your current total score is eight points away from where you'd like to be. One way to look at that gap is to think about what that means you'll need to accomplish *per section*. Gaining eight more raw score points means getting two more questions right per section. And that may not even mean doing more questions but simply trying to reduce your errors—if you made two careless mistakes in a section, that's where your improvement will come from. When you think of it in terms of how many more questions per section, instead of how many more questions overall, your goal score may seem much more attainable. And again, it's up to you as to where those extra points will come from. You may be at a saturation point with one question type, so instead of planning to get two more points in that section, you may opt to try for one more correct answer (or one fewer error) from there and three more from a different section. Design the approach that's most workable for *you*.

Okay, you've figured out how many more questions you need to get right to achieve your goal score. How do you go about fixing your errors? You want to keep track of your progress, preferably in a notebook, on each drill or timed section you do. Analysis is the key to better performance. After each drill or timed section, write down the drill or section number, and for each question you did, note the question number, question type, whether you got it right or wrong, and what happened if you did indeed miss it. After a while you may begin to see patterns emerge: Maybe you always miss questions that ask what "must be false" because you forget the "false;" or you constantly pick answer choices that go beyond the scope of a passage; or you lose focus when tackling EXCEPT questions. Or maybe there's a particular question type you keep misidentifying, or you're not picking the best questions for you to attempt. Whatever the problem is, you have to be able to diagnose it before you can fix it. Keeping track of your progress and reviewing the notes you make about questions you miss will help you further structure your preparation.

ADDITIONAL PRACTICE TIPS

A few final, extra things to think about.

- Try to time your LSAT practice to the time of day you'll be taking the real thing as much as possible. At the very least, start your practice tests at the same time that the real test will be given. For a June LSAT, this means you'll want to concentrate your study time during the afternoon; for all other administrations of the test, you'll want to practice in the morning.

- Although both the tests in this book and the real LSATs from LSAC have only four sections, the actual exam, as you know, has five. It's a really good idea to take an extra section from one of the real LSATs you've ordered and use it as an experimental section when taking full-length practice tests. It will build your stamina and it will give you a chance to practice with an extra section of each type of question because you never know what question type you could see as an experimental section on test day. Even when doing individual timed sections, try to do a couple of sections back-to-back before checking your answers. Get used to focusing for longer periods of time.

- If you've mastered what's in this book and are aiming for a score in the high 150s or above, consider purchasing our *LSAT Workout*, which focuses on higher-level skills and more difficult questions. For those students who need to get some of their points from tougher material, this book will provide ample opportunity to practice on some challenging questions.

- Don't forget to check out our free online tools at **www.PrincetonReview.com/cracking**. You just need to have this book handy when you log in for the first time.

THE DAY OF THE TEST

There is probably just as much bad advice as good advice dispensed about what to do on test day. A lot of the good advice is just common sense, but we're going to give it to you here just in case you're a bit distracted.

Visit your test center before test day

Why worry on test day about the best way to get to the test center? Visit the test center a few weeks or days before the test so you know exactly where to go on test day. Better yet, go there with a practice LSAT and try to get into the room where you're going to take the LSAT. Work the test in that room, if possible, so you're on familiar ground the day of the test. This will do wonders for your comfort and confidence. You'll know if the room is hot or cold, what the lighting is like, whether you'll be working at an individual desk or a long table, etc. Use the boy scout motto here: Be prepared.

Eat and drink what you normally eat and drink

People have many different ideas about what to eat and drink on the morning of the test. The most important thing is not to vary dramatically from what you normally ingest. Don't eat a big, heavy breakfast that will leave you sluggish. Don't skip breakfast completely. Eat a reasonable meal that will prepare you for a grueling three-and-a-half-hour test. And don't experiment with caffeine. If you don't normally have coffee in the morning, don't start on test day. If you do normally have coffee in the morning, don't stop on test day. The same advice applies if you get your caffeine from soda or any other caffeinated beverage.

Bring a snack

Maybe your proctor won't let you munch on anything during the break, but maybe he or she will. If so, be prepared by bringing a bottle of water and some granola bars or a banana. If you're subtle about it, chances are no one will care one way or the other. Even if you're not allowed to eat in the testing room, you can always go outside and fuel up for the second half of the test.

Bring a nonbeeping digital timer

Spend the 10 or 15 dollars and get yourself a digital timer. Use it as you practice so that you'll be familiar with it on test day. You can't use a timer that beeps, so either find one that doesn't or have someone disable the speaker. It's amazing what you can do with a small screwdriver, a pair of scissors, and some tape. If you absolutely *insist* on using an analog watch, do yourself a favor and reset it to twelve o'clock at the beginning of each section. That will take the guesswork out of determining when the section will be over. And don't forget the five-minute drill: Bubble in your "letter of the day" for any questions you haven't worked on and then change them one at a time as you pick up those last few questions.

Bring everything you'll need

Yes, you will be fingerprinted and will need to present proper identification. You'll also need your registration ticket. Refer to the registration booklet and follow the procedures outlined there. You'll also want to have plenty of sharp pencils and a separate eraser. Don't leave any room for the unexpected.

Get there nice and early and warm up your brain

You're going to be stressed out enough on test day without worrying that you'll be late for the test. Get there nice and early and warm up your brain by working out a game that you've already done and perhaps by running through a few arguments. And don't bother to check the answers; the purpose is warming up, not diagnosis. That way, you'll already be in gear by the time you open up the first section. You want to hit the ground running so you won't be warming up on questions that count toward your score.

Some stress is good; too much stress is bad

We know you're going to be stressed the day of the exam, and a little stress is not a bad thing—it will keep you on your toes. But if you tend to get *really* stressed by standardized tests, try a yoga or meditation class, or some other type of relaxation therapy, preferably a month before the test. This way, you'll have some techniques to calm you down, taught to you by people who know what they're doing. One Princeton Review student had a dream about test day—she went into the test, and the bubbles were about five feet in diameter. She hadn't even finished bubbling in one bubble before the proctor called time. If you're having dreams like this, relaxation therapy might help.

Wear layered clothing

Who knows how cold or how warm the test center will be on test day? Wear your most comfortable layered clothing, so you can put more layers on if you're cold or take layers off if you're hot.

Be confident, and be aggressive

Sometimes we'll talk to students after they've taken the LSAT and they'll say: "By the time I got to section 5, I just didn't care anymore. I just filled in whatever." Don't say that, don't think that—section 5 will probably count because the experimental section is usually in the first three sections of the exam. So when you open up your test to section 5, keep in mind that it's most likely a real section that will count toward your score. Your goal is to take three deep breaths and to fight your way through that last section, and approach it just as aggressively as you approached the other sections of the exam. It's going to count—don't lose your confidence and your energy here because it's almost over!

Here is another problem students have reported: "I was doing fine until I hit section 3. I didn't know how to do any of the games, and I couldn't concentrate on the last two sections of the test." Well, guess what? That was probably the experimental section! Don't let a complex or tough section get you down, especially if it's early in the test. Remember, they are using the experimental sections to test new questions—some of them invariably will be a bit strange. And even if it is a section that ultimately counts toward your score, getting stressed out over it will only hurt your performance on that section and potentially on subsequent scored sections as well. Just roll with the punches.

Always keep your pencil moving

Actively using your pencil will help you to stay engaged. Cross off all the wrong answer choices; circle and underline key words in reading comprehension and arguments passages; always diagram and symbolize in games. By constantly keeping your pencil moving, you'll be keeping your brain moving as well.

If you find that you're losing focus, stop working for a second and regroup. Never waste time working on a question if your mind has gone astray or if you find that you can't focus on the task at hand. The few seconds you invest in a short break will pay off in the long run.

And remember that you can always come back to a question that is giving you grief. Just mark it so that you can find it later if you have time to come back to it. Don't spend too much time on any one question. It will only lead to frustration and lost points.

Your Test Day "Top Ten"

Here are the tips mentioned above in a handy numbered list. Find some room on the fridge.

1. Visit your test center before test day.
2. Eat and drink what you normally eat and drink.
3. Bring a snack.
4. Bring a nonbeeping digital timer.
5. Bring everything you'll need.
6. Get there nice and early and warm up your brain.
7. Some stress is good; too much stress is bad.
8. Wear layered clothing.
9. Be confident, and be aggressive.
10. Always keep your pencil moving.

Good luck on test day!

7

Law School Admissions

INTRODUCTION

LSAC, LSAT, LSDAS

The Law School Admission Council (LSAC), headquartered in Newtown, Pennsylvania, is the governing body that oversees the creation, testing, and administration of the LSAT (Law School Admission Test). The LSAC also runs the Law School Data Assembly Service (LSDAS), which provides information (in a standard format) on law school applicants to the schools themselves. All American Bar Association (ABA)–approved law schools are members of LSAC.

The process of applying to law school, although simple enough in theory, is viewed by many to be about as painful as a root canal. The best way to avoid the pain is to start early. If you're reading this in December, hope to get into a law school for the following year, and haven't done anything about it, you're in big trouble. If you've got an LSAT score that you're happy with, you're in less trouble. However, your applications will get to the law schools after the optimum time and the applications themselves, even with the most cursory glance by an admissions officer, may appear rushed. The best way to think about applying is to start early in the year, take care of one thing at a time, and be totally finished by December.

This chapter is mainly a nuts-and-bolts manual on how to apply to law school and when to do it. A checklist, information about Law School Forums, fee waivers, the Law School Data Assembly Service (LSDAS), and several admissions calendars, which will show you when you need to take which step, is included.

LSAT Score Distribution

Most test takers are interested in knowing where their LSAT scores fall within the distribution of all scores. This chart should help you determine how well you did in comparison to fellow test takers over the last few years. Please be aware, however, that percentiles are not fixed values that remain constant over time. Unlike an LSAT score, a percentile rank associated with a given test score may vary slightly depending on the year in which it is reported. This chart is just to give you a roughly accurate idea where you rank compared to those competing for the same spot in law school.

LSAT Score	Percent Below	LSAT Score	Percent Below
180	100.0	160	62.7
179	100.0	159	58.8
178	100.0	158	55.4
177	100.0	157	51.0
176	100.0	156	43.6
175	100.0	155	37.3
174	100.0	154	30.9
173	100.0	153	23.5
172	100.0	152	16.7
171	99.0	151	13.7
170	97.5	150	10.8
169	95.1	149	7.8
168	94.6	148	4.9
167	93.6	147	3.9
166	91.7	146	3.9
165	89.7	145	1.5
164	84.8	144	1.5
163	81.9	143	1.5
162	76.0	142	1.0
161	72.1	141	0.5

Source: *The Complete Book of Law Schools*, 2006 Ed.

When to Apply

Consider these application deadlines for fall admission: Yale Law School, on or about January 10; New York University (NYU) Law School, on or about February 1; Loyola University Chicago School of Law, on or about April 1. Although some of this information may make starting the application process in December seem like a viable option, remember that law schools don't wait until they've received every application to start selecting students. In fact, the longer you wait to apply to a school, the worse your chances are of getting into that school. Maybe your chances will go only from 90 percent to 85 percent, but you shouldn't risk it if you don't have to.

Additionally, some schools have "early admissions decisions" options, so that you may know by December if you've been accepted (for instance, NYU's early admission deadline is on or about October 15). This option is good for a few reasons: It can give you an indication of what your chances are at other schools; it can relieve the stress of waiting until April to see where you're going to school; and, if you're waitlisted the first time around, you might be accepted a bit later on in the process—i.e., when everyone else is hearing from law schools for the first time. However, not every school has an early admission option, and not every school's option is the same, so check with your prospective institutions' policies before you write any deadlines on your calendar.

Law School Forums

Law School Forums are an excellent way to talk with representatives and gather information on almost every law school in the country simultaneously. More than 150 schools send admissions officers to these forums, which take place in major cities around the country between July and November. If possible, GO. For information about forum dates and locations check the LSAC website at www.lsac.org.

Let's take a look at the major steps in the application process.

- **Take the LSAT**. All ABA-approved and most non–ABA-approved law schools in the United States and Canada require an LSAT score from each applicant. The LSAT is given in February, June, October (occasionally very late September), and December of each year.
- **Register for LSDAS**. You can register for the Law School Data Assembly Service at the same time you register to take the LSAT—both forms are contained in the *LSAT & LSDAS Registration Information Book* (hence the name).
- **Select approximately seven schools**. After you've selected your schools, you'll be able to see which schools want what types of things on their applications—although almost all of them will want three basic things: a personal statement, recommendations, and a résumé. Each applicant should be thinking about putting law schools into three categories: (1) "reach" schools, (2) schools where you've got a good chance of being accepted, and (3) "safety" schools. As a minimum, each applicant should apply to two to three schools in each category. (Most admissions experts will say either 2-2-3 or 2-3-2.) It is not uncommon for those with extremely low grades or low LSAT scores (or both) to apply to 15 or 20 schools.
- **Write your personal statement(s)**. It may be that you'll only need to write one personal statement (many schools will ask that your personal statement be about why you want to obtain a law degree), but you may need to write several—which is why you need to select your schools fairly early.
- **Obtain two or three recommendations**. Some schools will ask for two recommendations, both of which must be academic. Others want more than two recommendations and want at least one of your recommenders to be someone who knows you outside traditional academic circles.

- **Update/create a résumé**. Most law school applications ask that you submit a résumé. Make sure yours is up to date and suitable for submission to an academic institution.
- **Get your academic transcripts sent to LSDAS**. A minor administrative detail, seemingly, but then again, if you forget to do this, LSDAS will not send your information to the law schools. LSDAS helps the law schools by acting as a clearinghouse for information—LSDAS, not you, sends the law schools your undergraduate and graduate school transcripts, your LSAT score(s), and an undergraduate academic summary.

Those are the major steps in applying to law school. From reading this chapter, or from reading the *LSAT & LSDAS Registration Information Book*, you might discover that there are other steps you need to take—such as preparing an addendum to your application, asking for application fee waivers, applying for a special administration of the LSAT, and so on. If you sense that you might need to do anything special, start your application process even earlier than what is recommended in the *LSAT & LSDAS Registration Information Book*, which is unquestionably the most useful tool in applying to law school. This information book not only contains the forms to apply for the LSAT and LSDAS, but also has a sample LSAT, admissions information, the Law School Forum schedule, and two sample application schedules. These schedules are very useful. For instance, one sample schedule recommends taking the June LSAT for fall admission. This schedule allows you to focus on the LSAT in the spring and early summer and then start the rest of your application process rolling. That's good advice—as mentioned in the LSAT portion of this book, the LSAT is one of the most important factors in getting into the best law school possible.

The sample schedule also indicates that you should research schools in late July/early August. While you are doing this, go ahead and subscribe to LSDAS and send your transcript request forms to your undergraduate and any other educational institutions—there's no reason to wait until September to do this (you should pay LSDAS for seven law school applications, unless you're positive you want to apply to only a few schools). Why do this? Because undergraduate institutions can and will screw up and delay the transcript process—even when you go there personally and pay them to provide your records. This is essential if you're applying for early decision at some law schools—the transcript process can be a nightmare.

Average LSAT Scores

Law School	Scores
University of North Dakota, School of Law	147–155
Widener University, School of Law	149–152
Gonzaga University, School of Law	150–156
The John Marshall Law School	151–155
Rutgers University–Newark, Rutgers School of Law	153–162
University of Tennessee, College of Law	155–161
University of Missouri-Columbia, School of Law	156–160
University of Florida, Levin College of Law	156–162
Southern Methodist University, School of Law	156–164
Case Western Reserve University, School of Law	157–161
Loyola University Chicago, School of Law	157–161
Northeastern University, School of Law	157–162
Temple University, James E. Beasley School of Law	157–162
University of Pittsburgh, School of Law	158–162
The University of Alabama, School of Law	159–163
Emory University, School of Law	161–165
Brigham Young University, J. Reuben Clark Law School	161–166
Boston University, School of Law	162–165
George Washington University, Law School	162–166
Duke University, School of Law	162–169
University of Southern California, The Law School	164–167
University of Michigan, Law School	164–169
Stanford University, School of Law	166–172
University of Chicago, Law School	167–171
New York University, School of Law	168–172
Yale University, Yale Law School	168–175

Source: *The Complete Book of Law Schools*, 2006 Ed.

Policies vary from school to school—check with the schools you're interested in to learn how they handle multiple LSAT scores.

Finally, you should send your applications to law schools between late September and early November. Naturally, if you bombed the LSAT the first time around, you're still in good shape to take the test again in October. Another good piece of news on that front is that more and more law schools are now just simply taking the highest LSAT score that each applicant has, rather than averaging multiple scores. If you've got to take the LSAT again, this is good news—but with proper preparation, you can avoid having to spend too much quality time with the LSAT.

A simple checklist

The following is a simple checklist for the major steps of the application process. Each shaded box indicates the recommended month during which you should complete that action.

	Jan.	Feb.	Mar.	Apr.	May	June	July	Aug.	Sept.	Oct.	Nov.	Dec.
Take practice LSAT												
Research LSAT prep companies												
Obtain *Registration Information Book**												
Register for June LSAT												
Take LSAT prep course												
Take LSAT												
Register for LSDAS												
Research law schools												
Obtain law school applications												
Get transcripts sent to LSDAS												
Write personal statement(s)												
Update/create résumé												
Get recommendations												
Send early decision applications												
Finish sending all applications												
Relax												

*The *LSAT & LSDAS Registration Information Book* is traditionally published in March of each year. Call 215-968-1001 to order your materials.

Helpful Hints on Personal Statements, Recommendations, Résumés, and Addenda

Although your LSAT score is one of the most important factors in the admissions process, you should still present a professional résumé, get excellent recommendations, and hone your personal statement when preparing your law school applications.

Many law schools still employ the "three-pile" system in the application process:

Pile 1 contains applicants with high enough LSAT scores and GPAs to admit them pretty much automatically.

Pile 2 contains applicants who are "borderline"—decent enough LSAT scores and GPAs for that school but not high enough for automatic admission. Admissions officers look at these applications thoroughly to sort out the best candidates.

Pile 3 contains applicants with "substandard" LSAT scores and GPAs for that school. These applicants are usually rejected without much further ado. There are circumstances in which admissions officers will look through pile 3 for any extraordinary applications, but it doesn't happen very often.

What does this mean? Well, if you're lucky, you are in pile 2 (and not pile 3!) for at least one of your "reach" schools. And if you are, there's a good possibility that your application will be thoroughly scrutinized by the admissions committee. Consequently, make sure the following four elements of your application are as strong as you can possibly make them.

Personal statement

Ideally, your personal statement should be two pages long. Often, law schools will ask you to identify exactly why you want to go to law school and obtain a law degree. "I love 'The Practice'" is not the answer to this question. There should be some moment in your life, some experience that you had, or some intellectual slant that you are interested in that is directing you to law school. Identify that, write about it, and make it compelling.

Then you should have three or four people read your personal statement and critique it. You should select people whom you respect intellectually, not people who will merely give it a cursory read and tell you it's fine. Also, your personal statement is not the place to make excuses, get on your soapbox, or try your hand at alliterative verse. Make it intelligent, persuasive, short, and powerful—those are the writing and analytical qualities law schools are looking for.

Make your personal statement intelligent, persuasive, short, and powerful—those are the writing and analytical qualities law schools are looking for.

Recommendations

Most law schools ask for two or three recommendations. Typically, the longer it has been since you've graduated, the tougher it is to obtain academic recommendations. However, if you've kept your papers and if your professors were tenured, chances are you'll still be able to find them and obtain good recommendations—just present your selected prof with your personal statement and a decent paper you did in his or her course. That way, the recommender has something tangible to work from. And that's the simple secret to great recommendations—if the people you're asking for recommendations don't know anything specific about you, how can the recommendation possibly be compelling? Getting the mayor of your town or a state senator to write a recommendation

Fee waivers

Even though the cost of taking the LSAT, subscribing to LSDAS, paying for LSAT prep materials, and paying application fees will probably be one-hundredth of your total law school outlay, it's still not just a drop in the bucket. The LSAT is $108 (late registrants must pay an additional $54), LSDAS is $99 (includes one report sent to an LSDAS-requiring law school and three letters of recommendation), plus $10 for each additional school you are applying to when ordered at the time that you register for LSDAS, and $12 for each additional report ordered after you register for LSDAS. And law school applications themselves are typically around $50 each. As a result, LSAC, as well as most law schools, offers a fee waiver program. If you're accepted into the LSAC program, you get one free LSAT per year, one LSDAS subscription, three LSDAS law school reports, and one TriplePrep Plus (which contains three previously administered LSATs). With proper documentation, you can also waive a good portion of your law school application fees. You can request a fee waiver packet from LSAC at 215-968-1001, or write to them at: Law School Admission Council, Attn: Fee Waiver Packet, Box 2000, 661 Penn Street, Newtown, PA, 18940-0998. You can also download a packet at www.lsac.org.

helps only if you have a personal and professional connection to them in some way. That way, the recommender will be able to present to the admissions committee actual qualities and accomplishments you have demonstrated.

If you've been out of school for some time and are having trouble finding academic recommendations, choose people from your workplace, from the community, or from any other area of your life that is important to you. You should respect the people you choose—you should view them as quality individuals who have in some way shaped your life. If they're half as good as you think they are, they will know, at least intuitively, that they in some way were responsible for part of your development or education, and they will then be able to talk intelligently about it. Simply put, these people should know who you are, where you live, what your background is, and what your desires and motivations are—otherwise, your recommendations will not distinguish you from the ten-foot-high pile that's on an admissions committee desk.

Résumés

Résumés are a fairly simple part of your application, but make sure yours is updated and proofed correctly. Errors on your résumé (and, indeed, anywhere on your application) will make you look as if you don't really care too much about going to law school. Just remember that this should be a more academically oriented résumé, because you are applying to an academic institution. Put your academic credentials and experiences first—no matter what they are.

Addenda

If your personal and academic life has run fairly smoothly, you shouldn't need to include any addenda with your application. Addenda are brief explanatory letters written to explain or support a "deficient" portion of your application. Some legitimate addenda topics are academic probation, low/discrepant GPA, low/discrepant LSAT score, arrests/convictions, DUI/DWI suspensions, a leave of absence or other "time gap," etc.

The addenda is not the place to go off on polemics about standardized testing—if you've taken the LSAT two or three times and simply did not do very well, after spending time preparing with a test prep company or private tutor, merely tell the admissions committee that that's what you've done—you worked as hard as you could to achieve a high score and explored all possibilities to help you achieve that goal. Then let them draw their own conclusions. Additionally, addenda should be brief and balanced—do not go into detailed descriptions of things. Explain the problem and state what you did about it. Simply put, do not whine.

Gathering Information and Making Decisions

There are some key questions that you should ask before randomly selecting law schools around the country or submitting your application to someone or other's list of the "top ten" law schools and saying, "If I don't get in to one of these schools, I'll go to B-School instead." Here are some questions to think about.

Where would you like to practice law?

For instance, if you were born and bred in the state of Nebraska, care deeply about it, wish to practice law there, and want to someday be governor, then it might be a better move to go to the University of Nebraska School of Law than, say, University of Virginia, even though UVA is considered a "top ten" law school. A law school's reputation is usually greater on its home turf than anywhere else (except for Harvard and Yale). Apply to the schools in the geographic area where you wish to practice law. You'll be integrated into the community, you may gain some experience in the region doing clinics during law school, and it should be easier for you to get more interviews and position yourself as someone who already knows, for instance, Nebraska.

What type of law would you like to practice?

Law schools *do* have specialties. For instance, if you are very interested in environmental law, it might be better to go to the University of Vermont School of Law than to go to NYU. The University of Vermont is one of the most highly regarded schools in the country when it comes to environmental law. So look at what you want to do in addition to where you want to do it.

Can you get in?

Many people apply to Harvard. Very few get in. Go right ahead and apply, if you wish, but unless you've got killer scores and/or have done some very outstanding things in your life, your chances are, well, *slim*. Apply to a few reach schools, but make sure they are schools you really want to go to.

Did you like the school when you went there?

What if you decided to go to Stanford, got in, went to Palo Alto, California, and decided that you hated it? The weather was horrible! The architecture was mundane! There's nothing to do nearby! Well, maybe Stanford wasn't the best example—but you get the point. Go to the school and check it out. Talk to students and faculty. Walk around. *Then* make a decision.

Applying by computer

Almost all law schools want their applications typed. Although typing is not exactly rocket science, it can be annoying. The Princeton Review's very own www.Princetonreview.com will allow you to fill out law school applications free on its site. The LSACD, a CD-ROM online service (215-968-1001 or www.lsac.org; $59), has a searchable database and applications to ABA-approved schools.

CONCLUSION

The application process, although detailed, is much easier than taking the extremely stressful LSAT, which in turn will be much easier than your first year of law school—no matter where you go. However, you've still got to want to go to law school. Applying to law school is a demanding process, and if you're not committed to doing it well, it will almost certainly come across in your applications. Be as thorough in preparing your applications as you were in preparing for the LSAT; otherwise you run the risk of turning in applications that are late or contain errors, thereby hurting your chances of getting accepted by the schools to which you really want to go.

If all this administrative stuff seems overwhelming (i.e., you're the type of person who dreads filling out a deposit slip), the major test-prep companies have designed law school application courses that force you to think about where you want to go and make sure you've got all your recommendations, résumés, personal statements, addenda, and everything else together.

Whatever your level of administrative facility, the choice of where you want to go to school is yours. You'll probably be paying a lot of money to go, so you should really make sure you go to the place that's best for you. Take the time to do research on the schools because you'll be paying for law school for a long, long time.

8

The Princeton Review LSAT Practice Test 1

ABOUT OUR PRINCETON REVIEW LSAT PRACTICE TEST

If you can't get your hands on some actual LSATs, our practice test is the next best thing. As we said in Chapter 1, you should practice on real LSATs only. Don't be fooled by the sample questions in the other books, which are only superficially similar to actual LSAT questions.

We have constructed our practice test using the same sophisticated procedures and statistical methods used in creating actual LSATs. Thousands of Princeton Review students have taken this test, so we know it is an excellent predictor of LSAT scores. It includes the four sections that contribute to your LSAT score; we have spared you the trouble of taking the unscored experimental section and Writing Sample.

How to Take This Test

Be sure to review the chapters in this book before sitting down to take this test. Clear some table space, take your phone off the hook, and try to complete these sections in one sitting. You may want to take a break after completing the first three sections. If possible, have a friend time you. Trust us: Timing yourself is not nearly the same experience.

SECTION I

Time—35 Minutes

24 Questions

Directions: Each group of questions in this section is based on a set of conditions. In answering some of the questions, it may be useful to draw a rough diagram. Choose the response that most accurately and completely answers each question and blacken the corresponding space on your answer sheet.

Questions 1–5

A veterinarian will be using four large animal cages for transport: Cage 1, Cage 2, Cage 3, and Cage 4. Each cage has an upper berth and a lower berth, and each berth will be occupied by exactly one animal, either male or female. The following rules govern assignment of animals to cage berths:

Exactly three berths will contain males.

The upper berths of Cages 1 and 2 will contain females.

If a cage has a male in one of its berths, it will carry a female in the other.

If a male is assigned to the lower berth of Cage 3, then the upper berth of Cage 4 will contain a male.

1. If a female is assigned to both berths of Cage 3, then which one of the following could be two other berths that also contain females?

(A) The upper berth of Cage 1 and the lower berth of Cage 2
(B) The lower berth of Cage 1 and the upper berth of Cage 4
(C) The lower berth of Cage 1 and the upper berth of Cage 2
(D) The upper berth of Cage 2 and the lower berth of Cage 4
(E) The lower berth of Cage 2 and the lower berth of Cage 4

2. It CANNOT be true that females are assigned to both

(A) the lower berth of Cage 1 and the lower berth of Cage 4
(B) the lower berth of Cage 1 and the lower berth of Cage 2
(C) the lower berth of Cage 1 and the upper berth of Cage 3
(D) the lower berth of Cage 2 and the lower berth of Cage 4
(E) the upper berth of Cage 3 and the lower berth of Cage 4

3. If the upper berth of Cage 4 contains a female, then a female must also be assigned to which one of the following berths?

(A) The lower berth of Cage 1
(B) The lower berth of Cage 4
(C) The lower berth of Cage 2
(D) The lower berth of Cage 3
(E) The upper berth of Cage 3

4. If a male is assigned to the lower berth of Cage 3, which one of the following is a complete and accurate list of the berths that CANNOT be assigned males?

(A) The upper berth of Cage 1, the upper berth of Cage 2
(B) The upper berth of Cage 1, the upper berth of Cage 2, the upper berth of Cage 3
(C) The upper berth of Cage 1, the upper berth of Cage 2, the lower berth of Cage 4
(D) The upper berth of Cage 1, the upper berth of Cage 2, the upper berth of Cage 3, the lower berth of Cage 4
(E) The upper berth of Cage 1, the lower berth of Cage 1, the upper berth of Cage 2, the upper berth of Cage 3, the lower berth of Cage 4

5. If the lower berth of Cage 2 contains a female, then it could be true that females are assigned to both

(A) the lower berth of Cage 1 and the upper berth of Cage 4
(B) the lower berth of Cage 1 and the lower berth of Cage 4
(C) the upper berth of Cage 3 and the upper berth of Cage 4
(D) the lower berth of Cage 3 and the lower berth of Cage 4
(E) the lower berth of Cage 3 and the upper berth of Cage 3

GO ON TO THE NEXT PAGE.

Questions 6–11

In a single day, exactly seven airplanes—J, K, L, M, N, P, and Q—are the only arrivals at an airport. No airplane arrives at the same time as any other plane, and no plane arrives more than once that day. Each airplane is either a prop or a jet (but not both). The following conditions apply:

No two consecutive arrivals are jets.
P arrives some time before both K and M.
Exactly two of the planes that arrive before P are jets.
J is the sixth arrival.
Q arrives sometime before L.

6. Which one of the following could be the order, from first to last, in which the airplanes arrive?

(A) N, Q, L, P, M, J, K
(B) N, P, Q, L, M, J, K
(C) Q, M, L, K, P, J, N
(D) Q, L, K, P, M, J, N
(E) L, Q, P, K, J, M, N

7. For which one of the following pairs of airplanes is it the case that they CANNOT both be jets?

(A) J and N
(B) K and J
(C) L and M
(D) M and K
(E) N and Q

8. If N is the third arrival, then which of the following airplanes must be a prop?

(A) J
(B) K
(C) L
(D) M
(E) Q

9. If exactly three of the airplanes are props, then which one of the following airplanes must be a prop?

(A) J
(B) K
(C) L
(D) M
(E) Q

10. For how many of the seven airplanes can one determine exactly how many airplanes arrived before it?

(A) one
(B) two
(C) three
(D) four
(E) five

11. Which one of the following pairs of airplanes CANNOT arrive consecutively at the airport?

(A) L and P
(B) N and P
(C) P and K
(D) P and M
(E) P and Q

GO ON TO THE NEXT PAGE.

Questions 12–18

A total of six pieces of fruit are found in three small baskets: one in the first basket, two in the second basket, and three in the third basket. Two of the fruits are pears—one Bosc, the other Forelle. Two others are apples—one Cortland, one Dudley. The remaining two fruits are oranges—one navel, one Valencia. The fruits' placement is consistent with the following:

There is at least one orange in the same basket as the Bosc pear.
The apples are not in the same basket.
The navel orange is not in the same basket as either apple.

12. Which of the following could be an accurate matching of the baskets to the pieces of fruit in each of them?

(A) basket one: Forelle pear
basket two: Dudley apple, navel orange
basket three: Bosc pear, Cortland apple, Valencia orange
(B) basket one: Dudley apple
basket two: Bosc pear, navel orange
basket three: Forelle pear, Cortland apple, Valencia orange
(C) basket one: navel orange
basket two: Cortland apple, Bosc pear
basket three: Forelle pear, Dudley apple, Valencia orange
(D) basket one: Valencia orange
basket two: Cortland and Dudley apples
basket three: navel orange, Bosc and Forelle pears
(E) basket one: Valencia orange
basket two: Bosc pear, navel orange
basket three: Forelle pear, Cortland and Dudley apples

13. Which one of the following CANNOT be true?

(A) A pear is in the first basket.
(B) An apple is in the same basket as the Forelle pear.
(C) An orange is in the first basket.
(D) The oranges are in the same basket as each other.
(E) Neither apple is in the first basket.

14. Which one of the following must be true?

(A) An apple and a pear are in the second basket.
(B) An orange and a pear are in the second basket.
(C) At least one apple and at least one pear are in the third basket.
(D) At least one orange and at least one pear are in the third basket.
(E) At least one orange and at least one apple are in the third basket.

15. If both pears are in the same basket, which one of the following could be true?

(A) The Cortland apple is in the third basket.
(B) An orange is in the first basket.
(C) Both oranges are in the second basket.
(D) The Bosc pear is in the second basket.
(E) The Cortland apple is in the first basket.

16. Which one of the following must be true?

(A) An apple is in the first basket.
(B) No more than one orange is in each basket.
(C) The pears are not in the same basket.
(D) The Dudley apple is not in the same basket as the Valencia orange.
(E) The Valencia orange is not in the first basket.

17. If the Bosc pear is not in the third basket, which of the following could be true?

(A) The Cortland apple is in the second basket.
(B) The Forelle pear is in the second basket.
(C) The Dudley apple is in the third basket.
(D) The navel orange is in the third basket.
(E) The Valencia orange is in the second basket.

18. If the Forelle pear and the Cortland apple are in the same basket, which one of the following must be true?

(A) The Cortland apple is in the second basket.
(B) The Valencia orange is in the second basket.
(C) The Dudley apple is in the second basket.
(D) The Dudley apple is in the first basket.
(E) The Valencia orange is in the third basket.

GO ON TO THE NEXT PAGE.

Questions 19–25

A live radio show features five bands—the Foghorns, the Geriatrics, the Hollowmen, the Inkstains, and the Jarheads—that will sing ten songs. Each band performs exactly two of the songs: one band performs songs 1 and 6, one band performs songs 2 and 7, one band performs songs 3 and 8, one band performs songs 4 and 9, and one band performs songs 5 and 10. The following conditions apply:

Neither of the Geriatrics's songs is performed immediately before either of the Hollowmen's.
The Foghorns do not sing the ninth song.
The Jarheads's first song is after (but not necessarily immediately after) the Inkstains's first song.
At least one of the Foghorns's songs is immediately after one of the Jarheads's songs.

19. Which one of the following could be an accurate list of the bands performing the first five songs, in order from song 1 to song 5?

(A) Foghorns, Geriatrics, Inkstains, Hollowmen, Jarheads
(B) Geriatrics, Inkstains, Jarheads, Foghorns, Hollowmen
(C) Hollowmen, Inkstains, Foghorns, Geriatrics, Jarheads
(D) Jarheads, Geriatrics, Inkstains, Hollowmen, Foghorns
(E) Inkstains, Jarheads, Foghorns, Geriatrics, Hollowmen

20. If the Foghorns sing the eighth song, then for exactly how many of the ten songs can one determine which band sings the song?

(A) ten
(B) eight
(C) six
(D) four
(E) two

21. If the Jarheads sing the fourth song, then which one of the following could be true?

(A) The Foghorns sing song 1.
(B) The Foghorns sing song 3.
(C) The Geriatrics sing song 5.
(D) The Hollowmen sing song 3.
(E) The Inkstains sing song 5.

22. Which one of the following could be true?

(A) The Foghorns sing song 4.
(B) The Geriatrics sing song 5.
(C) The Hollowmen sing song 5.
(D) The Inkstains sing song 10.
(E) The Jarheads sing song 6.

23. The Foghorns CANNOT perform which one of the following songs?

(A) song 1
(B) song 2
(C) song 3
(D) song 6
(E) song 10

24. Which one of the following could be an accurate list of the bands performing the last five songs, in order from song 6 to song 10?

(A) Foghorns, Inkstains, Geriatrics, Jarheads, Hollowmen
(B) Geriatrics, Hollowmen, Inkstains, Jarheads, Foghorns
(C) Hollowmen, Geriatrics, Inkstains, Jarheads, Foghorns
(D) Inkstains, Geriatrics, Jarheads, Foghorns, Hollowmen
(E) Jarheads, Foghorns, Geriatrics, Inkstains, Hollowmen

STOP

IF YOU FINISH BEFORE TIME IS CALLED, YOU MAY CHECK YOUR WORK ON THIS SECTION ONLY. DO NOT WORK ON ANY OTHER SECTION IN THE TEST.

SECTION II

Time—35 Minutes

25 Questions

Directions: The questions in this section are based on the reasoning contained in brief statements or passages. For some questions, more than one of the choices could conceivably answer the question. However, you are to choose the best answer; that is, the response that most accurately and completely answers the question. You should not make assumptions that are by commonsense standards implausible, superfluous, or incompatible with the passage. After you have chosen the best answer, blacken the corresponding space on your answer sheet.

1. Educator: By itself, the expert advice delivered in a workshop setting does not cause a young writer to be able to craft short stories; rather, the repeated effort of writing new stories in the context of a short-story workshop can be a cause. When any individual writes many short stories, the quality of that person's stories inevitably increases. As a result, the new short-story workshops offered by this school will increase the quality of short stories written by its students.

The conclusion drawn by the educator follows logically if which one of the following is assumed?

(A) The new short-story workshops offered by the school will increase the number of its students who write a significant number of new short stories.
(B) The advice delivered by instructors in the new short-story workshops will be superior to the advice previously offered by writing teachers in the school.
(C) The new short-story workshops will be attended by a large number of the school's students.
(D) The introduction on writing workshops represents a new emphasis in the school curriculum.
(E) Any young writer, regardless of his or her ability to craft short stories, can improve through repeated efforts at writing.

2. Last year, the challenger in this election proposed a plan to solve the city's waste-disposal problems. Just recently, the incumbent proposed a plan that is nearly the same. The incumbent claims that he was not aware of the challenger's plan, and that their similarities are due to the fact that the solution is merely a matter of common sense. Yet both plans involve similar increases in spending on recycling, both recommend the decommissioning of the same waste incinerators, and both rely on a system of so-called "green landfills," a revolutionary theory not employed by any other city in the world.

The main point of the argument is that

(A) the challenger's plan and the incumbent's plan have many similarities
(B) both plans have been advanced in an effort to attract the same large bloc of votes
(C) the incumbent's plan is similar to the challenger's in ways that suggest that this similarity is the product of more than coincidence
(D) the incumbent proposed his plan only after it was learned that the challenger's plan had wide popular support
(E) new plans that are introduced by political candidates sometimes take their opponents' plans into account

GO ON TO THE NEXT PAGE.

3. A physicist theorized that the present distribution of matter in the universe was largely determined by random clumping of primeval particles during the early stages of the universe's formation. When computer simulations developed by the physicist showed that several different clumping patterns led to substantially similar distributions of matter, the physicist did not report the results. A journalist who learned about the results of the simulations reported them and accused the physicist of suppressing experimental findings that contradict her theory. The physicist countered that the computer simulations were inconclusive because they depended in part upon present theories of the universe's formation.

Which one of the following, if true, most strengthens the physicist's counterargument?

(A) Other experiments conducted by the physicist showed that clumping of primeval particles could influence the later distribution of matter in the universe.
(B) The clumping patterns used by the physicist in the computer simulation were not randomly generated.
(C) Present theories of the universe's formation include principles that allow only slight variations in the distribution of matter.
(D) Every computer simulation yet devised to model the formation of the universe depends to some degree upon present theories of the universe's formation.
(E) It is impossible to determine the theoretical accuracy of the assumptions used in developing any computer simulation of the universe's formation.

4. Concerned citizen: The county government's new ordinance limiting the types of materials that can be disposed of in trash fires violates our rights as citizens. The fact that local environmental damage results from the burning of certain inorganic materials is not the primary issue. The real concern is the government's flagrant disregard for the right of the individual to establish what is acceptable on his or her own property.

Which one of the following principles, if accepted, would enable the concerned citizen's conclusion to be properly drawn?

(A) Legislative violation of an individual's right to privacy is not justifiable unless the actions of that individual put others at risk.
(B) The right of an individual to live in a safe environment takes precedence over the right of an individual to be exempt from legislative intrusion.
(C) An individual's personal rights supersede any right or responsibility the government may have to protect a community from harm.
(D) An individual has a moral obligation to act in the best interest of the community as a whole.
(E) A compromise must be found when the right of an individual to act independently conflicts with the responsibility of the government to provide protection for the local environment.

GO ON TO THE NEXT PAGE.

5. As part of a new commitment to customer satisfaction, an electronics company sent a survey to all customers who had purchased its electronic personal organizer in the previous month. The survey, which was sent through the mail, asked customers to give personal information and to rate their satisfaction with the product. Of customers who returned the survey, more indicated that they had a negative opinion of the product's performance than indicated a neutral or positive opinion. On the basis of these results, the company, hoping to increase customer satisfaction, decided to allocate a large amount of capital to redesigning the product.

Which one of the following, if true, indicates the most serious flaw in the method of research used by the company?

(A) The company relied on a numerical system of rating responses rather than on open-ended questions that allow for more detailed feedback.
(B) Customers who were dissatisfied with the information display of the organizer outnumbered customers who were dissatisfied with the variety of functions offered by the organizer.
(C) Studies show that customer dissatisfaction with a new product is highest during the first year of the product's release and gradually decreases over the following years.
(D) The marketing division has found that responses to their mail-in surveys are generally accurate.
(E) People who are satisfied with a product or have no strong opinion about it are less likely to be motivated to return a mail-in questionnaire.

6. Adolphus: The proposed system of computer control for the city's subway traffic, once it is implemented, will lead to greater on-time service and fewer accidents. We must secure whatever resources are required to implement the new system immediately.

Jean: The current financial state of the transit authority is such that the immediate implementation of the new system would require an increase in fares, which the public would not support. We should delay the implementation of the new system until the transit authority can set money aside for the transition and build support for it among riders.

Adolphus and Jean disagree with each other over whether

(A) the system of computer control will achieve its anticipated benefits
(B) the public would support higher fares to increase on-time service and reduce accidents
(C) it is possible to implement the proposed system of computer control quickly
(D) the proposed system of computer control could be implemented without increasing subway fares
(E) the existing system of control for the city's subways should be retained for some period of time

GO ON TO THE NEXT PAGE.

7. Because the consequences of an action intended to conserve the environment cannot be fully predicted, a wise principle is that such an action should be taken only when the likely consequence of inaction is less acceptable than any foreseeable negative consequence of the action.

Which one of the following provides the best illustration of the principle above?

(A) A system of canals is proposed to preserve threatened wetlands. Without the canals, the wetlands will vanish, so the objections of area farmers should not be allowed to prevent the canal system from being built.
(B) New roads are proposed to make it easier for conservationists to reach the areas inhabited by an endangered bird species. Because these same roads would increase the access of logging companies to these sensitive areas, the roads should not be built.
(C) A threatened moss thrives in a remote, uninhabited area that is not currently protected by law. Because the area is not important for either residential or industrial purposes, there is no possible negative consequence of passing a law to limit access to the area. Thus, such a law should be passed to protect the moss.
(D) A rare species of mink is found only in one area and has long been hunted for its fur. The proposal that all hunting be banned in the area, however, should not be implemented. Mule deer living in the same area contribute to destruction of the mink's habitat, and without hunting to limit the mule deer population, it is possible that the mink will die out completely.
(E) Tailings—the waste left over from mining—lead to severe water pollution in some mountain areas. Because most of the mining companies responsible for this pollution no longer exist, it is impossible to demand that they clean it up. Therefore, no matter how negatively taxpayers may react, taxes must be used to fund the cleanup of mine tailings.

8. Columnist: Our local public schools are desperately in need of community support, not just from tax revenues, but also from sources such as auxiliary fund-raisers and volunteer work. Although the mayor has often been seen participating in these activities and claims that the public schools are our community's most important assets, there is no reason to believe that his participation is sincere. After all, his own children attend a local private school instead of the public schools.

The columnist's reasoning is most vulnerable to criticism on the grounds that it presumes, without providing justification, that

(A) the mayor's participation in fund-raising activities for local public schools is motivated solely by a desire for positive public perception
(B) the mayor could lend greater support to the local public schools by having his children attend them
(C) the mayor sends his children to a local private school so that they will not contribute to the serious problems of overcrowding in the local public schools
(D) no politician can plausibly profess support for any public institution which the politician does not use
(E) there is no reason to believe that the mayor's support for the public schools is sincere if he has no direct personal interest in seeing their needs met

GO ON TO THE NEXT PAGE.

9. A recent study seems to suggest that, contrary to popular perception, vocational and technical programs do a better job of preparing their students for the workforce than traditional four-year colleges do. This study indicated that just below 60 percent of vocational and technical school graduates found full-time employment within two years of graduation, whereas only 50 percent of those who graduated from four-year colleges did. Nevertheless, the study's official conclusion was that four-year colleges are in fact better at preparing their students for the workforce than are vocational and technical programs.

Which one of the following, if true, most helps to resolve the apparent discrepancy between the study's findings and its official conclusion?

(A) Presidents and trustees of four-year colleges work to shape public perceptions of their institutions.
(B) The study investigated a wide variety of both four-year colleges and vocational and technical programs over a period of a decade.
(C) Most graduates of vocational and technical programs who find employment within two years of graduation work in the professions for which they were trained.
(D) Increased demand for health care workers, nearly all of whom attend schools that were classified by the study as vocational, caused the employment rate among graduates of these schools to exceed 90 percent.
(E) More than 20 percent of the graduates of four-year colleges go on to professional schools that require more than two years to complete but only admit graduates of four-year colleges, and the vast majority of these students find employment when they seek it.

10. Howard: Why is it that, in physics, the direction of electric field is defined as the direction in which a positive charge experiences force? Electrons, which are negatively charged, are the particles that move in electric current, yet by the standard definition, they move in a direction opposite to the electric field.

Linda: The standard definition was developed at a time when it was known that two types of charge existed, but not that only one of them was involved in the conduction of electric current. The definition of electric field, by chance, depends upon positive charge, which generally does not move in an electric circuit.

Howard: Your explanation cannot be correct. It has been known for some time now that electrons are the only charges involved in the conduction of current, yet the definition of electric field has remained unchanged.

Which one of the following additional items of information, if true, could best be used by Linda to counter Howard's objection to her explanation?

(A) Subsequent development of physical theories related to electricity led to the wide adoption of the standard definition before its shortcomings were known, and to change it now would cause widespread confusion.
(B) Theories of magnetism, which is related to electricity, also incorporate standard definitions that take the behavior of positive charge as their bases.
(C) Students who learn the theory of electricity may initially be frustrated by its conventional dependence on the behavior of positive charge, but it does not prevent students from comprehending and correctly using that theory.
(D) There exist presentations of the theory of electricity that base their definitions around the behavior of negative charge, but anyone learning physics according to these presentations must be aware of the standard definitions in order to interpret the scientific literature surrounding electricity correctly.
(E) The choice of either positive charge or negative charge as the basis for standard definitions in the physical theory of electricity is arbitrary, and has no effect on the accuracy or completeness of the results of that theory.

GO ON TO THE NEXT PAGE.

11. Once, dieticians advocated radically reducing the proportion of total dietary calories from fat and increasing the proportion from carbohydrates as a method of aiding weight loss. One result of this advice has been an increased incidence of diabetes. Now, dieticians advocate radically reducing the proportion of dietary calories from carbohydrate and increasing the proportion from proteins and fat as a method of aiding weight loss. There is already evidence that this advice is leading to an increase in the incidence of heart disease and certain kinds of cancer. There can be little doubt that, whatever dieticians may recommend, radical changes to diet made for the purpose of losing weight do not contribute to overall health.

The reasoning in the argument is flawed because the argument

(A) takes for granted that the only possible reason for making radical dietary changes is to increase overall health
(B) takes for granted that diabetes is a less serious condition for those who suffer from it than is heart disease or cancer
(C) fails to consider the role of exercise in conjunction with dietary changes as an important factor in successful weight loss
(D) ignores the possibility that, even without advice from dieticians, many people who do not change their eating habits will develop serious health problems
(E) fails to consider that a radical reduction in calories consumed from all dietary sources may lead both to weight loss and to improved overall health

12. Dentist: Many children today eat so much sugary processed food that tooth decay has become a more serious problem than ever. Periodic brushing can protect children's teeth only if they also receive regular twice-yearly professional cleanings. Hence, the dental reimbursement plans offered by most companies are inadequate to protect the dental health of at least some children.

Which one of the following is an assumption required by the dentist's argument?

(A) In the past, children did not require twice-yearly professional cleanings to protect their teeth from decay.
(B) Some dental reimbursement plans offered by companies are adequate to protect the dental health of children who do not consume sugary processed food.
(C) No single dental reimbursement plan suits the dental health needs of all families.
(D) The dental reimbursement plans offered by some companies do not provide for regular twice-yearly professional cleanings for children.
(E) Children now are more likely than ever before to experience serious problems as the result of tooth decay.

GO ON TO THE NEXT PAGE.

13. Recent media coverage indicates that the incidence of malfeasance and fraud among securities traders has increased over the past decade. Economists believe that this is due to changes in how securities traders are compensated. Whereas ten years ago most traders were paid only a fixed percentage of the value of each transaction, now virtually all of them also receive commissions on the basis of profit generated for their employers.

Which one of the following statements is most strongly supported by the information above?

(A) An increased incentive for trader malfeasance is associated with payment based on a fixed percentage of each transaction.
(B) A decreased risk of trader fraud is associated with paying traders an increased percentage of each transaction.
(C) A decreased propensity for malfeasance and fraud is caused by changes in trader compensation that place greater emphasis on making profit for their employers.
(D) Fraud by a securities trader may lead to an increased profit-related commission that more than offsets any loss in compensation associated with the decreased value of that transaction.
(E) Fraud and malfeasance would no longer be a problem if traders were compensated solely on the basis of the value of each trader's transactions.

14. A study of former college athletes revealed that, as a group, they are five times less likely to die before the age of fifty than are members of the population at large. The advice to derive from this is clear: Colleges should vastly expand their athletic departments so as to allow a greater proportion of all students to participate in athletics, thereby increasing the overall life expectancy of their student population.

Which one of the following, if true, most seriously weakens the argument above?

(A) Because participation in college athletics requires tremendous academic discipline, college athletes are better suited to succeed in society than are students who do not participate in college athletics.
(B) The students who voluntarily compete in college athletics are more predisposed to good health than are those who do not.
(C) Few colleges have the resources to increase spending on athletics, a nonessential university program.
(D) People who become active after leading sedentary lives can remarkably decrease their chances of contracting heart disease.
(E) Women, whose average life expectancies exceed men's by seven years, have traditionally had fewer opportunities to participate in college athletics than have men.

GO ON TO THE NEXT PAGE.

Questions 15–16

To determine the suitability of candidates for this position, the human resources director evaluates each candidate's advantages; job candidates with greater advantages are more likely to be offered the position. Factors such as work experience and relevant job skills are important in these evaluations, yet age should also be an important consideration. Younger candidates demand lower salaries and are less likely to have family obligations that would interfere with job responsibilities.

15. Which one of the following, if true, most undermines the argument?

(A) Younger workers are more likely to miss work due to social activities than they are to miss work due to family obligations.
(B) Younger workers are more likely to change jobs or quit on short notice if they do not like a new job than are older workers.
(C) Younger workers are more likely to be willing to work long hours and travel frequently than are older workers.
(D) Older workers are more likely to insist on regular working hours and reasonable compensation than are younger workers.
(E) Older workers without family obligations are more similar to younger workers in their professional behavior and expectations than they are to older workers with family obligations.

16. The claim that age should be an important consideration in evaluating job candidates plays which one of the following roles in the argument?

(A) a premise of the argument
(B) the conclusion of the argument
(C) support offered for one of the argument's premises
(D) a consideration that potentially calls the argument's conclusion into question
(E) an explanation of circumstances under which the argument's conclusion is true

17. An airline representative announced the introduction of a new pricing system that uses sophisticated computer technology. Based on up-to-the-minute information on sales, the system identifies and continually updates peak times of high demand and off-peak times of low demand, keeping prices high when demand is high and lowering prices to attract customers when demand is low. As a result, the airline anticipates that large numbers of customers will choose to travel off-peak to experience savings, whereas those who wish to travel at peak times will enjoy greater availability due to higher prices. The airline therefore anticipates that the majority of customers will experience significant benefits as a result of the new system.

Which one of the following indicates an error in the reasoning on the part of the airline?

(A) The airline's conclusion is based on an unproven premise.
(B) The airline displays a naive trust in the possibilities of technology.
(C) The airline fails to factor in the cost of implementing the new system.
(D) The airline's conclusion rests on a result that would necessarily cancel out the anticipated benefit.
(E) The airline fails to establish the percentage of customers who would benefit from the change.

GO ON TO THE NEXT PAGE.

18. Kristen: Compared to a direct business tax cut, a personal income tax cut is a better way to stimulate our state's economy. A personal income tax cut would give residents greater in-pocket income. With this increase in income, individuals will be encouraged to start their own businesses. In addition, individuals will be more likely to spend more money at existing businesses.

Mark: A personal income tax cut is not the most effective way to help business. There is no guarantee that individuals will in fact start new businesses, and the additional income may be used to purchase products from a different state or even a different country.

Mark objects to Kristen's argument by

(A) suggesting that a personal income tax cut is no more important than a direct business tax cut
(B) claiming that Kristen has reached a premature conclusion based on an inadequate understanding of the consequences of a business tax cut
(C) demonstrating that the negative impact of a personal income tax outweighs the positive effects
(D) questioning Kristen's use of the ambiguous phrase "in-pocket income"
(E) indicating that the positive consequences that Kristen predicts may not occur

19. Scholar: Only those who can tell the difference between right and wrong should be held responsible for their wrong actions. It is for this reason that defendants who have serious developmental disabilities or mental illnesses cannot be held responsible for their crimes. However, many children are able to tell the difference between right and wrong and yet are not held responsible for their crimes. Therefore, ________.

Which one of the following most logically completes the last sentence of the scholar's argument?

(A) it is the ability of the parent or parents to tell the difference between right and wrong that is most relevant to determining responsibility when a child is accused of a crime
(B) not all those who are held responsible for a wrong action can tell the difference between right and wrong
(C) it cannot be true that the ability to distinguish between right and wrong is sufficient to hold a defendant responsible for his or her criminal actions
(D) it is unjust for children, or for those who have serious developmental disabilities or mental illnesses, to be found guilty of any crime
(E) only those who can be held responsible for their criminal actions are able to tell the difference between right and wrong

GO ON TO THE NEXT PAGE.

20. Statistics show that there is a direct correlation between the ammonia content and the cleaning power of industrial-strength floor and tile cleaners; simply stated, the more ammonia, the better the cleaner. However, in a nationwide survey of commercial food services, cleaning supervisors uniformly replied that for any floor and tile cleaner to be effective, it must be used on a given surface twice a day with the right proportion of cleaner to water, and must be applied with well-maintained mops. The survey thus proves that ammonia content is not relevant to the efficacy of floor and tile cleaners after all.

Which one of the following best identifies the flawed reasoning in the passage above?

(A) There is no reason to assume that effective floor and tile cleaning is the only use for floor and tile cleaner.
(B) It cannot be assumed that industrial-strength floor and tile cleaners contain comparable levels of ammonia.
(C) It is unreasonable to conclude that the ammonia content is not relevant to a cleaner's efficacy just because there are requirements for the proper use of industrial-strength floor and tile cleaners.
(D) It cannot be assumed that the efficacy of all industrial-strength floor and tile cleaners depends on the same procedures for use.
(E) It is unreasonable to assume that the makers of industrial-strength floor and tile cleaners are unaware that food services don't always use them properly.

21. Products containing naproxen sodium produce relief from pain and fever by blocking prostaglandins. As a consequence of recent technological advances, production costs for pain and fever medications containing naproxen sodium, allowing for both packaging and marketing costs, are one-fifth of what they were ten years ago, while the corresponding cost for medications using the ingredient ibuprofen, which is produced by different means, has increased. Therefore, naproxen sodium is a less costly ingredient to use in medication for the prevention of pain and fever relief than ibuprofen.

The conclusion of the argument is properly drawn if which one of the following is assumed?

(A) The cost of producing pain and fever medication containing ibuprofen has increased over the past ten years.
(B) Ten years ago, ibuprofen was used more than five times as often as naproxen sodium.
(C) None of the recent technological advances in producing pain and fever medication with naproxen sodium can be applied to the production of medication using ibuprofen.
(D) Ten years ago, the cost of producing pain and fever medication with the ingredient naproxen sodium was less than five times the cost of producing medications with ibuprofen.
(E) The cost of producing pain and fever medication with naproxen sodium is expected to decrease further, while the cost of producing similar medications using ibuprofen is not expected to decrease.

GO ON TO THE NEXT PAGE.

22. Some critics of Western medicine blame medical schools for encouraging doctors to treat sick people as defective machines rather than as feeling humans. These critics believe that if medical schools dedicate a greater portion of their curriculum to teaching compassion and medical ethics, the overall quality of medical treatment will improve. But if doctors are trained to identify with their patients too strongly, they may be reluctant to recommend courses of treatment that, although painful, are necessary to maximize the patients' chances of recovery.

The critics' reasoning provides grounds for accepting which one of the following statements?

(A) It is easier for a doctor to recommend painful chemotherapy to a cancer patient when that doctor has an understanding of his or her ethical responsibilities to the patient.
(B) It is more difficult to know what course of treatment is appropriate for a patient with a liver disorder if a doctor does not identify with that patient as a defective machine.
(C) It is easier for a doctor to recommend a transplant for a patient who is experiencing kidney failure if the doctor feels sympathy for the difficulty that patient will experience in recovering from surgery.
(D) It is easier for a doctor who feels compassion for a patient experiencing chronic pain to treat that patient effectively, particularly when the chronic pain does not seem to be caused by any known medical disorder.
(E) It is easier for doctors to think of their patients as defective machines than it is to think of them as feeling humans.

23. Increasing the starting pay for our sales agents will allow us to attract and hire more new sales agents next year; unfortunately, such an increase would anger experienced sales agents, causing more of them to quit next year. The increase in new hires we would be able to attract at the higher pay rate does not exceed the increase in the number of experienced sales agents who would quit, so increasing the starting pay of our sales agents will not increase the overall number of sales agents we employ.

The reasoning in the argument above most closely parallels that in which one of the following?

(A) Building a dam on this river would decrease the incidence of flooding in the lowlands downstream, but a dam would destroy the river's natural beauty. Tourism is an important component of the area's economy, so the building of a dam on this river is not justified.
(B) Spending additional money on safety training would result in greatly increased costs for our manufacturing operation; because accidents in our manufacturing operation cost more on an annual basis than the increased costs associated with better safety training, improving that training will increase company profits.
(C) Increasing the speed of our assembly line will increase the rate at which goods are produced; at the same time, an increase in the speed of our assembly line will increase the rate of defects. The number of additional losses due to defects will be greater than the number of additional goods produced by the assembly line, so increasing the speed of our assembly line will not increase the number of finished goods we produce.
(D) A new interstate highway will allow travelers to bypass the downtown area, leading to an increase in the rate at which travelers pass through our city; the increased rate of travel will encourage travelers to select routes passing through our city, leading to an increase in patronage of local businesses outside downtown. Therefore, we should build a new interstate highway.
(E) An earlier harvest will allow our tomatoes to reach market shelves more quickly, and will also decrease the number of our tomatoes that spoil before they are sold. However, an earlier harvest will lead to unripe tomatoes being put on market shelves. Because an unripe tomato can be safely eaten, whereas a spoiled tomato cannot, an earlier harvest will make our tomatoes safer for consumers.

GO ON TO THE NEXT PAGE.

24. Spokesperson: Horror movies are extremely popular among young moviegoers. A recent study of teenagers and young adults concluded that, after attending horror movies, they were more likely to engage in aggressive or violent behavior. However, experts agree that the methodology of this study was seriously flawed. There can be no doubt, then, that horror movies do not contribute to aggressive or violent behavior among young people who watch them.

The reasoning in the spokesperson's argument is flawed because that argument

(A) takes one failure to prove a contention as confirmation of the falsity of that contention
(B) treats the occurrence of one event preceding a change in behavior as sufficient proof that the event contributed to causing the change in behavior
(C) accepts the judgment of experts as definitive proof of a contention when evidence suggests that the contention is untrue
(D) fails to consider the possibility that a lack of proof for one contention may constitute proof requiring the acceptance of some other contention
(E) neglects to specify that those conducting the study did not have an ulterior motive in reaching the study's erroneous conclusions

25. Those who read a book without having been exposed to any reviews of it are more likely to say they enjoyed the book than they are to say that they did not. Yet when readers who previously claimed to enjoy a book are exposed to several negative reviews of it and then are asked whether they would read the book again, a majority of them say they would not. Thus, exposure to reviews about a book may cause readers to change their opinions of that book.

Which one of the following is an assumption required by the argument?

(A) Readers with favorable opinions of a book they have read are not unlikely to say they would read that book again.
(B) Exposure to reviews of a book they have previously read causes readers to notice flaws in the book that they did not notice on a first reading.
(C) Readers are not more likely to enjoy reading a book they have purchased than they are to enjoy reading a book they have borrowed from a library or a friend.
(D) Readers who claim to have enjoyed a book and are subsequently exposed to positive reviews of it are also likely to say they will not read the book again.
(E) Whether a book receives positive or negative reviews is an accurate reflection of that book's quality.

STOP

IF YOU FINISH BEFORE TIME IS CALLED, YOU MAY CHECK YOUR WORK ON THIS SECTION ONLY.
DO NOT WORK ON ANY OTHER SECTION IN THE TEST.

SECTION III

Time—35 minutes

27 Questions

Directions: Each passage in this section is followed by a group of questions to be answered on the basis of what is stated or implied in the passage. For some questions, more than one of the choices could conceivably answer the question. However, you are to choose the best answer, that is, the response that most accurately and completely answers the question, and blacken the corresponding space on your answer sheet.

Questions 1–5 are based on the following passage:

One of the most prolific authors of all time, Isaac Asimov was influential both in science fiction and in the popularization of science during the twentieth century, but he is also justly famous for the scope of his interests. Although the common claim that Asimov is the only author to have written a book in every category of the Dewey decimal system is untrue, its spirit provides an accurate picture of the man: a dedicated humanist who lauded the far-reaching power of reason. His most famous work, the *Foundation* trilogy, can be read as an illustration of Asimov's belief in reason and science, but even while he expressed that belief, science itself was calling it into question.

Foundation describes a time in which a vast Empire spanning the galaxy is on the verge of collapse. Its inevitable doom is a consequence not of its size, but of the shortsightedness of its leaders. In this environment, a scientist named Hari Seldon devises an all-encompassing plan to help human civilization recover from the trauma of the Empire's coming collapse. Using mathematics, Seldon is able to predict the future course of history for thousands of years, and he takes steps that are geared toward guiding that future in a beneficial direction. The trope of the benevolent and paternalistic scientist shaping existence from behind the scenes, present in much of Asimov's fiction, is never more explicit than in the *Foundation* series, which describes with an epic sweep the course and progress of the Seldon Plan.

As naïve and, perhaps, self-serving as the conceit of *Foundation* may seem to contemporary readers, it retains to some degree its ability to comfort by offering an antidote to the complex and unpredictable nature of experience. Science in Asimov's time was, in popular conceptions, engaged in just this pursuit: discerning immutable laws that operate beneath a surface appearance of contingency, inexplicability, and change. But even while Asimov wrote, science itself was changing. In physics, the study of matter at the subatomic level showed that indeterminacy was not a transitory difficulty to be overcome, but an essential physical principle. In biology, the sense of evolution as a steady progress toward better-adapted forms was being disturbed by proof of a past large-scale evolution taking place in brief explosions of frantic change. At the time of Asimov's death, even mathematics was gaining popular notice for its interest in chaos and inexplicability. Usually summarized in terms of the so-called "butterfly effect," chaos theory showed that perfect prediction could take place only on the basis of perfect information, which was by nature impossible to obtain. Science had dispensed with the very assumptions that motivated Asimov's idealization of it in the Seldon Plan. Indeed, it was possible to see chaos at work in *Foundation* itself: As sequels multiplied and began to be tied into narrative threads from Asimov's other novels, the urge to weave one grand narrative spawned myriad internal inconsistencies that were never resolved.

1. Which one of the following most accurately expresses the main point of the passage?

(A) Isaac Asimov's greatest work, the *Foundation* trilogy, is an expression of the common trope of the benevolent and paternalistic scientist.
(B) Popularizations of science are always to some degree dependent on idealizations and simplifications of that science, as Isaac Asimov's work demonstrates.
(C) The impossibility of the conceit on which Isaac Asimov's *Foundation* trilogy is based demonstrates that Asimov's fiction was based on imperfect understandings of science.
(D) The central figure of Hari Seldon in Isaac Asimov's *Foundation* trilogy is a manifestation of humanism's idealization of reason and science.
(E) Isaac Asimov's idealization of science as revealed in his Foundation series was called into question by the science of his time, which was increasingly focused on chaos and indeterminacy.

2. Which one of the following statements most accurately expresses the purpose of the final paragraph?

(A) The ultimate failure of the *Foundation* series as a coherent scientific narrative is discussed.
(B) A claim is made about the purpose of Asimov's writing and then is finally rejected.
(C) A key theme of Asimov's *Foundation* series is described and discoveries in science that seem contrary to that theme are outlined.
(D) The history of science is used to demonstrate the falsity of a widely believed claim about the power of human reason.
(E) The works of Asimov are used as evidence against a popular belief that Asimov encouraged but may not have personally held.

3. The author's reference to a common claim made about Isaac Asimov (lines 5–7) serves to

(A) demonstrate that many untrue beliefs are held about him
(B) illustrate the broad scope of his interests and writings
(C) undermine the claim that he was a prolific writer
(D) substantiate his belief in the power of human reason
(E) indicate that he was only interested in science

4. With respect to the Seldon Plan, the author's attitude can most properly be described as

(A) amused at the naïve conception of history it implies
(B) uncertain of the practical impossibility of its application
(C) ambivalent because of the reliance on human reason it requires
(D) convinced that it illustrates Asimov's attitude toward science
(E) confident that continued scientific progress will make it practicable

5. Which one of the following statements best illustrates the "butterfly effect" as it is described in the passage's third paragraph?

(A) A system implemented to predict the weather worldwide for the next century is soon found to be inaccurate because it was supplied with incomplete data.
(B) Efforts to predict the result of a nuclear reaction fail because of indeterminacy inherent in the behavior of subatomic particles.
(C) The fossil record indicates that certain adaptations found in many organisms appeared soon after a past catastrophic event.
(D) Scientific predictions about the future course of human history are found to be reasonably accurate once existing social theories are reconciled.
(E) A map that is less detailed than the area it represents is found not to include all the important features of that area.

Questions 6–12 are based on the following passage:

Renowned for its canals and rich history, the Italian city of Venice is most famous for the singular peril it faces: The city is sinking. Situated in a lagoon, in the midst of a marsh bordering on the Adriatic Sea, Venice remained a capital of Mediterranean trade for centuries, in part because the few navigable channels through the lagoon were a closely guarded secret, and without that knowledge no enemy could hope to invade. In more recent times, Venice's distinctive character has become a threat to the city's future even as it draws millions of visitors every year.

In the fourteenth century, city leaders became concerned that silt deposited by the four rivers that once emptied into Venice's lagoon were threatening to clog the deep channels on which their trading ships depended. The solution was a public works project of staggering scope: Over the course of two centuries, the rivers were diverted through canals so that they emptied elsewhere. Although this expedient preserved the deep channels leading to the city itself, it had an unanticipated effect: The main source of new sediment entering the lagoon was cut off, removing one major contributor in the dynamic reformation of the lagoon's landscape.

The "bedrock" on which Venice is built is a mile-thick layer of river sediment, deposited over a period of millennia. Such sediments naturally compact under the weight of the material above, and as a result, the land in Venice's lagoon has been sinking throughout its history. With the rivers diverted, the major source of replenishment for the area's land is no longer operating, giving the upper hand to storm and tide in their efforts to reclaim the lagoon. But even were the rivers' former courses to be restored—an action no one seriously recommends—that by itself would not constitute a solution to Venice's problem.

Archaeological data indicate that Venice's residents have historically coped with the land's subsidence by rebuilding. Multiple layers of old foundations demonstrate that Venice has been racing against the loss of land throughout its history; some floors from Roman times are now five feet below sea level. Although such solutions worked well in an atmosphere where historical preservation was not a priority, Venice's economic strength rests now on the foundation of tourism. The fact that modern-day Venice has become more a museum than a working city lends particular urgency and difficulty to the efforts to preserve it.

There is reason to believe that these efforts must be undertaken soon. Even while the land sinks, sea levels in the Adriatic Sea rise. Prediction is difficult, but most estimates put the water-level rise in the next century in the range of fifteen to thirty inches. A century ago, Venice's signature landmark—St. Mark's square—was flooded an average of nine times a year; now, after roughly ten inches of loss versus sea level, it is flooded one hundred times in an average year. Unless radical steps are taken, within another century, most experts agree that it will be submerged year-round.

6. The primary purpose of the discussion in the second paragraph is to

(A) argue that the blame for Venice's current problems rests with its past leaders
(B) provide historical context that describes one contributing factor in Venice's dilemma
(C) explain why the problem Venice faces is unique among the world's cities
(D) show that human intervention in Venice's environment has taken place throughout its history
(E) prove that the landscape of Venice's lagoon is being dynamically reformed

7. Given the descriptions in the passage, which one of the following is most analogous to the method by which Venetians have historically coped with their sinking land?

(A) A Japanese shrine has stood in the same location for centuries, but because it has traditionally been constructed of materials that are not durable, it has been periodically rebuilt throughout its history.
(B) A German castle was originally built on a river island that experienced severe erosion, so within the past century, the castle was moved to more stable ground on the riverbank.
(C) A Roman temple was originally built of quarried marble, but since then, local residents have largely dismantled the building to use its marble in other construction.
(D) An American armory built in the nineteenth century is no longer used for its original purpose but has instead been converted into a convention hall.
(E) A Russian hotel which was a symbol of the former Soviet regime is demolished both because of its history and because contemporary residents now believe the building is an eyesore.

8. The passage's predictions about the likely future incidence of flooding in St. Mark's square would be most weakened if which one of the following were found to be true?

(A) Variations in water level attributable to storm surge are primarily responsible for the current flooding in St. Mark's square.
(B) The flooding in St. Mark's square could be mostly prevented by the installation of inflatable gates in the channels leading into the lagoon, a massive project opposed by environmentalists.
(C) Steps taken in the Low Countries of Europe, many parts of which are below sea level, are effective at preventing flooding there.
(D) A moderate increase in the height of the canal walls at the edges of St. Mark's square would prevent flooding, even if sea levels were to rise substantially.
(E) Although many proposed plans exist to halt the flooding of St. Mark's square, most are controversial either because they are too radical or because they are likely to be ineffective.

9. Each of the following can be inferred from the passage EXCEPT:

(A) The earliest buildings constructed in the lagoon of Venice are now below sea level.
(B) River sediments deposited in the lagoon of Venice compacted over time even before humans settled in the area.
(C) Venice's primary source of economic viability is no longer Mediterranean trade.
(D) Water levels in the Adriatic Sea are rising at a faster rate than are water levels in other large bodies of water worldwide.
(E) Some factor other than secrecy surrounding the navigable channels of the lagoon has contributed to Venice's economic security.

10. The passage's author would be most likely to agree with which one of the following statements concerning modern-day Venice?

(A) The preservation of its historic buildings should be a priority.
(B) The environmental health of the salt marshes in its lagoon must be protected.
(C) Its survival depends on stopping the subsidence of land on which it is built.
(D) Moderate measures are adequate to protect it from rising sea levels.
(E) It must become more of a working city than it currently is to survive.

11. Based on the passage, the author most likely holds which one of the following opinions concerning past alterations to Venice's environment?

(A) They are solely responsible for Venice's current difficulties.
(B) They were undertaken without full knowledge of their consequences.
(C) They must be reversed for Venice to survive.
(D) They have contributed to the rise in water levels in the Adriatic Sea.
(E) They could have been prevented by responsible city leadership.

12. From the passage, it can be inferred that

(A) water levels in the Adriatic Sea will rise more than twenty inches in the next century
(B) the level of land in Venice's lagoon will sink more than ten inches in the next century
(C) St. Mark's square will flood less than one hundred times per year over the next century
(D) Venice is likely to lose more elevation versus sea level in the next century than it did in the previous century
(E) some of Venice's historical landmarks will be lost in the next century

Questions 13–19 are based on the following passage:

The work of Amartya Sen, winner of the Nobel Prize for economics in 1998, has helped usher in a new era in the field as it is practically applied throughout the world. Institutions such as the United Nations have adopted his ideas in measuring and aiding the development of emerging economies, and the consequences of the social-choice theory he employs have garnered much public attention.

The classic defining work of social choice theory is Ken Arrow's careful investigation of voting through a series of thought experiments. The result—Arrow's Impossibility Theorem—showed that no method of conducting a majority-decision vote can be guaranteed to conform to the basic requirements of democracy. A simple example illustrates Arrow's idea: For an electorate of three voters—1, 2, and 3—there are three candidates—A, B, and C. Voter 1 prefers A to B, and B to C; voter 2 prefers B to C, and C to A; voter 3 prefers C to A, and A to B. In such an electorate, a runoff between A and B declares A the winner; a runoff between B and C is won by B; and a runoff between A and C is won by C. Whichever candidate wins, that candidate is actually less preferable to the electorate than the candidate who was not involved in the runoff.

The work for which Sen was awarded his Nobel Prize is, in essence, an application of such methods to national economies, politics, and public welfare. Just as Arrow focused on paradoxes within democratic systems, Sen investigated instances such as famine in which capitalist market systems seem not to function properly, according to traditional economic public-choice principles. Public choice focuses on self-interest as the driving factor in economics; Sen, in a famous quote, shows the flaw in this view: "'Can you direct me to the railway station?' asks the stranger. 'Certainly,' says the local, pointing in the opposite direction, towards the post office, 'and would you post this letter for me on your way?' 'Certainly,' says the stranger, resolving to open it to see if it contains anything worth stealing." Factors other than self-interest exert their influence at every level within a society, and only by incorporating them can a theory truly describe how economies function.

This departure from traditional views has made Sen's work a subject in the ongoing debate over globalization. Partisans who advocate the spread of capitalism and democracy have called Sen everything from an anarchist to a Marxist; opponents of globalization use his work as proof that these institutions are not the boon they are supposed to be. By doing so, both sides misrepresent Sen's concerns. One of his early works demonstrated the conditions under which Arrow's Impossibility Theorem does not apply to democratic elections, and Sen is most famous for his notion of "capability" as an antidote to economic injustice. The specific forms "capability" takes—education and equal access—are precisely those that are called for in theoretical formulations of how choice-driven markets and democracies are supposed to function. Sen's work is an examination of the failures of these core systems, but it is also a roadmap to realizing their promise.

13. Which one of the following most accurately expresses the main idea of the passage?

(A) Although the work of Amartya Sen has been viewed as opposing democracy and global capitalism, in fact it is a defense of these ideas.

(B) Amartya Sen's revolutionary use of social choice theory in economics has been widely misinterpreted but nevertheless offers hope that social justice can be achieved in capitalist and democratic systems.

(C) The work of social choice theorists such as Ken Arrow and Amartya Sen has helped their theories supplant public choice theory as the most widely accepted theoretical approach to economics.

(D) Amartya Sen's work delineates the circumstances under which commonly accepted notions of how economic and democratic systems operate can be said to be correct.

(E) Social choice theory does not include considerations of self-interest in its evaluation of economic and democratic institutions.

14. Which one of the following titles provides the most complete and accurate summary of the passage's contents?

(A) "Nobel Prizewinner Amartya Sen: Reluctant Economic Rebel"

(B) "Social Choice Theory: Moving Beyond Self-Interest"

(C) "Arrow's Impossibility Theorem: Why No Election Is Fair"

(D) "Economics and Social Justice: Amartya Sen's Groundbreaking Work"

(E) "Fighting the Future: The Rising Opposition to Globalization"

15. The passage supports the inference that the author most likely holds which one of the following views?

(A) Existing economic theories are incapable of explaining why self-interest fails to prevent famine and social injustice.
(B) No majority-decision election conducted under any circumstances is capable of fulfilling even the most basic promises of democracy.
(C) Those who believe that Amartya Sen's work is intended to oppose economic globalization misunderstand it.
(D) Social choice theory does not constitute a legitimate alternative to traditional theoretical explanations of economic action.
(E) Amartya Sen is the first economist to take social considerations into account in the analysis of institutions such as democratic elections and the free market.

16. As it is described in the passage, Ken Arrow's method for investigating democratic elections is most analogous to which one of the following?

(A) To discern universal physical principles, a physicist imagines what it would be like to ride a beam of light.
(B) To evaluate existing theories of evolution, a paleontologist undertakes a survey of the fossil record.
(C) To learn about daily life in an ancient civilization, an anthropologist studies the traditional culture of the civilization's descendants.
(D) To evaluate the success of market reforms, an economist studies changes in key indicators.
(E) To discover political attitudes within a local area, a sociologist interviews religious leaders in the area.

17. The author's attitude toward social choice theory can most accurately be described as being

(A) skeptical that it will ever gain wide acceptance
(B) uncertain whether it correctly describes economic realities
(C) ambivalent about its critique of globalization
(D) satisfied that it represents an advance in economic understanding
(E) enthusiastic about its usefulness in reforming democratic elections

18. The passage suggests that which one of the following would provide the best definition of Sen's idea of "capability?"

(A) willingness to fill multiple economic roles
(B) access to legal redress for injustice
(C) capacity to exercise democratic and economic choice
(D) knowledge of underlying principles of economics
(E) assistance through the redistribution of wealth

19. Each of the following is stated or implied by the passage EXCEPT:

(A) Arrow's Impossibility Theorem does not hold for all democratic elections.
(B) Public choice theory does not provide a complete description of all economic transactions.
(C) The policies of the United Nations are not primarily concerned with aiding developing nations to achieve social justice.
(D) Amartya Sen's economic beliefs cannot properly be called Marxist.
(E) The precepts of social choice theory have not always informed economic policies.

Questions 20–27 refer to the following passage:

Perhaps the most fascinating effort to reconcile the apparently contradictory principles of traditional religious law and secular Western law is underway in Indonesia. Indonesia provides a unique laboratory for such experiments: The most populous majority-Muslim nation in the world, Indonesia also has significant minorities with widely varying religious beliefs. Indonesia spent much of the twentieth century in the grip of a secular military dictatorship supported by Western countries, but with the advent of a more democratic civil society, the question of how their legal system should operate has become one of broad, serious public interest and debate.

Indonesia has, in effect, two legal systems. The dominant system is a secular Western-style code founded on the principles of individual human rights and capitalism. The second is founded on Islamic *Sharia* law, derived from key writings as interpreted by religious authorities. In Indonesia, questions of the implementation of *Sharia* law are colored by the presence of an alternative standard and the possibility, in some cases, of individuals choosing between them. The fact that the *Sharia* system must to some degree compete with the secular system leads to interesting tensions and cross-fertilizations between the two.

Although many religious leaders believe that Muslims should follow the precepts of *Sharia*, the latitude of interpretation within it and the fact that Muslim parties are strong within the secular system of representative government foster a variety of positions. Some believe that the two systems are not fundamentally incompatible and support a more liberal interpretation of *Sharia*; this strategy might help *Sharia* to become dominant within Indonesia by removing features that seem discriminatory or overly harsh. However, some conservative Muslims who wield secular power believe that it should be used to inject *Sharia* into daily life; attempts to pass secular laws requiring all Muslims to subject themselves to judgment by *Sharia* courts, or to require Islamic religious instruction of all Muslim children, even if they attend private Christian schools, are examples of ways the secular legal system can itself be used to ensure the primacy of *Sharia*.

In a democratic environment, it seems likely that neither of these approaches will predominate and that social institutions will promote a shifting compromise. The rise of *Sharia* banking provides an encouraging example. Because *Sharia* requires the sharing of profits and forbids charging interest, conventional Western banking models are distasteful to many Muslims. The rise of *Sharia* banks—those that voluntarily follow religious strictures and attract business on that basis—has been so rapid in Indonesia that Western banks have scrambled to provide services that also comply with these requirements. To regulate these banks, the secular authorities have passed laws and set up commissions to ensure compliance with both accepted Western practices and *Sharia* requirements. This instance of cooperation among secular authorities, religious leaders, and the market system offers hope that civil society can foster creative compromise in other areas as well.

20. Which one of the following most accurately expresses the main point of the passage?

(A) Tensions between *Sharia* law and traditional Western legal systems have led to a conflict within Indonesia that has not yet been resolved.

(B) The example of *Sharia* banking in Indonesia provides an example of how civil institutions can foster cultural compromise between competing legal standards.

(C) Indonesia represents a laboratory in which the ongoing conflict between Western secular and traditional religious views of culture can finally be resolved.

(D) Future efforts to resolve cultural conflict in all countries can only be effective if competition fosters cross-fertilization and compromise between legal standards that disagree.

(E) The existence of parallel legal standards in Indonesia represents an unusual circumstance that cannot be sustained and will ultimately be resolved by the fusion of Western and traditional religious principles.

21. Based on the information contained in the passage about the author's views, which one of the following would represent the most acceptable future compromise between the principles of *Sharia* law and traditional Western law in Indonesia?

(A) parallel legal systems in which defendants are able to choose the standard of judgment most beneficial to them
(B) a single legal system agreed on by democratic means that incorporates aspects of both systems without being excessively harsh or culturally offensive
(C) a set of multiple competing legal systems that operate in local areas depending on the cultural practices accepted in those areas
(D) a single system of liberally interpreted *Sharia* law that is made to apply to all residents by the exercise of Indonesia's secular power
(E) a single system of traditional Western law that makes allowances for the fact that Muslim religious authorities may wish to impose additional penalties on Muslim defendants who have violated the law

22. Which one of the following is mentioned in the passage as a characteristic of *Sharia* law?

(A) It contains some latitude for interpretation.
(B) It is marked by the application of precedent.
(C) It includes only weak protections of individual property rights.
(D) It does not provide for equal treatment of all citizens.
(E) It has never been successfully implemented as the basis of a modern legal system.

23. The rise of *Sharia* banking in Indonesia, as it is described in the passage, provides an illustration of which one of the following principles?

(A) When a particular business practice is legally required, that requirement may be justified by reference to religious authority.
(B) When a particular business practice is legally permissible but ethically distasteful, businesses may succeed by voluntarily refraining from that practice.
(C) When a particular business practice is legally required but ethically unacceptable, democratic means may be used to alter the applicable legal standards.
(D) When a particular business practice is neither legally nor ethically forbidden, some businesses may nevertheless choose not to engage in that practice.
(E) When a particular business practice is legally permissible but ethically prohibited, a business may nevertheless be forced to engage in that practice to remain viable.

24. Which one of the following questions is most directly answered in the passage?

(A) In what year did the standards of *Sharia* begin to play a role in Indonesian law?
(B) What protections for minorities are currently threatened by those who exercise secular power in Indonesia?
(C) What provisions of traditional Western law do Muslim religious authorities in Indonesia find most distasteful?
(D) What institutions aside from banks have succeeded by appealing to Muslim religious preferences?
(E) What methods have some religious leaders considered employing to increase the power of *Sharia* courts in Indonesia?

25. The purpose of the second paragraph is primarily to

(A) reconcile competing philosophies
(B) provide historical context
(C) describe a noteworthy set of circumstances
(D) indicate possibilities for resolving a dispute
(E) propose strategies for avoiding a problem

26. It can be most reasonably inferred from the passage that the author believes that an interpretation of *Sharia* law that conforms completely to the principles of Indonesian secular law will be

(A) unlikely to gain the full support of Indonesian religious leaders
(B) essential to the future health of Indonesian democracy
(C) able to prevent Western banks in Indonesia from profiting by charging interest on loans
(D) offensive to the majority of Muslims outside Indonesia
(E) promoted by the cooperative action of all Indonesian social institutions

27. Which one of the following can most reasonably be concluded from the information in the passage?

(A) The action of the free market in Indonesia is likely to ensure that the Indonesian economy eventually conforms to the principles outlined in *Sharia* law without requiring the intervention of secular authorities.
(B) Elected authorities in Indonesia are not forbidden from exercising secular power to ensure the compliance of some Indonesian businesses with the requirements of *Sharia* law.
(C) Religious leaders of Indonesia's minority groups will have a role in deciding whether any future modification of Indonesia's secular laws should incorporate principles of Islamic *Sharia* law.
(D) Religious authorities in Indonesia are prevented by the country's secular law from seeking elected office unless they agree not to use their secular power to pursue religious goals.
(E) Indonesia's many religious leaders must all work to foster cooperation among themselves if religious tensions in the country are to be minimized.

STOP

IF YOU FINISH BEFORE TIME IS CALLED, YOU MAY CHECK YOUR WORK ON THIS SECTION ONLY. DO NOT WORK ON ANY OTHER SECTION IN THE TEST.

SECTION IV

Time—35 Minutes

25 Questions

Directions: The questions in this section are based on the reasoning contained in brief statements or passages. For some questions, more than one of the choices could conceivably answer the question. However, you are to choose the best answer; that is, the response that most accurately and completely answers the question. You should not make assumptions that are by commonsense standards implausible, superfluous, or incompatible with the passage. After you have chosen the best answer, blacken the corresponding space on your answer sheet.

1. In France, children in preschool programs spend a portion of each day engaged in a program of stretching and exercise. Preschool programs in the United States, however, seldom devote time to a daily stretching and exercise program. In tests designed to measure cardiovascular fitness, children in the United States were outperformed by their French counterparts. It can therefore be determined that children attending preschool programs in the United States can achieve cardiovascular fitness only by engaging in a daily school program of stretching and exercise.

   Which one of the following is an assumption on which the argument depends?

   (A) A daily program of stretching and exercise will allow all children to achieve cardiovascular fitness.
   (B) Cardiovascular fitness is integral to one's overall health.
   (C) It has been proven that children who participate in stretching and exercise programs in preschool have better cardiovascular fitness than adults.
   (D) Stretching and exercise are necessary components of French children's superior cardiovascular fitness programs.
   (E) United States preschool children could make healthful dietary changes as well as changes to their daily fitness regimens.

2. In an effort to lessen the risk of liability, fertility clinics are seeking new methods of record-keeping and storage that would help avoid donor sperm that might contain dangerous genes. Toward this end, a database is being developed to aid the clients in their screening of donor sperm. The database is exhaustively thorough, containing the medical histories of more than twenty thousand people, approximately half of them men.

   Which one of the following, if true, best explains why the database contains the records of almost ten thousand women?

   (A) Small fertility clinics, located in remote areas, wish to have access to a large selection of donor sperm.
   (B) Keeping genetic information on women is a standard procedure for many scientific clinics.
   (C) Some genetic disorders are not expressed until the onset of puberty.
   (D) Some genetic disorders may be carried by, but not manifested in, men who inherited the dangerous gene from their mothers.
   (E) Some genetic disorders are due to the effects of drugs and alcohol during puberty.

GO ON TO THE NEXT PAGE.

3. If the Food and Drug Administration (FDA) does not relax some of its regulations governing the testing of experimental drugs, tens of thousands of U.S. citizens are sure to die as a result of certain diseases before an effective treatment is found and made generally available.

It follows logically from the statement above that if the FDA does relax some of its regulations governing the testing of experimental drugs, then tens of thousands of U.S. citizens

(A) will definitely die of certain diseases
(B) will probably die of certain diseases
(C) will probably not die of certain diseases
(D) will not die of certain diseases
(E) may still die of certain diseases

4. The level of blood sugar for many patients suffering from disease *Q* is slightly higher than the level of blood sugar in the general population. Nonetheless, most medical professionals believe that slightly increasing blood sugar levels is a successful means by which to treat disease *Q*.

This apparently contradictory argument can best be resolved by which one of the following statements?

(A) Blood sugar levels for patients who have been cured of disease *Q* are virtually identical to the levels of blood sugar found in the general population.
(B) Many of the symptoms associated with severe cases of disease *Q* have been recognized in laboratory animals with experimentally induced high blood pressure, but none of the animals developed disease *Q*.
(C) The movement from inactive to advanced states of disease *Q* often occurs because the virus that causes *Q* flourishes during periods when blood sugar levels are slightly low.
(D) The blood sugar level in patients with disease *Q* fluctuates abnormally in response to changes in blood chemistry.
(E) Low levels of blood sugar are symptomatic of many other diseases that are even more serious than disease *Q*.

5. Activist: There are countries in which the number of handgun deaths per capita is less than one-tenth of the number in our country. Although not all of these countries outlaw handguns, most of them do. Therefore, to reduce the number of handgun deaths in our country, we must outlaw handguns.

Which one of the following is an assumption on which the activist's argument depends?

(A) The number of handgun deaths in a country is primarily determined by the rate of handgun ownership in that country.
(B) Some countries in which handguns are not outlawed have low numbers of handgun deaths per capita because of conditions that cannot be replicated in all other countries.
(C) The number of handgun deaths in a country may be reduced without a corresponding decrease in the number of per capita handgun deaths in that country.
(D) Laws forbidding the ownership of handguns are justified only insofar as those laws are effective in preventing handgun deaths.
(E) Accidents are not a significant cause of handgun deaths in countries where the number of per capita handgun deaths is relatively low.

6. Medical studies indicate that the metabolic rates of professional athletes are substantially greater than those of the average person. So, most likely, a person's speed and strength are primarily determined by that person's metabolic rate.

Which one of the following, if true, most strengthens the argument?

(A) Some professional athletes are either faster or stronger than the average person.
(B) Some professional athletes do not have higher metabolic rates than some people who are not professional athletes.
(C) The speed and strength of people who are not professional athletes are not primarily determined by choices of diet and exercise.
(D) Intensive training such as that engaged in by professional athletes causes an increase in metabolic rate.
(E) Drugs that suppress metabolic rate have been shown to have the side-effect of diminishing the speed and strength of those who are not professional athletes.

GO ON TO THE NEXT PAGE.

7. Environmentalist: In most land ecologies, grasses are the basis of the food chain. Desertification of several North African areas over the past decade has caused the grasses there to die, leading to serious disruption of the ecology in those areas. Now it has been shown that warming in Antarctic waters is causing a die-off of krill there. Because krill is the basis of the food chain in ocean ecologies, we can anticipate that there will be serious disruption of the ecology in these waters.

The environmentalist's argument proceeds by

(A) demonstrating that ocean ecologies are more delicate than land ecologies
(B) using an analogy to reach the conclusion that some ocean ecologies are in danger
(C) proving that the population of krill in Antarctic waters is decreasing
(D) asserting the role that grasses play in the health of land ecologies
(E) demonstrating that changes in temperature have categorically negative effects on all ecologies

8. Some residents of Woodbridge work the late shift at the nearby factory. Because of the fact that all of the residents of Woodbridge who own cars are also members of the Area Auto Club, the Woodbridge city manager concluded that none of the residents who work the late shift at the nearby factory own cars.

The city manager's conclusion is properly drawn if which one of the following is assumed?

(A) None of the residents of Woodbridge who work the late shift at the nearby factory are members of the Area Auto Club.
(B) None of the residents of Woodbridge who owns a car has failed to join the Area Auto Club.
(C) Some of the residents of Woodbridge who do not work the late shift at the nearby factory do not own cars.
(D) All residents of Woodbridge who do not work the late shift at the nearby factory own cars.
(E) All residents of Woodbridge who are members of the Area Auto Club own cars.

9. Naturalist: It was once believed that only modern humans were capable of learning to use tools for obtaining food. Decades ago, archaeological evidence showed that extinct species of hominids closely related to modern humans also used tools for these purposes. What remained in doubt, however, was whether any existing nonhuman species could also learn to use tools. Some populations of chimpanzees use dried grasses to "fish" for termites, a high-protein delicacy. Moreover, evidence shows that this behavior is not instinctive but must be taught to and practiced by young chimpanzees. Some populations in the same area do not "fish" for termites in this way, although dried grasses and termite mounds are available to them.

Which one of the following most accurately expresses the conclusion of the naturalist's argument?

(A) At least some behaviors of chimpanzees are learned, not instinctive.
(B) Certain past assumptions about the uniqueness of modern humans have been shown to be false.
(C) Evidence exists that animals other than modern humans and their closest relatives are capable of learning to use tools.
(D) Only modern humans are capable of learning to use tools in ways that are not directly related to obtaining food.
(E) Some species of hominids became extinct for reasons unrelated to their ability to use tools.

GO ON TO THE NEXT PAGE.

10. Victor: Auto manufacturers report strong profit growth this year. This should not be taken to mean, however, that sales of new cars are increasing. Closer examination shows that the growth in auto manufacturers' profits is attributable solely to the financing of new-car sales.

Kim: I don't think that's right. After all, if they were not continuing to sell new cars, auto manufacturers could not profit from financing them, could they?

Kim's reply suggests that she misinterprets Victor's point to be that

(A) overall sales of new cars are not increasing
(B) auto manufacturers' profits this year were derived solely from financing
(C) the financing of the past year's sales is not solely responsible for this year's profit growth
(D) auto manufacturers should place increased emphasis on the sale and financing of used cars
(E) only new car sales should be considered in evaluating the financial health of auto manufacturers

11. Most people believe that obtaining a master's in business administration (MBA) leads to increased pay. A recent survey, however, suggests that this belief is unfounded. Among the top executives at the nation's most prominent companies, there is no indication that pay rates are any higher for employees with an MBA than they are for employees in similar positions without one.

The argument above is flawed because it neglects the possibility that

(A) an employee with an MBA may be more likely to attain a top executive position than a similarly able employee without one
(B) the pay of top executives in the nation's most prominent companies may be higher than the pay of other employees in those same companies
(C) pay rates for top executives may differ from company to company, even among the most prominent companies
(D) an employee who obtains an MBA may learn job skills that are critical to success in a top executive position
(E) top executives who obtain MBAs while holding their jobs may be better able than other executives to find similar positions in other companies in the event that they are laid off.

12. Since Oscar received extensive training in how to repair motorcycles, he is able to repair many of their most common mechanical problems. However, Oscar does not understand how internal combustion engines work. When Oscar was given Lucy's motorcycle to repair, he was able to fix the problem, despite the fact that he did not understand what was causing it.

From the statements above, which one of the following can be properly inferred?

(A) The problem with Lucy's motorcycle involved its engine.
(B) Not all mechanical problems can be repaired only by mechanics who understand how an internal combustion engine works.
(C) At least some good mechanics are able to fix mechanical problems without an understanding of what is causing them.
(D) Oscar's mechanical training in how to repair motorcycles was incomplete.
(E) Those common mechanical problems that Oscar cannot fix require an understanding of how an internal combustion engine works.

GO ON TO THE NEXT PAGE.

13. Dr. Jackson: Many people criticize the advertisement of prescription drugs because they believe it causes patients to form mistaken beliefs about how their conditions should be treated. Surveys show, however, that in more than 60 percent of cases when a patient requests a prescription for a particular drug from a doctor, the doctor writes a prescription for the drug he or she has requested.

Dr. Morris: True, patients often receive the treatment they request. But this is most often because patients refuse to follow medical advice that does not agree with the beliefs they form about how they should be treated, not because the treatment they request is correct.

Which one of the following, if true, most supports Dr. Morris's counter to Dr. Jackson?

(A) More than half of patients are sufficiently knowledgeable about their conditions to request the correct treatment for it.
(B) Many national organizations that work on behalf of doctors are opposed to the advertisement of prescription drugs.
(C) Studies show that more than half of patients receive incorrect or excessive treatment for their medical problems.
(D) More than half of patients who receive the prescriptions they request from their doctors have previously requested the same prescription from another doctor and have been refused.
(E) Only a very few of the most common medical maladies for which patients seek treatment are most appropriately treated with prescription drugs.

14. It cannot be true that the lack of success of third-party candidates in national elections is due to the difficulties such candidates encounter in securing space on national ballots. Everyone who identifies him- or herself as a supporter of a third party has voted for a major-party candidate in at least one national election when a third-party candidate was listed on the ballot.

Which one of the following most accurately describes a reasoning flaw in the argument?

(A) The argument overlooks the possibility that the lack of success of third-party candidates in national elections may be due to the fact that their views on major issues prevent them from gaining broad support.
(B) The argument takes for granted that the media coverage devoted to third-party candidates for national office is comparable to that devoted to major-party candidates for those same offices.
(C) The argument treats as contradictory to some claim evidence that may instead provide support for that claim.
(D) The argument draws its conclusion through the use of a set of facts, not all of which can be true.
(E) The argument derives a statement about the behavior of all voters on the basis of partial information about the past voting preferences of only a few voters.

GO ON TO THE NEXT PAGE.

15. Sara: Our government devotes billions of tax dollars every year to foreign aid, although most experts agree that our social and economic infrastructure is badly in need of that money. It is unconscionable that our elected representatives consider the needs of our own citizens less important than the needs of citizens of other countries.

Ross: Foreign aid helps our country by assuring its security. If money were not spent on foreign aid to the most threatened governments in the world, we would need to spend a great deal more in military interventions when those governments collapsed.

From their statements, it can most properly be inferred that Sara and Ross disagree about whether

(A) their country's spending on foreign aid ought to be increased
(B) failed governments pose a security threat to their country
(C) their country's social infrastructure is in need of additional investment
(D) their country's spending on foreign aid serves its citizens' needs
(E) decreased spending on foreign aid would necessitate additional military spending

16. In communities heavily affected by environmental regulation where such regulation directly benefits neither the companies that are most important to the community's economy nor the residents of that community, the government is perceived as being insensitive to the community's economic welfare. For this reason, the people in some communities heavily affected by environmental regulation are in favor of decreased taxes. When people believe that government considers the interests of others more important than their own, they tend to favor decreased taxes, believing this will limit the government's power over their lives.

Which one of the following is an assumption on which the argument depends?

(A) When government policy is perceived as being sensitive to a community's economic welfare, the people of that community do not wish to limit the government's power over their lives.
(B) Environmental regulation that directly benefits the companies that are most important to a community's economy leads to greater government support than environmental regulation that directly benefits only the residents of that community.
(C) A government's power over the lives of a community's residents depends on taxes collected from those residents.
(D) People in a community tend to believe that their government considers others' interests more important than their own unless that government is perceived as being sensitive to the community's economic welfare.
(E) Community members do not consider indirect benefits to themselves or to the companies that are most important to the community's economy in formulating their response to environmental regulation.

GO ON TO THE NEXT PAGE.

17. Researcher: Heavily insulated homes trap radon gas much better than do poorly insulated homes. Therefore, those who live in heavily insulated homes are at greater risk for certain types of brain cancer because evidence shows that those who are being treated for brain cancer have high blood levels of the radioactive compounds that are found in those who are exposed to high levels of radon gas.

Which one of the following, if true, most undermines the researcher's argument?

(A) Radon gas is commonly found even in homes that do not trap it well.
(B) Exposure to radiation is known to lead to an increased incidence of cancer of all kinds.
(C) Young people are particularly susceptible to the negative consequences of high levels of radon exposure.
(D) Radioactive compounds are used in many cases to help develop an initial diagnosis of medical problems.
(E) The most common brain cancer therapy involves radiation and leads to high blood levels of many radioactive compounds.

18. Food critic: Consumers should buy only wild salmon, not farmed salmon. Whereas the environmental damage associated with harvesting wild salmon is slight, salmon farms are significant causes of water pollution, and salmon that escape from the farms displace wild varieties, threatening biodiversity. The fact that farmed salmon is cheaper than wild varieties has led to a large increase in the popularity of salmon, which may eventually pose a threat to wild populations because of over-fishing.

Which one of the following most accurately describes a flaw in the food critic's argument?

(A) At least one of the potential disadvantages cited in arguing against a course of action applies at least as strongly to the alternative course of action the argument recommends.
(B) The argument is constructed in such a way that it precludes the possibility of reaching any logical conclusion, if all of its premises are accepted as true.
(C) It overlooks the possibility that some unspecified benefit of the choice argued against may outweigh any possible benefit of the choice argued for.
(D) It concludes that one course of action is not permissible on the basis of a principle that is in greater need of support than the conclusion it is advanced to defend.
(E) Its premises are presented in such a way that the argument presupposes the truth of the conclusion it is intended to support.

GO ON TO THE NEXT PAGE.

19. Resentment is not a reasonable response to rejection because rejection is merely an expression of preference: either a preference is purely personal, in which case the rejection could not have been anticipated, or else that preference is commonly held, in which case steps should have been taken in advance to avoid rejection.

Which one of the following, if assumed, enables the argument's conclusion to be properly drawn?

(A) No emotional response to any action that could not have been anticipated is reasonable.
(B) Resentment is not a reasonable response to any action which steps should have been taken in advance to avoid.
(C) Resentment is not a reasonable response to any preference that is either purely personal or commonly held.
(D) Responses to resentment indicate preferences that either could not have been anticipated or else could have been avoided.
(E) No response to an expression of preference that steps should have been taken to avoid could reasonably have been anticipated.

20. According to newspaper reviews, some of the films released this year were of superior artistic quality. According to audience surveys, some of the films released this year involved exciting plots. Therefore, some of the films this year which involved exciting plots were also of superior artistic quality.

The flawed reasoning in the argument above is most similar to that in which one of the following?

(A) Judging from automotive magazines, some of the cars released this year were exceptionally fast, but according to automotive enthusiasts, none of the cars released this year is likely to become a classic. Thus not even the fastest car released this year is likely to become a classic.
(B) According to consumer magazines, some of the new refrigerators introduced this year are exceptionally energy efficient. According to consumer surveys, energy efficiency plays some role in determining whether a customer is satisfied with a new refrigerator. Therefore, the reason some customers are satisfied with their new refrigerators is that they are exceptionally energy efficient.
(C) Art says that snow is forecast for some parts of our area tomorrow, and Lois says that rain is forecast for some parts of our area tomorrow. Thus, tomorrow it will neither snow nor rain in some parts of our area.
(D) Doctors say that some vaccines need be administered only once in a patient's lifetime, and drug companies say that some vaccines prevent measles, so some vaccine that prevents measles need be administered only once in a patient's lifetime.
(E) According to publishers, most of the works of fiction published this year were novels. According to book reviewers, most of the works of fiction published this year were of inferior quality. Therefore, some of the novels published this year were of inferior quality.

GO ON TO THE NEXT PAGE.

21. Stock options are the only investments that allow an individual investor to achieve high returns with limited liability. With relatively small risk, an individual investing in stock options can make profits of several hundred percent over a short period of time. Thus stock options represent a more efficient use of an individual's money than any other investment option.

Which one of the following, if assumed, enables the argument's conclusion to be properly inferred?

(A) Investments other than stock options do not allow an individual investor to achieve high returns with limited liability.
(B) The efficient use of an individual investor's money requires the possibility of achieving profit over a short period of time.
(C) A profit of several hundred percent over a short period of time is considered a high return on an individual's investment.
(D) An investment cannot be considered efficient unless it returns several hundred percent profit.
(E) Investments that allow an individual to achieve high returns with limited liability represent a more efficient use of money than any other potential use.

22. Only corporate executives who behave ethically are likely to be promoted, but no corporate executive who makes wise business decisions is a poor employee. All corporate executives who behave ethically are both well respected and make wise business decisions, qualities lacking in many corporate executives who do not behave ethically.

If all of the statements above are true, which one of the following must also be true?

(A) No corporate executive who makes wise business decisions but does not behave ethically is well respected.
(B) All corporate executives who are well respected but do not behave ethically make wise business decisions.
(C) No corporate executive who is likely to be promoted is a poor employee.
(D) All corporate executives who are not well respected are poor employees.
(E) All corporate executives who are good employees behave ethically.

23. It cannot be true that everyone who donates money to charity is concerned with the well-being of others. After all, it is possible that donating money to charity may help some people lessen their own feelings of guilt.

Which one of the following arguments employs a principle of reasoning most similar to that illustrated by the argument above?

(A) It cannot be true that the only reason for space exploration is scientific discovery. After all, there have been many space missions that have not contributed to scientific knowledge at all.
(B) It cannot be true that income taxes are justified by the government's obligation to redistribute wealth. After all, many government programs paid for by tax money benefit wealthy individuals.
(C) It cannot be true that Columbus was the one who discovered that the Earth was not flat. After all, ancient mathematicians had calculated the Earth's circumference centuries before Columbus was born.
(D) It cannot be true that all those who become actors desire wealth and fame. After all, some actors may perform so that they can share their artistic vision with others.
(E) It cannot be true that a meteor impact caused the extinction of the dinosaurs. After all, it is possible that climatic conditions similar to those following a meteor impact could have been created by a massive volcanic eruption.

GO ON TO THE NEXT PAGE.

24. Appraiser: We know the following about the pottery made by artisan A. Pieces with a metallic glaze always feature a floral pattern but never have an hourglass shape. Pieces that are signed always have an hourglass shape, and pieces made in this century are always signed. A piece of pottery made by artisan A has recently come to my attention; it has a floral pattern and is signed.

From the appraiser's statements, which one of the following can be properly concluded about the piece of pottery by artisan A that has recently come to the appraiser's attention?

(A) It has an hourglass shape and was made in this century.
(B) It has an hourglass shape but was not made in this century.
(C) It has an hourglass shape but does not have a metallic glaze.
(D) It has a metallic glaze and was made in this century.
(E) It lacks both an hourglass shape and a metallic glaze.

25. No doubt the presidential candidate who wins an election deserves credit for persistence and political aplomb, but the advisors who develop campaign strategy are often overlooked. Although presidential candidates sometimes take the lead in shaping their campaign's policy positions, most often it is political professionals who, in service to the campaign, devote their time and energy to crafting the candidate's message and persona. Campaign strategists play a crucial role in virtually every successful candidacy.

The claim that presidential candidates sometimes take the lead in shaping their campaign's policy positions plays which one of the following roles in the argument?

(A) It indicates the circumstances to which the argument's conclusion is to be understood to apply.
(B) It concedes that the shortcoming the argument intends to address does not exist in every instance.
(C) It supports the argument's contention that political professionals devote time and energy to crafting the candidate's message and persona.
(D) It suggests that the relationship between a candidate's policy and that candidate's persona is not as essential as some may believe it to be.
(E) It is a premise on which other premises supporting the conclusion is based.

STOP

IF YOU FINISH BEFORE TIME IS CALLED, YOU MAY CHECK YOUR WORK ON THIS SECTION ONLY. DO NOT WORK ON ANY OTHER SECTION IN THE TEST.

The Princeton Review

Completely darken bubbles with a No. 2 pencil. If you make a mistake, be sure to erase mark completely.

1. YOUR NAME: ______________________
(Print) Last First M.I.

SIGNATURE: ______________________ DATE: ___/___/___

HOME ADDRESS: ______________________
(Print) Number

____
City State Zip Code

PHONE NO.: ______________________
(Print)

IMPORTANT: Please fill in these boxes exactly as shown on the back cover of your test book.

2. TEST FORM

3. TEST CODE

4. REGISTRATION NUMBER

5. YOUR NAME

First 4 letters of last name | FIRST INIT | MID INIT

6. DATE OF BIRTH

Month	Day	Year
JAN		
FEB		
MAR		
APR		
MAY		
JUN		
JUL		
AUG		
SEP		
OCT		
NOV		
DEC		

7. SEX

MALE

FEMALE

The Princeton Review

FORM NO. 00001-PR

Test 1

Start with number 1 for each new section.
If a section has fewer questions than answer spaces, leave the extra answer spaces blank.

1. A B C D E
2. A B C D E
3. A B C D E
4. A B C D E
5. A B C D E
6. A B C D E
7. A B C D E
8. A B C D E
9. A B C D E
10. A B C D E
11. A B C D E
12. A B C D E
13. A B C D E
14. A B C D E
15. A B C D E
16. A B C D E
17. A B C D E
18. A B C D E
19. A B C D E
20. A B C D E
21. A B C D E
22. A B C D E
23. A B C D E
24. A B C D E

1. A B C D E
2. A B C D E
3. A B C D E
4. A B C D E
5. A B C D E
6. A B C D E
7. A B C D E
8. A B C D E
9. A B C D E
10. A B C D E
11. A B C D E
12. A B C D E
13. A B C D E
14. A B C D E
15. A B C D E
16. A B C D E
17. A B C D E
18. A B C D E
19. A B C D E
20. A B C D E
21. A B C D E
22. A B C D E
23. A B C D E
24. A B C D E
25. A B C D E

1. A B C D E
2. A B C D E
3. A B C D E
4. A B C D E
5. A B C D E
6. A B C D E
7. A B C D E
8. A B C D E
9. A B C D E
10. A B C D E
11. A B C D E
12. A B C D E
13. A B C D E
14. A B C D E
15. A B C D E
16. A B C D E
17. A B C D E
18. A B C D E
19. A B C D E
20. A B C D E
21. A B C D E
22. A B C D E
23. A B C D E
24. A B C D E
25. A B C D E
26. A B C D E
27. A B C D E

1. A B C D E
2. A B C D E
3. A B C D E
4. A B C D E
5. A B C D E
6. A B C D E
7. A B C D E
8. A B C D E
9. A B C D E
10. A B C D E
11. A B C D E
12. A B C D E
13. A B C D E
14. A B C D E
15. A B C D E
16. A B C D E
17. A B C D E
18. A B C D E
19. A B C D E
20. A B C D E
21. A B C D E
22. A B C D E
23. A B C D E
24. A B C D E
25. A B C D E

COMPUTING YOUR SCORE

Directions

1. Use the Answer Key on the next page to check your answers.
2. Use the Scoring Worksheet below to compute your raw score.
3. Use the Score Conversion Chart to convert your raw score into the 120–180 LSAT scale.

Your scaled score on this virtual test is for general guidance only.

Scores obtained by using the Score Conversion Chart can only approximate the score you would receive if this virtual test were an actual LSAT. Your score on an actual LSAT may differ from the score obtained on this virtual test.

In an actual test, final scores are computed using an equating method that makes scores earned on different editions of the LSAT comparable to one another. This virtual test has been constructed to reflect an actual LSAT as closely as possible, and the conversion of raw scores to the LSAT scale has been approximated.

What this means is that the Conversion Chart reflects only an estimate of how raw scores would translate into final LSAT scores.

Scoring Worksheet

1. Enter the number of questions you answered correctly in each section.

	Number Correct
Section I	______
Section II............	______
Section III	______
Section IV	______

2. Enter the sum here: ______

This is your raw score.

SCORE CONVERSION CHART

For Converting Raw Scores to the 120–180 LSAT Scaled Score

Reported Score	Raw Score Lowest	Raw Score Highest
180	99	101
179	—*	—*
178	98	98
177	97	97
176	96	96
175	95	95
174	94	94
173	93	93
172	92	92
171	91	91
170	90	90
169	89	89
168	88	88
167	86	87
166	85	85
165	84	84
164	82	83
163	81	81
162	79	80
161	77	78
160	76	76
159	74	75
158	72	73
157	71	71
156	69	70
155	67	68
154	65	66
153	63	64
152	61	62
151	59	60
150	58	58
149	56	57
148	54	55
147	52	53
146	50	51
145	48	49
144	46	47
143	44	45
142	43	43
141	41	42
140	39	40
139	37	38
138	36	36
137	34	35
136	32	33
135	30	31
134	29	29
133	27	28
132	26	26
131	24	25
130	23	23
129	22	22
128	20	21
127	19	19
126	18	18
125	17	17
124	16	16
123	15	15
122	14	14
121	13	13
120	0	12

*There is no raw score that will produce this scaled score for this form.

SECTION I

1. D	8. C	15. E	22. B
2. B	9. A	16. E	23. B
3. D	10. B	17. C	24. C
4. D	11. E	18. E	
5. D	12. B	19. A	
6. A	13. A	20. A	
7. B	14. D	21. D	

SECTION II

1. A	8. E	15. B	22. D
2. C	9. E	16. B	23. C
3. C	10. A	17. D	24. A
4. C	11. E	18. E	25. A
5. E	12. D	19. C	
6. E	13. D	20. C	
7. D	14. B	21. D	

SECTION III

1. E	8. D	15. C	22. A
2. C	9. D	16. A	23. B
3. B	10. A	17. D	24. E
4. D	11. B	18. C	25. C
5. A	12. D	19. C	26. A
6. B	13. B	20. B	27. B
7. A	14. D	21. B	

SECTION IV

1. D	8. A	15. D	22. C
2. D	9. C	16. D	23. D
3. E	10. B	17. E	24. C
4. C	11. A	18. A	25. B
5. B	12. B	19. C	
6. E	13. D	20. D	
7. B	14. C	21. E	

9

Answers and Explanations to Practice Test 1

QUESTIONS	EXPLANATIONS

Questions 1–5

A veterinarian will be using four large animal cages for transport: Cage 1, Cage 2, Cage 3, and Cage 4. Each cage has an upper berth and a lower berth, and each berth will be occupied by exactly one animal, either male or female. The following rules govern assignment of animals to cage berths:

Exactly three berths will contain males.
The upper berths of Cages 1 and 2 will contain females.
If a cage has a male in one of its berths, it will carry a female in the other.
If a male is assigned to the lower berth of Cage 3, then the upper berth of Cage 4 will contain a male.

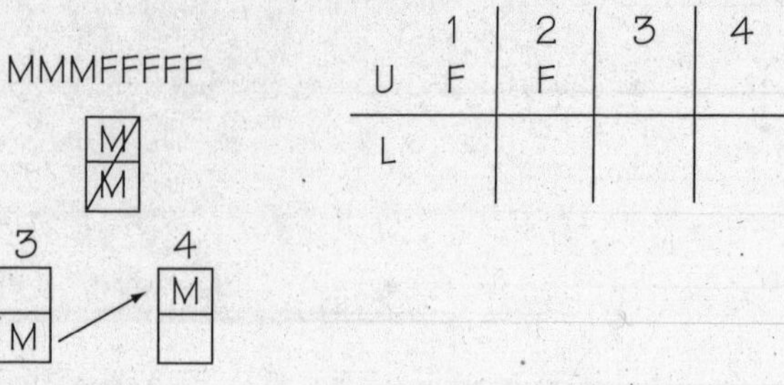

1. If a female is assigned to both berths of Cage 3, then which one of the following could be two other berths that also contain females?
   (A) The upper berth of Cage 1 and the lower berth of Cage 2
   (B) The lower berth of Cage 1 and the upper berth of Cage 4
   (C) The lower berth of Cage 1 and the upper berth of Cage 2
   (D) The upper berth of Cage 2 and the lower berth of Cage 4
   (E) The lower berth of Cage 2 and the lower berth of Cage 4

1. (A) No. This would leave two males in Cage 4.
   (B) No. This would make a total of six females.
   (C) No. This would leave two males in Cage 4.
   (D) Right. This is possible.
   (E) No. This would make a total of six females.

2. It CANNOT be true that females are assigned to both
   (A) the lower berth of Cage 1 and the lower berth of Cage 4
   (B) the lower berth of Cage 1 and the lower berth of Cage 2
   (C) the lower berth of Cage 1 and the upper berth of Cage 3
   (D) the lower berth of Cage 2 and the lower berth of Cage 4
   (E) the upper berth of Cage 3 and the lower berth of Cage 4

2. (A) No. This is possible.
   (B) Right. That would force males to double up in 3 or 4.
   (C) No. This is possible.
   (D) No. This is possible.
   (E) No. This is possible.

SECTION I

QUESTIONS	EXPLANATIONS

3. If the upper berth of Cage 4 contains a female, then a female must also be assigned to which one of the following berths?

   (A) The lower berth of Cage 1
   (B) The lower berth of Cage 4
   (C) The lower berth of Cage 2
   (D) The lower berth of Cage 3
   (E) The upper berth of Cage 3

3. (A) No. A male could go there.
   (B) No. A male could go there.
   (C) No. A male could go there.
   (D) Right. A male can't go there because of the conditional clue.
   (E) No. A male could go there.

4. If a male is assigned to the lower berth of Cage 3, which one of the following is a complete and accurate list of the berths that CANNOT be assigned males?

   (A) The upper berth of Cage 1, the upper berth of Cage 2
   (B) The upper berth of Cage 1, the upper berth of Cage 2, the upper berth of Cage 3
   (C) The upper berth of Cage 1, the upper berth of Cage 2, the lower berth of Cage 4
   (D) The upper berth of Cage 1, the upper berth of Cage 2, the upper berth of Cage 3, the lower berth of Cage 4
   (E) The upper berth of Cage 1, the lower berth of Cage 1, the upper berth of Cage 2, the upper berth of Cage 3, the lower berth of Cage 4

4. (A) This list is incomplete.
   (B) A male cannot go in the upper berth of Cage 3.
   (C) A male cannot go in the lower berth of Cage 4.
   (D) Right.
   (E) A male can go in the lower berth of Cage 1.

5. If the lower berth of Cage 2 contains a female, then it could be true that females are assigned to both

   (A) the lower berth of Cage 1 and the upper berth of Cage 4
   (B) the lower berth of Cage 1 and the lower berth of Cage 4
   (C) the upper berth of Cage 3 and the upper berth of Cage 4
   (D) the lower berth of Cage 3 and the lower berth of Cage 4
   (E) the lower berth of Cage 3 and the upper berth of Cage 3

5. (A) No. A female in the lower berth of Cage 1 would force males to double up somewhere else.
   (B) No. A female in the lower berth of Cage 1 would force males to double up somewhere else.
   (C) No. That would leave a male in the lower berth of 3, which would force a male into the upper berth of 4.
   (D) Right.
   (E) No. That would force males to double up in Cage 4.

SECTION I

QUESTIONS

Questions 6–11

In a single day, exactly seven airplanes—J, K, L, M, N, P, and Q—are the only arrivals at an airport. No airplane arrives at the same time as any other plane, and no plane arrives more than once that day. Each airplane is either a prop or a jet (but not both). The following conditions apply:

No two consecutive arrivals are jets.
P arrives some time before both K and M.
Exactly two of the planes that arrive before P are jets.
J is the sixth arrival.
Q arrives sometime before L.

6. Which one of the following could be the order, from first to last, in which the airplanes arrive?

(A) N, Q, L, P, M, J, K
(B) N, P, Q, L, M, J, K
(C) Q, M, L, K, P, J, N
(D) Q, L, K, P, M, J, N
(E) L, Q, P, K, J, M, N

7. For which one of the following pairs of airplanes is it the case that they CANNOT both be jets?

(A) J and N
(B) K and J
(C) L and M
(D) M and K
(E) N and Q

8. If N is the third arrival, then which of the following airplanes must be a prop?

(A) J
(B) K
(C) L
(D) M
(E) Q

9. If exactly three of the airplanes are props, then which one of the following airplanes must be a prop?

(A) J
(B) K
(C) L
(D) M
(E) Q

EXPLANATIONS

JKLMNPQ
j/p
~~jj~~

P—K
P—M
jjP
Q—L

	1	2	3	4	5	6	7
	–L		–Q		–P		–Q –P
				P	K/M	J	M/K
j/p:	j	p	j	P			

Many deductions can be made at the very beginning. Take a look at the chart above.

6. (A) Right. This is possible.
(B) No. P must be fourth.
(C) No. P must be fourth.
(D) No. M and K must be fifth and seventh in some order.
(E) No. P must be fourth.

7. (A) No. They could both be jets.
(B) Right. Either way, they must be next to each other.
(C) No. They could both be jets.
(D) No. They could both be jets.
(E) No. They could both be jets.

8. (A) No. J could be either.
(B) No. K could be either.
(C) Yes. L must be second, and is therefore a prop.
(D) No. M could be either.
(E) No. Q could be either.

9. (A) Yes. J would have to be between two jets.
(B) No. It would have to be a jet.
(C) No. It could be either.
(D) No. It would have to be a jet.
(E) No. It could be either.

SECTION I

QUESTIONS	EXPLANATIONS

10. For how many of the seven airplanes can one determine exactly how many airplanes arrived before it?

(A) one
(B) two
(C) three
(D) four
(E) five

10. (A) No. You can deduce both P and J's locations.
(B) Right. You can deduce both P and J's locations.
(C) No. You can deduce only P and J's locations.
(D) No. You can deduce only P and J's locations.
(E) No. You can deduce only P and J's locations.

11. Which one of the following pairs of airplanes CANNOT arrive consecutively at the airport?

(A) L and P
(B) N and P
(C) P and K
(D) P and M
(E) P and Q

11. (A) No. They could arrive consecutively.
(B) No. They could arrive consecutively.
(C) No. They could arrive consecutively.
(D) No. They could arrive consecutively.
(E) Right. Q can't be third.

SECTION I

QUESTIONS	EXPLANATIONS

Questions 12–18

A total of six pieces of fruit are found in three small baskets: one in the first basket, two in the second basket, and three in the third basket. Two of the fruits are pears—one Bosc, the other Forelle. Two others are apples—one Cortland, one Dudley. The remaining two fruits are oranges—one navel, one Valencia. The fruits' placement is consistent with the following:

There is at least one orange in the same basket as the Bosc pear.
The apples are not in the same basket.
The navel orange is not in the same basket as either apple.

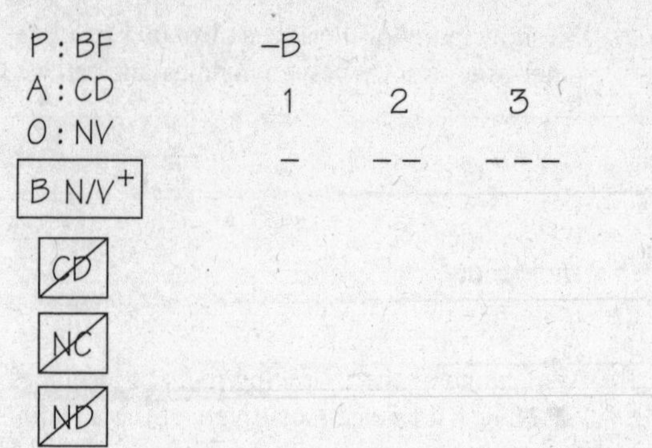

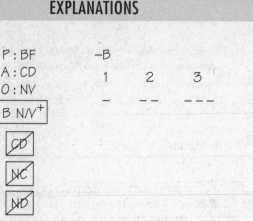

The most important deduction is that the navel orange, Cortland apple, and Dudley apple must all be in separate baskets.

12. Which of the following could be an accurate matching of the baskets to the pieces of fruit in each of them?

(A) basket one: Forelle pear
basket two: Dudley apple, navel orange
basket three: Bosc pear, Cortland apple, Valencia orange
(B) basket one: Dudley apple
basket two: Bosc pear, navel orange
basket three: Forelle pear, Cortland apple, Valencia orange
(C) basket one: navel orange
basket two: Cortland apple, Bosc pear
basket three: Forelle pear, Dudley apple, Valencia orange
(D) basket one: Valencia orange
basket two: Cortland and Dudley apples
basket three: navel orange, Bosc and Forelle pears
(E) basket one: Valencia orange
basket two: Bosc pear, navel orange
basket three: Forelle pear, Cortland and Dudley apples

12. (A) No. D and N can't be together.
(B) Right. This is possible.
(C) No. B must be with at least one of the oranges.
(D) No. C and D can't be together.
(E) No. C and D can't be together.

13. Which one of the following CANNOT be true?

(A) A pear is in the first basket.
(B) An apple is in the same basket as the Forelle pear.
(C) An orange is in the first basket.
(D) The oranges are in the same basket as each other.
(E) Neither apple is in the first basket.

13. (A) Right. Because N, C, and D must be separated, one of them must be in the first basket.
(B) No. This is possible.
(C) No. This is possible.
(D) No. This is possible.
(E) No. This is possible.

SECTION I

QUESTIONS	EXPLANATIONS

14. Which one of the following must be true?

(A) An apple and a pear are in the second basket.
(B) An orange and a pear are in the second basket.
(C) At least one apple and at least one pear are in the third basket.
(D) At least one orange and at least one pear are in the third basket.
(E) At least one orange and at least one apple are in the third basket.

14. (A) Not necessarily.
(B) Not necessarily.
(C) Not necessarily.
(D) Right.
(E) Not necessarily.

15. If both pears are in the same basket, which one of the following could be true?

(A) The Cortland apple is in the third basket.
(B) An orange is in the first basket.
(C) Both oranges are in the second basket.
(D) The Bosc pear is in the second basket.
(E) The Cortland apple is in the first basket.

15. (A) No. This can't be true.
(B) No. An apple must be in the first basket.
(C) No. The navel orange must be in the third basket.
(D) No. The Bosc pear must be in the third basket.
(E) Right. This is possible.

16. Which one of the following must be true?

(A) An apple is in the first basket.
(B) No more than one orange is in each basket.
(C) The pears are not in the same basket.
(D) The Dudley apple is not in the same basket as the Valencia orange.
(E) The Valencia orange is not in the first basket.

16. Which one of the following must be true?
(A) No. The navel orange could be, too.
(B) No. This is possible.
(C) No. This is possible.
(D) No. This is possible.
(E) Right. N, C, and D must be separated, so one of them must be in the first basket.

17. If the Bosc pear is not in the third basket, which of the following could be true?

(A) The Cortland apple is in the second basket.
(B) The Forelle pear is in the second basket.
(C) The Dudley apple is in the third basket.
(D) The navel orange is in the third basket.
(E) The Valencia orange is in the second basket.

17. (A) No. The second basket must hold B and N.
(B) No. The second basket must hold B and N.
(C) Right. This could be true.
(D) No. N must be in the second basket.
(E) No. The second basket must hold B and N.

18. If the Forelle pear and the Cortland apple are in the same basket, which one of the following must be true?

(A) The Cortland apple is in the second basket.
(B) The Valencia orange is in the second basket.
(C) The Dudley apple is in the second basket.
(D) The Dudley apple is in the first basket.
(E) The Valencia orange is in the third basket.

18. (A) No. It could be in the third basket, too.
(B) No. This can't be true.
(C) No. This can't be true.
(D) No. It could be in the third basket, too.
(E) Right. This must be true.

QUESTIONS | EXPLANATIONS

Questions 19–25

A live radio show features five bands—the Foghorns, the Geriatrics, the Hollowmen, the Inkstains, and the Jarheads—that will sing ten songs. Each band performs exactly two of the songs: one band performs songs 1 and 6, one band performs songs 2 and 7, one band performs songs 3 and 8, one band performs songs 4 and 9, and one band performs songs 5 and 10. The following conditions apply:

Neither of the Geriatrics's songs is performed immediately before either of the Hollowmen's.
The Foghorns do not sing the ninth song.
The Jarheads's first song is after (but not necessarily immediately after) the Inkstains's first song.
At least one of the Foghorns's songs is immediately after one of the Jarheads's songs.

FGHIJ

~~GH~~

I—J

JF +

	–J 1/6	–F 2/7	–J 3/8	–F 4/9	–I 5/10
(20)	I	J	F	H	G
(21)				J	F

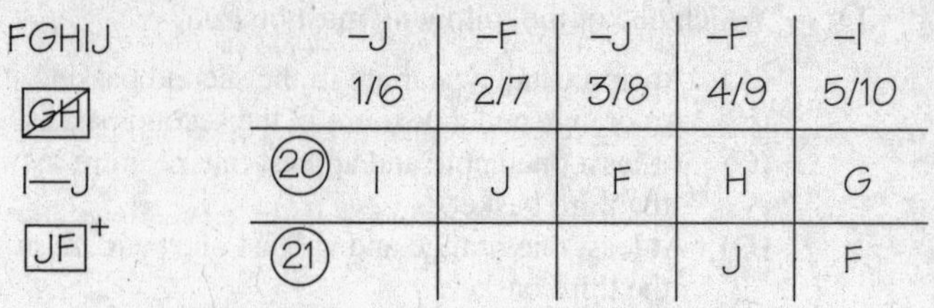

You can deduce that J can only be 2/7, 4/9, or 5/10.

19. Which one of the following could be an accurate list of the bands performing the first five songs, in order from song 1 to song 5?

(A) Foghorns, Geriatrics, Inkstains, Hollowmen, Jarheads
(B) Geriatrics, Inkstains, Jarheads, Foghorns, Hollowmen
(C) Hollowmen, Inkstains, Foghorns, Geriatrics, Jarheads
(D) Jarheads, Geriatrics, Inkstains, Hollowmen, Foghorns
(E) Inkstains, Jarheads, Foghorns, Geriatrics, Hollowmen

19. (A) Right. This is possible. Remember that this would still put one of the Foghorns's songs (the sixth) immediately after one of the Jarheads's (the fifth).
(B) No. Jarheads can't be 3/8.
(C) No. Jarheads must immediately precede Foghorns at least once.
(D) No. Jarheads can't be 1/6.
(E) No. Geriatrics can't immediately precede Hollowmen.

20. If the Foghorns sing the eighth song, then for exactly how many of the ten songs can one determine which band sings the song?

(A) ten
(B) eight
(C) six
(D) four
(E) two

20. (A) Right. You can determine them all. See diagram.
(B) No. You can determine them all.
(C) No. You can determine them all.
(D) No. You can determine them all.
(E) No. You can determine them all.

21. If the Jarheads sing the fourth song, then which one of the following could be true?

(A) The Foghorns sing song 1.
(B) The Foghorns sing song 3.
(C) The Geriatrics sing song 5.
(D) The Hollowmen sing song 3.
(E) The Inkstains sing song 5.

21. (A) No. They must sing songs 5/10.
(B) No. They must sing songs 5/10.
(C) No. The Foghorns sing song 5.
(D) Right. This is possible.
(E) No. The Foghorns sing song 5.

SECTION I

QUESTIONS	EXPLANATIONS

22. Which one of the following could be true?

    (A) The Foghorns sing song 4.
    (B) The Geriatrics sing song 5.
    (C) The Hollowmen sing song 5.
    (D) The Inkstains sing song 10.
    (E) The Jarheads sing song 6.

22. (A) No. This can't happen.
    (B) Right. We've already shown in our diagram that this could happen.
    (C) No. This can't happen.
    (D) No. This can't happen.
    (E) No. This can't happen.

23. The Foghorns CANNOT perform which one of the following songs?

    (A) song 1
    (B) song 2
    (C) song 3
    (D) song 6
    (E) song 10

23. (A) No. This could happen.
    (B) Right. This can't happen.
    (C) No. This could happen.
    (D) No. This could happen.
    (E) No. This could happen.

24. Which one of the following could be an accurate list of the bands performing the last five songs, in order from song 6 to song 10?

    (A) Foghorns, Inkstains, Geriatrics, Jarheads, Hollowmen
    (B) Geriatrics, Hollowmen, Inkstains, Jarheads, Foghorns
    (C) Hollowmen, Geriatrics, Inkstains, Jarheads, Foghorns
    (D) Inkstains, Geriatrics, Jarheads, Foghorns, Hollowmen
    (E) Jarheads, Foghorns, Geriatrics, Inkstains, Hollowmen

24. (A) No. Foghorns must immediately follow Jarheads at least once.
    (B) No. Geriatrics cannot immediately precede Hollowmen.
    (C) Right. This is possible.
    (D) No. Foghorns can't sing ninth.
    (E) No. Inkstains must always precede Jarheads.

SECTION II

QUESTIONS

1. Educator: By itself, the expert advice delivered in a workshop setting does not cause a young writer to be able to craft short stories; rather, the repeated effort of writing new stories in the context of a short-story workshop can be a cause. When any individual writes many short stories, the quality of that person's stories inevitably increases. As a result, the new short-story workshops offered by this school will increase the quality of short stories written by its students.

The conclusion drawn by the educator follows logically if which one of the following is assumed?

(A) The new short-story workshops offered by the school will increase the number of its students who write a significant number of new short stories.

(B) The advice delivered by instructors in the new short-story workshops will be superior to the advice previously offered by writing teachers in the school.

(C) The new short-story workshops will be attended by a large number of the school's students.

(D) The introduction on writing workshops represents a new emphasis in the school curriculum.

(E) Any young writer, regardless of his or her ability to craft short stories, can improve through repeated efforts at writing.

EXPLANATIONS

1. **Conclusion**: Workshops will increase the quality of the short stories written by students.

Premise: Anyone who repeatedly writes new stories will write better-quality stories.

Assumption: The workshops will cause an increase in the number of students who repeatedly write new stories.

This is a STRENGTHEN question. We want to pick the answer that, if true, guarantees the truth of the conclusion—most likely by filling the gap.

(A) Yes. This choice links the premise to the conclusion and fills the argument's main gap.

(B) This choice refers to advice; the argument states that advice isn't important for improving quality.

(C) Because the conclusion involves a comparison, we need to know how the number of students writing many new stories will compare to the number doing so now.

(D) This is too wishy-washy to guarantee the truth of the conclusion.

(E) This is a restatement of the main premise; it doesn't provide additional support to the conclusion.

SECTION II

QUESTIONS	EXPLANATIONS

QUESTIONS

2. Last year, the challenger in this election proposed a plan to solve the city's waste-disposal problems. Just recently, the incumbent proposed a plan that is nearly the same. The incumbent claims that he was not aware of the challenger's plan, and that their similarities are due to the fact that the solution is merely a matter of common sense. Yet both plans involve similar increases in spending on recycling, both recommend the decommissioning of the same waste incinerators, and both rely on a system of so-called "green landfills," a revolutionary theory not employed by any other city in the world.

   The main point of the argument is that

   (A) the challenger's plan and the incumbent's plan have many similarities
   (B) both plans have been advanced in an effort to attract the same large bloc of votes
   (C) the incumbent's plan is similar to the challenger's in ways that suggest that this similarity is the product of more than coincidence
   (D) the incumbent proposed his plan only after it was learned that the challenger's plan had wide popular support
   (E) new plans that are introduced by political candidates sometimes take their opponents' plans into account

EXPLANATIONS

2. This is a MAIN POINT question. We want to find the single thing the argument is constructed to make us believe.

   (A) The argument wants to explain the reasons for this similarity; this is a premise of the argument.
   (B) What the politicians hope to gain by introducing their plans isn't the issue here.
   (C) Yes. This is a gentle restatement of what the argument wants to say: The incumbent copied the challenger's plan.
   (D) Like (B), this choice goes to what gain the politicians hope to get.
   (E) This is far too general to the main point of this argument, which deals with a single situation.

QUESTIONS	EXPLANATIONS

3. A physicist theorized that the present distribution of matter in the universe was largely determined by random clumping of primeval particles during the early stages of the universe's formation. When computer simulations developed by the physicist showed that several different clumping patterns led to substantially similar distributions of matter, the physicist did not report the results. A journalist who learned about the results of the simulations reported them and accused the physicist of suppressing experimental findings that contradict her theory. The physicist countered that the computer simulations were inconclusive because they depended in part upon present theories of the universe's formation.

Which one of the following, if true, most strengthens the physicist's counterargument?

(A) Other experiments conducted by the physicist showed that clumping of primeval particles could influence the later distribution of matter in the universe.
(B) The clumping patterns used by the physicist in the computer simulation were not randomly generated.
(C) Present theories of the universe's formation include principles that allow only slight variations in the distribution of matter.
(D) Every computer simulation yet devised to model the formation of the universe depends to some degree upon present theories of the universe's formation.
(E) It is impossible to determine the theoretical accuracy of the assumptions used in developing any computer simulation of the universe's formation.

3. This is a STRENGTHEN question. We want the choice that provides the most additional support for the physicist's contention that the results were inconclusive.

(A) This provides only weak support; it doesn't deal with the results of the simulations.
(B) The issue here is whether changes in clumping could cause changes in the distribution of matter; the "random" factor in this choice is a red herring.
(C) Yes. This supports by reinforcing the physicist's explanation; the results were very similar because the theories used do not allow for much variation.
(D) The fact that this is a common attribute of all models doesn't support the physicist's statement about this case.
(E) This doesn't appear to affect the physicist's statements either way.

SECTION II

QUESTIONS	EXPLANATIONS

4. Concerned citizen: The county government's new ordinance limiting the types of materials that can be disposed of in trash fires violates our rights as citizens. The fact that local environmental damage results from the burning of certain inorganic materials is not the primary issue. The real concern is the government's flagrant disregard for the right of the individual to establish what is acceptable on his or her own property.

   Which one of the following principles, if accepted, would enable the concerned citizen's conclusion to be properly drawn?

   (A) Legislative violation of an individual's right to privacy is not justifiable unless the actions of that individual put others at risk.
   (B) The right of an individual to live in a safe environment takes precedence over the right of an individual to be exempt from legislative intrusion.
   (C) An individual's personal rights supersede any right or responsibility the government may have to protect a community from harm.
   (D) An individual has a moral obligation to act in the best interest of the community as a whole.
   (E) A compromise must be found when the right of an individual to act independently conflicts with the responsibility of the government to provide protection for the local environment.

4. This is a PRINCIPLE question. We are given five principles in the answer choices for this specific question, so we should come up with our own principle for the actions in the argument and match it to the answer choices.

   (A) If this were true, it would not match with the actions in the argument, because the argument says the local environmentenal risk isn't as important as individual rights.
   (B) This has the same problem as answer choice (A). It's the opposite of what the argument is saying.
   (C) Bingo. An individual's rights (such as privacy) are more important than environmental rights.
   (D) This would also go in the opposite direction from the argument.
   (E) This is nice, but it's not something that would strengthen the citizen's viewpoint. This is the politically correct response. Watch out—it's a trap.

SECTION II

QUESTIONS	EXPLANATIONS

5. As part of a new commitment to customer satisfaction, an electronics company sent a survey to all customers who had purchased its electronic personal organizer in the previous month. The survey, which was sent through the mail, asked customers to give personal information and to rate their satisfaction with the product. Of customers who returned the survey, more indicated that they had a negative opinion of the product's performance than indicated a neutral or positive opinion. On the basis of these results, the company, hoping to increase customer satisfaction, decided to allocate a large amount of capital to redesigning the product.

Which one of the following, if true, indicates the most serious flaw in the method of research used by the company?

(A) The company relied on a numerical system of rating responses rather than on open-ended questions that allow for more detailed feedback.

(B) Customers who were dissatisfied with the information display of the organizer outnumbered customers who were dissatisfied with the variety of functions offered by the organizer.

(C) Studies show that customer dissatisfaction with a new product is highest during the first year of the product's release and gradually decreases over the following years.

(D) The marketing division has found that responses to their mail-in surveys are generally accurate.

(E) People who are satisfied with a product or have no strong opinion about it are less likely to be motivated to return a mail-in questionnaire.

5. **Conclusion:** The company is going to redesign the product.

Premise: The surveys indicate that more people have a negative opinion of the product than have a neutral or positive one.

Assumption: The survey is representative of the opinions of all people who have used the product.

This is a WEAKEN question. Try and see which answer choice has the most negative impact on the conclusion of the argument. Remember to assume the hypothetical truth of each choice and apply it to the argument.

(A) We have no idea whether a numerical system or an open-ended system would be more appropriate for this survey.

(B) We're not concerned with what exactly about the product these customers didn't like. We're looking for something that would show why the conclusion might be wrong.

(C) This looks okay, but it doesn't really show that we should ignore the dissatisfaction of the customers. Let's eliminate it.

(D) This would strengthen the argument by showing how the survey was representative. It's the opposite of what we want in this case.

(E) This shows how the survey was not representative because there's a lot of happy, or at least not unhappy, people who aren't sending back the questionnaires, thereby skewing the data. It's the answer.

QUESTIONS	EXPLANATIONS

6. Adolphus: The proposed system of computer control for the city's subway traffic, once it is implemented, will lead to greater on-time service and fewer accidents. We must secure whatever resources are required to implement the new system immediately.

Jean: The current financial state of the transit authority is such that the immediate implementation of the new system would require an increase in fares, which the public would not support. We should delay the implementation of the new system until the transit authority can set money aside for the transition and build support for it among riders.

Adolphus and Jean disagree with each other over whether

(A) the system of computer control will achieve its anticipated benefits
(B) the public would support higher fares to increase on-time service and reduce accidents
(C) it is possible to implement the proposed system of computer control quickly
(D) the proposed system of computer control could be implemented without increasing subway fares
(E) the existing system of control for the city's subways should be retained for some period of time

6. This is basically an INFERENCE question. We want a statement about which both Adolphus and Jean definitely express different views.

(A) Jean never says that the new system won't do what Adolphus says it will.
(B) Adolphus does not address the issue of public support.
(C) Jean doesn't think it can't be implemented quickly; she just doesn't think that would be a good idea.
(D) Adolphus doesn't address the question of how to pay for the change.
(E) This is it. Adolphus would say "no": replace it immediately; Jean would say "yes": secure funding and build public support first.

SECTION II

QUESTIONS

7. Because the consequences of an action intended to conserve the environment cannot be fully predicted, a wise principle is that such an action should be taken only when the likely consequence of inaction is less acceptable than any foreseeable negative consequence of the action.

Which one of the following provides the best illustration of the principle above?

(A) A system of canals is proposed to preserve threatened wetlands. Without the canals, the wetlands will vanish, so the objections of area farmers should not be allowed to prevent the canal system from being built.

(B) New roads are proposed to make it easier for conservationists to reach the areas inhabited by an endangered bird species. Because these same roads would increase the access of logging companies to these sensitive areas, the roads should not be built.

(C) A threatened moss thrives in a remote, uninhabited area that is not currently protected by law. Because the area is not important for either residential or industrial purposes, there is no possible negative consequence of passing a law to limit access to the area. Thus, such a law should be passed to protect the moss.

(D) A rare species of mink is found only in one area and has long been hunted for its fur. The proposal that all hunting be banned in the area, however, should not be implemented. Mule deer living in the same area contribute to destruction of the mink's habitat, and without hunting to limit the mule deer population, it is possible that the mink will die out completely.

(E) Tailings—the waste left over from mining—lead to severe water pollution in some mountain areas. Because most of the mining companies responsible for this pollution no longer exist, it is impossible to demand that they clean it up. Therefore, no matter how negatively taxpayers may react, taxes must be used to fund the cleanup of mine tailings.

EXPLANATIONS

7. This is a (use-the-) PRINCIPLE question. Note that the condition used in this principle is a necessary ("only-if") condition.

(A) This choice does not address possible negative consequences of the canal system at all.

(B) This choice doesn't state that the negative consequences outweigh the consequences of inaction.

(C) Tough one. This demonstrates that the necessary condition in the principle is satisfied; however, that condition can only tell you when *not* to pass the law ("only pass it if..."). There may be further requirements we aren't told about.

(D) Yes. If the ban is instituted, it is possible that the mink will die out; if the ban is not instituted, it seems likely that the mink will continue to survive because it has been hunted for a long time. Because this doesn't satisfy the necessary condition, the ban should *not* be implemented. This is a correct use of the principle.

(E) This choice talks about funding for an environmental policy, which isn't relevant to the principle.

SECTION II

QUESTIONS	EXPLANATIONS

8. Columnist: Our local public schools are desperately in need of community support, not just from tax revenues, but also from sources such as auxiliary fund-raisers and volunteer work. Although the mayor has often been seen participating in these activities and claims that the public schools are our community's most important assets, there is no reason to believe that his participation is sincere. After all, his own children attend a local private school instead of the public schools.

The columnist's reasoning is most vulnerable to criticism on the grounds that it presumes, without providing justification, that

(A) the mayor's participation in fund-raising activities for local public schools is motivated solely by a desire for positive public perception
(B) the mayor could lend greater support to the local public schools by having his children attend them
(C) the mayor sends his children to a local private school so that they will not contribute to the serious problems of overcrowding in the local public schools
(D) no politician can plausibly profess support for any public institution that the politician does not use
(E) there is no reason to believe that the mayor's support for the public schools is sincere if he has no direct personal interest in seeing their needs met

8. **Conclusion**: The mayor's support for public schools is insincere.

Premise: The mayor sends his own children to private school.

Assumption: It is impossible for someone who doesn't send their own children to public schools to be sincere in their support for them.

This is an ASSUMPTION question. We want to pick something the argument needs for its conclusion to be correct.

(A) This is too specific in its description of the mayor's motives; some other factor may explain his behavior.
(B) Very close, but this doesn't go to the question of the mayor's sincerity in professing support, which is the issue in this argument.
(C) This is far too specific to be an assumption required by this argument.
(D) This is rather too sweeping to be an assumption required by this argument.
(E) Yes. This includes both the main issues: public schools and the mayor's sincerity. "No direct personal interest" is a reasonable paraphrase of the idea of sending his own children to public schools.

QUESTIONS	EXPLANATIONS

9. A recent study seems to suggest that, contrary to popular perception, vocational and technical programs do a better job of preparing their students for the workforce than traditional four-year colleges do. This study indicated that just below 60 percent of vocational and technical school graduates found full-time employment within two years of graduation, whereas only 50 percent of those who graduated from four-year colleges did. Nevertheless, the study's official conclusion was that four-year colleges are in fact better at preparing their students for the workforce than are vocational and technical programs.

Which one of the following, if true, most helps to resolve the apparent discrepancy between the study's findings and its official conclusion?

(A) Presidents and trustees of four-year colleges work to shape public perceptions of their institutions.
(B) The study investigated a wide variety of both four-year colleges and vocational and technical programs over a period of a decade.
(C) Most graduates of vocational and technical programs who find employment within two years of graduation work in the professions for which they were trained.
(D) Increased demand for health care workers, nearly all of whom attend schools that were classified by the study as vocational, caused the employment rate among graduates of these schools to exceed 90 percent.
(E) More than 20 percent of the graduates of four-year colleges go on to professional schools that require more than two years to complete but only admit graduates of four-year colleges, and the vast majority of these students find employment when they seek it.

9. This is a Resolve/Explain question. We want to find the choice that tells us why the study's official conclusion appears to contradict its statistic about employment rates.

(A) "Public perception" isn't clearly relevant to how the study's conclusion was reached.
(B) This makes the paradox worse by indicating that the study was properly conducted.
(C) This makes the paradox slightly worse by suggesting the vocational schools are successful in training students.
(D) This explains why the numbers for vocational schools were so high but not where the study's official conclusion came from.
(E) Yes. Many graduates of four-year colleges do not seek employment within two years because they go on to other schools, an option not open to anyone else. The number of students is large enough to account for the difference.

SECTION II

QUESTIONS

10. Howard: Why is it that, in physics, the direction of electric field is defined as the direction in which a positive charge experiences force? Electrons, which are negatively charged, are the particles that move in electric current, yet by the standard definition, they move in a direction opposite to the electric field.

Linda: The standard definition was developed at a time when it was known that two types of charge existed, but not that only one of them was involved in the conduction of electric current. The definition of electric field, by chance, depends upon positive charge, which generally does not move in an electric circuit.

Howard: Your explanation cannot be correct. It has been known for some time now that electrons are the only charges involved in the conduction of current, yet the definition of electric field has remained unchanged.

Which one of the following additional items of information, if true, could best be used by Linda to counter Howard's objection to her explanation?

(A) Subsequent development of physical theories related to electricity led to the wide adoption of the standard definition before its shortcomings were known, and to change it now would cause widespread confusion.

(B) Theories of magnetism, which is related to electricity, also incorporate standard definitions that take the behavior of positive charge as their bases.

(C) Students who learn the theory of electricity may initially be frustrated by its conventional dependence on the behavior of positive charge, but it does not prevent students from comprehending and correctly using that theory.

(D) There exist presentations of the theory of electricity that base their definitions around the behavior of negative charge, but anyone learning physics according to these presentations must be aware of the standard definitions in order to interpret the scientific literature surrounding electricity correctly.

(E) The choice of either positive charge or negative charge as the basis for standard definitions in the physical theory of electricity is arbitrary, and has no effect on the accuracy or completeness of the results of that theory.

EXPLANATIONS

10. This is most nearly a WEAKEN question. We want the choice that indicates why Howard's objection doesn't get to the heart of the matter.

(A) Yes. The standard definition, although inconvenient, was not changed once further evidence came to light because changing it would have caused problems.

(B) This is similar to (A), but it doesn't contain an explicit explanation of why the definition was not changed.

(C) This shows that the standard definition isn't unworkable, but it doesn't explain why the definition wasn't changed.

(D) This is similar to (A), but again it doesn't contain as explicit a statement of why the definition wasn't changed.

(E) This is like (C); it explains that the standard definition isn't absolutely unworkable, but nothing more.

QUESTIONS

11. Once, dieticians advocated radically reducing the proportion of total dietary calories from fat and increasing the proportion from carbohydrates as a method of aiding weight loss. One result of this advice has been an increased incidence of diabetes. Now, dieticians advocate radically reducing the proportion of dietary calories from carbohydrate and increasing the proportion from proteins and fat as a method of aiding weight loss. There is already evidence that this advice is leading to an increase in the incidence of heart disease and certain kinds of cancer. There can be little doubt that, whatever dieticians may recommend, radical changes to diet made for the purpose of losing weight do not contribute to overall health.

The reasoning in the argument is flawed because the argument

(A) takes for granted that the only possible reason for making radical dietary changes is to increase overall health
(B) takes for granted that diabetes is a less serious condition for those who suffer from it than is heart disease or cancer
(C) fails to consider the role of exercise in conjunction with dietary changes as an important factor in successful weight loss
(D) ignores the possibility that, even without advice from dieticians, many people who do not change their eating habits will develop serious health problems
(E) fails to consider that a radical reduction in calories consumed from all dietary sources may lead both to weight loss and to improved overall health

EXPLANATIONS

11. **Conclusion**: Radical dietary changes made to lose weight do not improve health.

Premises: Past radical dietary changes recommended for weight loss had negative health consequences; current ones are certain to do so as well.

Assumption: No radical change other than the ones discussed could improve health.

This is a FLAW question. We want a choice that indicates or describes the assumption.

(A) The argument accepts that people make changes for other reasons—weight loss; it claims that changes made for this purpose do not improve health.
(B) The relative severity of the problems discussed in the premises doesn't affect the conclusion.
(C) The issue in this argument is overall health, not whether weight-loss efforts are successful.
(D) The argument doesn't try to blame all health problems on dietary changes.
(E) Yes. Here is a diet plan that would reduce weight while improving health.

QUESTIONS

12. Dentist: Many children today eat so much sugary processed food that tooth decay has become a more serious problem than ever. Periodic brushing can protect children's teeth only if they also receive regular twice-yearly professional cleanings. Hence, the dental reimbursement plans offered by most companies are inadequate to protect the dental health of at least some children.

Which one of the following is an assumption required by the dentist's argument?

(A) In the past, children did not require twice-yearly professional cleanings to protect their teeth from decay.
(B) Some dental reimbursement plans offered by companies are adequate to protect the dental health of children who do not consume sugary processed food.
(C) No single dental reimbursement plan suits the dental health needs of all families.
(D) The dental reimbursement plans offered by some companies do not provide for regular twice-yearly professional cleanings for children.
(E) Children now are more likely than ever before to experience serious problems as the result of tooth decay.

EXPLANATIONS

12. **Conclusion:** Dental plans don't protect the dental health of children.

Premise: Dental health of children cannot be protected unless they receive regular twice-yearly cleanings.

Assumption: To be adequate, dental reimbursement plans must provide what is required to protect children's dental health.

This is an ASSUMPTION question. We want to pick a choice whose truth is essential for the conclusion.

(A) What was true in the past isn't relevant to this conclusion.
(B) The children for whom dental plans are adequate aren't relevant to this conclusion.
(C) This is far too sweeping to be an assumption required by this argument.
(D) Yes. If this is untrue, then there is still some possibility that the conclusion is right, but the premise certainly wouldn't support it.
(E) The argument says that tooth decay is a serious problem, but the problems that result from tooth decay aren't directly relevant to the conclusion.

SECTION II

QUESTIONS

13. Recent media coverage indicates that the incidence of malfeasance and fraud among securities traders has increased over the past decade. Economists believe that this is due to changes in how securities traders are compensated. Whereas ten years ago most traders were paid only a fixed percentage of the value of each transaction, now virtually all of them also receive commissions on the basis of profit generated for their employers.

    Which one of the following statements is most strongly supported by the information above?

    (A) An increased incentive for trader malfeasance is associated with payment based on a fixed percentage of each transaction.
    (B) A decreased risk of trader fraud is associated with paying traders an increased percentage of each transaction.
    (C) A decreased propensity for malfeasance and fraud is caused by changes in trader compensation that place greater emphasis on making profit for their employers.
    (D) Fraud by a securities trader may lead to an increased profit-related commission that more than offsets any loss in compensation associated with the decreased value of that transaction.
    (E) Fraud and malfeasance would no longer be a problem if traders were compensated solely on the basis of the value of each trader's transactions.

EXPLANATIONS

13. This is an INFERENCE question. The answer should be a logical consequence of the material in the passage.

    (A) This is the opposite of the passage; this is the method of compensation that was used before fraud began to grow.
    (B) Although the fixed-percentage method is associated with less fraud, we aren't told that a bigger percentage would give us even less fraud.
    (C) This is the opposite of the passage; this is the method of compensation that appears to have caused fraud to increase.
    (D) Yes. If fraud causes a decrease in one kind of compensation, then it must at least sometimes increase the other kind of compensation by a greater amount, or else the new compensation method wouldn't encourage fraud.
    (E) The problem here is the word *problem*; we're told that changes have increased the amount of fraud, but we don't know that it wasn't a problem before it increased.

SECTION II

QUESTIONS	EXPLANATIONS

14. A study of former college athletes revealed that, as a group, they are five times less likely to die before the age of fifty than are members of the population at large. The advice to derive from this is clear: Colleges should vastly expand their athletic departments so as to allow a greater proportion of all students to participate in athletics, thereby increasing the overall life expectancy of their student population.

Which one of the following, if true, most seriously weakens the argument above?

(A) Because participation in college athletics requires tremendous academic discipline, college athletes are better suited to succeed in society than are students who do not participate in college athletics.
(B) The students who voluntarily compete in college athletics are more predisposed to good health than are those who do not.
(C) Few colleges have the resources to increase spending on athletics, a nonessential university program.
(D) People who become active after leading sedentary lives can remarkably decrease their chances of contracting heart disease.
(E) Women, whose average life expectancies exceed men's by seven years, have traditionally had fewer opportunities to participate in college athletics than have men.

14. **Conclusion:** Colleges should expand their athletic departments.

Premises: College athletes are less likely to die young; expanded departments would allow more people to participate in college athletics.

Assumption: That it is participation in athletics that makes people live longer, rather than something inherent in the people who currently compete in college athletics.

This is a WEAKEN question. Figure out which answer choice has the most negative impact on the conclusion of the argument. Remember to assume the hypothetical truth of each choice and apply it to the argument.

(A) Succeeding in society has no impact on this argument. Eliminate this choice.
(B) This is it. It seems to be saying that the existing athlete population is different health-wise from the college population at large, which would weaken the argument that if we included more people in the program, more people would be healthy.
(C) This doesn't impact the argument that if colleges were able to expand athletic departments, people would be healthier.
(D) This would strengthen the argument, if anything, if we made nonathletes into athletes when they entered college.
(E) Comparing women to men is not revelant. There could be biological (or other) reasons why women live longer than men that are completely unrelated to athletics. For this answer to be relevant, it would need to compare women athletes to women nonathletetes.

SECTION II

QUESTIONS

Questions 15–16

To determine the suitability of candidates for this position, the human resources director evaluates each candidate's advantages; job candidates with greater advantages are more likely to be offered the position. Factors such as work experience and relevant job skills are important in these evaluations, yet age should also be an important consideration. Younger candidates demand lower salaries and are less likely to have family obligations that would interfere with job responsibilities.

15. Which one of the following, if true, most undermines the argument?

(A) Younger workers are more likely to miss work due to social activities than they are to miss work due to family obligations.
(B) Younger workers are more likely to change jobs or quit on short notice if they do not like a new job than are older workers.
(C) Younger workers are more likely to be willing to work long hours and travel frequently than are older workers.
(D) Older workers are more likely to insist on regular working hours and reasonable compensation than are younger workers.
(E) Older workers without family obligations are more similar to younger workers in their professional behavior and expectations than they are to older workers with family obligations.

16. The claim that age should be an important consideration in evaluating job candidates plays which one of the following roles in the argument?

(A) a premise of the argument
(B) the conclusion of the argument
(C) support offered for one of the argument's premises
(D) a consideration that potentially calls the argument's conclusion into question
(E) an explanation of circumstances under which the argument's conclusion is true

EXPLANATIONS

Questions 15–16

Conclusion: Youth should be considered an advantage in hiring.

Premises: Younger workers can be paid less; younger workers have fewer other commitments that detract from their jobs.

Assumption: The identified advantages of youth are not more than compensated for by disadvantages that are not mentioned.

15. This is a WEAKEN question. We want something that tells us why youth shouldn't really be considered an advantage.

(A) This compares two reasons a young employee might miss work; it doesn't involve a comparison between young workers and older workers.
(B) Yes. This identifies a disadvantage of younger workers that doesn't apply to older workers.
(C) This strengthens the argument by identifying an additional advantage of young workers.
(D) This strengthens by identifying a disadvantage of older workers.
(E) This weakens very slightly by showing that not all older workers have the cited disadvantages, but it isn't as clear or direct as (B).

16. This is a REASONING question. The claim mentioned is the conclusion of the argument. (B) is the only possible choice here.

(A) No. The claim mentioned is the conclusion, not a premise.
(B) Yes. This is the primary thing that the argument wants to establish.
(C) No. Anything that supports a premise would also be a premise of the argument; the claim mentioned is the conclusion.
(D) No. It states the conclusion, so it certainly doesn't call it into question.
(E) No. This statement is the conclusion, not a stipulation or a qualification of the conclusion.

SECTION II

QUESTIONS

17. An airline representative announced the introduction of a new pricing system that uses sophisticated computer technology. Based on up-to-the-minute information on sales, the system identifies and continually updates peak times of high demand and off-peak times of low demand, keeping prices high when demand is high and lowering prices to attract customers when demand is low. As a result, the airline anticipates that large numbers of customers will choose to travel off-peak to experience savings, whereas those who wish to travel at peak times will enjoy greater availability due to higher prices. The airline therefore anticipates that the majority of customers will experience significant benefits as a result of the new system.

Which one of the following indicates an error in the reasoning on the part of the airline?

(A) The airline's conclusion is based on an unproven premise.

(B) The airline displays a naive trust in the possibilities of technology.

(C) The airline fails to factor in the cost of implementing the new system.

(D) The airline's conclusion rests on a result that would necessarily cancel out the anticipated benefit.

(E) The airline fails to establish the percentage of customers who would benefit from the change.

EXPLANATIONS

17. **Conclusion:** People will be tempted to buy tickets at off-peak times since prices will be lower and will not buy at peak times since prices will be higher.

Premise: The computer will set the prices so that they are high when demand is high and low when demand is low.

Assumptions: That prices will stay low at off-peak times even though lots of people will want tickets, and will stay high at peak times even though fewer people will want tickets.

This is a FLAW question. Come up with your own description of why the author's conclusion is flawed before you go to the answer choices, and then match your description to the choices.

(A) No, the reason that this argument is flawed is actually much worse than this—the fact that the argument makes no sense, perhaps. Eliminate it.

(B) Assuming that the technology will work is not what's wrong with this line of reasoning. Eliminate it.

(C) This has no impact on the goal of the airline—to pass savings on to its customers. Eliminate it.

(D) Yes. The result, that a large number of people would choose to travel at off-peak times, would cancel the benefit that off-peak times would be cheaper because the system would increase the number of flights as a larger number of people sought to buy tickets.

(E) We're not concerned with the overall percentages here. Eliminate it.

SECTION II

QUESTIONS	EXPLANATIONS

18. Kristen: Compared to a direct business tax cut, a personal income tax cut is a better way to stimulate our state's economy. A personal income tax cut would give residents greater in-pocket income. With this increase in income, individuals will be encouraged to start their own businesses. In addition, individuals will be more likely to spend more money at existing businesses.

Mark: A personal income tax cut is not the most effective way to help business. There is no guarantee that individuals will in fact start new businesses, and the additional income may be used to purchase products from a different state or even a different country.

Mark objects to Kristen's argument by

(A) suggesting that a personal income tax cut is no more important than a direct business tax cut
(B) claiming that Kristen has reached a premature conclusion based on an inadequate understanding of the consequences of a business tax cut
(C) demonstrating that the negative impact of a personal income tax outweighs the positive effects
(D) questioning Kristen's use of the ambiguous phrase "in-pocket income"
(E) indicating that the positive consequences that Kristen predicts may not occur

18. This is a REASONING question. Come up with your own description of how Mark objects to Kristen before you go to the answer choices, and then match your description to the choices.

(A) Importance is not the issue here—effectiveness is. Eliminate it.
(B) No, she's making a mistake with regard to the personal income tax cut—not the business one. Eliminate it.
(C) He doesn't point out any negative impacts of the personal income tax. He just shows that Kristen's positive points may not be so positive.
(D) He doesn't ever question that.
(E) Exactly. He shows how it's possible that neither of Kristen's good outcomes could occur. It's the answer.

SECTION II

QUESTIONS

19. Scholar: Only those who can tell the difference between right and wrong should be held responsible for their wrong actions. It is for this reason that defendants who have serious developmental disabilities or mental illnesses cannot be held responsible for their crimes. However, many children are able to tell the difference between right and wrong and yet are not held responsible for their crimes. Therefore, ________.

Which one of the following most logically completes the last sentence of the scholar's argument?

(A) it is the ability of the parent or parents to tell the difference between right and wrong that is most relevant to determining responsibility when a child is accused of a crime
(B) not all those who are held responsible for a wrong action can tell the difference between right and wrong
(C) it cannot be true that the ability to distinguish between right and wrong is sufficient to hold a defendant responsible for his or her criminal actions
(D) it is unjust for children, or for those who have serious developmental disabilities or mental illnesses, to be found guilty of any crime
(E) only those who can be held responsible for their criminal actions are able to tell the difference between right and wrong

EXPLANATIONS

19. This is most similar to an INFERENCE question. We want to pick the statement that most clearly sums up the rest of the passage.

(A) This goes far beyond the material in the passage.
(B) This is the opposite of the direction the passage is going: children can tell the difference, yet they aren't always held responsible.
(C) Yes. If everyone who could tell the difference were held responsible, then many children would be held responsible.
(D) This brings in the concept "unjust," which isn't explicitly used in the passage.
(E) This contradicts the passage, which identifies some people who can tell the difference who aren't held responsible.

SECTION II

QUESTIONS

20. Statistics show that there is a direct correlation between the ammonia content and the cleaning power of industrial-strength floor and tile cleaners; simply stated, the more ammonia, the better the cleaner. However, in a nationwide survey of commercial food services, cleaning supervisors uniformly replied that for any floor and tile cleaner to be effective, it must be used on a given surface twice a day with the right proportion of cleaner to water, and must be applied with well-maintained mops. The survey thus proves that ammonia content is not relevant to the efficacy of floor and tile cleaners after all.

Which one of the following best identifies the flawed reasoning in the passage above?

(A) There is no reason to assume that effective floor and tile cleaning is the only use for floor and tile cleaner.

(B) It cannot be assumed that industrial-strength floor and tile cleaners contain comparable levels of ammonia.

(C) It is unreasonable to conclude that the ammonia content is not relevant to a cleaner's efficacy just because there are requirements for the proper use of industrial-strength floor and tile cleaners.

(D) It cannot be assumed that the efficacy of all industrial-strength floor and tile cleaners depends on the same procedures for use.

(E) It is unreasonable to assume that the makers of industrial-strength floor and tile cleaners are unaware that food services don't always use them properly.

EXPLANATIONS

20. **Conclusion:** Ammonia content is not relevant to cleaner efficacy.

Premise: For a cleaner to be effective, it must be used with the right proportion of water and applied with a mop twice a day.

Assumption: That because you must do other things to make a cleaner effective, ammonia has nothing to do with cleaner effectiveness.

This is a FLAW question. Come up with your own description of why the author's conclusion is flawed before you go to the answer choices, and then match your description to the choices.

(A) This answer choice is an excellent example of LSAT gibberish. Eliminate it.

(B) Why not? Because you know that's true in life? We're talking about the argument. Eliminate it.

(C) That's right. The other requirements don't just make the ammonia issue evaporate. No pun intended.

(D) The author is flawed in assuming that ammonia content isn't relevant, not in discussing procedure.

(E) The awareness of the cleaner makers is out of the scope of this argument.

SECTION II

QUESTIONS

21. Products containing naproxen sodium produce relief from pain and fever by blocking prostaglandins. As a consequence of recent technological advances, production costs for pain and fever medications containing naproxen sodium, allowing for both packaging and marketing costs, are one-fifth of what they were ten years ago, while the corresponding cost for medications using the ingredient ibuprofen, which is produced by different means, has increased. Therefore, naproxen sodium is a less costly ingredient to use in medication for the prevention of pain and fever relief than ibuprofen.

The conclusion of the argument is properly drawn if which one of the following is assumed?

(A) The cost of producing pain and fever medication containing ibuprofen has increased over the past ten years.
(B) Ten years ago, ibuprofen was used more than five times as often as naproxen sodium.
(C) None of the recent technological advances in producing pain and fever medication with naproxen sodium can be applied to the production of medication using ibuprofen.
(D) Ten years ago, the cost of producing pain and fever medication with the ingredient naproxen sodium was less than five times the cost of producing medications with ibuprofen.
(E) The cost of producing pain and fever medication with naproxen sodium is expected to decrease further, while the cost of producing similar medications using ibuprofen is not expected to decrease.

EXPLANATIONS

21. **Conclusion:** Naproxen sodium is less costly than is ibuprofen.

Premises: Naproxen sodium costs one fifth what it did ten years ago, while ibuprofen costs somewhat more.

Assumption: Naproxen sodium was not five times as expensive or more than was ibuprofen ten years ago.

This is a STRENGTHEN question. Figure out which answer choice has the most positive impact on the conclusion of the argument. Remember to assume the hypothetical truth of each choice and apply it to the argument.

(A) Nope. We need something that links the price of naproxen and ibuprofen. Eliminate it.
(B) The frequency of use of either product is outside the scope of the argument.
(C) Bummer, but we're not trying to help the ibuprofen makers here anyway. Eliminate it.
(D) Bingo. If you work out the math, you'll see that it's now a certainty that naproxen is less costly than ibuprofen.
(E) But if naproxen were *really* expensive as compared to the possibly super-cheap ibuprofen originally, this wouldn't necessarily make the conclusion work.

QUESTIONS

22. Some critics of Western medicine blame medical schools for encouraging doctors to treat sick people as defective machines rather than as feeling humans. These critics believe that if medical schools dedicate a greater portion of their curriculum to teaching compassion and medical ethics, the overall quality of medical treatment will improve. But if doctors are trained to identify with their patients too strongly, they may be reluctant to recommend courses of treatment that, although painful, are necessary to maximize the patients' chances of recovery.

The critics' reasoning provides grounds for accepting which one of the following statements?

(A) It is easier for a doctor to recommend painful chemotherapy to a cancer patient when that doctor has an understanding of his or her ethical responsibilities to the patient.

(B) It is more difficult to know what course of treatment is appropriate for a patient with a liver disorder if a doctor does not identify with that patient as a defective machine.

(C) It is easier for a doctor to recommend a transplant for a patient who is experiencing kidney failure if the doctor feels sympathy for the difficulty that patient will experience in recovering from surgery.

(D) It is easier for a doctor who feels compassion for a patient experiencing chronic pain to treat that patient effectively, particularly when the chronic pain does not seem to be caused by any known medical disorder.

(E) It is easier for doctors to think of their patients as defective machines than it is to think of them as feeling humans.

EXPLANATIONS

22. This is an INFERENCE question. We want something that is a correct conclusion from the passage material.

(A) "Medical ethics" is mentioned in the passage, but we aren't told how this would change a doctor's behavior.

(B) This mixes up the "identifying with a patient" and "defective machine" claims in the passage. There's no way we can conclude this.

(C) The only passage material about sympathy in treatment indicates it might be harder for a sympathetic doctor to recommend difficult treatment.

(D) Yes. This is a case in which sympathy leads to better care than treating the patient as a defective machine would.

(E) We have no information about which way of viewing a patient is easier for a doctor.

SECTION II

QUESTIONS

23. Increasing the starting pay for our sales agents will allow us to attract and hire more new sales agents next year; unfortunately, such an increase would anger experienced sales agents, causing more of them to quit next year. The increase in new hires we would be able to attract at the higher pay rate does not exceed the increase in the number of experienced sales agents who would quit, so increasing the starting pay of our sales agents will not increase the overall number of sales agents we employ.

The reasoning in the argument above most closely parallels that in which one of the following?

(A) Building a dam on this river would decrease the incidence of flooding in the lowlands downstream, but a dam would destroy the river's natural beauty. Tourism is an important component of the area's economy, so the building of a dam on this river is not justified.

(B) Spending additional money on safety training would result in greatly increased costs for our manufacturing operation; because accidents in our manufacturing operation cost more on an annual basis than the increased costs associated with better safety training, improving that training will increase company profits.

(C) Increasing the speed of our assembly line will increase the rate at which goods are produced; at the same time, an increase in the speed of our assembly line will increase the rate of defects. The number of additional losses due to defects will be greater than the number of additional goods produced by the assembly line, so increasing the speed of our assembly line will not increase the number of finished goods we produce.

(D) A new interstate highway will allow travelers to bypass the downtown area, leading to an increase in the rate at which travelers pass through our city; the increased rate of travel will encourage travelers to select routes passing through our city, leading to an increase in patronage of local businesses outside downtown. Therefore, we should build a new interstate highway.

(E) An earlier harvest will allow our tomatoes to reach market shelves more quickly, and will also decrease the number of our tomatoes that spoil before they are sold. however, an earlier harvest will lead to unripe tomatoes being put on market shelves. Because an unripe tomato can be safely eaten, whereas a spoiled tomato cannot, an earlier harvest will make our tomatoes safer for consumers.

EXPLANATIONS

23. **Conclusion:** Increasing starting pay wouldn't increase the overall number of sales agents.

Premises: Increasing starting pay would increase the number of new hires, but it would also increase the number of existing employees who leave; the number of additional new hires is no greater than the number who would be induced to quit.

This is a PARALLEL question. We want a choice that also talks about a measure that has two effects—one causing an increase and the other causing a decrease—in which the sizes of the two effects are compared.

(A) The comparison here isn't between similar quantitative things.

(B) The comparison here is between the increase in spending on training and the overall amount spent on accidents; this might have a chance if the anticipated *change* in the amount spent on accidents were mentioned, but it isn't.

(C) This is it. The increase due to faster production is offset by a decrease due to defects, so speeding up production wouldn't help.

(D) This one doesn't compare an increase and a decrease to the same quantity. This isn't quite parallel.

(E) This one brings in the issue of safety, which isn't quantitative.

SECTION II

QUESTIONS

24. Spokesperson: Horror movies are extremely popular among young moviegoers. A recent study of teenagers and young adults concluded that, after attending horror movies, they were more likely to engage in aggressive or violent behavior. However, experts agree that the methodology of this study was seriously flawed. There can be no doubt, then, that horror movies do not contribute to aggressive or violent behavior among young people who watch them.

The reasoning in the spokesperson's argument is flawed because that argument

(A) takes one failure to prove a contention as confirmation of the falsity of that contention
(B) treats the occurrence of one event preceding a change in behavior as sufficient proof that the event contributed to causing the change in behavior
(C) accepts the judgment of experts as definitive proof of a contention when evidence suggests that the contention is untrue
(D) fails to consider the possibility that a lack of proof for one contention may constitute proof requiring the acceptance of some other contention
(E) neglects to specify that those conducting the study did not have an ulterior motive in reaching the study's erroneous conclusions

EXPLANATIONS

24. **Conclusion**: Horror movies don't contribute to the bad behavior of young people.

Premises: A study concluded that horror movies contribute to bad behavior of young people; experts agree that the study was flawed.

Assumption: No evidence other than the mentioned study links horror movies to bad behavior; a contention that has not been proven cannot be true.

This is a FLAW question. We want a choice that exploits or describes the argument's assumptions.

(A) Yes. The argument does this, and this is indeed its problem.
(B) This relates to the flawed study, not to the spokesperson's argument.
(C) No evidence suggests that the experts' judgment about the study is incorrect.
(D) On the contrary, the argument doesn't fail to consider this fact; it's the (incorrect) method the argument uses to reach its conclusion.
(E) The motives of those who conducted the flawed study aren't relevant to the spokesperson's conclusion.

QUESTIONS

25. Those who read a book without having been exposed to any reviews of it are more likely to say they enjoyed the book than they are to say that they did not. Yet when readers who previously claimed to enjoy a book are exposed to several negative reviews of it and then are asked whether they would read the book again, a majority of them say they would not. Thus, exposure to reviews about a book may cause readers to change their opinions of that book.

    Which one of the following is an assumption required by the argument?

    (A) Readers with favorable opinions of a book they have read are not unlikely to say they would read that book again.
    (B) Exposure to reviews of a book they have previously read causes readers to notice flaws in the book that they did not notice on a first reading.
    (C) Readers are not more likely to enjoy reading a book they have purchased than they are to enjoy reading a book they have borrowed from a library or a friend.
    (D) Readers who claim to have enjoyed a book and are subsequently exposed to positive reviews of it are also likely to say they will not read the book again.
    (E) Whether a book receives positive or negative reviews is an accurate reflection of that book's quality.

EXPLANATIONS

25. **Conclusion**: Exposure to reviews of a book can change a reader's opinion of it.

    Premises: Most people say they enjoy a book when they read it without having read reviews; most people who say they enjoyed a book say they will not reread it after having read some reviews.

    Assumptions: Willingness to reread a book is a reliable indicator of whether a reader has a favorable opinion of that book.

    This is an ASSUMPTION question. We want to pick the choice that the argument requires for its conclusion to be correct.

    (A) Yes. If this is untrue—if a reader who likes a book is unlikely to say that he or she will reread it—then the argument's reasoning falls apart.
    (B) This would strengthen the argument, but it's too specific to be something the argument needs.
    (C) This brings in questions of how the reader got the book; this doesn't have any clear impact on the argument's reasoning.
    (D) This might weaken the argument, but it isn't an assumption.
    (E) How good the book actually is isn't relevant to the argument's conclusion.

SECTION III

Directions: Each passage in this section is followed by a group of questions to be answered on the basis of what is stated or implied in the passage. For some questions, more than one of the choices could conceivably answer the question. However, you are to choose the best answer, that is, the response that most accurately and completely answers the question, and blacken the corresponding space on your answer sheet.

Questions 1–5 refer to the following passage:

One of the most prolific authors of all time, Isaac Asimov was influential both in science fiction and in the popularization of science during the twentieth century, but he is also justly famous for the scope of his interests. Although the common claim that Asimov is the only author to have written a book in every category of the Dewey decimal system is untrue, its spirit provides an accurate picture of the man: a dedicated humanist who lauded the far-reaching power of reason. His most famous work, the *Foundation* trilogy, can be read as an illustration of Asimov's belief in reason and science, but even while he expressed that belief, science itself was calling it into question.

Foundation describes a time in which a vast Empire spanning the galaxy is on the verge of collapse. Its inevitable doom is a consequence not of its size, but of the shortsightedness of its leaders. In this environment, a scientist named Hari Seldon devises an all-encompassing plan to help human civilization recover from the trauma of the Empire's coming collapse. Using mathematics, Seldon is able to predict the future course of history for thousands of years, and he takes steps that are geared toward guiding that future in a beneficial direction. The trope of the benevolent and paternalistic scientist shaping existence from behind the scenes, present in much of Asimov's fiction, is never more explicit than in the *Foundation* series, which describes with an epic sweep the course and progress of the Seldon Plan.

As naïve and, perhaps, self-serving as the conceit of *Foundation* may seem to contemporary readers, it retains to some degree its ability to comfort by offering an antidote to the complex and unpredictable nature of experience. Science in Asimov's time was, in popular conceptions, engaged in just this pursuit: discerning immutable laws that operate beneath a surface appearance of contingency, inexplicability, and change. But even while Asimov wrote, science itself was changing. In physics, the study of matter at the subatomic level showed that indeterminacy was not a transitory difficulty to be overcome, but an essential physical principle. In biology, the sense of evolution as a steady progress toward better-adapted forms was being disturbed by proof of past large-scale evolution taking place in brief explosions of frantic change. At the time of Asimov's death, even mathematics was gaining popular notice for its interest in chaos and inexplicability. Usually summarized in terms of the so-called "butterfly effect," chaos theory showed that perfect prediction could take place only on the basis of perfect information, which was by nature impossible to obtain. Science had dispensed with the very assumptions that motivated Asimov's idealization of it in the Seldon Plan. Indeed, it was possible to see chaos at work in *Foundation* itself: as sequels multiplied and began to be tied into narrative threads from Asimov's other novels, the urge to weave one grand narrative spawned myriad internal inconsistencies that were never resolved.

SECTION III

QUESTIONS	EXPLANATIONS

1. Which one of the following most accurately expresses the main point of the passage?

   (A) Isaac Asimov's greatest work, the *Foundation* trilogy, is an expression of the common trope of the benevolent and paternalistic scientist.
   (B) Popularizations of science are always to some degree dependent on idealizations and simplifications of that science, as Isaac Asimov's work demonstrates.
   (C) The impossibility of the conceit on which Isaac Asimov's *Foundation* trilogy is based demonstrates that Asimov's fiction was based on imperfect understandings of science.
   (D) The central figure of Hari Seldon in Isaac Asimov's *Foundation* trilogy is a manifestation of humanism's idealization of reason and science.
   (E) Isaac Asimov's idealization of science as revealed in his Foundation series was called into question by the science of his time, which was increasingly focused on chaos and indeterminacy.

1. This is a GENERAL question. We're looking for the main point.

   (A) This is too narrow; it leaves out the material in the third paragraph.
   (B) The emphasis here is wrong; it focuses on popularizations of science and Asimov merely as one example, whereas the passage is primarily concerned with Asimov's work.
   (C) The tone here is wrong; the passage isn't concerned with showing that Asimov didn't understand science.
   (D) This is too narrow; it's too focused on Seldon specifically and leaves out the larger implications from the third paragraph.
   (E) Yes. This has pieces from all three paragraphs and is consistent with the author's tone.

2. Which one of the following statements most accurately expresses the purpose of the final paragraph?

   (A) The ultimate failure of the *Foundation* series as a coherent scientific narrative is discussed.
   (B) A claim is made about the purpose of Asimov's writing and then is finally rejected.
   (C) A key theme of Asimov's *Foundation* series is described and discoveries in science that seem contrary to that theme are outlined.
   (D) The history of science is used to demonstrate the falsity of a widely believed claim about the power of human reason.
   (E) The works of Asimov are used as evidence against a popular belief that Asimov encouraged but may not have personally held.

2. This is a GENERAL question. We're looking for a good summary of the third paragraph.

   (A) The tone here is wrong; "ultimate failure" is a bit too strong.
   (B) This isn't similar to the paragraph. No claim about Asimov's fiction is considered and rejected.
   (C) Yes. This contains the two main topics of the paragraph, and the tone matches the author's.
   (D) This is too general. It needs to include some reference to Asimov's work specifically.
   (E) This seems contrary to the passage; the themes of Asimov's works are represented as ones he definitely believed in.

3. The author's reference to a common claim made about Isaac Asimov (lines 5–7) serves to

   (A) demonstrate that many untrue beliefs are held about him
   (B) illustrate the broad scope of his interests and writings
   (C) undermine the claim that he was a prolific writer
   (D) substantiate his belief in the power of human reason
   (E) indicate that he was only interested in science

3. This is a SPECIFIC question. We're working with the statement that Asimov wrote at least one book in every Dewey decimal category.

   (A) The statement is untrue, but this isn't identified as one of many untrue things that are believed about him.
   (B) Yes. Although the statement is untrue, the passage says that "its spirit provides an accurate picture of the man."
   (C) The passage itself states that Asimov was prolific.
   (D) This isn't as directly related to the cited statement as (B) is.
   (E) This contradicts passage information.

SECTION III

QUESTIONS	EXPLANATIONS

4. With respect to the Seldon Plan, the author's attitude can most properly be described as

(A) amused at the naïve conception of history it implies
(B) uncertain of the practical impossibility of its application
(C) ambivalent because of the reliance on human reason it requires
(D) convinced that it illustrates Asimov's attitude toward science
(E) confident that continued scientific progress will make it practicable

4. This is a SPECIFIC question. We're dealing with statements in the second paragraph.

(A) "Amused" is the wrong tone here.
(B) On the contrary, the passage's whole point is to show that it's blatantly impossible.
(C) "Ambivalent" is the wrong tone here.
(D) Yes. This is a primary piece of evidence in the passage's description of Asimov's beliefs about the power of science.
(E) No; this is even worse than (B).

5. Which one of the following statements best illustrates the "butterfly effect" as it is described in the passage's third paragraph?

(A) A system implemented to predict the weather worldwide for the next century is soon found to be inaccurate because it was supplied with incomplete data.
(B) Efforts to predict the result of a nuclear reaction fail because of indeterminacy inherent in the behavior of subatomic particles.
(C) The fossil record indicates that certain adaptations found in many organisms appeared soon after a past catastrophic event.
(D) Scientific predictions about the future course of human history are found to be reasonably accurate once existing social theories are reconciled.
(E) A map that is less detailed than the area it represents is found not to include all the important features of that area.

5. This is a COMPLEX question. We're looking for an illustration of the effect described in the third paragraph.

(A) Yes. The referenced area of the passage explains the effect as showing that perfect prediction is impossible because perfect knowledge is.
(B) This has to do with described advances in physics, which are in a different part of this paragraph.
(C) This has to do with described advances in biology, which are in a different part of this paragraph.
(D) This contradicts the idea described in the passage.
(E) This doesn't have to do with inevitable errors in predictions.

SECTION III

Questions 6–12 refer to the following passage:

Renowned for its canals and rich history, the Italian city of Venice is most famous for the singular peril it faces: the city is sinking. Situated in a lagoon, in the midst of a marsh bordering on the Adriatic Sea, Venice remained a capital of Mediterranean trade for centuries, in part because the few navigable channels through the lagoon were a closely guarded secret, and without that knowledge no enemy could hope to invade. In more recent times, Venice's distinctive character has become a threat to the city's future even as it draws millions of visitors every year.

In the fourteenth century, city leaders became concerned that silt deposited by the four rivers that once emptied into Venice's lagoon were threatening to clog the deep channels on which their trading ships depended. The solution was a public works project of staggering scope: Over the course of two centuries, the rivers were diverted through canals so that they emptied elsewhere. Although this expedient preserved the deep channels leading to the city itself, it had an unanticipated effect: the main source of new sediment entering the lagoon was cut off, removing one major contributor in the dynamic reformation of the lagoon's landscape.

The "bedrock" on which Venice is built is a mile-thick layer of river sediment, deposited over a period of millennia. Such sediments naturally compact under the weight of the material above, and as a result, the land in Venice's lagoon has been sinking throughout its history. With the rivers diverted, the major source of replenishment for the area's land is no longer operating, giving the upper hand to storm and tide in their efforts to reclaim the lagoon. But even were the rivers' former courses to be restored—an action no one seriously recommends—that by itself would not constitute a solution to Venice's problem.

Archaeological data indicate that Venice's residents have historically coped with the land's subsidence by rebuilding. Multiple layers of old foundations demonstrate that Venice has been racing against the loss of land throughout its history; some floors from Roman times are now five feet below sea level. Although such solutions worked well in an atmosphere where historical preservation was not a priority, Venice's economic strength rests now on the foundation of tourism. The fact that modern-day Venice has become more a museum than a working city lends particular urgency and difficulty to the efforts to preserve it.

There is reason to believe that these efforts must be undertaken soon. Even while the land sinks, sea levels in the Adriatic Sea rise. Prediction is difficult, but most estimates put the water-level rise in the next century in the range of fifteen to thirty inches. A century ago, Venice's signature landmark—St. Mark's square—was flooded an average of nine times a year; now, after roughly ten inches of loss versus sea level, it is flooded one hundred times in an average year. Unless radical steps are taken, within another century, most experts agree that it will be submerged year-round.

SECTION III

QUESTIONS	EXPLANATIONS

6. The primary purpose of the discussion in the second paragraph is to

(A) argue that the blame for Venice's current problems rests with its past leaders
(B) provide historical context that describes one contributing factor in Venice's dilemma
(C) explain why the problem Venice faces is unique among the world's cities
(D) show that human intervention in Venice's environment has taken place throughout its history
(E) prove that the landscape of Venice's lagoon is being dynamically reformed

6. This is a GENERAL question. We want the choice that provides a good summary of the second paragraph.

(A) The tone here is wrong; the material in this paragraph describes one source of the problem, but it isn't solely responsible for the problem.
(B) Yes. History is used to describe one reason for the severity of the current problem.
(C) The problem's uniqueness is described most clearly in the first paragraph; this is the wrong emphasis.
(D) The emphasis here is wrong; certainly the discussion supports this contention, but this isn't the direction the passage takes this material.
(E) The emphasis here is wrong; this has always been true of the lagoon, but this paragraph describes a past event that influenced how it is happening.

7. Given the descriptions in the passage, which one of the following is most analogous to the method by which Venetians have historically coped with their sinking land?

(A) A Japanese shrine has stood in the same location for centuries, but because it has traditionally been constructed of materials that are not durable, it has been periodically rebuilt throughout its history.
(B) A German castle was originally built on a river island that experienced severe erosion, so within the past century, the castle was moved to more stable ground on the riverbank.
(C) A Roman temple was originally built of quarried marble, but since then, local residents have largely dismantled the building to use its marble in other construction.
(D) An American armory built in the nineteenth century is no longer used for its original purpose but has instead been converted into a convention hall.
(E) A Russian hotel that was a symbol of the former Soviet regime is demolished both because of its history and because contemporary residents now believe the building is an eyesore.

7. This is a COMPLEX question. We're looking for a situation similar to the one described in the fourth paragraph.

(A) Yes. This describes another situation in which loss is compensated for by new building on the same spot.
(B) This describes a situation in which loss is compensated for by moving a building elsewhere.
(C) This describes a situation in which new building leads directly to loss.
(D) This describes a situation in which an old building is adapted to suit new purposes.
(E) This describes a situation in which intentional demolition leads to loss of a building.

SECTION III

QUESTIONS

8. The passage's predictions about the likely future incidence of flooding in St. Mark's square would be most weakened if which one of the following were found to be true?

(A) Variations in water level attributable to storm surge are primarily responsible for the current flooding in St. Mark's square.
(B) The flooding in St. Mark's square could be mostly prevented by the installation of inflatable gates in the channels leading into the lagoon, a massive project opposed by environmentalists.
(C) Steps taken in the Low Countries of Europe, many parts of which are below sea level, are effective at preventing flooding there.
(D) A moderate increase in the height of the canal walls at the edges of St. Mark's square would prevent flooding, even if sea levels were to rise substantially.
(E) Although many proposed plans exist to halt the flooding of St. Mark's square, most are controversial either because they are too radical or because they are likely to be ineffective.

9. Each of the following can be inferred from the passage EXCEPT:

(A) The earliest buildings constructed in the lagoon of Venice are now below sea level.
(B) River sediments deposited in the lagoon of Venice compacted over time even before humans settled in the area.
(C) Venice's primary source of economic viability is no longer Mediterranean trade.
(D) Water levels in the Adriatic Sea are rising at a faster rate than are water levels in other large bodies of water worldwide.
(E) Some factor other than secrecy surrounding the navigable channels of the lagoon has contributed to Venice's economic security.

EXPLANATIONS

8. This is a COMPLEX question. We want a statement that weakens the last sentence of the passage.

(A) This doesn't tell us that radical measures may not be required to prevent flooding.
(B) This strengthens the statement by indicating that radical measures may be required.
(C) This suggests that the problem may be prevented, but we don't know how radical the preventive measures will need to be.
(D) Yes. This describes a relatively modest measure that, according to the choice, would solve the problem.
(E) This strengthens by suggesting that effective solutions may have to be radical.

9. This is a SPECIFIC question. Four of these statements will be supported by the passage, and the fifth will be our answer.

(A) This can be concluded from the statements about Roman construction in the fourth paragraph.
(B) This can be concluded from the statements about natural compaction of river sediments in the third paragraph.
(C) This can be concluded from the statements about Venice's current economy in the fourth paragraph, or alternatively from statements about its history in the first paragraph.
(D) Here we go. We're told that water levels are rising, but not how the rate of the rise compares to the rate elsewhere.
(E) This can be concluded from the statements in the first paragraph describing the factors that "in part" led to Venice's trade success, or the statement in the fourth paragraph that "Venice's economic strength rests now on the foundation of tourism."

QUESTIONS

10. The passage's author would be most likely to agree with which one of the following statements concerning modern-day Venice?

(A) The preservation of its historic buildings should be a priority.
(B) The environmental health of the salt marshes in its lagoon must be protected.
(C) Its survival depends on stopping the subsidence of land on which it is built.
(D) Moderate measures are adequate to protect it from rising sea levels.
(E) It must become more of a working city than it currently is to survive.

11. Based on the passage, the author most likely holds which one of the following opinions concerning past alterations to Venice's environment?

(A) They are solely responsible for Venice's current difficulties.
(B) They were undertaken without full knowledge of their consequences.
(C) They must be reversed for Venice to survive.
(D) They have contributed to the rise in water levels in the Adriatic Sea.
(E) They could have been prevented by responsible city leadership.

12. From the passage, it can be inferred that

(A) water levels in the Adriatic Sea will rise more than twenty inches in the next century
(B) the level of land in Venice's lagoon will sink more than ten inches in the next century
(C) St. Mark's square will flood less than one hundred times per year over the next century
(D) Venice is likely to lose more elevation versus sea level in the next century than it did in the previous century
(E) some of Venice's historical landmarks will be lost in the next century

EXPLANATIONS

10. This is a SPECIFIC question. The phrase "modern-day" points to the last sentence in the fourth paragraph.

(A) Yes. This relates to the nearby claim about the "foundation" of "Venice's economic strength."
(B) Environmental effects on the salt marshes aren't discussed in the passage.
(C) The passage indicates that this can't be stopped.
(D) This contradicts statements in the passage.
(E) This is not a recommendation the author ever makes.

11. This is a SPECIFIC question. The stem points us to the discussion in the second paragraph of diverting rivers.

(A) No, the passage says that this contributes to the problem but is not solely responsible for it.
(B) Yes. This comes from the comment that diverting the rivers had "an unanticipated effect."
(C) The passage says that no one has seriously recommended restoring the rivers' courses, and that this change wouldn't solve the problem anyway.
(D) This is not said anywhere in the passage.
(E) The tone here is wrong. The author's point in this paragraph isn't to show that past city leaders were irresponsible.

12. This is a SPECIFIC question. We're looking for direct passage report for one of the choices.

(A) The passage says that the water-level rise will most likely be from fifteen to thirty inches.
(B) Although the passage talks about the loss of elevation versus sea level, it seems to focus on rising water as the cause of this, rather than sinking land.
(C) On the contrary, the passage predicts it will flood more often if nothing is done.
(D) Yes. The passage says that sea-level rises are likely to be in the range of fifteen to thirty inches; taking the sinking land into account, the loss versus sea level would be larger. The passage says it lost ten inches versus sea level in the last century. This leaves us plenty of wiggle room.
(E) This is a danger identified by the passage, but it doesn't predict that this will definitely happen.

SECTION III

Questions 13–19 refer to the following passage:

The work of Amartya Sen, winner of the Nobel Prize for economics in 1998, has helped usher in a new era in the field as it is practically applied throughout the world. Institutions such as the United Nations have adopted his ideas in measuring and aiding the development of emerging economies, and the consequences of the social-choice theory he employs have garnered much public attention.

The classic defining work of social choice theory is Ken Arrow's careful investigation of voting through a series of thought experiments. The result—Arrow's Impossibility Theorem—showed that no method of conducting a majority-decision vote can be guaranteed to conform to the basic requirements of democracy. A simple example illustrates Arrow's idea: For an electorate of three voters—1, 2, and 3—there are three candidates—A, B, and C. Voter 1 prefers A to B, and B to C; voter 2 prefers B to C, and C to A; voter 3 prefers C to A, and A to B. In such an electorate, a runoff between A and B declares A the winner; a runoff between B and C is won by B; and a runoff between A and C is won by C. Whichever candidate wins, that candidate is actually less preferable to the electorate than the candidate who was not involved in the runoff.

The work for which Sen was awarded his Nobel Prize is, in essence, an application of such methods to national economies, politics, and public welfare. Just as Arrow focused on paradoxes within democratic systems, Sen investigated instances such as famine in which capitalist market systems seem not to function properly, according to traditional economic public-choice principles. Public choice focuses on self-interest as the driving factor in economics; Sen, in a famous quote, shows the flaw in this view: "'Can you direct me to the railway station?' asks the stranger. 'Certainly,' says the local, pointing in the opposite direction, towards the post office, 'and would you post this letter for me on your way?' 'Certainly,' says the stranger, resolving to open it to see if it contains anything worth stealing." Factors other than self-interest exert their influence at every level within a society, and only by incorporating them can a theory truly describe how economies function.

This departure from traditional views has made Sen's work a subject in the ongoing debate over globalization. Partisans who advocate the spread of capitalism and democracy have called Sen everything from an anarchist to a Marxist; opponents of globalization use his work as proof that these institutions are not the boon they are supposed to be. By doing so, both sides misrepresent Sen's concerns. One of his early works demonstrated the conditions under which Arrow's Impossibility Theorem does not apply to democratic elections, and Sen is most famous for his notion of "capability" as an antidote to economic injustice. The specific forms "capability" takes—education and equal access—are precisely those that are called for in theoretical formulations of how choice-driven markets and democracies are supposed to function. Sen's work is an examination of the failures of these core systems, but it is also a roadmap to realizing their promise.

SECTION III

QUESTIONS	EXPLANATIONS

13. Which one of the following most accurately expresses the main idea of the passage?

(A) Although the work of Amartya Sen has been viewed as opposing democracy and global capitalism, in fact it is a defense of these ideas.
(B) Amartya Sen's revolutionary use of social choice theory in economics has been widely misinterpreted but nevertheless offers hope that social justice can be achieved in capitalist and democratic systems.
(C) The work of social choice theorists such as Ken Arrow and Amartya Sen has helped their theories supplant public choice theory as the most widely accepted theoretical approach to economics.
(D) Amartya Sen's work delineates the circumstances under which commonly accepted notions of how economic and democratic systems operate can be said to be correct.
(E) Social choice theory does not include considerations of self-interest in its evaluation of economic and democratic institutions.

13. This is a GENERAL question. We're looking for the main point.

(A) The tone here is wrong. It's too much to say that the passage represents Sen's work as a "defense" of these ideas.
(B) This is it. It includes all the major components of the passage and is appropriately qualified.
(C) The emphasis here is wrong; the passage isn't just about social choice. Also, we're never told that it's replaced other theories.
(D) The tone here is wrong. This is too neutral to represent the author's views correctly.
(E) The emphasis here is wrong; it's too narrowly focused on one issue in the passage, and it overstates the passage's treatment of that issue.

14. Which one of the following titles provides the most complete and accurate summary of the passage's contents?

(A) "Nobel Prizewinner Amartya Sen: Reluctant Economic Rebel"
(B) "Social Choice Theory: Moving Beyond Self-Interest"
(C) "Arrow's Impossibility Theorem: Why No Election Is Fair"
(D) "Economics and Social Justice: Amartya Sen's Groundbreaking Work"
(E) "Fighting the Future: The Rising Opposition to Globalization"

14. This is a GENERAL question. We're looking for a title that comes closest to encapsulating the passage.

(A) The tone here is wrong; calling Sen a "rebel" isn't consistent with the passage's treatment of him.
(B) This is a bit too general. It would be nice to have a choice that focuses on Sen.
(C) The emphasis here is really wrong. The passage isn't primarily about Arrow.
(D) Yes. This has Sen, social justice, and a positive spin on both.
(E) This is far too general, has the wrong emphasis, and doesn't even mention Sen or social choice.

QUESTIONS	EXPLANATIONS

15. The passage supports the inference that the author most likely holds which one of the following views?

(A) Existing economic theories are incapable of explaining why self-interest fails to prevent famine and social injustice.
(B) No majority-decision election conducted under any circumstances is capable of fulfilling even the most basic promises of democracy.
(C) Those who believe that Amartya Sen's work is intended to oppose economic globalization misunderstand it.
(D) Social choice theory does not constitute a legitimate alternative to traditional theoretical explanations of economic action.
(E) Amartya Sen is the first economist to take social considerations into account in the analysis of institutions such as democratic elections and the free market.

15. You can't be sure, but this is most likely a SPECIFIC question. We'd like direct passage support for our answer.

(A) "Incapable" is an overstatement of information about Sen's work in the third paragraph.
(B) This contradicts statements about Sen's work in the fourth paragraph, which in part says that the Arrow's theorem doesn't always apply.
(C) Yes. This is directly supported by statements in the fourth paragraph.
(D) This contradicts the passage's third paragraph.
(E) This contradicts the passage's second paragraph, in which we learn that Arrow worked in social choice before Sen.

16. As it is described in the passage, Ken Arrow's method for investigating democratic elections is most analogous to which one of the following?

(A) To discern universal physical principles, a physicist imagines what it would be like to ride a beam of light.
(B) To evaluate existing theories of evolution, a paleontologist undertakes a survey of the fossil record.
(C) To learn about daily life in an ancient civilization, an anthropologist studies the traditional culture of the civilization's descendants.
(D) To evaluate the success of market reforms, an economist studies changes in key indicators.
(E) To discover political attitudes within a local area, a sociologist interviews religious leaders in the area.

16. This is a COMPLEX question. The reference is to the second paragraph.

(A) Yes. Arrow's work is described as "a series of thought experiments."
(B) This choice involves using evidence from the past, not thought experiments.
(C) This choice involves using specific observations, not thought experiments.
(D) This choice involves using measurement tools, not thought experiments.
(E) This choice involves using personal statements, not thought experiments.

17. The author's attitude toward social choice theory can most accurately be described as being

(A) skeptical that it will ever gain wide acceptance
(B) uncertain whether it correctly describes economic realities
(C) ambivalent about its critique of globalization
(D) satisfied that it represents an advance in economic understanding
(E) enthusiastic about its usefulness in reforming democratic elections

17. This is likely to be a SPECIFIC question. We're hoping for direct passage support for our answer.

(A) This seems to contradict statements in the first paragraph.
(B) The tone here is wrong; the author seems to think social choice theory is pretty nifty.
(C) The tone here is wrong; the author doesn't seem to be unable to come to a conclusion.
(D) Yes. This is most clearly indicated in the first and third paragraphs, although there isn't an outright statement of the fact.
(E) Practical applications for election reform aren't really addressed by the passage.

QUESTIONS	EXPLANATIONS

18. The passage suggests that which one of the following would provide the best definition of Sen's idea of "capability?"

(A) willingness to fill multiple economic roles
(B) access to legal redress for injustice
(C) capacity to exercise democratic and economic choice
(D) knowledge of underlying principles of economics
(E) assistance through the redistribution of wealth

18. This is a SPECIFIC question. The reference is to the fourth paragraph.

(A) Mobility and adaptability aren't really the ideas described here.
(B) "Access" and "justice" are key terms in the description, but "legal redress" doesn't really come out of the passage.
(C) Yes. Markets and democracies are described as "choice-driven" in this area of the passage.
(D) The passage doesn't require that everyone be an economist.
(E) This goes too far; the passage doesn't say that Sen is in favor of anything like this.

19. Each of the following is stated or implied by the passage EXCEPT:

(A) Arrow's Impossibility Theorem does not hold for all democratic elections.
(B) Public choice theory does not provide a complete description of all economic transactions.
(C) The policies of the United Nations are not primarily concerned with aiding developing nations to achieve social justice.
(D) Amartya Sen's economic beliefs cannot properly be called Marxist.
(E) The precepts of social choice theory have not always informed economic policies.

19. This is a SPECIFIC question. We'll find passage support for four of the choices, and the fifth will be our answer.

(A) This is stated in the fourth paragraph, in a description of Sen's early work.
(B) This is stated at the end of the third paragraph.
(C) Yes. We aren't given complete enough information about the UN to know this.
(D) This is stated near the beginning of the fourth paragraph.
(E) This is stated right at the beginning of the passage.

Questions 20–27 refer to the following passage:

Perhaps the most fascinating effort to reconcile the apparently contradictory principles of traditional religious law and secular Western law is underway in Indonesia. Indonesia provides a unique laboratory for such experiments: the most populous majority-Muslim nation in the world, Indonesia also has significant minorities with widely varying religious beliefs. Indonesia spent much of the twentieth century in the grip of a secular military dictatorship supported by Western countries, but with the advent of a more democratic civil society, the question of how their legal system should operate has become one of broad, serious public interest and debate.

Indonesia has, in effect, two legal systems. The dominant system is a secular Western-style code founded on the principles of individual human rights and capitalism. The second is founded on Islamic *Sharia* law, derived from key writings as interpreted by religious authorities. In Indonesia, questions of the implementation of *Sharia* law are colored by the presence of an alternative standard and the possibility, in some cases, of individuals choosing between them. The fact that the *Sharia* system must to some degree compete with the secular system leads to interesting tensions and cross-fertilizations between the two.

Although many religious leaders believe that Muslims should follow the precepts of *Sharia*, the latitude of interpretation within it and the fact that Muslim parties are strong within the secular system of representative government foster a variety of positions. Some believe that the two systems are not fundamentally incompatible and support a more liberal interpretation of *Sharia*; this strategy might help *Sharia* to become dominant within Indonesia by removing features that seem discriminatory or overly harsh. However, some conservative Muslims who wield secular power believe that it should be used to inject *Sharia* into daily life; attempts to pass secular laws requiring all Muslims to subject themselves to judgment by *Sharia* courts, or to require Islamic religious instruction of all Muslim children, even if they attend private Christian schools, are examples of ways the secular legal system can itself be used to ensure the primacy of *Sharia*.

In a democratic environment, it seems likely that neither of these approaches will predominate and that social institutions will promote a shifting compromise. The rise of *Sharia* banking provides an encouraging example. Because *Sharia* requires the sharing of profits and forbids charging interest, conventional Western banking models are distasteful to many Muslims. The rise of *Sharia* banks—those that voluntarily follow religious strictures and attract business on that basis—has been so rapid in Indonesia that Western banks have scrambled to provide services that also comply with these requirements. To regulate these banks, the secular authorities have passed laws and set up commissions to ensure compliance with both accepted Western practices and *Sharia* requirements. This instance of cooperation among secular authorities, religious leaders, and the market system offers hope that civil society can foster creative compromise in other areas as well.

SECTION III

QUESTIONS	EXPLANATIONS

20. Which one of the following most accurately expresses the main point of the passage?

(A) Tensions between *Sharia* law and traditional Western legal systems have led to a conflict within Indonesia that has not yet been resolved.
(B) The example of *Sharia* banking in Indonesia provides an example of how civil institutions can foster cultural compromise between competing legal standards.
(C) Indonesia represents a laboratory in which the ongoing conflict between Western secular and traditional religious views of culture can finally be resolved.
(D) Future efforts to resolve cultural conflict in all countries can only be effective if competition fosters cross-fertilization and compromise between legal standards that disagree.
(E) The existence of parallel legal standards in Indonesia represents an unusual circumstance that cannot be sustained and will ultimately be resolved by the fusion of Western and traditional religious principles.

20. This is a GENERAL question. We're looking for the main point of the passage.

(A) The tone here is wrong. It's a bit too neutral and also doesn't include the idea of compromise.
(B) Yes. This places a lot of emphasis on the passage's primary example, but it also includes the idea of competing legal standards.
(C) This is far too general.
(D) This is far too general.
(E) The tone here is wrong. The passage doesn't say that the current state of affairs is unsustainable or that it will be resolved through "fusion," whatever that means.

21. Based on the information contained in the passage about the author's views, which one of the following would represent the most acceptable future compromise between the principles of *Sharia* law and traditional Western law in Indonesia?

(A) parallel legal systems in which defendants are able to choose the standard of judgment most beneficial to them
(B) a single legal system agreed on by democratic means that incorporates aspects of both systems without being excessively harsh or culturally offensive
(C) a set of multiple competing legal systems that operate in local areas depending on the cultural practices accepted in those areas
(D) a single system of liberally interpreted *Sharia* law that is made to apply to all residents by the exercise of Indonesia's secular power
(E) a single system of traditional Western law that makes allowances for the fact that Muslim religious authorities may wish to impose additional penalties on Muslim defendants who have violated the law

21. This is a COMPLEX question. Our general understanding of the author's views will help.

(A) This is the current situation, but it doesn't really represent a future compromise.
(B) Yes. This involves "democratic" institutions and represents a compromise that's more or less acceptable by both Western and religious standards.
(C) This kind of fragmentation isn't what the author is arguing in favor of.
(D) This privileges one system over the other; it isn't the kind of compromise the author seems to want.
(E) This privileges one system over the other; it isn't the kind of compromise the author seems to want.

SECTION III

QUESTIONS	EXPLANATIONS

22. Which one of the following is mentioned in the passage as a characteristic of *Sharia* law?

(A) It contains some latitude for interpretation.
(B) It is marked by the application of precedent.
(C) It includes only weak protections of individual property rights.
(D) It does not provide for equal treatment of all citizens.
(E) It has never been successfully implemented as the basis of a modern legal system.

22. This is a SPECIFIC question. This subject is discussed in several places.

(A) Yes. This statement is included most directly in the third paragraph.
(B) Precedent is not mentioned in connection with *Sharia* law.
(C) Property rights aren't specifically mentioned in connection with *Sharia* law.
(D) Although it is identified as being less concerned with "individual rights" and perhaps, in some views, discriminatory, this seems a bit of an overstatement.
(E) Whether *Sharia* is used elsewhere is not explicitly discussed.

23. The rise of *Sharia* banking in Indonesia, as it is described in the passage, provides an illustration of which one of the following principles?

(A) When a particular business practice is legally required, that requirement may be justified by reference to religious authority.
(B) When a particular business practice is legally permissible but ethically distasteful, businesses may succeed by voluntarily refraining from that practice.
(C) When a particular business practice is legally required but ethically unacceptable, democratic means may be used to alter the applicable legal standards.
(D) When a particular business practice is neither legally nor ethically forbidden, some businesses may nevertheless choose not to engage in that practice.
(E) When a particular business practice is legally permissible but ethically prohibited, a business may nevertheless be forced to engage in that practice to remain viable.

23. This is a COMPLEX question. We're looking for the general statement that's most consistent with the example described in the passage's last paragraph.

(A) The example of *Sharia* banking doesn't demonstrate this kind of compromise.
(B) Yes. *Sharia* banks initially succeeded by voluntarily refusing to engage in certain practices that were legal but not ethical.
(C) No ethically unacceptable practice in this case could be called "legally required."
(D) The example in hand describes a practice that is ethically forbidden, or at least frowned upon.
(E) This is precisely the opposite of the force of this example.

24. Which one of the following questions is most directly answered in the passage?

(A) In what year did the standards of *Sharia* begin to play a role in Indonesian law?
(B) What protections for minorities are currently threatened by those who exercise secular power in Indonesia?
(C) What provisions of traditional Western law do Muslim religious authorities in Indonesia find most distasteful?
(D) What institutions aside from banks have succeeded by appealing to Muslim religious preferences?
(E) What methods have some religious leaders considered employing to increase the power of *Sharia* courts in Indonesia?

24. This is a SPECIFIC question. We're looking for passage material that directly answers one of these questions.

(A) We don't know the precise chronology of the development of Indonesia's system.
(B) We don't know exactly what minority rights may be threatened.
(C) We don't know which of the Western standards is considered the worst.
(D) We don't know of other instances similar to the example of banks.
(E) Yes. This is described near the end of the third paragraph.

SECTION III

QUESTIONS	EXPLANATIONS

25. The purpose of the second paragraph is primarily to

(A) reconcile competing philosophies
(B) provide historical context
(C) describe a noteworthy set of circumstances
(D) indicate possibilities for resolving a dispute
(E) propose strategies for avoiding a problem

25. This is a GENERAL question. We want something that describes the general contents of the second paragraph.

(A) Competing philosophies are mentioned but not reconciled.
(B) Historical context is presented in the first paragraph.
(C) Yes. This is a vanilla but clearly correct description of what the second paragraph does.
(D) Possible resolutions are described in the third and fourth paragraphs.
(E) The passage never tries to propose a way of avoiding problems.

26. It can be most reasonably inferred from the passage that the author believes that an interpretation of *Sharia* law that conforms completely to the principles of Indonesian secular law will be

(A) unlikely to gain the full support of Indonesian religious leaders
(B) essential to the future health of Indonesian democracy
(C) able to prevent Western banks in Indonesia from profiting by charging interest on loans
(D) offensive to the majority of Muslims outside Indonesia
(E) promoted by the cooperative action of all Indonesian social institutions

26. This is a SPECIFIC question. We don't know exactly where passage support will come from, but we want to find it for whatever choice we pick.

(A) Yes. As is mentioned in the third paragraph, some religious leaders believe *Sharia* and secular law aren't "fundamentally incompatible," but some believe they are.
(B) The passage says compromise is necessary, but not that it would have to fit all the principles of secular law.
(C) This goes way too far in trying to use passage material.
(D) Muslims outside Indonesia don't figure in the passage.
(E) The passage says that compromise should be promoted by social institutions, but not that it would have to conform to all secular principles.

QUESTIONS	EXPLANATIONS

27. Which one of the following can most reasonably be concluded from the information in the passage?

(A) The action of the free market in Indonesia is likely to ensure that the Indonesian economy eventually conforms to the principles outlined in *Sharia* law without requiring the intervention of secular authorities.

(B) Elected authorities in Indonesia are not forbidden from exercising secular power to ensure the compliance of some Indonesian businesses with the requirements of *Sharia* law.

(C) Religious leaders of Indonesia's minority groups will have a role in deciding whether any future modification of Indonesia's secular laws should incorporate principles of Islamic *Sharia* law.

(D) Religious authorities in Indonesia are prevented by the country's secular law from seeking elected office unless they agree not to use their secular power to pursue religious goals.

(E) Indonesia's many religious leaders must all work to foster cooperation among themselves if religious tensions in the country are to be minimized.

27. This is a SPECIFIC question. We're looking for direct passage support for our answer.

(A) This goes a bit too far. The free market by itself isn't said to be likely to lead to this result in all cases.

(B) Yes. This comes from the discussion in the last paragraph that the secular authorities set up commissions to ensure compliance with *Sharia* principles.

(C) We don't know much about how minority groups fit into this whole process.

(D) This seems to contradict passage information directly.

(E) The passage doesn't have much to say about religious tensions.

SECTION IV

QUESTIONS

1. In France, children in preschool programs spend a portion of each day engaged in a program of stretching and exercise. Preschool programs in the United States, however, seldom devote time to a daily stretching and exercise program. In tests designed to measure cardiovascular fitness, children in the United States were outperformed by their French counterparts. It can therefore be determined that children attending preschool programs in the United States can achieve cardiovascular fitness only by engaging in a daily school program of stretching and exercise.

   Which one of the following is an assumption on which the argument depends?

   (A) A daily program of stretching and exercise will allow all children to achieve cardiovascular fitness.
   (B) Cardiovascular fitness is integral to one's overall health.
   (C) It has been proven that children who participate in stretching and exercise programs in preschool have better cardiovascular fitness than adults.
   (D) Stretching and exercise are necessary components of French children's superior cardiovascular fitness programs.
   (E) United States preschool children could make healthful dietary changes as well as changes to their daily fitness regimens.

EXPLANATIONS

1. **Conclusion:** U.S. children can achieve cardiovascular fitness only by engaging in daily stretching and exercise.

   Premises: French children are more fit than are U.S. children, and French children engage in daily stretching and exercise.

   Assumptions: There is no other reason that French children have greater cardiovascular fitness; if U.S. children start such a program, they will achieve greater fitness; the reason French children are more fit has something to do with daily stretching and exercise.

   This is an ASSUMPTION question. The correct answer will be something necessary for the conclusion to be true, and, if made false, will make the argument fall apart.

   (A) This certainly strengthens the conclusion that stretching and fitness, applied to children anywhere, will help them achieve cardiovascular nirvana. Is it necessary though? We're only concerned with kids in the United States, so "all" is too extreme.
   (B) We're not concerned with the overall health of the children in this argument. Eliminate it.
   (C) We're not concerned with how fit the children will become when they are adults. Eliminate it.
   (D) If stretching *weren't* a necessary part of the French children's fitness, then the argument that doing the same thing in the United States would have the same result would fall apart. So it's the answer.
   (E) Dietary changes are outside the scope of the argument. Eliminate it.

SECTION IV

QUESTIONS

2. In an effort to lessen the risk of liability, fertility clinics are seeking new methods of record-keeping and storage that would help avoid donor sperm that might contain dangerous genes. Toward this end, a database is being developed to aid the clients in their screening of donor sperm. The database is exhaustively thorough, containing the medical histories of more than twenty thousand people, approximately half of them men.

   Which one of the following, if true, best explains why the database contains the records of almost ten thousand women?

   (A) Small fertility clinics, located in remote areas, wish to have access to a large selection of donor sperm.
   (B) Keeping genetic information on women is a standard procedure for many scientific clinics.
   (C) Some genetic disorders are not expressed until the onset of puberty.
   (D) Some genetic disorders may be carried by, but not manifested in, men who inherited the dangerous gene from their mothers.
   (E) Some genetic disorders are due to the effects of drugs and alcohol during puberty.

3. If the Food and Drug Administration (FDA) does not relax some of its regulations governing the testing of experimental drugs, tens of thousands of U.S. citizens are sure to die as a result of certain diseases before an effective treatment is found and made generally available.

   It follows logically from the statement above that if the FDA does relax some of its regulations governing the testing of experimental drugs, then tens of thousands of U.S. citizens

   (A) will definitely die of certain diseases
   (B) will probably die of certain diseases
   (C) will probably not die of certain diseases
   (D) will not die of certain diseases
   (E) may still die of certain diseases

EXPLANATIONS

2. This is a PARADOX question. Look for an answer choice that allows both parts of the argument to be true, and remember to assume the hypothetical truth of each of the answer choices.

   (A) This doesn't explain why half the records are of women. Eliminate it.
   (B) This looks pretty good, but it doesn't actually explain why this is "standard procedure." Also, it's a bit too general because it says "scientific clinics," and we're talking specifically about fertility clinics. Eliminate it.
   (C) Puberty is outside the scope of the argument. Eliminate it.
   (D) Ah, so we have an example of why the records of the same number of women are kept as of men. It's the answer.
   (E) Puberty is outside the scope of the argument. Eliminate it.

3. This is an INFERENCE question. Your goal is to find the one choice that must be true based on the information in the passage.

   (A) We don't know for sure what will happen if they do relax regulations, only what will happen if they don't. Therefore, look for a wishy-washy answer. This is too extreme.
   (B) This is less extreme than (A), so let's leave it in for right now.
   (C) This has a similar structure to (B), so we now have to eliminate both (B) and (C).
   (D) Too extreme. Eliminate.
   (E) This is the most wishy-washy choice, and therefore, it's the answer.

SECTION IV

QUESTIONS

4. The level of blood sugar for many patients suffering from disease *Q* is slightly higher than the level of blood sugar in the general population. Nonetheless, most medical professionals believe that slightly increasing blood sugar levels is a successful means by which to treat disease *Q*.

This apparently contradictory argument can best be resolved by which one of the following statements?

(A) Blood sugar levels for patients who have been cured of disease *Q* are virtually identical to the levels of blood sugar found in the general population.
(B) Many of the symptoms associated with severe cases of disease *Q* have been recognized in laboratory animals with experimentally induced high blood pressure, but none of the animals developed disease *Q*.
(C) The movement from inactive to advanced states of disease *Q* often occurs because the virus that causes *Q* flourishes during periods when blood sugar levels are slightly low.
(D) The blood sugar level in patients with disease *Q* fluctuates abnormally in response to changes in blood chemistry.
(E) Low levels of blood sugar are symptomatic of many other diseases that are even more serious than disease *Q*.

EXPLANATIONS

4. This is a PARADOX question. Look for an answer choice that allows both parts of the argument to be true, and remember to assume the hypothetical truth of each of the answer choices.

(A) This would exacerbate the paradox, if anything. Eliminate it.
(B) This doesn't do anything to explain the paradox, and blood pressure is out of the scope here. Eliminate it.
(C) So if we are always making sure to keep blood sugar levels high, then we won't ever have these slightly low periods where the virus will flourish. It's the answer.
(D) We don't care why the blood sugar fluctuates. We just want to know why we should keep it high.
(E) Other diseases are outside the scope of the argument.

SECTION IV

QUESTIONS	EXPLANATIONS

5. Activist: There are countries in which the number of handgun deaths per capita is less than one-tenth of the number in our country. Although not all of these countries outlaw handguns, most of them do. Therefore, to reduce the number of handgun deaths in our country, we must outlaw handguns.

Which one of the following is an assumption on which the activist's argument depends?

(A) The number of handgun deaths in a country is primarily determined by the rate of handgun ownership in that country.
(B) Some countries in which handguns are not outlawed have low numbers of handgun deaths per capita because of conditions that cannot be replicated in all other countries.
(C) The number of handgun deaths in a country may be reduced without a corresponding decrease in the number of per capita handgun deaths in that country.
(D) Laws forbidding the ownership of handguns are justified only insofar as those laws are effective in preventing handgun deaths.
(E) Accidents are not a significant cause of handgun deaths in countries where the number of per capita handgun deaths is relatively low.

5. **Conclusion**: We must outlaw handguns to reduce handgun deaths.

Premise: Most of the countries in which handgun deaths are substantially lower outlaw handguns.

Assumptions: Other countries are similar enough that a ban may have similar effects; no means other than a ban will work.

This is an ASSUMPTION question. We're looking for something that's necessary for the argument's conclusion to be true.

(A) The rate of ownership isn't relevant to the conclusion in the strictest sense; the argument doesn't depend on bans working in this specific way.
(B) Yes. If this isn't true—if the result of few gun deaths can be replicated in all countries without banning handguns—then the conclusion is definitely wrong.
(C) Although there is a language shift like this in the argument, the conclusion doesn't depend on this statement being true.
(D) The question of the basis on which a ban is justified is not relevant to the conclusion, which only concerns the ban's effect.
(E) Like (A), this one tries to deal with how a ban would work; the argument doesn't depend on anything that specific.

6. Medical studies indicate that the metabolic rates of professional athletes are substantially greater than those of the average person. So, most likely, a person's speed and strength are primarily determined by that person's metabolic rate.

Which one of the following, if true, most strengthens the argument?

(A) Some professional athletes are either faster or stronger than the average person.
(B) Some professional athletes do not have higher metabolic rates than some people who are not professional athletes.
(C) The speed and strength of people who are not professional athletes are not primarily determined by choices of diet and exercise.
(D) Intensive training such as that engaged in by professional athletes causes an increase in metabolic rate.
(E) Drugs that suppress metabolic rate have been shown to have the side-effect of diminishing the speed and strength of those who are not professional athletes.

6. **Conclusion**: A person's speed and strength are mostly determined by metabolic rate.

Premise: The metabolic rates of professional athletes are higher than those of average people.

Assumptions: Speed and strength are determining factors in whether a person is a professional athlete; no third factor is responsible for speed and strength as well as metabolic rate.

This is a STRENGTHEN question. We want something that supports the conclusion.

(A) This provides very weak support for the argument's causal conclusion.
(B) This choice weakens the argument slightly.
(C) At best, this provides exceptionally weak support for the conclusion.
(D) This choice seems to weaken by suggesting that the causation may be reverse.
(E) Yes. This makes a strong causal connection between metabolic rate and the other factors discussed.

SECTION IV

QUESTIONS

7. Environmentalist: In most land ecologies, grasses are the basis of the food chain. Desertification of several North African areas over the past decade has caused the grasses there to die, leading to serious disruption of the ecology in those areas. Now it has been shown that warming in Antarctic waters is causing a die-off of krill there. Because krill is the basis of the food chain in ocean ecologies, we can anticipate that there will be serious disruption of the ecology in these waters.

The environmentalist's argument proceeds by

(A) demonstrating that ocean ecologies are more delicate than land ecologies
(B) using an analogy to reach the conclusion that some ocean ecologies are in danger
(C) proving that the population of krill in Antarctic waters is decreasing
(D) asserting the role that grasses play in the health of land ecologies
(E) demonstrating that changes in temperature have categorically negative effects on all ecologies

8. Some residents of Woodbridge work the late shift at the nearby factory. Because of the fact that all of the residents of Woodbridge who own cars are also members of the Area Auto Club, the Woodbridge city manager concluded that none of the residents who work the late shift at the nearby factory own cars.

The city manager's conclusion is properly drawn if which one of the following is assumed?

(A) None of the residents of Woodbridge who work the late shift at the nearby factory are members of the Area Auto Club.
(B) None of the residents of Woodbridge who own cars have failed to join the Area Auto Club.
(C) Some of the residents of Woodbridge who do not work the late shift at the nearby factory do not own cars.
(D) All residents of Woodbridge who do not work the late shift at the nearby factory own cars.
(E) All residents of Woodbridge who are members of the Area Auto Club own cars.

EXPLANATIONS

7. This is a REASONING question. We're looking for a choice that refers to the similarity between past developments on land and likely future developments in the ocean.

(A) The two are presented as similar, not different, in this way.
(B) Yes. The analogy is between grasses in land ecologies and krill in ocean ecologies.
(C) This is a premise of the argument; this choice leaves out the conclusion.
(D) Like (C), this choice covers only a part of the argument, leaving out the conclusion.
(E) The argument doesn't make any statement that is this sweeping.

8. **Conclusion**: work late shift → - own car

Premise: own car → AAC member

This is a STRENGTHEN question. We're looking for the additional item of information that would most strongly support the conclusion.

(A) Yes. This choice—work late shift - AAC member—gives us a piece that, when connected to the contrapositive of the premise, guarantees us that the conclusion is correct.
(B) This is a restatement of our premise; it doesn't provide any additional strength.
(C) This tells us about people who don't work the late shift—information that isn't relevant to our conclusion.
(D) Like (C), this tells us about people who don't work the late shift. We need definite information about those who do.
(E) This includes no information about those who work the late shift.

SECTION IV

QUESTIONS

9. Naturalist: It was once believed that only modern humans were capable of learning to use tools for obtaining food. Decades ago, archaeological evidence showed that extinct species of hominids closely related to modern humans also used tools for these purposes. What remained in doubt, however, was whether any existing nonhuman species could also learn to use tools. Some populations of chimpanzees use dried grasses to "fish" for termites, a high-protein delicacy. Moreover, evidence shows that this behavior is not instinctive but must be taught to and practiced by young chimpanzees. Some populations in the same area do not "fish" for termites in this way, although dried grasses and termite mounds are available to them.

   Which one of the following most accurately expresses the conclusion of the naturalist's argument?

   (A) At least some behaviors of chimpanzees are learned, not instinctive.
   (B) Certain past assumptions about the uniqueness of modern humans have been shown to be false.
   (C) Evidence exists that animals other than modern humans and their closest relatives are capable of learning to use tools.
   (D) Only modern humans are capable of learning to use tools in ways that are not directly related to obtaining food.
   (E) Some species of hominids became extinct for reasons unrelated to their ability to use tools.

10. Victor: Auto manufacturers report strong profit growth this year. This should not be taken to mean, however, that sales of new cars are increasing. Closer examination shows that the growth in auto manufacturers' profits is attributable solely to the financing of new-car sales.

    Kim: I don't think that's right. After all, if they were not continuing to sell new cars, auto manufacturers could not profit from financing them, could they?

    Kim's reply suggests that she misinterprets Victor's point to be that

    (A) overall sales of new cars are not increasing
    (B) auto manufacturers' profits this year were derived solely from financing
    (C) the financing of the past year's sales is not solely responsible for this year's profit growth
    (D) auto manufacturers should place increased emphasis on the sale and financing of used cars
    (E) only new car sales should be considered in evaluating the financial health of auto manufacturers

EXPLANATIONS

9. This is a MAIN POINT question. We're looking for the best statement of the single thing the argument wants us to believe.

   (A) This choice leaves out the notion of using tools.
   (B) This choice is a bit too general to be the best available expression of the point.
   (C) Yes. This includes the two main pieces of the argument: using tools and animals other than humans.
   (D) Tool use not related to getting food isn't addressed by this argument.
   (E) This isn't the thing the argument is trying to prove.

10. This is a REASONING question; it doesn't fit well in any strict category. We want the choice that correctly describes what Kim seems to think Victor is saying.

    (A) This is Victor's point. Kim interprets Victor to be saying something stronger.
    (B) Yes. Kim appears to think that Victor's comments apply to profits, not the *growth* in profits.
    (C) This choice introduces considerations of chronology that aren't included in the argument.
    (D) Used cars aren't mentioned by either of them.
    (E) "Financial health" isn't an issue that either of them addresses.

SECTION IV

QUESTIONS

11. Most people believe that obtaining a master's in business administration (MBA) leads to increased pay. A recent survey, however, suggests that this belief is unfounded. Among the top executives at the nation's most prominent companies, there is no indication that pay rates are any higher for employees with an MBA than they are for employees in similar positions without one.

The argument above is flawed because it neglects the possibility that

(A) an employee with an MBA may be more likely to attain a top executive position than a similarly able employee without one
(B) the pay of top executives in the nation's most prominent companies may be higher than the pay of other employees in those same companies
(C) pay rates for top executives may differ from company to company, even among the most prominent companies
(D) an employee who obtains an MBA may learn job skills that are critical to success in a top executive position
(E) top executives who obtain MBAs while holding their jobs may be better able than other executives to find similar positions in other companies in the event that they are laid off.

12. Since Oscar received extensive training in how to repair motorcycles, he is able to repair many of their most common mechanical problems. However, Oscar does not understand how internal combustion engines work. When Oscar was given Lucy's motorcycle to repair, he was able to fix the problem, despite the fact that he did not understand what was causing it.

From the statements above, which one of the following can be properly inferred?

(A) The problem with Lucy's motorcycle involved its engine.
(B) Not all mechanical problems can be repaired only by mechanics who understand how an internal combustion engine works.
(C) At least some good mechanics are able to fix mechanical problems without an understanding of what is causing them.
(D) Oscar's mechanical training in how to repair motorcycles was incomplete.
(E) Those common mechanical problems that Oscar cannot fix require an understanding of how an internal combustion engine works.

EXPLANATIONS

11. **Conclusion**: Having an MBA doesn't lead to increased pay.

Premise: A recent survey shows that top executives with MBAs are paid the same amount as top executives without MBAs.

Assumption: Pay rates among top executives reliably show what the effect of having an MBA is on the salaries of all workers.

This is a WEAKEN question. We're looking for new information suggesting that the conclusion may not be true.

(A) Yes. If this is the case, then having an MBA might have the effect of increasing pay because it's a matter of common sense that top executives get paid more than other workers.
(B) This choice doesn't provide us any new information about the effect of having an MBA.
(C) This choice doesn't provide us any new information about the effect of having an MBA.
(D) The success of those who already have a top job doesn't have a clear impact on pay rates.
(E) This involves a comparison of those who already have top executive positions.

12. This is an INFERENCE question. We want the choice that must be true, given the information in the passage.

(A) We know that Oscar didn't understand the cause of Lucy's problem, but that doesn't guarantee us that the problem was with the engine.
(B) Yes. Oscar repaired Lucy's problem; Oscar doesn't understand engines; this has to be true.
(C) We don't know enough about "good" mechanics from the passage to conclude this.
(D) We can't judge the completeness of Oscar's training just because he doesn't understand engines.
(E) We don't know that the only problems Oscar can't fix pertain to engines.

SECTION IV

QUESTIONS

13. Dr. Jackson: Many people criticize the advertisement of prescription drugs because they believe it causes patients to form mistaken beliefs about how their conditions should be treated. Surveys show, however, that in more than 60 percent of cases when a patient requests a prescription for a particular drug from a doctor, the doctor writes a prescription for the drug he or she has requested.

Dr. Morris: True, patients often receive the treatment they request. But this is most often because patients refuse to follow medical advice that does not agree with the beliefs they form about how they should be treated, not because the treatment they request is correct.

Which one of the following, if true, most supports Dr. Morris's counter to Dr. Jackson?

(A) More than half of patients are sufficiently knowledgeable about their conditions to request the correct treatment for it.
(B) Many national organizations that work on behalf of doctors are opposed to the advertisement of prescription drugs.
(C) Studies show that more than half of patients receive incorrect or excessive treatment for their medical problems.
(D) More than half of patients who receive the prescriptions they request from their doctors have previously requested the same prescription from another doctor and have been refused.
(E) Only a very few of the most common medical maladies for which patients seek treatment are most appropriately treated with prescription drugs.

EXPLANATIONS

13. This is a STRENGTHEN question. We're looking to provide further support for Dr. Morris's part of the conversation.

(A) This would weaken Dr. Morris's argument.
(B) The opinions of organizations aren't relevant to Dr. Morris's point.
(C) This is suggestive, but it doesn't strengthen Dr. Morris's argument directly.
(D) Yes. This provides further support for Dr. Morris's contention that patients refuse to accept any treatment other than the one they request.
(E) The impact of this choice isn't clear; certainly it doesn't directly support Dr. Morris's point about what patients will accept as treatment.

SECTION IV

QUESTIONS

14. It cannot be true that the lack of success of third-party candidates in national elections is due to the difficulties such candidates encounter in securing space on national ballots. Everyone who identifies him- or herself as a supporter of a third party has voted for a major-party candidate in at least one national election when a third-party candidate was listed on the ballot.

Which one of the following most accurately describes a reasoning flaw in the argument?

(A) The argument overlooks the possibility that the lack of success of third-party candidates in national elections may be due to the fact that their views on major issues prevent them from gaining broad support.
(B) The argument takes for granted that the media coverage devoted to third-party candidates for national office is comparable to that devoted to major-party candidates for those same offices.
(C) The argument treats as contradictory to some claim evidence that may instead provide support for that claim.
(D) The argument draws its conclusion through the use of a set of facts, not all of which can be true.
(E) The argument derives a statement about the behavior of all voters on the basis of partial information about the past voting preferences of only a few voters.

EXPLANATIONS

14. **Conclusion**: The difficulty third-party candidates have in getting on the ballot in national elections isn't the reason they haven't had much success.

Premise: Self-identified supporters of third parties have all at some point voted for a major-party candidate in a national election when a third-party candidate was listed on the ballot.

Assumption: The third-party candidates listed on the ballot in national elections are always members of the party supported by the voters mentioned in the premise.

This is a FLAW question. We're looking for a choice that describes or exploits the argument's assumption.

(A) On the contrary, the argument concludes that some factor other than difficulty getting on the ballot must be responsible.
(B) As with (A), this choice concerns a possible reason other than difficulty getting on the ballot that may be responsible; that's the argument's point!
(C) Yes. The fact that third-party supporters sometimes vote for major-party candidates may well be explained by the fact that candidates they support can't get on the ballot.
(D) There are no internal contradictions here.
(E) The behavior of all voters isn't relevant to the conclusion here.

SECTION IV

QUESTIONS

15. Sara: Our government devotes billions of tax dollars every year to foreign aid, although most experts agree that our social and economic infrastructure is badly in need of that money. It is unconscionable that our elected representatives consider the needs of our own citizens less important than the needs of citizens of other countries.

    Ross: Foreign aid helps our country by assuring its security. If money were not spent on foreign aid to the most threatened governments in the world, we would need to spend a great deal more in military interventions when those governments collapsed.

    From their statements, it can most properly be inferred that Sara and Ross disagree about whether

    (A) their country's spending on foreign aid ought to be increased
    (B) failed governments pose a security threat to their country
    (C) their country's social infrastructure is in need of additional investment
    (D) their country's spending on foreign aid serves its citizens' needs
    (E) decreased spending on foreign aid would necessitate additional military spending

EXPLANATIONS

15. This is an INFERENCE question. We're looking for a statement about which Sara and Ross definitely express different views.

    (A) Ross doesn't go so far as to say that foreign aid spending should be increased.
    (B) Sara registers no opinion on this question.
    (C) Ross registers no opinion on this question.
    (D) Yes. Sara would say it doesn't; Ross would say it does.
    (E) Sara registers no opinion on this question.

SECTION IV

QUESTIONS

16. In communities heavily affected by environmental regulation where such regulation directly benefits neither the companies that are most important to the community's economy nor the residents of that community, the government is perceived as being insensitive to the community's economic welfare. For this reason, the people in some communities heavily affected by environmental regulation are in favor of decreased taxes. When people believe that government considers the interests of others more important than their own, they tend to favor decreased taxes, believing this will limit the government's power over their lives.

    Which one of the following is an assumption on which the argument depends?

    (A) When government policy is perceived as being sensitive to a community's economic welfare, the people of that community do not wish to limit the government's power over their lives.
    (B) Environmental regulation that directly benefits the companies that are most important to a community's economy leads to greater government support than environmental regulation that directly benefits only the residents of that community.
    (C) A government's power over the lives of a community's residents depends on taxes collected from those residents.
    (D) People in a community tend to believe that their government considers others' interests more important than their own unless that government is perceived as being sensitive to the community's economic welfare.
    (E) Community members do not consider indirect benefits to themselves or to the companies that are most important to the community's economy in formulating their response to environmental regulation.

EXPLANATIONS

16. **Conclusion**: People in communities affected by environmental regulation often favor decreased taxes.

    Premises: When environmental regulation doesn't have direct economic benefits for the community, the government is perceived as being insensitive; when government seems to consider other people's interests more important, people in an area tend to favor less taxation.

    Assumption: The perception that government is insensitive leads to the belief that the government considers others' interests more important.

    This is an ASSUMPTION question. We're looking for a statement that is needed for the conclusion to be true.

    (A) This concerns what happens when government is perceived as being sensitive but no information about what happens when it's insensitive; this doesn't provide the needed link.
    (B) This compares two possible sources of perceived insensitivity in a way that isn't essential to the argument.
    (C) This relates to the beliefs that people have about the results of decreased taxation, but those beliefs could be wrong without affecting the argument.
    (D) Yes. Suppose this isn't true, and that people may not hold this belief even if the government is perceived as being insensitive. Under those circumstances, the argument doesn't work.
    (E) Even if they do consider indirect benefits, the reasoning in the argument may still stand. This isn't a factor that's essential to the argument's reasoning.

SECTION IV

QUESTIONS

17. Researcher: Heavily insulated homes trap radon gas much better than do poorly insulated homes. Therefore, those who live in heavily insulated homes are at greater risk for certain types of brain cancer because evidence shows that those who are being treated for brain cancer have high blood levels of the radioactive compounds that are found in those who are exposed to high levels of radon gas.

Which one of the following, if true, most undermines the researcher's argument?

(A) Radon gas is commonly found even in homes that do not trap it well.
(B) Exposure to radiation is known to lead to an increased incidence of cancer of all kinds.
(C) Young people are particularly susceptible to the negative consequences of high levels of radon exposure.
(D) Radioactive compounds are used in many cases to help develop an initial diagnosis of medical problems.
(E) The most common brain cancer therapy involves radiation and leads to high blood levels of many radioactive compounds.

EXPLANATIONS

17. **Conclusion**: Those who live in heavily insulated homes are at greater risk for brain cancer.

Premises: Heavily insulated homes trap more radon gas; radon gas exposure leads to high blood levels of radioactive compounds found in those who are being treated for brain cancer.

Assumptions: The radioactive compounds are somehow involved in the causation of brain cancer.

This is a WEAKEN question. We want to break the assumption or otherwise make the conclusion seem less likely.

(A) The argument concerns only those exposed to high levels of radon; the fact that everyone is exposed to some radon doesn't hurt the argument.
(B) This would slightly strengthen the argument.
(C) The relative susceptibility of certain people to these problems isn't relevant here.
(D) This seems to be trying to identify an alternate source of the compounds, but it's a weak answer; why, if these are used only initially, do patients with brain cancer continue to have them in their blood?
(E) Yes. The brain-cancer treatment is the source of these radioactive compounds, suggesting that they aren't involved in causing brain cancer.

QUESTIONS

18. Food critic: Consumers should buy only wild salmon, not farmed salmon. Whereas the environmental damage associated with harvesting wild salmon is slight, salmon farms are significant causes of water pollution, and salmon that escape from the farms displace wild varieties, threatening biodiversity. The fact that farmed salmon is cheaper than wild varieties has led to a large increase in the popularity of salmon, which may eventually pose a threat to wild populations because of over-fishing.

Which one of the following most accurately describes a flaw in the food critic's argument?

(A) At least one of the potential disadvantages cited in arguing against a course of action applies at least as strongly to the alternative course of action the argument recommends.
(B) The argument is constructed in such a way that it precludes the possibility of reaching any logical conclusion, if all of its premises are accepted as true.
(C) It overlooks the possibility that some unspecified benefit of the choice argued against may outweigh any possible benefit of the choice argued for.
(D) It concludes that one course of action is not permissible on the basis of a principle that is in greater need of support than the conclusion it is advanced to defend.
(E) Its premises are presented in such a way that the argument presupposes the truth of the conclusion it is intended to support.

EXPLANATIONS

18. **Conclusion:** People should buy wild salmon instead of farmed salmon.

Premises: Farmed salmon has many more bad environmental effects than wild salmon; cheapness of farmed salmon has increased the popularity of the fish, which may eventually threaten wild populations.

Assumption: Buying only wild salmon could somehow prevent these bad effects; especially notable in this regard is the strange assumption that buying only wild salmon could somehow prevent them from being over-fished.

This is a FLAW question. We're looking for the choice that describes or exploits an assumption.

(A) Yes. This refers to the strange idea that buying more wild salmon could help prevent it from being over-fished.
(B) The premises aren't contradictory; they just don't support the conclusion the argument is trying to draw from them.
(C) It's not evident what these benefits may be.
(D) No questionable principle is employed here.
(E) The argument is not circular.

SECTION IV

QUESTIONS

19. Resentment is not a reasonable response to rejection because rejection is merely an expression of preference: either a preference is purely personal, in which case the rejection could not have been anticipated, or that preference is commonly held, in which case steps should have been taken in advance to avoid rejection.

Which one of the following, if assumed, enables the argument's conclusion to be properly drawn?

(A) No emotional response to any action that could not have been anticipated is reasonable.
(B) Resentment is not a reasonable response to any action which steps should have been taken in advance to avoid.
(C) Resentment is not a reasonable response to any preference which is either purely personal or commonly held.
(D) Responses to resentment indicate preferences that either could not have been anticipated or else could have been avoided.
(E) No response to an expression of preference that steps should have been taken to avoid could reasonably have been anticipated.

EXPLANATIONS

19. **Conclusion**: Resentment isn't a reasonable response to rejection.

Premise: Rejection is the expression of either a purely personal preference or else a commonly held one; if purely personal, it could not have been predicted; if commonly held, it could have been taken into account.

This is a STRENGTHEN question. We're looking for the statement that makes our conclusion certain.

(A) This gets only one of the two possibilities mentioned; it leaves out the question of commonly held preferences.
(B) This gets only one of the two possibilities mentioned; it leaves out the question of purely personal preferences.
(C) Yes. This assures us the conclusion is right in both of the possible cases.
(D) This describes responses to resentment, not rejection.
(E) This mixes up the two possibilities described in the argument.

SECTION IV

QUESTIONS

20. According to newspaper reviews, some of the films released this year were of superior artistic quality. According to audience surveys, some of the films released this year involved exciting plots. Therefore, some of the films this year which involved exciting plots were also of superior artistic quality.

The flawed reasoning in the argument above is most similar to that in which one of the following?

(A) Judging from automotive magazines, some of the cars released this year were exceptionally fast, but according to automotive enthusiasts, none of the cars released this year is likely to become a classic. Thus not even the fastest car released this year is likely to become a classic.

(B) According to consumer magazines, some of the new refrigerators introduced this year are exceptionally energy efficient. According to consumer surveys, energy efficiency plays some role in determining whether a customer is satisfied with a new refrigerator. Therefore, the reason some customers are satisfied with their new refrigerators is that they are exceptionally energy efficient.

(C) Art says that snow is forecast for some parts of our area tomorrow, and Lois says that rain is forecast for some parts of our area tomorrow. Thus, tomorrow it will neither snow nor rain in some parts of our area.

(D) Doctors say that some vaccines need be administered only once in a patient's lifetime, and drug companies say that some vaccines prevent measles, so some vaccine that prevents measles need be administered only once in a patient's lifetime.

(E) According to publishers, most of the works of fiction published this year were novels. According to book reviewers, most of the works of fiction published this year were of inferior quality. Therefore, some of the novels published this year were of inferior quality.

EXPLANATIONS

20. **Conclusion**: Some things with quality A also have quality B.

Premises: Some things in a group have quality A; some things in the same group have quality B.

Flaw: "Some" is too small a proportion to guarantee that there is a member of the group with both qualities.

This is a PARALLEL-FLAW question. We're looking for another argument that has the problem described above.

(A) The premises here involve one "some" statement and one "none" statement.

(B) The premises here don't involve two things that are each true of "some refrigerators."

(C) The conclusion here isn't similar; it talks about cases where neither quality is present.

(D) Yes. Quality A is "prevents measles"; quality B is "needs to be administered only once."

(E) The premises here involve two "most" statements.

SECTION IV

QUESTIONS

21. Stock options are the only investments that allow an individual investor to achieve high returns with limited liability. With relatively small risk, an individual investing in stock options can make profits of several hundred percent over a short period of time. Thus stock options represent a more efficient use of an individual's money than any other investment option.

    Which one of the following, if assumed, enables the argument's conclusion to be properly inferred?

    (A) Investments other than stock options do not allow an individual investor to achieve high returns with limited liability.
    (B) The efficient use of an individual investor's money requires the possibility of achieving profit over a short period of time.
    (C) A profit of several hundred percent over a short period of time is considered a high return on an individual's investment.
    (D) An investment cannot be considered efficient unless it returns several hundred percent profit.
    (E) Investments that allow an individual to achieve high returns with limited liability represent a more efficient use of money than any other potential use.

EXPLANATIONS

21. **Conclusion**: Stock options are the most efficient use of an individual's investment money.

    Premise: Stock options are the only investment in which an individual can get high returns with limited liability.

    This is a STRENGTHEN question. We're looking for the choice that makes the argument's conclusion certain.

    (A) This is a restatement of the argument's premise and provides no further support.
    (B) This strengthens somewhat, but it doesn't make the conclusion airtight. A short time period is identified as an advantage, but we don't know that this is the only investment with that advantage.
    (C) This seems to be a fact that's indicated by the premises; restating it doesn't offer further support to the conclusion.
    (D) We're told that this is an attribute of stock options, but we don't know that options are the only investment with this attribute.
    (E) Yes. In addition to our premise, this fact would guarantee the truth of the conclusion.

SECTION IV

QUESTIONS

22. Only corporate executives who behave ethically are likely to be promoted, but no corporate executive who makes wise business decisions is a poor employee. All corporate executives who behave ethically are both well respected and make wise business decisions, qualities lacking in many corporate executives who do not behave ethically.

If all of the statements above are true, which one of the following must also be true?

(A) No corporate executive who makes wise business decisions but does not behave ethically is well respected.
(B) All corporate executives who are well respected but do not behave ethically make wise business decisions.
(C) No corporate executive who is likely to be promoted is a poor employee.
(D) All corporate executives who are not well respected are poor employees.
(E) All corporate executives who are good employees behave ethically.

EXPLANATIONS

22. likely to be promoted → behave ethically

makes wise decisions → - poor employee

behave ethically → well respected AND makes wise decisions

This is an INFERENCE question. We're looking for a statement that's definitely true, given the facts in the passage.

(A) The only thing we know for certain about executives who don't behave ethically is that they're not likely to be promoted. The last phrase of the passage guarantees us that there are some who lack both the quality of being well-respected and the quality of making wise decisions, but it leaves open the possibility that there are some executives who don't behave ethically who have either one or even possibly both of these qualities.
(B) See the explanation above in (A).
(C) Yes. This is a correct use of this chain from the passage: likely to be promoted → behave ethically → makes wise decisions → - poor employee.
(D) The only things we know about executives who aren't well respected is that they don't behave ethically and aren't likely to be promoted.
(E) We aren't able to draw any definite conclusions about executives who aren't poor employees.

SECTION IV

QUESTIONS

23. It cannot be true that everyone who donates money to charity is concerned with the well-being of others. After all, it is possible that donating money to charity may help some people lessen their own feelings of guilt.

Which one of the following arguments employs a principle of reasoning most similar to that illustrated by the argument above?

(A) It cannot be true that the only reason for space exploration is scientific discovery. After all, there have been many space missions that have not contributed to scientific knowledge at all.
(B) It cannot be true that income taxes are justified by the government's obligation to redistribute wealth. After all, many government programs paid for by tax money benefit wealthy individuals.
(C) It cannot be true that Columbus was the one who discovered that the Earth was not flat. After all, ancient mathematicians had calculated the Earth's circumference centuries before Columbus was born.
(D) It cannot be true that all those who become actors desire wealth and fame. After all, some actors may perform so that they can share their artistic vision with others.
(E) It cannot be true that a meteor impact caused the extinction of the dinosaurs. After all, it is possible that climatic conditions similar to those following a meteor impact could have been created by a massive volcanic eruption.

EXPLANATIONS

23. **Conclusion**: It cannot be true that everyone who engages in an activity (donating to charity) does so out of the same motive (concern for others).

Premise: Another motive (lessening guilt) may also be a reason to engage in the activity.

This is a PARALLEL question. We're looking for the choice that uses the same basic method of reasoning as the original.

(A) The premise here is that the purpose wasn't achieved in all cases; it doesn't have to do with another possible purpose.
(B) Like (A), the premise here has to do with the purpose not being achieved.
(C) This doesn't have to do with motives at all.
(D) Yes. One motive (wealth and fame) is rejected as the explanation for all cases because another possible motive (sharing artistic vision) could explain it as well.
(E) This has to do with causes, which seems close, but this argument talks about a single instance, whereas our original talks about a whole group of instances.

SECTION IV

QUESTIONS	EXPLANATIONS

24. Appraiser: We know the following about the pottery made by artisan A. Pieces with a metallic glaze always feature a floral pattern but never have an hourglass shape. Pieces that are signed always have an hourglass shape, and pieces made in this century are always signed. A piece of pottery made by artisan A has recently come to my attention; it has a floral pattern and is signed.

From the appraiser's statements, which one of the following can be properly concluded about the piece of pottery by artisan A that has recently come to the appraiser's attention?

(A) It has an hourglass shape and was made in this century.
(B) It has an hourglass shape but was not made in this century.
(C) It has an hourglass shape but does not have a metallic glaze.
(D) It has a metallic glaze and was made in this century.
(E) It lacks both an hourglass shape and a metallic glaze.

24. metallic glaze → floral pattern AND - hourglass shape

signed → hourglass shape

made this century → signed

This piece: floral pattern AND signed

This is an INFERENCE question. We can predict the answer on this one using the conditionals. We cannot conclude anything for certain from the fact that the piece has a floral pattern. From the fact that the piece is signed, we can conclude that it has an hourglass shape; from the fact that it has an hourglass shape, we can conclude that it does not have a metallic glaze. We cannot conclude anything more about the piece.

The only choice that's consistent with our conclusions is (C).

25. No doubt the presidential candidate who wins an election deserves credit for persistence and political aplomb, but the advisors who develop campaign strategy are often overlooked. Although presidential candidates sometimes take the lead in shaping their campaign's policy positions, most often it is political professionals who, in service to the campaign, devote their time and energy to crafting the candidate's message and persona. Campaign strategists play a crucial role in virtually every successful candidacy.

The claim that presidential candidates sometimes take the lead in shaping their campaign's policy positions plays which one of the following roles in the argument?

(A) It indicates the circumstances to which the argument's conclusion is to be understood to apply.
(B) It concedes that the shortcoming the argument intends to address does not exist in every instance.
(C) It supports the argument's contention that political professionals devote time and energy to crafting the candidate's message and persona.
(D) It suggests that the relationship between a candidate's policy and that candidate's persona is not as essential as some may believe it to be.
(E) It is a premise on which other premises supporting the conclusion is based.

25. This is a REASONING question. We're looking for the choice that correctly describes the cited statement.

(A) On the contrary, the statement in question describes the cases when the conclusion *doesn't* apply.
(B) Yes. In cases when the candidate takes the lead on policy, you can't say that strategists don't get the credit they deserve. In every other case, however, you can.
(C) This statement doesn't provide support for any other statement in the argument.
(D) This doesn't seem to be an accurate description of the argument's contents.
(E) This is similar to (C). This statement doesn't provide support for any other.

10

The Princeton Review LSAT Practice Test 2

SECTION I

Time—35 Minutes

27 Questions

Directions: Each passage in this section is followed by a group of questions to be answered on the basis of what is stated or implied in the passage. For some questions, more than one of the choices could conceivably answer the question. However, you are to choose the best answer, that is, the response that most accurately and completely answers the question, and blacken the corresponding space on your answer sheet.

Questions 1–8 are based on the following passage:

Perhaps no figure from the Reconstruction era in the aftermath of the U.S. Civil War exemplifies the failed promise of those times better than Tunis Campbell. Campbell, born free in New Jersey, came to postwar Georgia as a superintendent in the Freedmen's Bureau. He was assigned to organize the settlement of three of the sea islands off Georgia's coast, in accordance with General William T. Sherman's Special Field Order 15, which famously granted forty acres and a mule to each of forty thousand freed slaves in the coastal areas of Georgia and South Carolina.

Campbell, a champion of black equality and self-determination, set up one of the islands—St. Catherine's—as an effectively independent black principality. Taking possession of the abandoned plantation lands granted by Sherman's order, the residents of St. Catherine's set up their own constitution, education system, and militia, and allowed no whites on the island. Within a year, however, the effects of Lincoln's assassination were felt throughout the occupied South, and the Union army seized the land back from residents, either returning it to its former owners or selling it to white investors in the North. A sharecropping system was instituted, whereby many of the practical realities of slavery, if not their precise form, took hold again. Campbell himself was exiled.

Determined to continue fighting for the freed slaves, Campbell worked tirelessly on their behalf. Resettling in MacIntosh County, he organized farm labor to help them gain power in negotiations with white landowners, and he worked tirelessly to register black voters. Within a few years his efforts paid off, and he became one of three African Americans to be elected to the Georgia state senate, where against all odds he managed to secure some few legal protections for black Georgians. His stature, however, was a serious irritant to the white power structure of the state, and Campbell was eventually driven out of the senate as the result of a concerted campaign of election fraud and the preferment of false charges against him.

Campbell continued to work on the former slaves' behalf, but the rising power of white supremacists and the indifference of the federal government to the fate of former slaves steadily eroded what progress he was able to make. Eventually, with the help of a judge sympathetic to their cause, Campbell's enemies were able to convict him on a trumped-up charge, and Campbell was sentenced to a year of hard labor on a chain gang. The plantation owner who bought his labor for that year paid the state of Georgia the meager sum of $8.75. Annual mortality rates for chain-gang laborers then averaged between 16 and 25 percent, and at age 63, it seems almost miraculous that Campbell survived. After his release Campbell left Georgia, and returned only once more before his death in 1891. In Georgia as in most of the former Confederate states, efforts to implement reform during Reconstruction were systematically foiled by those who sought to preserve white power and relegate black Americans to a permanent underclass.

1. The passage is primarily concerned with

(A) assessing the accomplishments of a well-known historical figure
(B) criticizing conventional views of a contentious historical era
(C) correcting mistaken understandings of an important geographical region
(D) detailing the obstacles faced by a leader who sought self-determination for a group
(E) asserting the importance of laws in reevaluating views of a historical era

2. The passage supports which one of the following statements concerning the lives of freed slaves in South Carolina and Georgia soon after the conclusion of the Civil War?

(A) Some owned land and were able to participate in government.
(B) Many were able to live independent of white influence.
(C) Most were forced to continue working for their former owners.
(D) All were able to exercise the freedoms afforded to other citizens.
(E) No effort was made to assure their representation in national government.

GO ON TO THE NEXT PAGE.

3. Which one of the following best describes the function of the second paragraph of the passage?

(A) It describes developments during Reconstruction that led to Campbell's eventual failure.
(B) It describes an effort to establish self-determination for freed slaves and the ways in which that effort was foiled.
(C) It summarizes the reasons Sherman's Special Field Order 15 was not fully implemented and indicates its limited effects.
(D) It shows an instance of efforts to maintain freed slaves as a permanent underclass not being entirely successful.
(E) It describes the outcome of the only effort during Reconstruction to respect the freed slaves' new legal equality.

4. In the fourth paragraph, the author mentions that a plantation owner paid $8.75 for a year of Campbell's labor while he was imprisoned primarily to

(A) demonstrate the ways in which institutions of slavery remained operative during Reconstruction
(B) quantify the dangerous conditions under which chain-gang laborers worked
(C) suggest that Campbell's punishment was demeaning
(D) prove the claim that the state of Georgia profited from Campbell's imprisonment
(E) indicate why Campbell returned to Georgia only once after he had served out the term of his imprisonment

5. Which one of the following, if true, would provide the LEAST support for the author's statements concerning the sharecropping system that was instituted after the Civil War?

(A) Black farmers were often subject to violence and intimidation by white landowners, both as slave laborers and as sharecroppers.
(B) The rents that white landowners demanded from black sharecropping farmers were so high that it was impossible for most of them to accumulate any property or money of their own as the result of their labor.
(C) The children of sharecropping farmers only rarely had access to education, and most of them were forced to work in the fields from a young age, just as they had during slavery.
(D) Legal means were used to prevent sharecropping farmers from organizing to demand lower rents and better treatment from the white landowners whose land they farmed.
(E) Sharecropping farmers were able to keep their families together and make other significant life decisions that were not available to slaves.

6. It can be inferred from the passage that each of the following is true of the political system in Georgia during the initial stages of Reconstruction EXCEPT:

(A) Some freed slaves cast votes in state elections.
(B) African-American legislators were able to pass laws protecting some rights of freed slaves.
(C) No white legislators supported Campbell's efforts to extend important freedoms to freed slaves.
(D) White leaders were not all pleased at the stature achieved by some black politicians.
(E) White judges at times served purposes approved of by white supremacists.

7. The passage does NOT provide an answer to which one of the following questions?

(A) Was land ever given to freed slaves as a result of Special Field Order 15?
(B) Was forced labor used as a means of punishment during Reconstruction?
(C) Were African Americans elected to positions in state government at any time during Reconstruction?
(D) For how long did the sharecropping system remain the primary means by which Southern landowners profited from their land?
(E) Did the laborers who were former slaves negotiate with white landowners?

8. The author would most likely agree with which one of the following statements about Campbell's importance to a full understanding of Reconstruction?

(A) Campbell was the only leader during Reconstruction who attempted to secure a full range of citizens' rights for freed slaves.
(B) Campbell's story is emblematic of the reasons why Reconstruction did not deliver on its promise of freedom and equal rights for former slaves.
(C) Campbell did not succeed in Georgia because he himself was not a freed slave and was not fully trusted by those he sought to help.
(D) Campbell's effort at protecting freed slaves in Georgia from white supremacists exemplifies the fact that Southern state governments were weak during Reconstruction.
(E) The analysis of Reconstruction requires that its failures as well as its successes be studied in detail, and Campbell provides ample illustrations of both.

GO ON TO THE NEXT PAGE.

Questions 9–14 are based on the following passage:

The crucial discovery that opened the way for modern advances in biochemistry was the role of DNA and protein in the biological activity of cells. After much debate and experimentation, it was eventually learned that DNA serves as the genetic blueprint for proteins, which are the compounds upon which all cellular activity depends. Thus, although no living cell can function without protein, DNA and its chemical cousin RNA serve as the driving force for its organization and use. This led to a proper understanding of viruses. Although pathogens such as parasites and bacteria are cellular and are thus by conventional definitions living organisms, viruses are not. They have no cells of their own; instead, they are composed of DNA or RNA material accompanied by only a small amount of protein. A virus uses its genetic instruction set to commandeer the machinery of other cells, and therefore was thought to demonstrate that although a pathogen can exist without protein, it must at a bare minimum include DNA or RNA.

In 1982, however, the biologist Stanley Prusiner hypothesized that there might exist proteins that were themselves pathogenic. Prusiner's idea of "prions" (proteinaceous infectious particles) was controversial because it contradicted the central dogma of modern biology. This hypothesis was, however, strengthened by further study of a class of encephalopathies that exist in many mammals: Called scrapie in sheep and goats, chronic wasting disease in elk and mule deer, and bovine spongiform encephalopathy in cattle ("mad cow disease"), these diseases are also found in humans—kuru, Creutzfeldt-Jakob Disease (CJD), and Fatal Familial Insomnia, to name a few. The fact that these diseases all lead to similar types of brain damage was interesting, but even more interesting was the fact that material from infected individuals could transmit disease even after sterilization in an autoclave. DNA could not survive such treatment, but some proteins could, leading to the speculation that the pathogens in these cases were special forms of protein acting alone, without genetic direction.

A prion protein is not a foreign protein, but a variant conformation of a protein normally produced by cells. Because a protein's conformation—its folding and physical shape—determines its biological activity, the prion protein no longer serves its normal purpose. Instead, prion proteins replicate themselves by catalyzing the conversion of normal copies of the protein into the prion conformation, and they may also alter the synthesis of new protein to favor that conformation. This mechanism helps explain why a disorder such as scrapie may develop spontaneously in a sheep that has never been exposed to an external source of the prion protein that causes it because a normal protein may slip into its prion conformation by chance. This mechanism also explains how humans exposed to cattle prion proteins in their food may subsequently develop disease because it has been shown that cattle prions can cause a similar human protein to shift from its normal conformation into a prion form.

9. Which one of the following best expresses the main idea of the passage?

(A) Recent discoveries suggest that the understandings of DNA and protein on which modern biochemistry is based are incomplete.
(B) The hypothesis that prions cause certain classes of disease shows that there may be pathogens that do not possess genetic material.
(C) The central dogma of modern biology is that the presence of genetic material is necessary for an organism to be considered alive.
(D) Although pathogens have been found that are composed primarily of DNA or RNA with little protein, no pathogen can exist completely without protein.
(E) The discovery that prions cause certain encephalopathies holds out hope that hitherto untreatable diseases may soon be cured.

10. The passage indicates that one consequence for a person who ingests food products derived from cattle with bovine spongiform encephalopathy may be

(A) the contraction of a virus
(B) the spontaneous development of scrapie
(C) the contraction of a prion disease
(D) resistance to certain types of parasites
(E) the expression of genes that do not operate normally

GO ON TO THE NEXT PAGE.

11. Which one of the following best describes the organization of the passage?

(A) A commonly held belief is introduced, scientific evidence against the belief is offered, and the belief is finally rejected as untrue.
(B) A new area of biology is described, possible benefits of study in this area are hypothesized, and further directions for study in this area are recommended.
(C) One potential cause of a class of diseases is hypothesized, evidence both for and against this hypothesis is presented, and the hypothesis is finally accepted.
(D) The basis of a scientific belief is introduced, a class of diseases this belief may not be adequate to explain is described, and a proposed cause of the diseases that does not conform to the belief is outlined.
(E) An alternative mechanism for a commonly observed phenomenon is posited, evidence in favor of that mechanism is considered, and arguments against the mechanism are ultimately accepted.

12. The author refers to the fact that material from individuals infected with certain encephalopathies may remain infectious even after sterilization in an autoclave primarily in order to

(A) provide evidence that the conventional belief that all pathogens contain genetic material may not be true
(B) reinforce the claim that the class of encephalopathies discussed are all caused by the same prion
(C) indicate that it remains possible that these encephalopathies may be caused by viruses
(D) undermine conventional views of encephalopathy that state that these diseases can only develop spontaneously
(E) show how normal proteins may in some cases become pathogenic

13. By the author's statements, it can be inferred that the author would be most likely to agree with which one of the following statements?

(A) Not all diseases are caused by parasites, bacteria, viruses, or prions.
(B) Not all prion diseases involve changes to the conformation of a naturally produced protein.
(C) Not all proteins that exist in a prion form have detrimental biological effects in that form.
(D) Most diseases that are thought to be caused by prions can be spread from one species to another.
(E) Not all cases of prion disease can be explained by exposure to an external source of the pathogen that causes it.

14. Which one of the following is most analogous to the proposed mechanism by which a prion replicates itself, as that mechanism is described in the passage?

(A) A teacher who advocates a new method of teaching reading to students is more successful with her method than are other teachers using more conventional methods.
(B) An artisan who produces works that other artisans consider to be of inferior quality is nevertheless successful because he can produce his works very cheaply.
(C) A scientist who has always accepted the theory that protein is involved in heredity changes her mind when it is discovered that genetic traits cannot be transmitted by a cell with its DNA removed.
(D) A criminal who has developed a safe and lucrative scheme for cheating investment banks convinces many other individuals who have previously obeyed the law to use the same scheme to make money, who then convince others to do so.
(E) A high-school graduate who goes into business for himself instead of going to college is extremely successful and becomes a role model for other graduates who chose not to attend college.

GO ON TO THE NEXT PAGE.

Questions 15–20 are based on the following passage:

The Sherman Antitrust Act was initially passed to curb the power of corporations that had established monopolies over the most important resources for the U.S. economy. These companies protected their position by engaging in predatory pricing and other anticompetitive practices that were seen as antithetical to free-market principles and threatening to civil authority. One industry that has managed to avoid regulation under the act, however, is Major League Baseball, and although the anomalous legal status of this organization can be understood in terms of its history, it seems unlikely to last forever.

The basis in precedent for baseball's status stems from a 1922 Supreme Court decision in which the two major leagues were adjudged to be exempt from antitrust regulation because their business did not constitute interstate commerce and thus was not subject to federal regulation. Even at the time, this argument was tenuous: Although baseball teams crossed state lines to participate in games, this fact was found to be incidental to the conduct of baseball exhibitions, which according to the court did not fit a narrow definition of commerce anyway. By the time baseball's exemption was once again taken up by the Supreme Court—in 1953, in the context of a labor dispute—it could no longer plausibly be argued that baseball's special treatment was justifiable on these grounds. However, the Supreme Court at the time declined to overturn the exemption because doing so was not part of the manifest intent of the law: Although antitrust law did technically cover baseball, its purpose was to curb socially harmful concentrations of power in the hands of robber-barons, and a breakup of the baseball monopoly would not serve this purpose. Even so, the Supreme Court declined to extend the protections afforded to Major League Baseball to similar organizations in other sports, and by the 1970s the Supreme Court seemed to have settled on the curious position that, even though it no longer believed that Major League Baseball merited exemption, it would continue to honor the precedent unless legislative bodies specifically withdrew it.

Certain aspects of the exemption, especially those concerning teams' contracts with baseball players, have been redefined, but it remains for the most part intact. Not until the end of the twentieth century was a full-scale withdrawal threatened, when Major League Baseball proposed unilaterally dissolving two of its least financially viable teams. Without its antitrust exemption, league management could never have contemplated such a move; legislators made it clear to the league that following through with it would likely cost baseball its special status. Although the teams were saved, however, in the end it seems that baseball's exemption may be more a vulnerability than an asset. As baseball's competitive position with regard to other professional sports grows weaker, the need for significant steps to improve that position grows. The fact that legislative bodies exercise a unique brand of veto power over league decisions may, in the end, dictate that baseball must risk the voiding of its exemption to take steps required to assure its financial viability.

15. It can be inferred from the passage that by referring to its "anomalous legal status" (line 9–10) the author means that Major League Baseball is

(A) not subject to direct interference by legislators in the same way that other similar organizations are
(B) not accountable to the voters and consumers in the same way that all powerful business organizations should be
(C) not constrained to follow laws to which other similar organizations have been found to be subject
(D) not involved in the conduct of anything that can correctly be called "interstate commerce"
(E) not required to consider the consequences of its actions in the same way that legislators are

16. The passage indicates that each of the following has at some time served as a justification for Major League Baseball's exemption from the Sherman Antitrust Act EXCEPT:

(A) the precedent established by a 1922 Supreme Court decision
(B) the fact that staging baseball exhibitions could not be classified as "commerce"
(C) the assertion that a monopoly over baseball does not represent a socially harmful concentration of power
(D) the fact that other professional sports are also not subject to regulation under the act
(E) the assurance that legislators may withdraw Major League Baseball's exemption if they choose to do so

GO ON TO THE NEXT PAGE.

17. It can be inferred from the passage that the author considers the unique role legislators play with regard to Major League Baseball to be

(A) a violation of the Sherman Antitrust Act
(B) more of a hindrance to the sport's success than a help
(C) a primary factor in its financial decline
(D) responsible for its indeterminate legal status
(E) the product of a weak and vacillating Supreme Court

18. The author implies that which of the following is true of the companies that antitrust legislation was intended to regulate?

(A) The business practices they sometimes employed included the manipulation of prices to harm competitors.
(B) They did not pose a threat to the ability of legislative bodies to govern effectively.
(C) Their monopolies represented an aberration in the history of the free market.
(D) At least some of them could have been allowed to retain their monopolies without causing harm.
(E) They created circumstances that directly led to legislative interference in all professional sports leagues.

19. The author's characterization of the basis for a 1922 Supreme Court decision as "tenuous" (line 17) indicates the author's belief that

(A) professional sports exhibitions do not constitute interstate commerce
(B) the concentration of economic power represented by professional sports monopolies is not socially harmful
(C) sports organizations other than those associated with professional baseball are not exempt from antitrust legislation
(D) the labor practices engaged in by Major League Baseball represent an abuse of its special legal status
(E) the precedent that established baseball's exemption from antitrust legislation was legally questionable

20. According to the passage, the future financial health of Major League Baseball may depend on which one of the following courses of action?

(A) provoking legislators to revisit the limitations placed on the league's exemption from certain laws
(B) taking potentially risky measures to ensure the league's competitive strength
(C) concentrating greater power in the hands of the league's leadership
(D) taking steps that would not be possible for any organization without an exemption from antitrust laws
(E) voluntarily conceding the right of other sports leagues to be protected against antitrust enforcement

GO ON TO THE NEXT PAGE.

Questions 21–27 are based on the following passage:

Like many aspects of public life in the former Soviet Union, the production of visual art was sanctioned and closely controlled by the central government and the Communist party. Most Soviet-era work is thus dismissed by critics as mere propaganda, not worthy of the same consideration due to Western works of the same period. Interest in Soviet artists has traditionally focused on those who resisted the regime and, in many cases, were persecuted for doing so. Yet it is difficult to avoid seeing, in this interest, not an objection to art as propaganda, but rather a preference for one kind of propaganda over another. In the highly charged political atmosphere of the Cold War, works produced both inside and outside the Soviet Union tended to take on ideological dimensions, whether the artist intended them.

Soviet art took shape at a time when governments worldwide were beginning to make full use of the power of propaganda. Although the Nazi regime in Germany is typically identified as leading the way in this pursuit, over the same period Stalin was expanding the Soviet Union's propaganda apparatus. With regard to visual arts, this apparatus operated in the contexts of both "high culture" and "low culture." Stalin's government sponsored a style of painting called Socialist Realism, which used conventional sentimental tropes and a lexicon of Communist imagery to portray life in the Soviet Union, and Stalin himself, in idealized and inspirational ways. At the same time, the production of posters was vastly expanded; these posters used cartoonish and overblown imagery to evoke such ideas as the greed of capitalism, the savagery of fascism, and the bravery of factory workers and collective farmers. Today, the Soviet-era posters that survive are collector's items, and a modest market remains for the high-culture works of painting and sculpture that survived the overthrow of the Soviet regime.

An examination of cultural production in the United States over the same period yields surprising similarities. Throughout the thirties, the government sponsored production of public art through the Works Progress Administration. Often these works celebrated the dignity of work and the enduring spirit of the people. World War II poster propaganda yielded images that linger in the popular culture even now: Rosie the Riveter, Uncle Sam, and caricatured racist portrayals of people living in fascist countries. Even the most famous high-culture painting in the United States—the abstract expressionist work of such painters as Pollock and Rothko—took on political dimensions that are striking in light of their apparent lack of ideological content. Triumphal showings of these artists' work, represented as "cultural exchange," were organized within the Soviet Union during the Cold War with the purpose of lauding freedom of expression. Soviet officials, at the same time, pointed to them as proof of capitalist decadence. Even these works, meant to exemplify the aesthetic in its purest form, became weapons in an arms race of propaganda that mirrored other political contests taking place throughout the Cold War.

21. According to the passage, which one of the following opinions would art critics be most likely to hold concerning Socialist Realist paintings produced in the Soviet Union under Stalin's regime?

(A) They cannot be considered as artistically valuable as other works produced during the same period because of their status as government propaganda.
(B) They are at least as ideologically motivated as paintings made under the Works Progress Administration during the same time.
(C) Their market value exceeds the market value of some serious paintings made outside the Soviet Union during the same time.
(D) Their popularity in the contemporary market indicates that they are of less artistic value than other paintings made during that time.
(E) Although they are propaganda, they cannot be completely dismissed because much of the art made during that period served similar purposes.

GO ON TO THE NEXT PAGE.

22. Which one of the following, if true, would most undermine the author's interpretation of the fact that the U.S. government sponsored the production of art through the Works Progress Administration?

(A) U.S. painters who produced government-sponsored works were not subject to direct oversight by government representatives during the planning stages of their work.
(B) Soviet painters who worked in the officially approved style were paid for their work only after it had been accepted by the Communist party.
(C) U.S. painters were free to choose whether they wished to seek government funding for works that might have been considered subversive.
(D) Soviet painters were able to gain at least some public attention for paintings produced outside the auspices of the government and the Communist party.
(E) U.S. painters who were funded by the Works Progress Administration were not prevented from producing work critical of the U.S. government, and they often did.

23. Which one of the following best describes the organization of the second paragraph?

(A) A general claim about a historical period is presented and then illustrated with the use of supporting examples from several countries.
(B) A contention concerning one country is used as proof of the truth of this contention for all countries.
(C) A particular strategy by a government is shown to operate in two separate contexts for similar purposes.
(D) The ongoing popularity of the results of a particular policy is used to demonstrate the efficacy of that policy.
(E) Two governments that are considered similar in one way are shown to be dissimilar in other important ways.

24. According to the passage, which one of the following is true of abstract expressionist paintings?

(A) They were aesthetically superior to any paintings being produced in the Soviet Union at the same time.
(B) Their apparent lack of ideological content did not prevent them from being used as propaganda.
(C) The artists intended for them to be interpreted as lauding free expression.
(D) Their production was sponsored by the U.S. government through the Works Progress Administration.
(E) Their decadence is a primary reason they are considered among the greatest paintings of the twentieth century.

25. It can be inferred that the author would most likely agree with which one of the following statements concerning posters produced in the Soviet Union during World War II?

(A) They dealt with the same subjects used in propaganda posters produced in Nazi Germany during the same time.
(B) They employed the same deceptive practices that Socialist Realist paintings of the period employed.
(C) They attributed characteristics to factory and farm workers that those workers normally did not possess.
(D) They served similar purposes to the purposes served by some posters produced in the U.S. during the same period.
(E) These posters are not as desirable to collectors today as are propaganda posters produced in other countries during the same period.

GO ON TO THE NEXT PAGE.

26. Which one of the following is most analogous to the passage's discussion of the "preference" (line 11) ascribed to art critics?

(A) Literary reviewers prefer literary novels to popular novels because the tastes of literary reviewers are more refined than the tastes of most readers.
(B) Economists who prefer capitalism to socialism focus on the inefficiencies of a socialist government's policies and the successes of a rich venture capitalist who has been imprisoned by that government.
(C) Fashion designers who prefer creativity to practicality make garments that are exceptionally inconvenient to wear and maintain.
(D) Archaeologists who subscribe to a particular view of a civilization's history commence an investigation of a major site inhabited by that civilization with hopes of finding support for their view.
(E) A landscape designer who prefers shrubs to flowers nevertheless must accommodate a client's wishes to have a substantial number of flowers in a garden she is designing.

27. Which one of the following best expresses the main idea of the passage?

(A) The use of propaganda in both high-culture and low-culture contexts was prevalent in many countries during the twentieth century.
(B) Critics who dismiss Soviet art as being excessively ideological are incapable of seeing the ideological content of art produced at the same time in the United States.
(C) Paintings and posters were the primary means by which the governments fighting World War II sought to motivate their public to endure hardships associated with that war.
(D) Those who dismiss visual art produced in the Soviet Union as propaganda reveal their biases by doing so because even the greatest works by U.S. artists during the same period could also be used as propaganda.
(E) All art, regardless of the time and place of its production, has a political dimension that may be exploited by governments in their effort to produce propaganda.

STOP

IF YOU FINISH BEFORE TIME IS CALLED, YOU MAY CHECK YOUR WORK ON THIS SECTION ONLY.
DO NOT WORK ON ANY OTHER SECTION IN THE TEST.

NO TEST MATERIAL ON THIS PAGE

SECTION II

Time—35 Minutes

26 Questions

Directions: The questions in this section are based on the reasoning contained in brief statements or passages. For some questions, more than one of the choices could conceivably answer the question. However, you are to choose the best answer; that is, the response that most accurately and completely answers the question. You should not make assumptions that are by commonsense standards implausible, superfluous, or incompatible with the passage. After you have chosen the best answer, blacken the corresponding space on your answer sheet.

1. Some analysts believe that changes in the price of oil are never appreciably influenced by long-term weather forecasts. Last year, however, the prediction of an especially violent hurricane season for this year was followed by a sharp increase in oil prices because in the past large hurricanes have been known to disrupt oil production in the Gulf of Mexico. Hence, the predicted incidence of hurricanes—only one of many aspects of long-term weather forecasts—can cause changes in the price of oil, which means that other aspects of weather forecasting can as well.

   The statement that large hurricanes in the past have disrupted oil production in the Gulf of Mexico is intended to support the contention that

   (A) the predicted violence of the upcoming hurricane season is the most important weather-related factor in determining oil prices
   (B) long-term weather forecasts usually do not influence oil prices at the time they are issued
   (C) any long-term weather forecasting must take into account the likely effect of fluctuations in the price of oil
   (D) a variety of predictions made in long-term weather forecasts can influence the price of oil
   (E) the usual effect of long-term predictions concerning the severity of the next year's hurricane season is to cause a sharp increase in the price of oil

2. In an experiment, first-year college students were asked to listen to a tape of someone speaking French. When asked to repeat the sounds they had heard, students who had studied French in high school could repeat more of the sounds than could students who had no knowledge of French. When asked to listen to a tape of only meaningless sounds, none of the students were able to repeat more than a few seconds' worth of the sounds made on the tape.

   Which one of the following conclusions is best supported by the information above?

   (A) Knowledge of a foreign language interferes with one's ability to repeat unfamiliar sounds.
   (B) People who have a knowledge of French have better memories than do people who have no knowledge of French.
   (C) The ability to repeat unrelated sounds is not improved by frequent practice.
   (D) The ability to repeat sounds is influenced by one's ability to comprehend the meaning of the sounds.
   (E) Learning a foreign language requires an ability to distinguish unfamiliar sounds from gibberish.

GO ON TO THE NEXT PAGE.

3. Many species of animals that have evolved poison as a protection from predators contain extremely large amounts of those poisons. It might seem that a poisonous animal would need to contain only enough poison to sicken or kill most animals, but there are some amphibians whose bodies contain enough poison to kill an elephant. This can be explained by the fact that the most common predators of these amphibians have evolved resistance to the defensive poisons, so that over time the prey has continually become more poisonous, while the predator has developed ever greater resistance to the poison.

Which one of the following most accurately expresses the main conclusion of the argument?

(A) The seemingly excessive amount of poison contained in some prey animals' bodies can be explained by the co-evolution of predator and prey.
(B) Some animals that protect themselves from predation by being poisonous contain more than enough poison to kill any predator.
(C) An animal that protects itself against predators by being poisonous is likely to contain much more poison than is a predator that kills its prey with the use of poison.
(D) The evolution of poison is not completely effective at preventing an animal from being preyed upon.
(E) Poison is the most effective method available for prey animals to protect themselves from predators.

4. Gardener M: High levels of nitrogen-containing compounds are necessary for any plant to grow well. Therefore, to aid in this plant's growth, you must be sure to add plenty of fertilizer.

Gardener O: That would be pointless. The soil in which this plant is growing already contains a high level of nitrogen-containing compounds, and it is also receiving plenty of light and water.

Which one of the following, if true, provides the strongest basis for Gardener M to respond to the objection raised by Gardener O?

(A) The fact that the plant is receiving all of the things necessary for its growth does not necessarily ensure that it will grow well.
(B) Without the addition of plenty of fertilizer, the plant will soon deplete the supply of nitrogen-containing compounds currently found in its soil.
(C) A steady supply of light and water, although important for a plant's growth, is not as essential to a plant's growth as the supply of nitrogen-containing compounds.
(D) No measure that guarantees a plant's growth should be neglected, even if it is possible that the plant may grow without that measure being taken.
(E) The addition of excessive amounts of fertilizer may harm a plant, even if that plant requires nitrogen-containing compounds to grow.

GO ON TO THE NEXT PAGE.

5. Medical Researcher: If I don't get another research grant soon, I'll never be able to discover a cure for phlebitis.

Assistant: But that's great. If your grant does come through, that dreaded disease will finally be eradicated.

Which one of the following statements best describes the flaw in the assistant's reasoning?

(A) The assistant believes the researcher will be unable to cure phlebitis unless the grant comes through.
(B) The assistant thinks the researcher will use the grant to find a cure for phlebitis, rather than for some other purpose.
(C) The assistant believes it is more important to cure phlebitis than to eradicate other, more deadly conditions.
(D) The assistant believes that all the researcher needs to cure phlebitis is another research grant.
(E) The assistant thinks the researcher will cure phlebitis even if the grant does not come through.

6. Commentator: Projections indicate that our nation's Gross Domestic Product (GDP) will shrink next year, leading to a 2 percent loss in tax revenues collected by the federal government. Therefore, we should pass a 2 percent cut in all federal taxes for next year. That way, the federal government's lost tax revenue will at least serve to stimulate the economy.

Which one of the following indicates a flaw in the commentator's argument?

(A) A cut in federal taxes may necessitate a decrease in federal spending, which in turn may necessitate further tax cuts.
(B) The economic stimulus offered by the proposed tax cut may not be great enough to ensure that the loss in federal taxes collected is no greater than 2 percent.
(C) Tax cuts that are adequate to increase the rate of GDP growth in a healthy economy may not suffice to prevent the shrinkage of GDP when the economy is weak.
(D) Money that is spent for one purpose cannot also be spent for another purpose.
(E) There is no assurance given that the benefits of the proposed tax cut will not accrue primarily to the wealthiest individuals in society.

7. Due to the increasing number of part-time adjuncts hired to teach university courses, it has become increasingly difficult for people who have recently earned PhDs to find full-time employment in universities.

Which one of the following conforms most closely to the principle illustrated above?

(A) Because the number of trees cut down in this area exceeds the number of new trees that have been planted, deforestation is a growing problem in the area.
(B) Because the number of teachers who are qualified to teach science and math is declining, the quality of instruction students receive in those subjects is suffering.
(C) Because individual songs can now be downloaded cheaply and easily from the internet, sales of new albums in record stores have significantly declined.
(D) Because two new computer programs appeal to the same market and include the same features, neither of these programs will be cost-effective for the companies that sell them.
(E) Due to the increasing number of coffee growers who are going out of business, it has become increasingly difficult for those who supply equipment to coffee growers to find a market for their products.

8. Sheet for sheet, Brand A paper towels cost less than Brand B paper towels and are more absorbent. Yet a roll of Brand A paper towels costs more than a roll of Brand B paper towels.

Which one of the following, if true, explains how the statements above can both be true?

(A) Both Brand A and Brand B towels are manufactured by the same company, which often creates artificial competition for its expensive products.
(B) A roll of Brand B paper towels is more absorbent than a roll of Brand A paper towels.
(C) A roll of Brand A paper towels is more absorbent than a roll of Brand B paper towels.
(D) The cost of a roll of Brand A towels has risen every year for the last five years.
(E) A roll of Brand A paper towels has more sheets than a roll of Brand B paper towels.

GO ON TO THE NEXT PAGE.

9. State agricultural officials are hoping to save California's $30 billion-a-year fruit industry from destruction by the Mediterranean fruit fly by releasing nearly one billion sterile female fruit flies throughout the state. In the past, this has been shown to be the only effective means of limiting the spread of this destructive pest, outside of large-scale pesticide spraying.

Which one of the following best explains the intended effect of the program described above?

(A) to drastically increase the number of potential mates for the male fruit flies, requiring them to devote more of their energies to mating rather than eating fruit
(B) to saturate a given area with fruit flies, creating greater competition for food and thereby containing the damage done by the fruit fly to a smaller area
(C) to ensure that a large number of fruit flies in succeeding generations are born infertile
(D) to limit the growth of the population by reducing the number of successful matings between fruit flies
(E) to encourage overpopulation of the fruit fly in the hopes that nature will correct the situation itself

10. Small businesses, which are essential to our country's economy, are more likely to fail when the price of health insurance increases unexpectedly. A recent bill introduced in parliament would reimburse health insurers who agree to limit the growth of the prices they charge to a set amount each year. Although this would effectively control the price of health insurance, there is no reason to pass the bill because only a small proportion of the small businesses that fail in this country do so because of sudden increases in insurance rates.

Which one of the following, if true, most seriously weakens the argument?

(A) Sudden increases in costs not associated with health insurance are equally harmful to small businesses.
(B) Changes to the market that result from lowering the risk of sudden increases in health insurance prices will increase the vulnerability of small businesses to sudden increases in other costs.
(C) Employees of small businesses who become unemployed as the result of the failure of the companies they work for are less likely to accept employment in other small businesses.
(D) The reimbursements to health insurers mandated by the bill will be funded by increased taxation that will significantly harm the overall economy.
(E) Decreasing the risk to employers associated with sudden increases in health insurance costs would induce many more people to start their own small businesses.

GO ON TO THE NEXT PAGE.

11. Marie: I just found out that it is cheaper for me to heat my home with gas or oil than for me to use any of the alternative methods available. I don't understand why environmentalists insist that the cost of fossil fuels is so high.

Louise: That's because you are confusing the price of fossil fuels with their cost. Gas and oil release tremendous amounts of pollution into the water and air, causing great damage to the environment. Not only does this pose a threat to the ecological balance that will affect the quality of life for future generations, but it also causes health problems that may be related to the consumption of these fuels. Once you add in these factors, it is clear that there are many alternatives that are actually cheaper than gas or oil, and consumers should adopt them.

According to her argument above, if an alternative energy source were to be found, under which one of the following conditions would Louise definitely object to its use?

(A) if its price and cost were equal
(B) if its cost were higher than the price of fossil fuels
(C) if its cost were higher than the cost of fossil fuels
(D) if the price of fossil fuels were to fall
(E) if it were less efficient than fossil fuels

12. Company president: Many shareholders believe that, rather than developing products of our own to compete in new markets, our company should instead acquire existing companies that offer products of that type. This would be unwise. Any company that is willing to be acquired cannot be in a healthy competitive position in its market, and any company that is unwilling to be acquired would cost too much for our company to acquire without incurring substantial risk.

The company president's argument proceeds by

(A) advocating one course of action because a potential alternative course of action offers fewer advantages
(B) determining that a course of action is unwise because it cannot be undertaken without incurring unacceptable costs
(C) arguing against a course of action because there exist potential alternative courses of action that have not been definitively ruled out
(D) dismissing the course of action recommended by a group of shareholders because the members of that group do not have the best interests of the company at heart
(E) rejecting a course of action because the two possible situations in which it could be pursued are both unacceptable

GO ON TO THE NEXT PAGE.

13. Pollster: In one survey of the electorate, a representative sample of likely voters was initially presented with information about the candidates' positions on several important issues. Months later in a second survey, these same voters were presented with information concerning the positions held by these candidates on the same issues, which in some cases had changed substantially. Despite this fact, the proportion of the sample that supported each candidate remained virtually unchanged. It can be concluded, therefore, that new information received about the candidates cannot appreciably change a voter's decision of which candidate to support.

Which one of the following, if true, most undermines the pollster's argument?

(A) The number of issues on which either candidate had completely reversed his or her earlier position was relatively small.

(B) It is not reasonable to expect voters to remember every detail of a political candidate's position on every significant issue.

(C) The issues covered by the survey were not those that had been most widely reported in media coverage of the election.

(D) More than a third of the survey group indicated that they supported a different candidate at the time of the second survey than they had at the time of the initial survey.

(E) At the time of the initial survey, a majority of the survey group indicated that the candidates' positions on issues were not the most important determining factor in their decision of which candidate to support.

14. Oil exploration cannot be efficiently conducted by geological methods alone. The information gained through geological methods is useful for obtaining an accurate estimate of the likelihood of finding oil in a particular area, but only invasive surveys can determine with certainty the quantity of oil that will be produced by any area where it is found, and geological methods of oil exploration never include invasive surveys.

Which one of the following is an assumption on which the argument depends?

(A) Oil exploration, to be successful, must include considerations of how practical it is to extract oil from a given area where it is found.

(B) Oil exploration in an area cannot be conducted efficiently without an accurate estimate of the likelihood of finding oil in that area.

(C) Knowledge of both the likelihood of finding oil in an area and the quantity of oil produced by that area are required by most oil companies before they will decide to drill there.

(D) Oil exploration can be efficiently conducted only with certain knowledge of the quantity of oil that will be produced by any area where oil can be found.

(E) Certain knowledge of the amount of oil that will be produced by any area where oil is likely to be found can be obtained solely through geological methods.

GO ON TO THE NEXT PAGE.

15. Although all societies have some form of class system, there are systems that are based on neither wealth nor power. Still, there is no society that does not divide its population into the privileged and the common.

If the above statements are correct, it can be properly concluded that

(A) making distinctions between haves and have-nots is a part of human nature
(B) there are some people in all cultures who are considered privileged
(C) every society has its own unique hierarchy
(D) privileged people must have money
(E) all societies have a tradition of seeing themselves as either privileged or common

GO ON TO THE NEXT PAGE.

Questions 16-17

On the basis of our understanding of ancient geography, it has long been accepted that the Americas were initially settled by people from eastern Asia who crossed into North America on a land bridge that once spanned the Bering Strait. Under this belief, all the native peoples of North and South America have been thought to be descendents of these first colonists. Yet genetic analysis of surviving native populations in the Americas indicates that most of them are much more closely related to the native populations of the Philippines and other Pacific islands. It seems clear that Pacific islanders must have been the first to reach the Americas. It has been shown that, using traditional construction methods, a group could have crossed the Pacific Ocean and reached South America.

16. Which one of the following is the main conclusion of the argument?

(A) The native populations in the Americas are no longer generally thought to be descended from settlers who came from eastern Asia.
(B) The genetic makeup of native populations in the Americas is substantially similar to that of native populations in the Philippines and other Pacific islands.
(C) The first human settlers in the Americas were Pacific islanders.
(D) At least some Pacific islanders reached the South American continent by traveling on boats that were constructed using traditional methods.
(E) Pacific islanders originating in the Philippines were the ancestors of all native populations in North and South America.

17. The reasoning in the argument is most vulnerable to which one of the following criticisms?

(A) That a stated belief has been traditionally held to be true is taken as evidence that the belief must, in fact, be false.
(B) That a given explanation of a set of facts is possible in some cases is taken as positive proof that this explanation is correct in all cases.
(C) The statement of a set of conditions under which some correction to a set of long-held beliefs would be required is confused with the establishment of the fact that such a set of conditions actually arose.
(D) The historical cause of a particular set of facts is mistakenly assumed to be the only possible cause of a similar set of facts elsewhere.
(E) Facts that may only support the claim that a particular historic event occurred are taken to show that this event occurred before other similar events that could possibly have occurred earlier.

18. The current method of powering aircraft, the burning of fuel by internal-combustion engines, cannot be maintained indefinitely. Internal-combustion engines now burn refined petroleum, and the world's supply of petroleum is necessarily limited.

Which one of the following is an assumption required by the argument?

(A) Some means of powering aircraft other than the burning of fuels in internal-combustion engines could be successfully adopted.
(B) Internal-combustion engines cannot be designed so that they burn some fuel not derived from limited resources.
(C) Products from refined petroleum other than those currently burned in aircraft engines could not be chemically modified to replace the fuels used in aircraft today.
(D) Engines that do not operate by internal combustion could not be designed to operate using fuels derived from petroleum.
(E) No method of powering aircraft that relies on a finite resource is practical.

19. Evidence seems to indicate that people's faith in some mystical practices increases when these practices offer relief in frightening or challenging situations. One significant piece of evidence is the observation that the use of "healing crystals" is more prevalent among people who suffer from life-threatening diseases such as cancer than it is among people who have minor health problems such as colds or the flu.

Which one of the following, if true, would most seriously weaken the conclusion drawn in the passage above?

(A) Rapid social change has alienated people and has led to an overall increase in people's adoption of mystical practices.
(B) Many mystical practices are never used by more than a small number of extremely ill people.
(C) Those who are diagnosed with life-threatening diseases may seek nontraditional treatments for those diseases without having faith in their effectiveness.
(D) Psychics and mediums do not experience a surge in business after the occurrence of earthquakes and plane crashes.
(E) The use of crystals is one of the most ancient methods utilized for healing.

20. Executive: Nearly everyone can become a consultant, for there are no formal requirements that must be satisfied to be called a consultant. Anyone who convinces a company to hire him or her to perform an advisory function—no matter what its nature—is by definition a consultant.

The executive's conclusion can be properly drawn if which one of the following is assumed?

(A) Nearly everyone can convince a company to hire him or her to perform an advisory function.
(B) Some consultants satisfy a set of formal requirements not directly related to any advisory function they perform for a business.
(C) Those who convince companies to hire them to perform advisory functions satisfy their employers' requirements for the performance of those functions.
(D) Every consultant has convinced some company that he or she satisfies a set of informal requirements.
(E) Some consultants could convince any company to hire them to perform certain advisory functions.

21. An editor found that the manuscript of a new novel contained many grammatical errors and misused words. Despite this fact, the editor did not recommend that the manuscript be rejected.

Each of the following, if true, would explain the editor's decision EXCEPT:

(A) The manuscript in question had already been accepted by the publisher, a decision that could not be reversed on the editor's advice.
(B) The author of the manuscript was a first-time author whose work was not expected to attract much critical notice.
(C) The prose style used in the manuscript, although unorthodox, was groundbreaking and enjoyable to read.
(D) The errors in the manuscript could easily be corrected in the editing process, and the novel's story was gripping and dramatic.
(E) Correct grammar and word usage are not the most important factors in an editor's decision of whether to recommend a manuscript's rejection.

22. If a candidate is to win an election easily, that candidate must respond to the electorate's emotional demands—demands that the opponent either does not see or cannot act upon. Although these emotional demands are often not directly articulated by the electorate or by the candidate responding to them, they are an integral part of any landslide victory.

Which one of the following conclusions can most logically be drawn from the passage above?

(A) If neither candidate responds to the emotional demands of the electorate, either candidate might win in a landslide.
(B) If an election was close, the emotional demands of the electorate were conflicting.
(C) If a candidate responds to the emotional demands of the electorate, that candidate will have a landslide victory.
(D) An election during which neither candidate responds to the emotional demands of the electorate will not result in a landslide.
(E) Emotional demands are the only inarticulated issues in an election.

23. A well-known philosopher once articulated the method by which an action can be judged to be unethical: Imagine the consequences of everyone in society taking that action; if those consequences would be harmful to society, then the action is unethical. Yet it cannot be denied that, at times in the past, the intentional breaking of laws to draw attention to injustice has had beneficial effects in many societies. By the philosopher's standard, however, these actions would be judged unethical because if everyone in a society disregarded its laws, chaos would result. Because it is every person's ethical responsibility to fight against injustice in society, the philosopher's method must be incorrect.

The argument is flawed because it

(A) confuses what is ethically impermissible with what is merely not forbidden
(B) treats actions that have characteristics in common with a larger class as members of that class without recognizing a relevant distinction
(C) derives a conclusion about all the actions of a certain class on the basis of a principle whose relevance to those actions is doubtful
(D) mistakenly ascribes a characteristic to a class of actions that can properly be said to apply only to the individual actions that make up that class
(E) incorrectly assumes the truth of its conclusion that the philosopher's method is flawed

24. For every known physical phenomenon, physicists have posited laws that govern the occurrence of that phenomenon. It can be concluded, therefore, that every known physical phenomenon is governed by the same law.

The flawed reasoning in the argument above is most similar to that in which one of the following?

(A) The trunk of every tree is a body of tissue that contains both xylem and phloem. Therefore, any body of tissue that contains both xylem and phloem is the trunk of a tree.
(B) Every house has a unique mailing address. Therefore, because these packages are all marked with the same mailing address, they will all be sent to the same house.
(C) Because every action taken by a person can be explained by unconscious motives, a single motive explains all of the actions taken by any person.
(D) No violin that was made in the twentieth century is remarkably valuable. Because this violin is remarkably valuable, it must not have been made in the twentieth century.
(E) For every known star, astronomers can determine that star's elemental composition. Because a star's elemental composition determines its exact color, no two stars are the same exact color.

25. No iconoclasts are public figures, and all politicians are public figures. It follows that no politicians are fanatics.

The conclusion above follows logically if which one of the following is assumed?

(A) All fanatics are public figures.
(B) All fanatics are iconoclasts.
(C) All public figures are politicians.
(D) No fanatics are iconoclasts.
(E) No iconoclasts are politicians.

26. Wendy: Young people in our country are lagging behind the young people in other countries in science and math. With the increasing importance of technology in the world economy, it seems all but certain that our country's economic stature is in jeopardy.

Thomas: You forget that our country's strong economy allows us to attract new immigrants easily. Although the young people in our country may not fill the need for employees in technology companies, we will always be able to satisfy it by allowing those with the needed skills to emigrate from other countries, thereby maintaining our crucial competitive position in the world economy.

By their statements, it can be most reasonably inferred that Wendy and Thomas would agree with which one of the following statements?

(A) Efforts should be made to encourage the growth of the country's economy in areas that do not rely as heavily on technical knowledge.
(B) Continued efforts to ensure that the country's future workforce includes those who have the skills needed by technology companies are warranted.
(C) The quality of math and science education offered to the country's young people can be improved only if the rate of immigration is limited.
(D) In the future, the country's economic stature is likely to decline.
(E) Technology companies will adapt their business operations so that they can successfully employ people in many different countries who have needed skills.

STOP

IF YOU FINISH BEFORE TIME IS CALLED, YOU MAY CHECK YOUR WORK ON THIS SECTION ONLY. DO NOT WORK ON ANY OTHER SECTION IN THE TEST.

NO TEST MATERIAL ON THIS PAGE

SECTION III

Time—35 Minutes

25 Questions

Directions: The questions in this section are based on the reasoning contained in brief statements or passages. For some questions, more than one of the choices could conceivably answer the question. However, you are to choose the best answer; that is, the response that most accurately and completely answers the question. You should not make assumptions that are by commonsense standards implausible, superfluous, or incompatible with the passage. After you have chosen the best answer, blacken the corresponding space on your answer sheet.

1. Senator: For economic issues, I base my responses on logic. For political issues, I base my responses either on logic or gut instinct. For moral issues, I never base my responses on logic.

   Which one of the following can be correctly inferred from the statements above?

   (A) If the senator relies on logic, he may be responding to a moral issue.
   (B) If the senator relies on logic, he is not responding to an economic issue.
   (C) If the senator does not rely on logic, he is responding to a political issue.
   (D) If the senator does not rely on logic, he must be responding to an economic issue.
   (E) If the senator does not rely on logic, he might be responding to a political issue.

2. Social institutions are organized in such a way that they reinforce the need for their continued existence. Thus, although many political candidates claim that they will do away with certain social institutions that are not universally supported, it is unlikely that these candidates will be able to deliver on their promises.

   The statement that social institutions are organized in such a way that they reinforce the need for their continued existence functions in the argument in which one of the following ways?

   (A) It is a premise offered to lend support to the claim that political candidates will be unable to deliver on their promises to eliminate certain social institutions.
   (B) It is a conclusion supported by the premise that many political candidates claim that they will do away with some social institutions.
   (C) It is an assertion despite which the argument says that political candidates will succeed in doing away with the least popular of social institutions.
   (D) It is offered as evidence against the belief that political candidates are sincere when they promise to do away with certain social institutions.
   (E) It is the main conclusion of the argument.

3. An electronics manufacturer in financial trouble decided last year that, to survive, it needed to eliminate its least popular product lines to save on production costs. The product lines it eliminated accounted for 20 percent of all products produced by the manufacturer at that time. Yet, one year after their elimination, production costs directly related to the manufacture of their products have decreased by only 15 percent.

   Which one of the following, if true, contributes most to an explanation of the difference between the reduction in manufacturing output and the cost savings achieved as a result of that reduction?

   (A) The product lines eliminated by the manufacturer were also the most expensive products to produce.
   (B) Production of products in the lines that were not eliminated were significantly cut back over the past year.
   (C) Raw materials for the manufacturer's products constitute a far greater share of the products' direct production costs than expenses such as labor and maintenance.
   (D) The total direct production costs associated with manufacturing components used in all of the manufacturer's products were not changed by the elimination of some product lines that used those components.
   (E) The manufacturer's contract with the union to which its employees belong required the reassignment of workers who had previously been employed in producing the eliminated product lines to administrative departments not directly related to manufacturing operations.

GO ON TO THE NEXT PAGE.

4. Advertisement: Professional exterminators will tell you that to rid your home of roaches, you must do more than kill all the roaches you see. This is why the system that professional exterminators use most includes a poison that inhibits the development of roach eggs already laid, as well as a chemical that kills all adult roaches. This same combination is now available to the nonprofessional in new Extirm. When you're ready to get rid of roaches once and for all, get Extirm in your corner.

All of the following are implied by the advertisement above EXCEPT:

(A) Professional exterminators asked about roach extermination recommended Extirm.
(B) Extirm contains a chemical that inhibits the development of roach eggs.
(C) More than one chemical is required to rid a home of roaches.
(D) Inhibiting the development of roach eggs may not eliminate roaches from the home.
(E) Roaches reproduce by laying eggs.

5. The use of genetically engineered bacteria to process some types of radioactive waste is preferable to the traditional method of burying it in sealed containers. Whereas waste disposed of by traditional means remains radioactive for thousands of years, the engineered bacteria can render radioactive waste safe within a matter of months. Also, breaches or flaws in the containment of buried waste can lead to harmful contamination of soil and water that may be extremely difficult to detect.

Which one of the following statements, if true, most weakens the argument?

(A) The by-products generated by the genetically engineered bacteria in processing radioactive waste are not more harmful to the environment than the radioactive waste itself would be.
(B) No type of genetically engineered bacteria has yet been discovered that can process all types of radioactive waste.
(C) The processes that produce radioactive waste also lead to radioactive contamination of equipment that cannot be reduced through the use of genetically engineered bacteria.
(D) The environmental conditions required by the genetically engineered bacteria in processing radioactive waste make harmful soil and water contamination likely.
(E) There is a risk that some of the genetically engineered bacteria, when used, will give rise to mutant progeny that are unable to process radioactive waste.

6. On Tuesday night, we observed that comet X was moving in the direction of star P. On Wednesday night, a flare was observed that could have been caused by a comet colliding with a star. Therefore, the flare that was observed on Wednesday night was caused by comet X colliding with star P.

The questionable method of reasoning in the argument above is most similar to that in which one of the following arguments?

(A) At three o'clock, a trash can was standing upright at the corner of the intersection of Myrtle and Carleton. At four o'clock, a trash can was lying in the center of that same intersection. Because at four o'clock there was no longer a trash can standing upright on the corner, it is likely that a passing automobile collided with the trash can and knocked it into the intersection.
(B) This morning, Stewart was in downtown Frostburg. This afternoon, Stewart was in downtown Augusta. Because Stewart could not have traveled so far in so short a time without traveling by airplane, Stewart must have traveled in an airplane today.
(C) Yesterday, Misty expressed her intention to make an offer on a house that is for sale through realtor V. Today, an offer was made on a house that is for sale through a realtor. Therefore, that offer was made by Misty on a house that is for sale through realtor V.
(D) Either May or Kathleen will be the next CEO of Thiscorp. Because media reports suggest that the one chosen will not be May, Kathleen is certain to be the next CEO of Thiscorp.
(E) Ten minutes ago, a red car was moving down this country road at excessive speed. No one else has used the road all day. A car has just collided with a large tree along this country road; there can be no doubt that the car involved in the collision is red.

GO ON TO THE NEXT PAGE.

7. Sales representative: Our nutritional supplement treats mold allergies at least as well as any prescription drug does. Unfortunately, we have no study results to prove this claim, but the supplement is clearly effective: Our customer satisfaction surveys show that people with mold allergies who take our supplement all report a lessening of symptoms. No study conducted by any maker of a prescription drug has ever refuted this evidence.

The sales representative's argument is flawed because it reasons that

(A) the fact that the supplement is effective does not necessarily imply that it is as effective as any prescription drug
(B) the results of a survey conducted by an organization with commercial interest in its findings may be biased
(C) because no evidence demonstrates that a survey's results are inaccurate, the results must therefore be accurate
(D) the experiences of those who seek treatment for a condition are relevant to an evaluation of the relative efficacy of those treatments
(E) the lessening of symptoms does not necessarily constitute effective treatment of the malady responsible for those symptoms

8. It is widely believed that the consumption of certain cold medicines may impair a driver's ability to operate a vehicle safely. However, the results of examinations administered during the process of obtaining a driver's license show that this is a misconception. The rate at which examinees who were taking cold medicines were awarded driver's licenses was no different from the rate at which examinees in the population at large received driver's licenses.

The reasoning above is fallacious because it fails to consider the possibility that

(A) the number of those taking cold medicines during the examination process represented a relatively small proportion of the total number of examinees
(B) not all cold medicines have similar effects on a driver's ability to operate a vehicle safely
(C) an individual who is able to operate a vehicle safely may fail one or more of the examinations on which the decision to award a driver's license is based
(D) the belief that cold medicines impair coordination has been refuted by other studies not directly related to operating vehicles
(E) an individual who takes cold medicine may be able to operate a vehicle more safely than that individual would if he or she left the cold untreated

GO ON TO THE NEXT PAGE.

9. The fact that many animals preyed upon by large carnivores are herd animals does not therefore imply that their herding behavior confers protection from predation. When hunting prey that lives in herds, large carnivores routinely target the weakest members of the herd, and unless the targeted animal is a juvenile, even the closest relatives of the targeted animal do not act to protect it. The closest relatives of most juvenile animals, whether or not they live in herds, will most often act to protect them from predators.

Which one of the following most accurately expresses the main conclusion of the argument?

(A) The closest relatives of juvenile animals most often act to protect those animals from predators.
(B) Living in herds offers advantages that do not stem from the decreased likelihood of being killed by a predator.
(C) Large carnivores tend to prefer prey that lives in herds.
(D) The reason that many animals live in herds cannot be that herding behavior increases the number of animals that will act to protect the herd's members from large carnivores.
(E) The confusion engendered when a herd flees from a large carnivore provides protection for the targeted member of that herd, even when no other herd member actively protects that animal.

10. Recent history in many former dictatorships suggests that the introduction of democratic reforms and market reforms at the same time is ultimately counterproductive. Although many countries in which one of these types of reform was carried out independent of the other have in time embraced liberalization of both types, almost all countries in which both political and economic continuity are interrupted eventually slip back into authoritarian styles of government that exert strong control over the market. It can be concluded that the best strategy for reform in a country that was formerly a dictatorship is to promote increased democracy, or more freedom in the market, but not both.

Which one of the following statements, if true, would provide the greatest additional support for the argument above?

(A) Economic reform in countries that were not formerly dictatorships is usually more difficult to promote than is political reform.
(B) Some authoritarian governments oppress their populations by exerting control over their countries' markets.
(C) Reform efforts that do not address the fundamental humanitarian needs of a country's citizenry are unlikely to succeed.
(D) Reform in a former dictatorship cannot be successful without including aspects of political or economic continuity as well as political or economic liberalization.
(E) Countries with both democratic governments and market economies may also benefit from reform to one or the other of these systems.

GO ON TO THE NEXT PAGE.

11. In mathematics, different definitions of key concepts may be advanced, but no new definition is considered correct if it conflicts with the accepted definition. In some cases, however, it is possible that a new correct definition is able to solve some problem that the accepted definition cannot. In this case, because the accepted definition should always be the correct definition that is capable of solving the greatest number of problems, the new definition should become the accepted definition.

Which one of the following principles, if valid, most helps to justify the reasoning above?

(A) Any new definition of a mathematical concept that can solve some problem that the accepted definition cannot must be correct.
(B) No new correct definition that is able to solve some problem that the accepted definition cannot solve fails to solve any problem that the accepted definition can solve.
(C) It is possible that a new incorrect definition of some mathematical concept is capable of solving problems that the currently accepted definition cannot.
(D) The definitions of mathematical concepts cannot be evaluated in terms of their truth, only their correctness.
(E) Any existing correct definition of a mathematical concept that is not the accepted definition must fail to solve at least one problem that the accepted definition can.

12. Computer Technician: This system has either a software problem or a hardware problem. None of the available diagnostic tests has been able to determine where the problem lies. The software can be replaced, but the hardware cannot be altered in any way, which means that if the problem lies in the hardware, the entire system will have to be scrapped. We must begin work to solve the problem by presupposing that the problem is with the software.

On which one of the following principles could the technician's reasoning be based?

(A) In fixing a problem that has two possible causes, it makes more sense to deal with both causes rather than spend time trying to determine which is the actual cause of the problem.
(B) If events outside one's control bear on a decision, the best course of action is to assume the "worst-case" scenario.
(C) When the soundness of an approach depends on the validity of an assumption, one's first task must be to test that assumption's validity.
(D) When circumstances must be favorable in order for a strategy to succeed, the strategy must be based on the assumption that conditions are indeed favorable until proved otherwise.
(E) When only one strategy can be successful, the circumstances affecting that strategy must be altered so that strategy may be employed.

GO ON TO THE NEXT PAGE.

13. To become a master at chess, a person must play. If a person plays for at least four hours a day, that person will inevitably become a master of the game. Thus, if a person is a master at the game of chess, that person must have played each day for at least four hours.

The error in the logic of the argument above is most accurately described by which one of the following?

(A) The conclusion is inadequate because it fails to acknowledge that people who play for four hours each day might not develop a degree of skill for the game that others view as masterful.
(B) The conclusion is inadequate because it fails to acknowledge that playing one hour a day might be sufficient for some people to become masters.
(C) The conclusion is inadequate because it fails to acknowledge that if a person has not played four hours a day, that person has not become a master.
(D) The conclusion is inadequate because it fails to acknowledge that four hours of playing time each day is not a strategy recommended by any world-champion chess players.
(E) The conclusion is inadequate because it fails to acknowledge that most people are not in a position to devote four hours each day to playing chess.

14. Prescriptive grammar is not a natural science. We know this because prescriptive grammar relies upon a set of axiomatic principles, and no science that relies upon a set of axiomatic principles depends primarily on experimentation.

The conclusion of the argument follows logically if which one of the following is assumed?

(A) Some natural sciences rely on a set of axiomatic principles.
(B) All natural sciences depend primarily on experimentation.
(C) No science that depends primarily on experimentation relies on a set of axiomatic principles.
(D) All sciences that depend primarily on experimentation are natural sciences.
(E) No grammar that relies on a set of axiomatic principles is a science.

15. Last year, Marcel enjoyed a high income from exactly two places: his sporting goods store and his stock market investments. Although Marcel earns far more from his store than from his investments, the money he earns from the stock market is an important part of his income. Because of a series of drops in the stock market, Marcel will not earn as much from his investments this year. It follows then that Marcel will make less money this year than he did last year.

Which one of the following is an assumption necessary to the author's argument?

(A) Increased profits at Marcel's sporting goods store will not offset any loss in stock market income.
(B) Sporting goods stores earn lower profits when the stock market drops.
(C) Drops in the stock market do not always affect all of a particular investor's stocks.
(D) Marcel's stock market investments will be subject to increased volatility.
(E) If his income is lower, Marcel will not be able to meet his expenses.

GO ON TO THE NEXT PAGE.

16. Efforts to encourage conservation by individuals are unlikely to address the world's most pressing energy problems, for although individuals have some knowledge of the amount of energy they use directly, there are hidden energy costs to everything an individual does. Every product purchased and every service received has an attendant energy cost, and the cumulative total of these costs far exceeds the amount of energy used directly by individuals.

Which one of the following is an assumption on which the argument relies?

(A) The most pressing energy problems involve consumption of energy that cannot be attributed to individual behavior.
(B) The prices of goods and services do not incorporate the hidden energy costs involved in their production and delivery.
(C) Conservation efforts are most effective when individuals have control over the amount of energy they consume.
(D) The world's most pressing energy problems cannot be solved by reliance on the actions of individuals.
(E) Individuals can effectively conserve energy in only those cases when they have some knowledge of the energy costs attendant upon their actions.

17. Activist: All nations that base their economic policy on unbridled competition encourage dishonest business practices, and all nations in which dishonest business practices are common lose the trust on which international investment is based. Any nation that, because of factors beyond the government's control or because of shortsighted policies, loses the respect of its trading partners is unlikely to be able to secure needed aid in the event of economic hardship. Thus, if a nation wishes to maintain economic stability, it is essential that the activities of banks be heavily regulated.

Each of the following, if true, weakens the activist's argument EXCEPT:

(A) Moderate regulation of banks is adequate to ensure that dishonest business practices do not become commonplace.
(B) Unbridled competition, in the absence of other contributing factors, only leads to a low incidence of dishonest business practices in an economy.
(C) Those nations that lose the trust on which international investment is based do not necessarily lose the respect of their trading partners.
(D) It is possible for a nation to maintain economic stability without securing aid in the event of economic hardship.
(E) An economic policy based on unbridled competition is not the only shortsighted government policy that may lead to a loss of respect among a country's trading partners.

GO ON TO THE NEXT PAGE.

18. Columnist: Labor unions claim that they take tough negotiating positions to secure fair treatment for workers, but they have self-interested motives in doing so. A union that gets higher wages for its members can collect higher union dues, thus allowing the union to make more political contributions and gain influence. There can be little doubt that the purpose of the labor movement is primarily to amass political power and only incidentally to help workers.

The reasoning in the columnist's argument is flawed because the argument

(A) incorrectly concludes that every union is interested in gaining political power based on the fact that many unions are interested in doing so
(B) improperly derives a conclusion about the labor movement as a whole on the basis of information concerning the behavior of individual labor unions
(C) assumes without warrant that two goals are mutually exclusive when a premise of the argument states that the pursuit of one goal may be furthered by pursuit of the other
(D) makes ambiguous use of the term "labor"
(E) rejects the arguments made by a group on the basis of information concerning the political preferences of that group

19. In concluding that there has been a shift in the sense of parental responsibility in the United States since the 1960s, researchers point to the increase in the frequency with which fathers tend to the daily needs of their children. However, this increase cannot be attributed exclusively to a shift in parental mores, for during the same period there has been an increase in the percentage of mothers who have jobs. With this in mind, the increased participation of fathers in childrearing may well be only a symptom of a more fundamental change in society.

The author of the passage criticizes the conclusion of the researchers by

(A) offering a clearer definition of the researchers' premises, thereby compromising their argument
(B) attacking the integrity of the researchers rather than their reasoning
(C) showing that the researchers have reversed cause and effect in making their argument
(D) pointing out that their criteria for "parental responsibility" are not a logical basis for their argument
(E) suggesting an alternative cause for the effect cited by the researchers

GO ON TO THE NEXT PAGE.

Questions 20–21

Upon exiting an exhibit, some visitors to art museums find it difficult to describe what it was that they liked and didn't like about the paintings. Yet because these visitors feel strongly about which art they believed to be good and which art they believed to be bad, appreciating a work of art obviously does not require the ability to articulate what, specifically, was perceived to be good or bad.

20. The argument above assumes which one of the following?

(A) The fact that some people find it difficult to articulate what they like about a work of art does not mean that no one can.
(B) If an individual feels strongly about a work of art, then he or she is capable of appreciating that work of art.
(C) The vocabulary of visual art is not a part of common knowledge, but rather is known only to those who study the arts.
(D) When a person can articulate what he or she likes about a particular painting, he or she is able to appreciate that work of art.
(E) Paintings can be discussed only in general terms of good and bad.

21. According to the passage above, all of the following could be true EXCEPT:

(A) Some museum visitors can explain with great precision what they liked and didn't like about a certain painting.
(B) If a person studies art, then that person will be able to articulate her opinion about paintings.
(C) If a person can't say why she likes a piece of art, it doesn't necessarily mean that she doesn't appreciate that piece.
(D) Some visitors can explain what they liked about a piece, but are unable to explain what they didn't like.
(E) The inability to express the reason for a particular preference indicates that the preference must not be strong.

22. Evan: Earlier this year, the *Stockton Free Press* reported that residents consider Mayor Dalton more concerned with his image than with advancing the cause of the less fortunate of Stockton.

Dalia: But the mayor appointed a new director of the public television station, and almost immediately the station began running a documentary series promoting the mayor's antipoverty program.

Evan: Clearly the mayor has, by this appointment, attempted to manipulate public opinion through the media.

Evan's second statement counters Dalia's argument by

(A) disputing the relevancy of her statement
(B) suggesting that Dalia is less informed about the issue than he
(C) confusing the argument she presents with his own
(D) appealing to popular opinion that the mayor should not misuse his access to the media
(E) claiming that Dalia's argument is an example that actually strengthens his own argument

GO ON TO THE NEXT PAGE.

23. Naturalist: Every year, thousands of animals already on the endangered species list are killed for their hides, furs, or horns. These illegal and often cruel deaths serve to push these species further toward the brink of extinction. The products made from these animals, such as articles of clothing and quack medical remedies, are goods no one really needs. What is needed is a large-scale media campaign to make the facts of the killings known and lessen the demand for these animal products. Such a campaign would be a good start in the effort to save endangered species from extinction.

Environmentalist: For the overwhelming majority of currently endangered species, the true threat of extinction comes not from hunting and poaching, but from continually shrinking habitats. Concentrating attention on the dangers of poaching for a very few high-visibility species would be counterproductive, leading people to believe that a boycott of a few frivolous items is enough to protect endangered species, when what is needed is a truly global environmental policy.

The point at issue between the naturalist and the environmentalist is which one of the following?

(A) whether the poaching of some endangered species actually increases that species' chances of becoming extinct
(B) whether a large-scale media campaign can affect the demand for some products
(C) whether more endangered species are threatened by poaching and hunting or shrinking of habitat
(D) whether some species could be saved from extinction by eliminating all commercial demand for that species
(E) whether a large-scale media campaign that lessens the demand for products made from endangered species is a good strategy for saving endangered species

24. Historian: Excavations in the ancient city of Ouz have uncovered a massive bronze statue. No other bronze object has ever been found in the city's ruins. Thus, because it appears that the ancient inhabitants of Ouz lacked either the ability to make bronze or the knowledge of how to shape it, it seems clear that the statue was looted and brought back during one of its many raids on neighboring cities.

Which one of the following, if true, most seriously weakens the historian's argument?

(A) Although all of Ouz's neighboring cities have been excavated, none has been found to include any bronze objects.
(B) The bronze statue is of a peacock, an animal that was widely found throughout the geographic region where Ouz was situated.
(C) No historical or archaeological evidence indicates that smaller bronze objects made in Ouz were removed by subsequent visitors to the site.
(D) A nearby city known to be frequently at war with Ouz contains signs that its inhabitants were able to shape bronze.
(E) Bronze was used in many regions as a material for making weapons throughout the era in which the city of Ouz was inhabited.

GO ON TO THE NEXT PAGE.

25. Studies of fighter pilots reveal the surprising fact that they are much less likely to die of heart attacks than are members of the population at large, despite the stressful nature of their work and the rigorous selection process to which they are subjected. These results hold even when the data are adjusted to compensate for the fact that piloting fighter jets is dangerous work and leads to some premature deaths. It seems doubtful, then, that recent studies purporting to show that job stress leads to an increased risk of heart attack can be correct.

Which one of the following, if true, lends the strongest support to the argument's conclusion?

(A) The average life expectancy of male fighter pilots is nearly five years shorter than the life expectancy of the general male population.
(B) The characteristics that allow fighter pilots to pass through the rigorous selection process to which they are subjected do not also allow them to avoid suffering the negative consequences of stress.
(C) Fighter pilots are in general fitter and more physically strong than are the members of the population at large, allowing them to survive more of the heart attacks they experience.
(D) Other studies of high-stress jobs outside the military have shown that the risk of heart attack triples for people who hold those jobs.
(E) Factors other than job stress, such as heredity, exercise, and diet, are known to be more important determining factors in whether or not an individual suffers a heart attack than is job stress.

S T O P

IF YOU FINISH BEFORE TIME IS CALLED, YOU MAY CHECK YOUR WORK ON THIS SECTION ONLY.
DO NOT WORK ON ANY OTHER SECTION IN THE TEST.

NO TEST MATERIAL ON THIS PAGE

SECTION IV

Time—35 Minutes

23 Questions

Directions: Each group of questions in this section is based on a set of conditions. In answering some of the questions, it may be useful to draw a rough diagram. Choose the response that most accurately and completely answers each question and blacken the corresponding space on your answer sheet.

Questions 1–6

An interior decorator is designing a color scheme using at least one of the following colors: red, orange, yellow, indigo, green, and violet. No other colors will be used. The selection of colors for the scheme is consistent with the following conditions:

If the scheme uses orange, then it does not use indigo.
If the scheme does not use green, then it uses orange.
If the scheme uses yellow, then it uses both indigo and violet.
If the scheme uses violet, then it uses red or green or both.

1. Which one of the following could be a complete and accurate list of the colors the scheme includes?

(A) yellow, indigo
(B) indigo, green
(C) yellow, indigo, violet
(D) yellow, green, violet
(E) orange, yellow, indigo, violet

2. Which one of the following could be the only color the scheme uses?

(A) red
(B) yellow
(C) indigo
(D) green
(E) violet

3. Which one of the following CANNOT be a complete and accurate list of the colors the scheme uses?

(A) orange, green
(B) green, violet
(C) red, orange, violet
(D) yellow, indigo, green, violet
(E) red, orange, yellow, indigo, violet

4. If the scheme doesn't use violet, then which one of the following must be true?

(A) The scheme uses orange.
(B) The scheme uses at least two colors.
(C) The scheme at most three colors.
(D) The scheme uses neither yellow nor indigo.
(E) The scheme uses neither yellow nor orange.

5. If the scheme uses violet, then which of the following must be false?

(A) The scheme does not use red.
(B) The scheme does not use green.
(C) The scheme does not use indigo.
(D) The scheme uses indigo but not yellow.
(E) The scheme uses indigo but not green.

6. If the condition that if the scheme doesn't use green then it does use orange is suspended, and all the other conditions remain in effect, then which one of the following CANNOT be a complete and accurate list of the colors the scheme uses?

(A) indigo
(B) red, indigo
(C) yellow, indigo, violet
(D) red, indigo, violet
(E) red, yellow, indigo, violet

GO ON TO THE NEXT PAGE.

Questions 7–13

Five runners—Fanny, Gina, Henrietta, Isabelle, and Mona—are assigned to lanes numbered 1 through 5 on a track. Each runner has the option of wearing a knee brace during the competition. Two of the runners are from Palo Alto, two are from San Jose, and one is from Newcastle. The following conditions must apply:

Isabelle and Mona are assigned to the first two lanes, but not necessarily in that order.
The runner in the third lane is from Newcastle and wears a knee brace.
Neither runner from San Jose wears a knee brace.
Both Gina and Fanny are assigned higher-numbered lanes than that of Henrietta.
Neither Mona nor Fanny comes from San Jose.

7. Which one the following could be an accurate list of the runners, in order from lane 1 to lane 5?

(A) Isabelle, Henrietta, Fanny, Mona, Gina
(B) Isabelle, Mona, Gina, Henrietta, Fanny
(C) Mona, Gina, Henrietta, Isabelle, Fanny
(D) Mona, Isabelle, Gina, Henrietta, Fanny
(E) Mona, Isabelle, Henrietta, Fanny, Gina

8. Which one of the following could be true?

(A) Fanny runs in lane 5.
(B) Gina runs in lane 1.
(C) Henrietta runs in lane 2.
(D) Isabelle runs in lane 3.
(E) Mona runs in lane 5.

9. If the runner in lane 1 is from San Jose, then which one of the following could be true?

(A) Fanny runs in a lane numbered one higher than Isabelle's.
(B) Henrietta runs in a lane numbered one higher than Fanny's.
(C) Henrietta runs in a lane numbered one higher than Mona's.
(D) Henrietta runs in a lane numbered one higher than Isabelle's.
(E) Isabelle runs in a lane numbered one higher than Mona's.

10. If a runner with a knee brace runs in lane 1, then which one of the following CANNOT be true?

(A) Fanny runs in lane 4.
(B) Gina runs in lane 5.
(C) A runner with a knee brace runs in lane 2.
(D) A runner with a knee brace runs in lane 3.
(E) A runner with a knee brace runs in lane 4.

11. Which one of the following must be true?

(A) Gina runs without a knee brace.
(B) Henrietta runs without a knee brace.
(C) Mona runs without a knee brace.
(D) Fanny runs with a knee brace.
(E) Isabelle runs with a knee brace.

12. If runners wearing knee braces do not run in consecutively-numbered lanes, and runners not wearing knee braces do not run in consecutively-numbered lanes, then in exactly how many distinct orders could the runners be assigned to lanes?

(A) one
(B) two
(C) three
(D) four
(E) five

13. If a runner with a knee brace runs in lane 2, then which one of the following CANNOT be true?

(A) The runner in lane 1 is from San Jose.
(B) The runner in lane 1 is from Palo Alto.
(C) The runner in lane 4 is from San Jose.
(D) The runner in lane 5 is from San Jose.
(E) The runner in lane 5 is from Palo Alto.

GO ON TO THE NEXT PAGE.

Questions 14–18

The Paulson, Rideau, Stevenson, Tisch, Van Pelt, and Wong families have each rented a time-share in a six-unit condominium. The condominium has three floors, labeled first to third from bottom to top. Each floor has an identical layout consisting of two units: a garden view apartment on the west side of the building and an ocean view apartment on the east side of the building. The following conditions must apply:

The Rideaus rent the unit immediately beneath the Paulsons's ocean-view unit.
If the Wongs rent an ocean-view apartment, the Rideaus occupy the same floor as the Van Pelts.
If the Paulsons and the Tisches occupy the same floor, the Wongs rent the unit immediately and directly beneath the Stevensons's unit.
If the Tisches rent a garden-view unit, the Wongs occupy a unit on the first floor.
If the Tisches occupy a first-floor unit, the Stevensons occupy a third-floor unit.

14. Which of the following could be true?

(A) The Stevensons occupy a second-floor unit, whereas the Tisches occupy a first-floor unit.
(B) The Paulsons occupy a unit immediately and directly below the Wongs, and share a floor with the Tisches.
(C) The Paulsons rent a garden-view unit on the same floor as the Van Pelts.
(D) The Wongs rent an ocean-view unit on the same floor as the Van Pelts.
(E) The Tisches and Wongs both occupy the third floor.

15. If the Van Pelts and the Tisches both rent garden-view units, then which of the following could be true?

(A) The Wongs rent the first-floor ocean-view unit.
(B) The Stevensons rent the first-floor garden-view unit.
(C) The Paulsons and the Tisches occupy the same floor.
(D) The Paulsons and the Wongs occupy the same floor.
(E) The Van Pelts and the Wongs occupy the same floor.

16. If the Wongs rent a third-floor unit, then which of the following must be true?

(A) The Rideaus rent a second-floor unit.
(B) The Stevensons rent a second-floor unit.
(C) The Stevensons rent a first-floor unit.
(D) The Tisches rent a third-floor unit.
(E) The Van Pelts rent a first-floor unit.

17. If the Tisches rent the first-floor ocean-view unit, then each of the following must be true EXCEPT:

(A) The Paulsons and the Stevensons occupy the same floor.
(B) The Rideaus and the Van Pelts occupy the same floor.
(C) The Van Pelts rent a garden-view unit.
(D) The Wongs rent a garden-view unit.
(E) The Paulsons rent a third-floor unit.

18. If neither the Paulsons nor the Stevensons rent a third-floor unit, then which one of the following could be true?

(A) The Rideaus rent a second-floor unit.
(B) The Tisches rent a second-floor unit.
(C) The Wongs rent a second-floor unit.
(D) The Stevensons rent an ocean-view unit.
(E) The Wongs rent an ocean-view unit.

GO ON TO THE NEXT PAGE.

Questions 19–23

Four racehorses and their four jockeys are assigned to consecutive tracks at a racetrack—tracks 1, 2, 3, and 4. Each horse has exactly one jockey, and each pair is assigned to exactly one track. The horses are Ficklehoof, Galloper, Knackerbound, and Lackluster; the jockeys are Ramos, Simon, Tonka, and Urbach. The following conditions apply:

Ficklehoof is assigned to a lower-numbered track than is Galloper, and at least one track separates the two.
Knackerbound is assigned to track 2.
Lackluster's jockey is Urbach.

19. Which one of the following horse and jockey teams could be assigned to track 1?

(A) Ficklehoof and Ramos
(B) Ficklehoof and Urbach
(C) Galloper and Ramos
(D) Galloper and Urbach
(E) Lackluster and Tonka

20. If Ramos is assigned to a higher-numbered track than is Urbach, which one of the following statements cannot be true?

(A) Ficklehoof is assigned to a lower-numbered track than is Simon.
(B) Knackerbound is assigned to a lower-numbered track than is Ramos.
(C) Knackerbound is assigned to a lower-numbered track than is Tonka.
(D) Simon is assigned to a lower-numbered track than is Ramos.
(E) Tonka is assigned to a lower-numbered track than is Knackerbound.

21. If Lackluster is assigned to a lower-numbered track than is Galloper, which one of the following statements could be false?

(A) Ficklehoof is assigned to a lower-numbered track than is Urbach.
(B) Galloper is assigned to track 4.
(C) Either Ramos or Tonka is assigned to a lower-numbered track than is Urbach.
(D) Simon is assigned to a lower-numbered track than is Urbach.
(E) Urbach is assigned to track 3.

22. What is the maximum possible number of different horse and jockey teams, any one of which could be assigned to track 4?

(A) 2
(B) 3
(C) 4
(D) 5
(E) 6

23. If Simon is assigned to a higher-numbered track than is Lackluster, then which one of the following statements could be false?

(A) Galloper is assigned to a higher-numbered track than is Ramos.
(B) Galloper is assigned to a higher-numbered track than is Tonka.
(C) Lackluster is assigned to a higher-numbered track than is Tonka.
(D) Tonka is assigned to a higher-numbered track than is Ramos.
(E) Urbach is assigned to a higher-numbered track than is Ramos.

STOP

IF YOU FINISH BEFORE TIME IS CALLED, YOU MAY CHECK YOUR WORK ON THIS SECTION ONLY.
DO NOT WORK ON ANY OTHER SECTION IN THE TEST.

The Princeton Review

Completely darken bubbles with a No. 2 pencil. If you make a mistake, be sure to erase mark completely.

1. YOUR NAME: (Print) Last First M.I.

SIGNATURE: **DATE:** / /

HOME ADDRESS: (Print) Number

City State Zip Code

PHONE NO.: (Print)

IMPORTANT: Please fill in these boxes exactly as shown on the back cover of your test book.

2. TEST FORM

3. TEST CODE

0	A	0	0	0
1	B	1	1	1
2	C	2	2	2
3	D	3	3	3
4	E	4	4	4
5	F	5	5	5
6	G	6	6	6
7		7	7	7
8		8	8	8
9		9	9	9

4. REGISTRATION NUMBER

0	0	0	0	0	0
1	1	1	1	1	1
2	2	2	2	2	2
3	3	3	3	3	3
4	4	4	4	4	4
5	5	5	5	5	5
6	6	6	6	6	6
7	7	7	7	7	7
8	8	8	8	8	8
9	9	9	9	9	9

5. YOUR NAME

First 4 letters of last name | FIRST INIT | MID INIT

A B C D E F G H I J K L M N O P Q R S T U V W X Y Z (each column)

6. DATE OF BIRTH

Month	Day		Year	
JAN				
FEB				
MAR	0	0	0	0
APR	1	1	1	1
MAY	2	2	2	2
JUN	3	3	3	3
JUL		4	4	4
AUG		5	5	5
SEP		6	6	6
OCT		7	7	7
NOV		8	8	8
DEC		9	9	9

7. SEX

MALE

FEMALE

The Princeton Review

FORM NO. 00001-PR

Test 2

Start with number 1 for each new section.
If a section has fewer questions than answer spaces, leave the extra answer spaces blank.

1. A B C D E
2. A B C D E
3. A B C D E
4. A B C D E
5. A B C D E
6. A B C D E
7. A B C D E
8. A B C D E
9. A B C D E
10. A B C D E
11. A B C D E
12. A B C D E
13. A B C D E
14. A B C D E
15. A B C D E
16. A B C D E
17. A B C D E
18. A B C D E
19. A B C D E
20. A B C D E
21. A B C D E
22. A B C D E
23. A B C D E
24. A B C D E
25. A B C D E
26. A B C D E
27. A B C D E

1. A B C D E
2. A B C D E
3. A B C D E
4. A B C D E
5. A B C D E
6. A B C D E
7. A B C D E
8. A B C D E
9. A B C D E
10. A B C D E
11. A B C D E
12. A B C D E
13. A B C D E
14. A B C D E
15. A B C D E
16. A B C D E
17. A B C D E
18. A B C D E
19. A B C D E
20. A B C D E
21. A B C D E
22. A B C D E
23. A B C D E
24. A B C D E
25. A B C D E
26. A B C D E

1. A B C D E
2. A B C D E
3. A B C D E
4. A B C D E
5. A B C D E
6. A B C D E
7. A B C D E
8. A B C D E
9. A B C D E
10. A B C D E
11. A B C D E
12. A B C D E
13. A B C D E
14. A B C D E
15. A B C D E
16. A B C D E
17. A B C D E
18. A B C D E
19. A B C D E
20. A B C D E
21. A B C D E
22. A B C D E
23. A B C D E
24. A B C D E
25. A B C D E

1. A B C D E
2. A B C D E
3. A B C D E
4. A B C D E
5. A B C D E
6. A B C D E
7. A B C D E
8. A B C D E
9. A B C D E
10. A B C D E
11. A B C D E
12. A B C D E
13. A B C D E
14. A B C D E
15. A B C D E
16. A B C D E
17. A B C D E
18. A B C D E
19. A B C D E
20. A B C D E
21. A B C D E
22. A B C D E
23. A B C D E

COMPUTING YOUR SCORE

Directions

1. Use the Answer Key on the next page to check your answers.
2. Use the Scoring Worksheet below to compute your raw score.
3. Use the Score Conversion Chart to convert your raw score into the 120–180 LSAT scale.

Your scaled score on this virtual test is for general guidance only.

Scores obtained by using the Score Conversion Chart can only approximate the score you would receive if this virtual test were an actual LSAT. Your score on an actual LSAT may differ from the score obtained on this virtual test.

In an actual test, final scores are computed using an equating method that makes scores earned on different editions of the LSAT comparable to one another. This virtual test has been constructed to reflect an actual LSAT as closely as possible, and the conversion of raw scores to the LSAT scale has been approximated.

What this means is that the Conversion Chart reflects only an estimate of how raw scores would translate into final LSAT scores.

Scoring Worksheet

1. Enter the number of questions you answered correctly in each section.

	Number Correct
Section I	______
Section II.	______
Section III	______
Section IV	______

2. Enter the sum here: ______

This is your raw score.

CONVERSION CHART FOR TEST 2

For Converting Raw Scores to the 120–180 LSAT Scaled Score

Reported Score	Raw Score Lowest	Raw Score Highest
180	99	101
179	—*	—*
178	98	98
177	97	97
176	96	96
175	—*	—*
174	95	95
173	94	94
172	93	93
171	92	92
170	91	91
169	89	90
168	88	88
167	87	87
166	85	86
165	84	84
164	83	83
163	81	82
162	79	80
161	78	78
160	76	77
159	74	75
158	73	73
157	71	72
156	69	70
155	67	68
154	66	66
153	64	65
152	62	63
151	60	61
150	58	59
149	57	57
148	55	56
147	53	54
146	51	52
145	50	50
144	48	49
143	46	47
142	44	45
141	42	43
140	41	41
139	39	40
138	37	38
137	36	36
136	34	35
135	33	33
134	31	32
133	29	30
132	28	28
131	27	27
130	25	26
129	24	24
128	22	23
127	21	21
126	20	20
125	19	19
124	18	18
123	16	17
122	15	15
121	—*	—*
120	0	14

*There is no raw score that will produce this scaled score for this form.

SECTION I

1. D	8. B	15. C	22. E
2. A	9. B	16. D	23. C
3. B	10. C	17. B	24. B
4. C	11. D	18. A	25. D
5. E	12. A	19. E	26. B
6. C	13. E	20. B	27. D
7. D	14. D	21. A	

SECTION II

1. D	8. E	15. B	22. D
2. D	9. D	16. C	23. B
3. A	10. E	17. E	24. C
4. B	11. C	18. B	25. B
5. D	12. E	19. C	26. B
6. B	13. D	20. A	
7. C	14. D	21. B	

SECTION III

1. E	8. B	15. A	22. E
2. A	9. D	16. E	23. E
3. D	10. D	17. E	24. A
4. A	11. B	18. B	25. B
5. D	12. D	19. E	
6. C	13. B	20. B	
7. C	14. B	21. E	

SECTION IV

1. B	8. A	15. A	22. C
2. D	9. C	16. D	23. D
3. E	10. C	17. B	
4. C	11. A	18. C	
5. E	12. A	19. A	
6. C	13. B	20. C	
7. E	14. E	21. D	

11

Answers and Explanations to Practice Test 2

SECTION I

Questions 1–6 are based on the following passage:

Perhaps no figure from the Reconstruction era in the aftermath of the US Civil War exemplifies the failed promise of those times better than Tunis Campbell. Campbell, born free in New Jersey, came to postwar Georgia as a superintendent in the Freedmen's Bureau. He was assigned to organize the settlement of three of the sea islands off Georgia's coast, in accordance with General William T. Sherman's Special Field Order 15, which famously granted forty acres and a mule to each of forty thousand freed slaves in the coastal areas of Georgia and South Carolina.

Campbell, a champion of black equality and self-determination, set up one of the islands—St. Catherine's—as an effectively independent black principality. Taking possession of the abandoned plantation lands granted by Sherman's order, the residents of St. Catherine's set up their own constitution, education system, and militia, and allowed no whites on the island. Within a year, however, the effects of Lincoln's assassination were felt throughout the occupied South, and the Union army seized the land back from residents, either returning it to its former owners or selling it to white investors in the North. A sharecropping system was instituted, whereby many of the practical realities of slavery, if not their precise form, took hold again. Campbell himself was exiled.

Determined to continue fighting for the freed slaves, Campbell worked tirelessly on their behalf. Resettling in MacIntosh County, he organized farm labor to help them gain power in negotiations with white landowners, and he worked tirelessly to register black voters. Within a few years his efforts paid off, and he became one of three African Americans to be elected to the Georgia state senate, where against all odds he managed to secure some few legal protections for black Georgians. His stature, however, was a serious irritant to the white power structure of the state, and Campbell was eventually driven out of the senate as the result of a concerted campaign of election fraud and the preferment of false charges against him.

Campbell continued to work on the former slaves' behalf, but the rising power of white supremacists and the indifference of the federal government to the fate of former slaves steadily eroded what progress he was able to make. Eventually, with the help of a judge sympathetic to their cause, Campbell's enemies were able to convict him on a trumped-up charge, and Campbell was sentenced to a year of hard labor on a chain gang. The plantation owner who bought his labor for that year paid the state of Georgia the meager sum of $8.75. Annual mortality rates for chain-gang laborers then averaged between 16 and 25 percent, and at age 63, it seems almost miraculous that Campbell survived. After his release Campbell left Georgia, and returned only once more before his death in 1891. In Georgia as in most of the former Confederate states, efforts to implement reform during Reconstruction were systematically foiled by those who sought to preserve white power and relegate black Americans to a permanent underclass.

SECTION I

QUESTIONS

1. The passage is primarily concerned with

(A) assessing the accomplishments of a well-known historical figure
(B) criticizing conventional views of a contentious historical era
(C) correcting mistaken understandings of an important geographical region
(D) detailing the obstacles faced by a leader who sought self-determination for a group
(E) asserting the importance of laws in reevaluating views of a historical era

2. The passage supports which one of the following statements concerning the lives of freed slaves in South Carolina and Georgia soon after the conclusion of the Civil War?

(A) Some owned land and were able to participate in government.
(B) Many were able to live independent of white influence.
(C) Most were forced to continue working for their former owners.
(D) All were able to exercise the freedoms afforded to other citizens.
(E) No effort was made to assure their representation in national government.

EXPLANATIONS

1. This is a GENERAL question. We're looking for a description of the passage's purpose.

(A) The tone here is off; it's a bit too neutral.
(B) Conventional views aren't discussed in the passage.
(C) The primary emphasis in the passage is less on a region than it is on a person and an era.
(D) Yes. This has the proper emphasis and tone.
(E) Laws are not the primary focus of this passage.

2. This is most likely a SPECIFIC question. It seems to be referring to the end of the first paragraph.

(A) Yes. This answer doesn't stick right to the reference, but St. Catherine's does provide an example of each of these.
(B) This is too strong. "Many" and "independent" are both overstatements of passage material.
(C) This is also too strong. Although it seems clear that some did, we aren't told how many.
(D) This is far too strong; nothing this positive took place.
(E) National government is not explicitly dealt with by the passage.

SECTION I

QUESTIONS

3. Which one of the following best describes the function of the second paragraph of the passage?

   (A) It describes developments during Reconstruction that led to Campbell's eventual failure.
   (B) It describes an effort to establish self-determination for freed slaves and the ways in which that effort was foiled.
   (C) It summarizes the reasons Sherman's Special Field Order 15 was not fully implemented and indicates its limited effects.
   (D) It shows an instance of efforts to maintain freed slaves as a permanent underclass not being entirely successful.
   (E) It describes the outcome of the only effort during Reconstruction to respect the freed slaves' new legal equality.

4. In the fourth paragraph, the author mentions that a plantation owner paid $8.75 for a year of Campbell's labor while he was imprisoned primarily to

   (A) demonstrate the ways in which institutions of slavery remained operative during Reconstruction
   (B) quantify the dangerous conditions under which chain-gang laborers worked
   (C) suggest that Campbell's punishment was demeaning
   (D) prove the claim that the state of Georgia profited from Campbell's imprisonment
   (E) indicate why Campbell returned to Georgia only once after he had served out the term of his imprisonment

EXPLANATIONS

3. This is a GENERAL question. We want the choice that matches our summary of the second paragraph.

   (A) Close, but this paragraph isn't broad enough to include all the territory in this answer choice.
   (B) Yes. This is similar to (A), but it includes both a description of what St. Catherine's was and limits its scope to just that part of Campbell's story.
   (C) The emphasis here is wrong. The paragraph is concerned with St. Catherine's and Campbell, not Sherman's order generally.
   (D) This picks up on material not mentioned until much later, and it's a stretch to say that St. Catherine's shows this.
   (E) This is an overstatement. We don't know that this was the only such effort.

4. This is a SPECIFIC question. We're looking for the choice that's most consistent with passage material.

   (A) This is an overstatement. It is not an example of slavery *per se*.
   (B) This seems to refer more to the following statement about mortality rates.
   (C) Yes. Although this isn't by any means perfect, this choice is consistent with the passage's tone.
   (D) The passage doesn't claim that Georgia profited from Campbell's punishment—not monetarily, anyway.
   (E) This seems too speculative to be as good an answer as (C).

SECTION I

QUESTIONS

5. Which one of the following, if true, would provide the LEAST support for the author's statements concerning the sharecropping system that was instituted after the Civil War?
   (A) Black farmers were often subject to violence and intimidation by white landowners, both as slave laborers and as sharecroppers.
   (B) The rents that white landowners demanded from black sharecropping farmers were so high that it was impossible for most of them to accumulate any property or money of their own as the result of their labor.
   (C) The children of sharecropping farmers only rarely had access to education, and most of them were forced to work in the fields from a young age, just as they had during slavery.
   (D) Legal means were used to prevent sharecropping farmers from organizing to demand lower rents and better treatment from the white landowners whose land they farmed.
   (E) Sharecropping farmers were able to keep their families together and make other significant life decisions that were not available to slaves.

6. It can be inferred from the passage that each of the following is true of the political system in Georgia during the initial stages of Reconstruction EXCEPT:
   (A) Some freed slaves cast votes in state elections.
   (B) African-American legislators were able to pass laws protecting some rights of freed slaves.
   (C) No white legislators supported Campbell's efforts to extend important freedoms to freed slaves.
   (D) White leaders were not all pleased at the stature achieved by some black politicians.
   (E) White judges at times served purposes approved of by white supremacists.

EXPLANATIONS

5. This is a COMPLEX question. We're looking for four choices that lend additional support to the statement at hand.
   (A) This identifies a similarity between slavery and sharecropping: Conditions were terrible.
   (B) This identifies a similarity between slavery and sharecropping: It was impossible to earn money with work under either system.
   (C) This identifies a similarity between slavery and sharecropping: Education was very difficult to obtain.
   (D) This identifies a similarity between slavery and sharecropping: Laws prevented workers from organizing to demand better conditions.
   (E) Yes. This is the odd choice out; it identifies an improvement, however slight, in sharecropping over slavery.

6. This is a SPECIFIC question. Four of these answers will have direct passage support; the odd one out is the answer.
   (A) This is stated in the passage's third paragraph.
   (B) This is stated in the passage's third paragraph.
   (C) Yes. This is the odd choice out. We aren't told that absolutely no white legislators supported these measures.
   (D) This is stated in the passage's third paragraph.
   (E) This is stated in the passage's fourth paragraph.

SECTION I

QUESTIONS

7. The passage does NOT provide an answer to which one of the following questions?

(A) Was land ever given to freed slaves as a result of Special Field Order 15?
(B) Was forced labor used as a means of punishment during Reconstruction?
(C) Were African Americans elected to positions in state government at any time during Reconstruction?
(D) For how long did the sharecropping system remain the primary means by which Southern landowners profited from their land?
(E) Did the laborers who were former slaves negotiate with white landowners?

8. The author would most likely agree with which one of the following statements about Campbell's importance to a full understanding of Reconstruction?

(A) Campbell was the only leader during Reconstruction who attempted to secure a full range of citizens' rights for freed slaves.
(B) Campbell's story is emblematic of the reasons why Reconstruction did not deliver on its promise of freedom and equal rights for former slaves.
(C) Campbell did not succeed in Georgia because he himself was not a freed slave, and was not fully trusted by those he sought to help.
(D) Campbell's effort at protecting freed slaves in Georgia from white supremacists exemplifies the fact that Southern state governments were weak during Reconstruction.
(E) The analysis of Reconstruction requires that its failures as well as its successes be studied in detail, and Campbell provides ample illustrations of both.

EXPLANATIONS

7. This is a SPECIFIC question. The passage will provide answers to four of these questions; the fifth will be the answer.

(A) This question is answered in the second paragraph.
(B) This question is answered in the fourth paragraph.
(C) This question is answered in the third paragraph.
(D) Yes. This question is not answered in the passage.
(E) This question is answered in the third paragraph.

8. This sounds like a GENERAL question. An understanding of the passage's main point should suffice to find the answer.

(A) This is too broad; we aren't told that Campbell was the only one.
(B) Yes. This is a reasonable statement of the passage's main point.
(C) This is said nowhere in the passage.
(D) The weakness of state governments seems not to have been the problem.
(E) The tone here is off. The passage is not this neutral.

Questions 9–14 are based on the following passage:

The crucial discovery that opened the way for modern advances in biochemistry was the role of DNA and protein in the biological activity of cells. After much debate and experimentation, it was eventually learned that DNA serves as the genetic blueprint for proteins, which are the compounds upon which all cellular activity depends. Thus, although no living cell can function without protein, DNA and its chemical cousin RNA serve as the driving force for its organization and use. This led to a proper understanding of viruses. Although pathogens such as parasites and bacteria are cellular and are thus by conventional definitions living organisms, viruses are not. They have no cells of their own; instead, they are composed of DNA or RNA material accompanied by only a small amount of protein. A virus uses its genetic instruction set to commandeer the machinery of other cells, and therefore was thought to demonstrate that although a pathogen can exist without protein, it must at a bare minimum include DNA or RNA.

In 1982, however, the biologist Stanley Prusiner hypothesized that there might exist proteins that were themselves pathogenic. Prusiner's idea of "prions" (proteinaceous infectious particles) was controversial because it contradicted the central dogma of modern biology. This hypothesis was, however, strengthened by further study of a class of encephalopathies that exist in many mammals: Called scrapie in sheep and goats, chronic wasting disease in elk and mule deer, and bovine spongiform encephalopathy in cattle ("mad cow disease"), these diseases are also found in humans—kuru, Creutzfeldt-Jakob Disease (CJD), and Fatal Familial Insomnia to name a few. The fact that these diseases all lead to similar types of brain damage was interesting, but even more interesting was the fact that material from infected individuals could transmit disease even after sterilization in an autoclave. DNA could not survive such treatment, but some proteins could, leading to the speculation that the pathogens in these cases were special forms of protein acting alone, without genetic direction.

A prion protein is not a foreign protein, but a variant conformation of a protein normally produced by cells. Because a protein's conformation—its folding and physical shape—determines its biological activity, the prion protein no longer serves its normal purpose. Instead, prion proteins replicate themselves by catalyzing the conversion of normal copies of the protein into the prion conformation, and they may also alter the synthesis of new protein to favor that conformation. This mechanism helps explain why a disorder such as scrapie may develop spontaneously in a sheep that has never been exposed to an external source of the prion protein that causes it because a normal protein may slip into its prion conformation by chance. This mechanism also explains how humans exposed to cattle prion proteins in their food may subsequently develop disease, because it has been shown that cattle prions can cause a similar human protein to shift from its normal conformation into a prion form.

SECTION I

QUESTIONS	EXPLANATIONS

9. Which one of the following best expresses the main idea of the passage?

(A) Recent discoveries suggest that the understandings of DNA and protein on which modern biochemistry is based are incomplete.
(B) The hypothesis that prions cause certain classes of disease shows that there may be pathogens that do not possess genetic material.
(C) The central dogma of modern biology is that the presence of genetic material is necessary for an organism to be considered alive.
(D) Although pathogens have been found that are composed primarily of DNA or RNA with little protein, no pathogen can exist completely without protein.
(E) The discovery that prions cause certain encephalopathies holds out hope that hitherto untreatable diseases may soon be cured.

9. This is a GENERAL question. We're looking for the main idea.

(A) The emphasis here is wrong; we'd like something that mentions prions and disease.
(B) Yes. This is a succinct statement of the passage's contents.
(C) This is far too general.
(D) The emphasis here is wrong; the passage's purpose is not to indicate that protein is absolutely necessary.
(E) Cures for these diseases are not discussed.

10. The passage indicates that one consequence for a person who ingests food products derived from cattle with bovine spongiform encephalopathy may be

(A) the contraction of a virus
(B) the spontaneous development of scrapie
(C) the contraction of a prion disease
(D) resistance to certain types of parasites
(E) the expression of genes that do not operate normally

10. This is a SPECIFIC question. The reference is to the final sentence of the passage.

(A) According to the passage, this disease is not caused by a virus.
(B) Scrapie is a disease of sheep, not humans.
(C) Yes. This is consistent with the statement in question.
(D) Parasites are mentioned only briefly in the first paragraph.
(E) Abnormal genes are not discussed in the passage.

11. Which one of the following best describes the organization of the passage?

(A) A commonly held belief is introduced, scientific evidence against the belief is offered, and the belief is finally rejected as untrue.
(B) A new area of biology is described, possible benefits of study in this area are hypothesized, and further directions for study in this area are recommended.
(C) One potential cause of a class of diseases is hypothesized, evidence both for and against this hypothesis is presented, and the hypothesis is finally accepted.
(D) The basis of a scientific belief is introduced, a class of diseases this belief may not be adequate to explain is described, and a proposed cause of the diseases that does not conform to the belief is outlined.
(E) An alternative mechanism for a commonly observed phenomenon is posited, evidence in favor of that mechanism is considered, and arguments against the mechanism are ultimately accepted.

11. This is a GENERAL question. We're looking for the choice that best agrees with a paragraph-by-paragraph summary of the passage.

(A) No belief is rejected at the end of the passage.
(B) No further directions for study are recommended.
(C) Evidence against the prion hypothesis is never mentioned.
(D) Yes. This is the closest fit to the contents and structure of the passage.
(E) No argument against the mechanism is even mentioned.

SECTION I

QUESTIONS

12. The author refers to the fact that material from individuals infected with certain encephalopathies may remain infectious even after sterilization in an autoclave primarily to

(A) provide evidence that the conventional belief that all pathogens contain genetic material may not be true
(B) reinforce the claim that the class of encephalopathies discussed are all caused by the same prion
(C) indicate that it remains possible that these encephalopathies may be caused by viruses
(D) undermine conventional views of encephalopathy that state that these diseases can only develop spontaneously
(E) show how normal proteins may in some cases become pathogenic

13. By the author's statements, it can be inferred that the author would be most likely to agree with which one of the following statements?

(A) Not all diseases are caused by parasites, bacteria, viruses, or prions.
(B) Not all prion diseases involve changes to the conformation of a naturally produced protein.
(C) Not all proteins that exist in a prion form have detrimental biological effects in that form.
(D) Most diseases that are thought to be caused by prions can be spread from one species to another.
(E) Not all cases of prion disease can be explained by exposure to an external source of the pathogen that causes it.

EXPLANATIONS

12. This is a SPECIFIC question. We're looking for the answer that's most consistent with the cited statement, which is in the second paragraph.

(A) Yes. The key is that sterilization in an autoclave destroys DNA and RNA.
(B) This is an overstatement of the passage's identification of similarities among these diseases.
(C) This is not discussed in the passage.
(D) This is not described in the passage as the conventional belief about them.
(E) The mechanism of a prion's action is not described until the following paragraph.

13. This seems likely to be a SPECIFIC question. We're hoping for direct passage support of our answer.

(A) No other potential cause of disease is mentioned.
(B) This would seem to contradict material in the third paragraph.
(C) This is not said in the passage.
(D) This is too strong a conclusion to draw from the passage's discussion of mad cow disease.
(E) Yes. The passage mentions in the third paragraph that scrapie can develop spontaneously.

QUESTIONS

14. Which one of the following is most analogous to the proposed mechanism by which a prion replicates itself, as that mechanism is described in the passage?

(A) A teacher who advocates a new method of teaching reading to students is more successful with her method than are other teachers using more conventional methods.
(B) An artisan who produces works that other artisans consider to be of inferior quality is nevertheless successful because he can produce his works very cheaply.
(C) A scientist who has always accepted the theory that protein is involved in heredity changes her mind when it is discovered that genetic traits cannot be transmitted by a cell with its DNA removed.
(D) A criminal who has developed a safe and lucrative scheme for cheating investment banks convinces many other individuals who have previously obeyed the law to use the same scheme to make money, who then convince others to do so.
(E) A high-school graduate who goes into business for himself instead of going to college is extremely successful and becomes a role model for other graduates who chose not to attend college.

EXPLANATIONS

14. This is a COMPLEX question. We're looking for something that's similar to the mechanism described in the third paragraph.

(A) This does not involve conversion from one thing to another.
(B) Like (A), this doesn't include any kind of conversion.
(C) This talks about an individual changing her mind in the face of evidence; there is no sense of spreading or replication here.
(D) Yes. This talks about a pathological change caused by a single example and indicates that the change spreads from that individual.
(E) This does not describe a conversion or change.

Questions 15–20 are based on the following passage:

The Sherman Antitrust Act was initially passed to curb the power of corporations that had established monopolies over the most important resources for the U.S. economy. These companies protected their position by engaging in predatory pricing and other anticompetitive practices that were seen as antithetical to free-market principles and threatening to civil authority. One industry that has managed to avoid regulation under the act, however, is Major League Baseball, and although the anomalous legal status of this organization can be understood in terms of its history, it seems unlikely to last forever.

The basis in precedent for baseball's status stems from a 1922 Supreme Court decision in which the two major leagues were adjudged to be exempt from antitrust regulation because their business did not constitute interstate commerce, and thus was not subject to federal regulation. Even at the time, this argument was tenuous: Although baseball teams crossed state lines to participate in games, this fact was found to be incidental to the conduct of baseball exhibitions, which according to the court did not fit a narrow definition of commerce anyway. By the time baseball's exemption was once again taken up by the Supreme Court—in 1953, in the context of a labor dispute—it could no longer plausibly be argued that baseball's special treatment was justifiable on these grounds. However, the Supreme Court at the time declined to overturn the exemption because doing so was not part of the manifest intent of the law: Although antitrust law did technically cover baseball, its purpose was to curb socially harmful concentrations of power in the hands of robber-barons, and a breakup of the baseball monopoly would not serve this purpose. Even so, the Supreme Court declined to extend the protections afforded to Major League Baseball to similar organizations in other sports, and by the 1970's the Supreme Court seemed to have settled on the curious position that, even though it no longer believed that Major League Baseball merited exemption, it would continue to honor the precedent unless legislative bodies specifically withdrew it.

Certain aspects of the exemption, especially those concerning teams' contracts with baseball players, have been redefined, but it remains for the most part intact. Not until the end of the twentieth century was a full-scale withdrawal threatened, when Major League Baseball proposed unilaterally dissolving two of its least financially viable teams. Without its antitrust exemption, league management could never have contemplated such a move; legislators made it clear to the league that following through with it would likely cost baseball its special status. Although the teams were saved, however, in the end it seems that baseball's exemption may be more a vulnerability than an asset. As baseball's competitive position with regard to other professional sports grows weaker, the need for significant steps to improve that position grows. The fact that legislative bodies exercise a unique brand of veto power over league decisions may, in the end, dictate that baseball must risk the voiding of its exemption to take steps required to assure its financial viability.

QUESTIONS	EXPLANATIONS

15. It can be inferred from the passage that by referring to its "anomalous legal status" (line 9–10) the author means that Major League Baseball is

(A) not subject to direct interference by legislators in the same way that other similar organizations are
(B) not accountable to the voters and consumers in the same way that all powerful business organizations should be
(C) not constrained to follow laws to which other similar organizations have been found to be subject
(D) not involved in the conduct of anything that can correctly be called "interstate commerce"
(E) not required to consider the consequences of its actions in the same way that legislators are

15. This seems to be a SPECIFIC question. The cited text is in the first paragraph; we're looking for a choice that's consistent with the passage.

(A) This seems opposite to the passage's opinion on the matter.
(B) The tone here is wrong. This is too openly critical.
(C) Yes. This actually comes from the second paragraph, some distance away from the citation.
(D) This is described as a rationale for the initial Supreme Court decision, but the author evidently does not agree with it.
(E) This is a strange comparison not made in the passage.

16. The passage indicates that each of the following has at some time served as a justification for Major League Baseball's exemption from the Sherman Anti-trust Act EXCEPT:

(A) the precedent established by a 1922 Supreme Court decision
(B) the fact that staging baseball exhibitions could not be classified as "commerce"
(C) the assertion that a monopoly over baseball does not represent a socially harmful concentration of power
(D) the fact that other professional sports are also not subject to regulation under the act
(E) the assurance that legislators may withdraw Major League Baseball's exemption if they choose to do so

16. This is a SPECIFIC question. It seems likely that four of these answer choices will be found in the second paragraph; the odd choice out will be our answer.

(A) This is mentioned as a reason in the second paragraph.
(B) This is mentioned as a reason in the second paragraph.
(C) This is mentioned as a reason in the second paragraph.
(D) Yes. This contradicts passage material.
(E) This is mentioned as a reason in the second paragraph.

17. It can be inferred from the passage that the author considers the unique role legislators play with regard to Major League Baseball to be

(A) a violation of the Sherman Anti-trust Act
(B) more of a hindrance to the sport's success than a help
(C) a primary factor in its financial decline
(D) responsible for its indeterminate legal status
(E) the product of a weak and vacillating Supreme Court

17. This is a SPECIFIC question. We want to pick the choice that's supported by material in the third paragraph.

(A) This refers to the exemption (at best), not legislators' role.
(B) Yes. This is a good paraphrase of material in the third paragraph.
(C) This is an overstatement of the passage's idea that baseball may have to risk losing its exemption in order to survive.
(D) The Supreme Court is to blame for this.
(E) This is a bit strong to characterize the passage's attitude correctly.

SECTION I

QUESTIONS

18. The author implies that which of the following is true of the companies that antitrust legislation was intended to regulate?

(A) The business practices they sometimes employed included the manipulation of prices to harm competitors.
(B) They did not pose a threat to the ability of legislative bodies to govern effectively.
(C) Their monopolies represented an aberration in the history of the free market.
(D) At least some of them could have been allowed to retain their monopolies without causing harm.
(E) They created circumstances that directly led to legislative interference in all professional sports leagues.

19. The author's characterization of the basis for a 1922 Supreme Court decision as "tenuous" (line 17) indicates the author's belief that

(A) professional sports exhibitions do not constitute interstate commerce
(B) the concentration of economic power represented by professional sports monopolies is not socially harmful
(C) sports organizations other than those associated with professional baseball are not exempt from antitrust legislation
(D) the labor practices engaged in by Major League Baseball represent an abuse of its special legal status
(E) the precedent that established baseball's exemption from antitrust legislation was legally questionable

20. According to the passage, the future financial health of Major League Baseball may depend on which one of the following courses of action?

(A) provoking legislators to revisit the limitations placed on the league's exemption from certain laws
(B) taking potentially risky measures to ensure the league's competitive strength
(C) concentrating greater power in the hands of the league's leadership
(D) taking steps that would not be possible for any organization without an exemption from antitrust laws
(E) voluntarily conceding the right of other sports leagues to be protected against antitrust enforcement

EXPLANATIONS

18. This is a SPECIFIC question; support for the answer could come from statements in either the first or second paragraphs.

(A) Yes. This is a good paraphrase of "predatory pricing and other anticompetitive practices."
(B) If anything, this seems the opposite of passage material.
(C) This requires far more general knowledge than we get from the passage.
(D) This is speculative; baseball retained its monopolies without causing problems, but the legislation was not intended specifically to break up baseball's monopoly.
(E) Legislative interference is mentioned only in connection with baseball.

19. This is a SPECIFIC question. The cited text is in the second paragraph.

(A) This appears to be the opposite of the author's belief.
(B) This is not mentioned in the area cited.
(C) This does not refer to the specific nature of the decision concerning baseball described in the cited portion of the passage.
(D) Labor practices are mentioned in passing much later.
(E) Yes. This seems about as clear a paraphrase of "tenuous" as you can get.

20. This is a SPECIFIC question. It refers us directly to the third paragraph.

(A) The emphasis here is backward; actions taken by the league may cause legislators to revoke the exemption completely, not revisit the limitations on that exemption.
(B) Yes. This is a good paraphrase of the passage's last sentence.
(C) This is not said anywhere in the passage.
(D) This is off the main point of the passage; the point here is that they must take steps that might risk the exemption, not that they need to exploit the exemption.
(E) This is not a possibility mentioned anywhere in the passage.

SECTION I

Questions 21–27 are based on the following passage:

Like many aspects of public life in the former Soviet Union, the production of visual art was sanctioned and closely controlled by the central government and the Communist party. Most Soviet-era work is thus dismissed by critics as mere propaganda, not worthy of the same consideration due to Western works of the same period. Interest in Soviet artists has traditionally focused on those who resisted the regime and, in many cases, were persecuted for doing so. Yet it is difficult to avoid seeing, in this interest, not an objection to art as propaganda, but rather a preference for one kind of propaganda over another. In the highly charged political atmosphere of the Cold War, works produced both inside and outside the Soviet Union tended to take on ideological dimensions, whether the artist intended them.

Soviet art took shape at a time when governments worldwide were beginning to make full use of the power of propaganda. Although the Nazi regime in Germany is typically identified as leading the way in this pursuit, over the same period Stalin was expanding the Soviet Union's propaganda apparatus. With regard to visual arts, this apparatus operated in the contexts of both "high culture" and "low culture." Stalin's government sponsored a style of painting called Socialist Realism, which used conventional sentimental tropes and a lexicon of Communist imagery to portray life in the Soviet Union, and Stalin himself, in idealized and inspirational ways. At the same time, the production of posters was vastly expanded; these posters used cartoonish and overblown imagery to evoke such ideas as the greed of capitalism, the savagery of fascism, and the bravery of factory workers and collective farmers. Today, the Soviet-era posters that survive are collector's items, and a modest market remains for the high-culture works of painting and sculpture that survived the overthrow of the Soviet regime.

An examination of cultural production in the United States over the same period yields surprising similarities. Throughout the thirties, the government sponsored production of public art through the Works Progress Administration. Often these works celebrated the dignity of work and the enduring spirit of the people. World War II poster propaganda yielded images that linger in the popular culture even now: Rosie the Riveter, Uncle Sam, and caricatured racist portrayals of people living in fascist countries. Even the most famous high-culture painting in the United States—the abstract expressionist work of such painters as Pollock and Rothko—took on political dimensions that are striking in light of their apparent lack of ideological content. Triumphal showings of these artists' work, represented as "cultural exchange," were organized within the Soviet Union during the Cold War with the purpose of lauding freedom of expression. Soviet officials, at the same time, pointed to them as proof of capitalist decadence. Even these works, meant to exemplify the aesthetic in its purest form, became weapons in an arms race of propaganda that mirrored other political contests taking place throughout the Cold War.

SECTION I

QUESTIONS

21. According to the passage, which one of the following opinions would art critics be most likely to hold concerning Socialist Realist paintings produced in the Soviet Union under Stalin's regime?

(A) They cannot be considered as artistically valuable as other works produced during the same period because of their status as government propaganda.
(B) They are at least as ideologically motivated as paintings made under the Works Progress Administration during the same time.
(C) Their market value exceeds the market value of some serious paintings made outside the Soviet Union during the same time.
(D) Their popularity in the contemporary market indicates that they are of less artistic value than other paintings made during that time.
(E) Although they are propaganda, they cannot be completely dismissed because much of the art made during that period served similar purposes.

22. Which one of the following, if true, would most undermine the author's interpretation of the fact that the U.S. government sponsored the production of art through the Works Progress Administration?

(A) U.S. painters who produced government-sponsored works were not subject to direct oversight by government representatives during the planning stages of their work.
(B) Soviet painters who worked in the officially approved style were paid for their work only after it had been accepted by the Communist party.
(C) U.S. painters were free to choose whether they wished to seek government funding for works that might have been considered subversive.
(D) Soviet painters were able to gain at least some public attention for paintings produced outside the auspices of the government and the Communist party.
(E) U.S. painters who were funded by the Works Progress Administration were not prevented from producing work critical of the U.S. government, and they often did.

EXPLANATIONS

21. This is a SPECFIC question. There is a dual reference here—to the critics in the first paragraph and to Socialist Realism in the second.

(A) Yes. This is a good paraphrase of the material in the first paragraph.
(B) This may be an overstatement of passage material; certainly this is not mentioned in either part of the passage to which the question refers.
(C) The passage says the market is "modest" but nothing more.
(D) The critics mentioned in the passage don't explicitly base their judgment on the value of the paintings.
(E) This is the author's idea, not the critics'.

22. This is a COMPLEX question. We're looking for something that goes against the author's purpose in including the cited information, which appears in the third paragraph.

(A) This is suggestive of a difference, but we don't know that the Soviet Union controlled the art that was produced in this way, either.
(B) This is suggestive of a difference, but it doesn't very directly undermine the passage's suggestion that the works produced under WPA could be considered propaganda.
(C) This is suggestive of a difference, but it isn't clear that absolutely every artist working in the Soviet Union had to seek government funding.
(D) This doesn't really attack the idea we're looking for: that the government in the U.S. also exerted some control over the production of art.
(E) Yes. This is the best choice. Although the government sponsored production of art, this choice lets us know that it didn't exert control over its content.

SECTION I

QUESTIONS

23. Which one of the following best describes the organization of the second paragraph?

(A) A general claim about a historical period is presented and then illustrated with the use of supporting examples from several countries.
(B) A contention concerning one country is used as proof of the truth of this contention for all countries.
(C) A particular strategy by a government is shown to operate in two separate contexts for similar purposes.
(D) The ongoing popularity of the results of a particular policy is used to demonstrate the efficacy of that policy.
(E) Two governments that are considered similar in one way are shown to be dissimilar in other important ways.

24. According to the passage, which one of the following is true of abstract expressionist paintings?

(A) They were aesthetically superior to any paintings being produced in the Soviet Union at the same time.
(B) Their apparent lack of ideological content did not prevent them from being used as propaganda.
(C) The artists intended for them to be interpreted as lauding free expression.
(D) Their production was sponsored by the U.S. government through the Works Progress Administration.
(E) Their decadence is a primary reason they are considered among the greatest paintings of the twentieth century.

25. It can be inferred that the author would most likely agree with which one of the following statements concerning posters produced in the Soviet Union during World War II?

(A) They dealt with the same subjects used in propaganda posters produced in Nazi Germany during the same time.
(B) They employed the same deceptive practices that Socialist Realist paintings of the period employed.
(C) They attributed characteristics to factory and farm workers that those workers normally did not possess.
(D) They served similar purposes to the purposes served by some posters produced in the U.S. during the same period.
(E) These posters are not as desirable to collectors today as are propaganda posters produced in other countries during the same period.

EXPLANATIONS

23. This is a GENERAL question. We're looking for the choice that best fits a general summary of the second paragraph.

(A) We don't have specific examples from several countries here.
(B) The paragraph isn't concerned with proving something about all countries.
(C) Yes. The contexts mentioned here are "high culture" and "low culture."
(D) The tone here is off. The purpose isn't really to praise the popularity of the works and the effectiveness of the policy.
(E) Dissimilarities are never emphasized in this paragraph.

24. This is a SPECIFIC question. The reference is to the third paragraph.

(A) This is not a judgment that the passage explicitly makes.
(B) Yes. This is a safe paraphrase of the cited text.
(C) This is how they were used as propaganda, but we're not sure that this was the artists' intent in producing them.
(D) This isn't said in the passage.
(E) Decadence is a quality ascribed to these paintings by Soviet officials, not the author.

25. This is a SPECIFIC question. The cited text is in the second paragraph.

(A) We aren't told that the subjects were the same.
(B) The tone here is wrong; "deceptive" is a judgment that the author doesn't make.
(C) The tone here is wrong; we don't know that these workers didn't deserve their portrayals in the posters.
(D) Yes. At the very least, both are said to have been against fascism.
(E) This is not a comparison that the passage makes.

SECTION I

QUESTIONS	EXPLANATIONS

26. Which one of the following is most analogous to the passage's discussion of the "preference" (line 11) ascribed to art critics?

(A) Literary reviewers prefer literary novels to popular novels because the tastes of literary reviewers are more refined than the tastes of most readers.
(B) Economists who prefer capitalism to socialism focus on the inefficiencies of a socialist government's policies and the successes of a rich venture capitalist who has been imprisoned by that government.
(C) Fashion designers who prefer creativity to practicality make garments that are exceptionally inconvenient to wear and maintain.
(D) Archaeologists who subscribe to a particular view of a civilization's history commence an investigation of a major site inhabited by that civilization with hopes of finding support for their view.
(E) A landscape designer who prefers shrubs to flowers nevertheless must accommodate a client's wishes to have a substantial number of flowers in a garden she is designing.

26. This is a COMPLEX question. The cited text is in the first paragraph.

(A) We're not looking for refined tastes; we're looking for preferences that can be interpreted as political.
(B) Yes. This is a political preference that influences the decision of what positive and negative aspects will be emphasized.
(C) This has to do with making things, not with making judgments about them.
(D) This is too neutral to be similar to the situation described in the passage.
(E) This has to do with going against preferences. It isn't similar.

27. Which one of the following best expresses the main idea of the passage?

(A) The use of propaganda in both high-culture and low-culture contexts was prevalent in many countries during the twentieth century.
(B) Critics who dismiss Soviet art as being excessively ideological are incapable of seeing the ideological content of art produced at the same time in the United States.
(C) Paintings and posters were the primary means by which the governments fighting World War II sought to motivate their public to endure hardships associated with that war.
(D) Those who dismiss visual art produced in the Soviet Union as propaganda reveal their biases by doing so because even the greatest works by U.S. artists during the same period could also be used as propaganda.
(E) All art, regardless of the time and place of its production, has a political dimension that may be exploited by governments in their effort to produce propaganda.

27. This is a GENERAL question. We're looking for the main point.

(A) This is too general to be the main point of this passage.
(B) This is too focused on the failings of the critics to be the best choice available.
(C) This is too general to be the main point of this passage.
(D) Yes. This has the Soviet/U.S. comparison on which the passage is focused, the notion of propaganda, and its tone is closer than (B)'s.
(E) This is too general to be the main point of the passage.

SECTION II

QUESTIONS

1. Some analysts believe that changes in the price of oil are never appreciably influenced by long-term weather forecasts. Last year, however, the prediction of an especially violent hurricane season for this year was followed by a sharp increase in oil prices because in the past large hurricanes have been known to disrupt oil production in the Gulf of Mexico. Hence, the predicted incidence of hurricanes—only one of many aspects of long-term weather forecasts—can cause changes in the price of oil, which means that other aspects of weather forecasting can as well.

   The statement that large hurricanes in the past have disrupted oil production in the Gulf of Mexico is intended to support the contention that

   (A) the predicted violence of the upcoming hurricane season is the most important weather-related factor in determining oil prices
   (B) long-term weather forecasts usually do not influence oil prices at the time they are issued
   (C) any long-term weather forecasting must take into account the likely effect of fluctuations in the price of oil
   (D) a variety of predictions made in long-term weather forecasts can influence the price of oil
   (E) the usual effect of long-term predictions concerning the severity of the next year's hurricane season is to cause a sharp increase in the price of oil

2. In an experiment, first-year college students were asked to listen to a tape of someone speaking French. When asked to repeat the sounds they had heard, students who had studied French in high school could repeat more of the sounds than could students who had no knowledge of French. When asked to listen to a tape of only meaningless sounds, none of the students were able to repeat more than a few seconds' worth of the sounds made on the tape.

   Which one of the following conclusions is best supported by the information above?

   (A) Knowledge of a foreign language interferes with one's ability to repeat unfamiliar sounds.
   (B) People who have a knowledge of French have better memories than do people who have no knowledge of French.
   (C) The ability to repeat unrelated sounds is not improved by frequent practice.
   (D) The ability to repeat sounds is influenced by one's ability to comprehend the meaning of the sounds.
   (E) Learning a foreign language requires an ability to distinguish unfamiliar sounds from gibberish.

EXPLANATIONS

1. This is a REASONING question. We're looking for a correct description of the mentioned statement, which is a premise of the argument.

   (A) It's too much to say that hurricane forecasts are the most important factor.
   (B) This contradicts information in the argument.
   (C) This is not a conclusion stated anywhere in the argument.
   (D) Yes. This is the main conclusion of the argument, and even if the cited statement doesn't support it directly, nevertheless the statement is part of the reasoning supporting this conclusion.
   (E) The argument doesn't conclude that every forecast causes an increase in prices.

2. This is an INFERENCE question. Your goal is to find the one choice that must be true based on the information in the passage.

   (A) No, because none of the students was able to repeat the sounds for more than a few seconds.
   (B) General memory is not related to an ability to speak French.
   (C) Maybe, but we don't know about practice.
   (D) Do we have proof of this? Yes—the French-speaking students remembered more of the sounds that were the French language than they did of the gibberish language. Plus, it's nice and wishy-washy—"is influenced by." This is the answer.
   (E) Maybe, but we don't know about learning a foreign language.

QUESTIONS	EXPLANATIONS

3. Many species of animals that have evolved poison as a protection from predators contain extremely large amounts of those poisons. It might seem that a poisonous animal would need to contain only enough poison to sicken or kill most animals, but there are some amphibians whose bodies contain enough poison to kill an elephant. This can be explained by the fact that the most common predators of these amphibians have evolved resistance to the defensive poisons, so that over time the prey has continually become more poisonous, while the predator has developed ever greater resistance to the poison.

   Which one of the following most accurately expresses the main conclusion of the argument?

   (A) The seemingly excessive amount of poison contained in some prey animals' bodies can be explained by the co-evolution of predator and prey.
   (B) Some animals that protect themselves from predation by being poisonous contain more than enough poison to kill any predator.
   (C) An animal that protects itself against predators by being poisonous is likely to contain much more poison than is a predator that kills its prey with the use of poison.
   (D) The evolution of poison is not completely effective at preventing an animal from being preyed upon.
   (E) Poison is the most effective method available for prey animals to protect themselves from predators.

3. This is a MAIN POINT question. We're looking for the statement of the single thing the argument most wants us to accept.

   (A) Yes. "Co-evolution" seems a good paraphrase of the escalating increases in the amount of poison in the prey's body along with the predator's resistance to that poison.
   (B) This is a premise of the argument, not its conclusion.
   (C) Predators that use poison are not even mentioned.
   (D) This is not the thing that the argument is trying to get us to believe.
   (E) No comparison to other methods is made.

QUESTIONS	EXPLANATIONS

4. Gardener M: High levels of nitrogen-containing compounds are necessary for any plant to grow well. Therefore, to aid in this plant's growth, you must be sure to add plenty of fertilizer.

Gardener O: That would be pointless. The soil in which this plant is growing already contains a high level of nitrogen-containing compounds, and it is also receiving plenty of light and water.

Which one of the following, if true, provides the strongest basis for Gardener M to respond to the objection raised by Gardener O?

(A) The fact that the plant is receiving all of the things necessary for its growth does not necessarily ensure that it will grow well.
(B) Without the addition of plenty of fertilizer, the plant will soon deplete the supply of nitrogen-containing compounds currently found in its soil.
(C) A steady supply of light and water, although important for a plant's growth, is not as essential to a plant's growth as the supply of nitrogen-containing compounds.
(D) No measure that guarantees a plant's growth should be neglected, even if it is possible that the plant may grow without that measure being taken.
(E) The addition of excessive amounts of fertilizer may harm a plant, even if that plant requires nitrogen-containing compounds to grow.

4. This is most nearly a WEAKEN question. We're looking for something that would counter Gardener O's objection to Gardener M.

(A) This does not address O's primary objection, which concerns nitrogen-containing compounds.
(B) Yes. This lets us know that, although there are enough nitrogen-containing compounds in the soil now, fertilizer must nevertheless be added.
(C) This does not address O's objection, which is that enough of these compounds are currently present.
(D) The addition of fertilizer is not presented as guaranteeing growth; also, this doesn't directly address O's statement that there would seem to be no purpose in adding fertilizer.
(E) If anything, this would help O's argument.

SECTION II

QUESTIONS

5. Medical Researcher: If I don't get another research grant soon, I'll never be able to discover a cure for phlebitis.

Assistant: But that's great. If your grant does come through, that dreaded disease will finally be eradicated.

Which one of the following statements best describes the flaw in the assistant's reasoning?

(A) The assistant believes the researcher will be unable to cure phlebitis unless the grant comes through.
(B) The assistant thinks the researcher will use the grant to find a cure for phlebitis, rather than for some other purpose.
(C) The assistant believes it is more important to cure phlebitis than to eradicate other, more deadly conditions.
(D) The assistant believes that all the researcher needs to cure phlebitis is another research grant.
(E) The assistant thinks the researcher will cure phlebitis even if the grant does not come through.

6. Commentator: Projections indicate that our nation's Gross Domestic Product (GDP) will shrink next year, leading to a 2 percent loss in tax revenues collected by the federal government. Therefore, we should pass a 2 percent cut in all federal taxes for next year. That way, the federal government's lost tax revenue will at least serve to stimulate the economy.

Which one of the following indicates a flaw in the commentator's argument?

(A) A cut in federal taxes may necessitate a decrease in federal spending, which in turn may necessitate further tax cuts.
(B) The economic stimulus offered by the proposed tax cut may not be great enough to ensure that the loss in federal taxes collected is no greater than 2 percent.
(C) Tax cuts that are adequate to increase the rate of GDP growth in a healthy economy may not suffice to prevent the shrinkage of GDP when the economy is weak.
(D) Money that is spent for one purpose cannot also be spent for another purpose.
(E) There is no assurance given that the benefits of the proposed tax cut will not accrue primarily to the wealthiest individuals in society.

EXPLANATIONS

5. **Conclusion:** If the researcher gets the grant, the disease will be eradicated.

Premise: If the researcher doesn't get the grant, she'll never discover a cure.

Assumption: There's no other factor preventing her from discovering a cure.

This is a FLAW question. Come up with your own description of how the assistant made a mistake before you go to the answer choices, and then match your description to the choices.

(A) No, this is what the medical researcher said. Look for something that mentions how the assistant thinks the researcher said that the grant was sufficient to ensure success.
(B) This isn't a flaw in the argument—it's accurate.
(C) Other diseases weren't mentioned by anyone.
(D) Yes, he confused *necessary* with *sufficient* in this case—the researcher said it was necessary for her to get the grant, the assistant assumed that the grant will be sufficient to effect the cure.
(E) No, neither person said this.

6. **Conclusion**: Cutting taxes by 2 percent will allow lost revenue to help stimulate the economy.

Premise: Tax revenues are projected to decline by 2 percent next year because of shrinkage in GDP

Assumption: It's a little hazy, but the commentator appears to think that a cut in taxes of 2 percent will somehow only result in a loss of 2 percent to tax revenues, although the GDP is projected to decrease.

This is a FLAW question. We're looking for a choice that describes or exploits the argument's assumption.

(A) The argument doesn't depend on the fact that no further tax cuts will be required.
(B) Yes. This is the best available statement of the flaw here.
(C) It isn't clear how this choice is relevant to the particular tax cuts under discussion here.
(D) Very interesting. It's difficult to see how this expresses the argument's problem.
(E) To whom the benefits of a tax cut primarily accrue is not a relevant issue in this argument.

SECTION II

QUESTIONS

7. Due to the increasing number of part-time adjuncts hired to teach university courses, it has become increasingly difficult for people who have recently earned PhDs to find full-time employment in universities.

Which one of the following conforms most closely to the principle illustrated above?

(A) Because the number of trees cut down in this area exceeds the number of new trees that have been planted, deforestation is a growing problem in the area.

(B) Because the number of teachers who are qualified to teach science and math is declining, the quality of instruction students receive in those subjects is suffering.

(C) Because individual songs can now be downloaded cheaply and easily from the internet, sales of new albums in record stores have significantly declined.

(D) Because two new computer programs appeal to the same market and include the same features, neither of these programs will be cost-effective for the companies that sell them.

(E) Due to the increasing number of coffee growers who are going out of business, it has become increasingly difficult for those who supply equipment to coffee growers to find a market for their products.

8. Sheet for sheet, Brand A paper towels cost less than Brand B paper towels and are more absorbent. Yet a roll of Brand A paper towels costs more than a roll of Brand B paper towels.

Which one of the following, if true, explains how the statements above can both be true?

(A) Both Brand A and Brand B towels are manufactured by the same company, which often creates artificial competition for its expensive products.

(B) A roll of Brand B paper towels is more absorbent than a roll of Brand A paper towels.

(C) A roll of Brand A paper towels is more absorbent than a roll of Brand B paper towels.

(D) The cost of a roll of Brand A towels has risen every year for the last five years.

(E) A roll of Brand A paper towels has more sheets than a roll of Brand B paper towels.

EXPLANATIONS

7. This is a PARALLEL-PRINCIPLE question. We're looking for the argument that illustrates the same principle that the initial argument illustrates.

(A) This has to do with competing factors, but whereas the initial argument involves things of different types (full-time jobs versus part-time jobs), this one involves only one thing: trees.

(B) This does not deal with competing factors.

(C) Yes. This reproduces the competing factors—downloading of individual songs versus buying complete albums—and indicates that the cheaper option that includes less is displacing the more expensive one that includes more.

(D) This involves competing factors, but it does not have one winning out over another.

(E) This does not involve competing factors.

8. This is a PARADOX question. Look for an answer choice that allows both parts of the argument to be true, and remember to assume the hypothetical truth of each of the answer choices.

(A) This doesn't explain the discrepancy in the per sheet versus overall price issue.

(B) Absorbency is totally out of the scope here. Eliminate it.

(C) Same problem as (B). Eliminate it.

(D) What about Brand B? Without anything to compare this information to, it's useless. Eliminate it.

(E) Can this explain why the overall price is higher? Yes—there are more sheets on Brand A. It's the answer.

SECTION II

QUESTIONS	EXPLANATIONS

9. State agricultural officials are hoping to save California's $30 billion-a-year fruit industry from destruction by the Mediterranean fruit fly by releasing nearly one billion sterile female fruit flies throughout the state. In the past, this has been shown to be the only effective means of limiting the spread of this destructive pest, outside of large-scale pesticide spraying.

   Which one of the following best explains the intended effect of the program described above?

   (A) to drastically increase the number of potential mates for the male fruit flies, requiring them to devote more of their energies to mating rather than eating fruit
   (B) to saturate a given area with fruit flies, creating greater competition for food and thereby containing the damage done by the fruit fly to a smaller area
   (C) to ensure that a large number of fruit flies in succeeding generations are born infertile
   (D) to limit the growth of the population by reducing the number of successful matings between fruit flies
   (E) to encourage overpopulation of the fruit fly in the hopes that nature will correct the situation itself

9. This is a CONCLUSION question. Look for the answer that is the goal of the agricultural officials. What are they trying to do here?

   (A) This looks okay, but they're still going to eat some fruit. Let's see if there is something better.
   (B) Still not all that great, is it? At least part of the state isn't going to have any fruit left at all. Let's keep looking.
   (C) But if we're releasing sterile flies, there won't be succeeding generations. Eliminate it.
   (D) This looks really good. By releasing sterile flies, we should be able to reduce the population of fruit flies. It's the answer.
   (E) Overpopulation is the opposite of what we want here. Eliminate it.

SECTION II

QUESTIONS

10. Small businesses, which are essential to our country's economy, are more likely to fail when the price of health insurance increases unexpectedly. A recent bill introduced in parliament would reimburse health insurers who agree to limit the growth of the prices they charge to a set amount each year. Although this would effectively control the price of health insurance, there is no reason to pass the bill because only a small proportion of the small businesses that fail in this country do so because of sudden increases in insurance rates.

Which one of the following, if true, most seriously weakens the argument?

(A) Sudden increases in costs not associated with health insurance are equally harmful to small businesses.
(B) Changes to the market that result from lowering the risk of sudden increases in health insurance prices will increase the vulnerability of small businesses to sudden increases in other costs.
(C) Employees of small businesses who become unemployed as the result of the failure of the companies they work for are less likely to accept employment in other small businesses.
(D) The reimbursements to health insurers mandated by the bill will be funded by increased taxation that will significantly harm the overall economy.
(E) Decreasing the risk to employers associated with sudden increases in health insurance costs would induce many more people to start their own small businesses.

EXPLANATIONS

10. **Conclusion**: There is no reason to pass the bill.

Premise: The bill would prevent a problem that is only responsible for a small proportion of small-business failures.

Assumptions: The bill would not help the economy in other ways than preventing the failure of a small proportion of small businesses.

This is a WEAKEN question. We're looking for the choice that attacks the assumption or, failing that, gives us a reason to believe the conclusion might not be right.

(A) At best, this would strengthen the conclusion.
(B) This would strengthen the conclusion.
(C) This doesn't seem to be relevant to the bill at the center of this argument.
(D) This would strengthen the conclusion.
(E) Yes. Because we're told that small businesses are crucial to the country's economy, this would be a beneficial effect of the bill in question.

SECTION II

QUESTIONS

11. Marie: I just found out that it is cheaper for me to heat my home with gas or oil than for me to use any of the alternative methods available. I don't understand why environmentalists insist that the cost of fossil fuels is so high.

Louise: That's because you are confusing the price of fossil fuels with their cost. Gas and oil release tremendous amounts of pollution into the water and air, causing great damage to the environment. Not only does this pose a threat to the ecological balance that will affect the quality of life for future generations, but it also causes health problems that may be related to the consumption of these fuels. Once you add in these factors, it is clear that there are many alternatives that are actually cheaper than gas or oil, and consumers should adopt them.

According to her argument above, if an alternative energy source were to be found, under which one of the following conditions would Louise definitely object to its use?

(A) if its price and cost were equal
(B) if its cost were higher than the price of fossil fuels
(C) if its cost were higher than the cost of fossil fuels
(D) if the price of fossil fuels were to fall
(E) if it were less efficient than fossil fuels

EXPLANATIONS

11. This is most like a WEAKEN or STRENGTHEN or PARADOX question because you're looking for the one thing in the answer choices that, if known, will have the most IMPACT on the argument. So let's go looking for that.

(A) It depends. If they were equal at current cost levels? No. At current price levels? Maybe. Eliminate it.
(B) This confuses "cost" and "price." Eliminate it.
(C) Yep. We know she doesn't like the current situation, and this would make it worse. She would object to this.
(D) This would have no impact on the argument either way. Eliminate it.
(E) Efficiency is not the issue—cost is.

QUESTIONS	EXPLANATIONS

12. Company president: Many shareholders believe that, rather than developing products of our own to compete in new markets, our company should instead acquire existing companies that offer products of that type. This would be unwise. Any company that is willing to be acquired cannot be in a healthy competitive position in its market, and any company that is unwilling to be acquired would cost too much for our company to acquire without incurring substantial risk.

The company president's argument proceeds by

(A) advocating one course of action because a potential alternative course of action offers fewer advantages
(B) determining that a course of action is unwise because it cannot be undertaken without incurring unacceptable costs
(C) arguing against a course of action because there exist potential alternative courses of action that have not been definitively ruled out
(D) dismissing the course of action recommended by a group of shareholders because the members of that group do not have the best interests of the company at heart
(E) rejecting a course of action because the two possible situations in which it could be pursued are both unacceptable

12. This is a REASONING question. We're looking for the choice that correctly describes the argument.

(A) It's not the advantages, but the disadvantages, of the course of action that are mentioned.
(B) One of the bad results concerns cost, but not both of them.
(C) Failure to eliminate other possibilities is not the reason the course of action mentioned is considered unwise.
(D) The motives of the shareholders are not discussed.
(E) Yes. This mentions the two possibilities discussed in the argument and matches the argument's conclusion.

SECTION II

QUESTIONS

13. Pollster: In one survey of the electorate, a representative sample of likely voters was initially presented with information about the candidates' positions on several important issues. Months later in a second survey, these same voters were presented with information concerning the positions held by these candidates on the same issues, which in some cases had changed substantially. Despite this fact, the proportion of the sample that supported each candidate remained virtually unchanged. It can be concluded, therefore, that new information received about the candidates cannot appreciably change a voter's decision of which candidate to support.

Which one of the following, if true, most undermines the pollster's argument?

(A) The number of issues on which either candidate had completely reversed his or her earlier position was relatively small.
(B) It is not reasonable to expect voters to remember every detail of a political candidate's position on every significant issue.
(C) The issues covered by the survey were not those that had been most widely reported in media coverage of the election.
(D) More than a third of the survey group indicated that they supported a different candidate at the time of the second survey than they had at the time of the initial survey.
(E) At the time of the initial survey, a majority of the survey group indicated that the candidates' positions on issues were not the most important determining factor in their decision of which candidate to support.

EXPLANATIONS

13. **Conclusion**: New information received about candidates doesn't affect a voter's decision of which candidate to support.

Premises: An initial survey in which information was presented yielded the same proportion of voters who support each candidate as a later poll in which further information was presented to the same voter.

Assumptions: The primary assumption here is that we can conclude that voters didn't change their opinions on the basis of the fact that the proportion of the group that supported each candidate didn't change.

This is a WEAKEN question. We're looking for a choice that attacks the assumption, or else generally contradicts the conclusion.

(A) Although this suggests that the new information wasn't of too major a nature, it doesn't contradict the conclusion very strongly.
(B) This doesn't have a definite impact on the question of whether new information changes opinions.
(C) If anything, this strengthens the conclusion by showing that the information conveyed in the survey was in fact new.
(D) Yes. This indicates that, although the proportions were the same, many individual voters changed their mind. Although this doesn't definitively contradict the conclusion, it does destroy the evidence's relevance to it.
(E) This doesn't attack the relevance of the evidence to the conclusion; new information other than that provided in the survey may still have changed the voters' decisions.

SECTION II

QUESTIONS	EXPLANATIONS

14. Oil exploration cannot be efficiently conducted by geological methods alone. The information gained through geological methods is useful for obtaining an accurate estimate of the likelihood of finding oil in a particular area, but only invasive surveys can determine with certainty the quantity of oil that will be produced by any area where it is found, and geological methods of oil exploration never include invasive surveys.

Which one of the following is an assumption on which the argument depends?

(A) Oil exploration, to be successful, must include considerations of how practical it is to extract oil from a given area where it is found.
(B) Oil exploration in an area cannot be conducted efficiently without an accurate estimate of the likelihood of finding oil in that area.
(C) Knowledge of both the likelihood of finding oil in an area and the quantity of oil produced by that area are required by most oil companies before they will decide to drill there.
(D) Oil exploration can be efficiently conducted only with certain knowledge of the quantity of oil that will be produced by any area where oil can be found.
(E) Certain knowledge of the amount of oil that will be produced by any area where oil is likely to be found can be obtained solely through geological methods.

14. **Conclusion:** Oil exploration can't be efficiently conducted if it only uses geological methods.

Premises: Geological methods can find oil, but they can't tell you how much is there.

Assumption: Efficient oil exploration requires being able to tell how much oil is in a place where you find it.

This is an ASSUMPTION question. We're looking for something that the conclusion requires in order to be correct.

(A) The practicality of extraction isn't clearly related to either geological or invasive methods.
(B) Geological methods give you this, so this isn't really relevant to the conclusion.
(C) The issue here is conducting exploration efficiently, not making the decision to drill.
(D) Yes. If efficient exploration can be conducted without this knowledge, then it remains possible that it could be conducted with geological methods alone.
(E) This contradicts a premise of the argument.

15. Although all societies have some form of class system, there are systems that are based on neither wealth nor power. Still, there is no society that does not divide its population into the privileged and the common.

If the above statements are correct, it can be properly concluded that

(A) making distinctions between haves and have-nots is a part of human nature
(B) there are some people in all cultures who are considered privileged
(C) every society has its own unique hierarchy
(D) privileged people must have money
(E) all societies have a tradition of seeing themselves as either privileged or common

15. This is an INFERENCE question. Your goal is to find the one choice that must be true based on the information in the passage.

(A) "Human nature" is a little too general here. Eliminate it.
(B) "Some" is nice and wishy-washy. Let's leave it. (B) is our best answer here.
(C) It doesn't have to be true that every society's hierarchy is "unique." Eliminate it.
(D) Money is out of the scope of the argument. Eliminate it.
(E) Each society has BOTH privileged and common categories. Eliminate it.

SECTION II

QUESTIONS	EXPLANATIONS

Questions 16-17

On the basis of our understanding of ancient geography, it has long been accepted that the Americas were initially settled by people from eastern Asia who crossed into North America on a land bridge that once spanned the Bering Strait. Under this belief, all the native peoples of North and South America have been thought to be descendents of these first colonists. Yet genetic analysis of surviving native populations in the Americas indicates that most of them are much more closely related to the native populations of the Philippines and other Pacific islands. It seems clear that Pacific islanders must have been the first to reach the Americas. It has been shown that, using traditional construction methods, a group could have crossed the Pacific Ocean and reached South America.

16. Which one of the following is the main conclusion of the argument?

(A) The native populations in the Americas are no longer generally thought to be descended from settlers who came from eastern Asia.
(B) The genetic makeup of native populations in the Americas is substantially similar to that of native populations in the Philippines and other Pacific islands.
(C) The first human settlers in the Americas were Pacific islanders.
(D) At least some Pacific islanders reached the South American continent by traveling on boats that were constructed using traditional methods.
(E) Pacific islanders originating in the Philippines were the ancestors of all native populations in North and South America.

16. **Conclusion:** Pacific islanders were the first humans to settle the Americas.

Premise: The vast majority of native peoples are much more closely related to Pacific islanders than they are to the group widely believed to have been the first to settle the Amerias.

Assumption: The group from which a majority of the native inhabitants are descended must have been the first one to arrive.

This is a MAIN POINT question. We're looking for the thing that the argument wants us to believe.

(A) The conclusion here doesn't explicitly say that this belief is no longer held.
(B) This is a premise of the argument, not its conclusion.
(C) Yes. This is a good paraphrase of the main point as it is stated in the argument.
(D) The conclusion here doesn't concern how they got here first, only that they did.
(E) This is more extreme than the similar statement made in the argument, and it isn't its main conclusion.

SECTION II

QUESTIONS	EXPLANATIONS

17. The reasoning in the argument is most vulnerable to which one of the following criticisms?

(A) That a stated belief has been traditionally held to be true is taken as evidence that the belief must, in fact, be false.
(B) That a given explanation of a set of facts is possible in some cases is taken as positive proof that this explanation is correct in all cases.
(C) The statement of a set of conditions under which some correction to a set of long-held beliefs would be required is confused with the establishment of the fact that such a set of conditions actually arose.
(D) The historical cause of a particular set of facts is mistakenly assumed to be the only possible cause of a similar set of facts elsewhere.
(E) Facts that may only support the claim that a particular historic event occurred are taken to show that this event occurred before other similar events that could possibly have occurred earlier.

17. This is a FLAW question. We want the choice that describes or exploits an assumption of the argument.

(A) Acceptance of the other theory is not the reason that the argument concludes it is false.
(B) The fact that this is a possible explanation is not the reason that the argument concludes it is correct.
(C) There is no hypothetical statement anywhere in the argument similar to the one described in this choice.
(D) The argument doesn't use a conclusion about one place to draw conclusions about another.
(E) Yes. The evidence only supports the conclusion that descendents of Pacific islanders came to the Americas; it doesn't directly show that they came to the Americas first.

18. The current method of powering aircraft, the burning of fuel by internal-combustion engines, cannot be maintained indefinitely. Internal-combustion engines now burn refined petroleum, and the world's supply of petroleum is necessarily limited.

Which one of the following is an assumption required by the argument?

(A) Some means of powering aircraft other than the burning of fuels in internal-combustion engines could be successfully adopted.
(B) Internal-combustion engines cannot be designed so that they burn some fuel not derived from limited resources.
(C) Products from refined petroleum other than those currently burned in aircraft engines could not be chemically modified to replace the fuels used in aircraft today.
(D) Engines that do not operate by internal combustion could not be designed to operate using fuels derived from petroleum.
(E) No method of powering aircraft that relies on a finite resource is practical.

18. **Conclusion**: Internal-combustion engines cannot be indefinitely used to power aircraft.

Premises: Current internal-combustion engines burn refined petroleum; the supply of petroleum is limited.

Assumption: Internal-combustion engines cannot burn, instead of petroleum, some resource whose supply is not limited.

This is an ASSUMPTION question. We're looking for something that the argument needs for its conclusion to be correct.

(A) This is not within the scope of the argument; the conclusion only concerns internal-combustion engines.
(B) Yes. If this is untrue—if internal-combustion engines can be designed to burn fuel from renewable resources—then it's possible that they could be used to power aircraft indefinitely.
(C) Other fuels derived from petroleum have no effect on the force of this argument.
(D) Other types of engines are not strictly relevant to this argument's conclusion.
(E) Practicality is not an explicit issue of this argument.

SECTION II

QUESTIONS

19. Evidence seems to indicate that people's faith in some mystical practices increases when these practices offer relief in frightening or challenging situations. One significant piece of evidence is the observation that the use of "healing crystals" is more prevalent among people who suffer from life-threatening diseases such as cancer than it is among people who have minor health problems such as colds or the flu.

Which one of the following, if true, would most seriously weaken the conclusion drawn in the passage above?

(A) Rapid social change has alienated people and has led to an overall increase in people's adoption of mystical practices.
(B) Many mystical practices are never used by more than a small number of extremely ill people.
(C) Those who are diagnosed with life-threatening diseases may seek nontraditional treatments for those diseases without having faith in their effectiveness.
(D) Psychics and mediums do not experience a surge in business after the occurrence of earthquakes and plane crashes.
(E) The use of crystals is one of the most ancient methods utilized for healing.

20. Executive: Nearly everyone can become a consultant, for there are no formal requirements that must be satisfied to be called a consultant. Anyone who convinces a company to hire him or her to perform an advisory function—no matter what its nature—is by definition a consultant.

The executive's conclusion can be properly drawn if which one of the following is assumed?

(A) Nearly everyone can convince a company to hire him or her to perform an advisory function.
(B) Some consultants satisfy a set of formal requirements not directly related to any advisory function they perform for a business.
(C) Those who convince companies to hire them to perform advisory functions satisfy their employers' requirements for the performance of those functions.
(D) Every consultant has convinced some company that he or she satisfies a set of informal requirements.
(E) Some consultants could convince any company to hire them to perform certain advisory functions.

EXPLANATIONS

19. **Conclusion:** Faith in mystical practices increases in life-threatening situations.

Premise: People are more likely to use healing crystals for cancer than for a cold or flu.

Assumption: The people who use healing crystals actually believe they will work.

This is a WEAKEN question. Figure out which answer choice has the most negative impact on the conclusion of the argument. Remember to assume the hypothetical truth of each choice and apply it to the argument.

(A) We're concerned more with crystals and specific diseases—this is a little too general.
(B) Mystical practices that are not used are not the issue.
(C) Ah, so while they are trying these cures, their faith in them hasn't necessarily increased—this would weaken the argument. This is the answer.
(D) None of this is talking about anything in the argument. Eliminate it.
(E) The ancientness of crystals has no impact on the argument. Eliminate it.

20. **Conclusion**: Nearly everyone can become a consultant.

Premise: Anyone who convinces a company to hire him or her to perform an advisory function is a consultant.

This is a STRENGTHEN question. We're looking for the choice that makes the conclusion certain.

(A) Yes. If we assume this, then the conclusion definitely follows.
(B) The argument says that no formal requirements are relevant to the issue.
(C) This wouldn't help us conclude that nearly everyone can do this.
(D) This restates a premise, and as such provides no additional support to the conclusion.
(E) This doesn't help us conclude that nearly anyone can become a consultant.

SECTION II

QUESTIONS

21. An editor found that the manuscript of a new novel contained many grammatical errors and misused words. Despite this fact, the editor did not recommend that the manuscript be rejected.

    Each of the following, if true, would explain the editor's decision EXCEPT:

    (A) The manuscript in question had already been accepted by the publisher, a decision that could not be reversed on the editor's advice.
    (B) The author of the manuscript was a first-time author whose work was not expected to attract much critical notice.
    (C) The prose style used in the manuscript, although unorthodox, was groundbreaking and enjoyable to read.
    (D) The errors in the manuscript could easily be corrected in the editing process, and the novel's story was gripping and dramatic.
    (E) Correct grammar and word usage are not the most important factors in an editor's decision of whether to recommend a manuscript's rejection.

22. If a candidate is to win an election easily, that candidate must respond to the electorate's emotional demands—demands that the opponent either does not see or cannot act upon. Although these emotional demands are often not directly articulated by the electorate or by the candidate responding to them, they are an integral part of any landslide victory.

    Which one of the following conclusions can most logically be drawn from the passage above?

    (A) If neither candidate responds to the emotional demands of the electorate, either candidate might win in a landslide.
    (B) If an election was close, the emotional demands of the electorate were conflicting.
    (C) If a candidate responds to the emotional demands of the electorate, that candidate will have a landslide victory.
    (D) An election during which neither candidate responds to the emotional demands of the electorate will not result in a landslide.
    (E) Emotional demands are the only inarticulated issues in an election.

EXPLANATIONS

21. This is a RESOLVE/EXPLAIN EXCEPT question. Four of these choices will explain the decision; the odd choice out is our answer.

    (A) This would help to explain why the editor didn't suggest that the manuscript be rejected. The suggestion wouldn't have mattered.
    (B) Yes. This doesn't offer a clear reason for not rejecting a manuscript with so many problems.
    (C) This would help to explain why the editor didn't suggest that the manuscript be rejected. Although it contained what could be called errors, the errors were features of a good style.
    (D) This would help to explain why the editor didn't suggest that the manuscript be rejected. Its good qualities were very good, and the errors were easy to correct.
    (E) This would help to explain why the editor didn't suggest that the manuscript be rejected. Its flaws didn't relate to the important factors for making the decision.

22. This is an INFERENCE question. Your goal is to find the one choice that must be true based on the information in the passage.

    (A) No, because if candidates don't respond, there can't be a landslide.
    (B) We have no idea what would happen if the election were close. Eliminate it.
    (C) This is the invalid contrapositive of the first sentence. Eliminate it.
    (D) Bingo—it's the contrapositive of the first sentence—that if you don't respond, you can't have a landslide.
    (E) "Only" is too extreme here. Eliminate it.

SECTION II

QUESTIONS	EXPLANATIONS

23. A well-known philosopher once articulated the method by which an action can be judged to be unethical: Imagine the consequences of everyone in society taking that action; if those consequences would be harmful to society, then the action is unethical. Yet it cannot be denied that, at times in the past, the intentional breaking of laws to draw attention to injustice has had beneficial effects in many societies. By the philosopher's standard, however, these actions would be judged unethical because if everyone in a society disregarded its laws, chaos would result. Because it is every person's ethical responsibility to fight against injustice in society, the philosopher's method must be incorrect.

The argument is flawed because it

(A) confuses what is ethically impermissible with what is merely not forbidden
(B) treats actions that have characteristics in common with a larger class as members of that class without recognizing a relevant distinction
(C) derives a conclusion about all the actions of a certain class on the basis of a principle whose relevance to those actions is doubtful
(D) mistakenly ascribes a characteristic to a class of actions that can properly be said to apply only to the individual actions that make up that class
(E) incorrectly assumes the truth of its conclusion that the philosopher's method is flawed

23. **Conclusion**: The philosopher's rule for deciding when an action is unethical is incorrect.

Premises: Sometimes, disobeying laws serves to fight injustice in society; it is everyone's ethical responsibility to fight injustice; by the philosopher's rule, however, breaking laws is unethical.

Assumption: The philosopher's rule, when applied to the cases in question, would consider only the fact that they are examples of breaking the law, rather than examples of breaking the law for the purpose of fighting injustice.

This is a FLAW question. We're looking for a choice that either describes or exploits an assumption of the argument.

(A) This is not a distinction that is relevant to the argument's conclusion.
(B) Yes. The relevant distinction is that these instances of breaking the law are intended to help society.
(C) The relevance of the principle isn't in doubt; the method of its application is.
(D) This argument does not confuse characteristics of an individual with characteristics of a group or collection.
(E) No, the argument attempts to support its conclusion with premises that differ from it.

SECTION II

QUESTIONS

24. For every known physical phenomenon, physicists have posited laws that govern the occurrence of that phenomenon. It can be concluded, therefore, that every known physical phenomenon is governed by the same law.

The flawed reasoning in the argument above is most similar to that in which one of the following?

(A) The trunk of every tree is a body of tissue that contains both xylem and phloem. Therefore, any body of tissue that contains both xylem and phloem is the trunk of a tree.
(B) Every house has a unique mailing address. Therefore, because these packages are all marked with the same mailing address, they will all be sent to the same house.
(C) Because every action taken by a person can be explained by unconscious motives, a single motive explains all of the actions taken by any person.
(D) No violin that was made in the twentieth century is remarkably valuable. Because this violin is remarkably valuable, it must not have been made in the twentieth century.
(E) For every known star, astronomers can determine that star's elemental composition. Because a star's elemental composition determines its exact color, no two stars are the same exact color.

EXPLANATIONS

24. **Conclusion:** All known physical phenomena are governed by the same law.

Premise: Each known physical phenomenon is governed by physical laws.

Flaw: There may be more than one physical law, yet all are called "the same law."

This is a PARALLEL-FLAW question. We're looking for the answer choice that has the same problem.

(A) No. This one is flawed because it misuses the conditional "all" statement: The fact that all tree trunks have xylem and phloem doesn't exclude the possibility that some tissues with xylem and phloem are not tree trunks. This is not the same as the problem with the original argument.
(B) No. This argument is not flawed.
(C) Yes. In this argument, "action taken by a person" corresponds to "known physical phenomenon," and "can be explained by unconscious motives" corresponds to "is governed by physical laws."
(D) No. This argument is not flawed.
(E) No. The conclusion of this argument is not at all similar to the conclusion of the original argument.

SECTION II

QUESTIONS

25. No iconoclasts are public figures, and all politicians are public figures. It follows that no politicians are fanatics.

The conclusion above follows logically if which one of the following is assumed?

(A) All fanatics are public figures.
(B) All fanatics are iconoclasts.
(C) All public figures are politicians.
(D) No fanatics are iconoclasts.
(E) No iconoclasts are politicians.

EXPLANATIONS

25. **Conclusion**: politician → - fanatic

Premises: iconoclast → - public figure; politician → public figure

This is a STRENGTHEN question. We're looking for the choice that makes the conclusion certain by completing a chain of conditional statements leading from "politician" to "- fanatic."

Note that the two premises given allow us to form part of such a chain, using the contrapositive of the second statement listed above. We have this chain: politician → public figure → - iconoclast. We need to extend it by one link to "- fanatic."

(A) Fanatic → public figure. Neither this statement nor its contrapositive allows us to extend the chain.

(B) Fanatic → iconoclast. This is it. Note its contrapositive: - iconoclast → - fanatic. This allows us to extend the chain to reach the desired conclusion.

(C) Public figure → politician. This doesn't involve the missing term—"fanatic"—at all.

(D) Fanatic → - iconoclast. Neither this statement nor its contrapositive allows us to extend the chain.

(E) Iconoclast → - politician. We already know this from our premises; also, this doesn't include the missing term: "fanatic."

SECTION II

QUESTIONS

26. Wendy: Young people in our country are lagging behind the young people in other countries in science and math. With the increasing importance of technology in the world economy, it seems all but certain that our country's economic stature is in jeopardy.

    Thomas: You forget that our country's strong economy allows us to attract new immigrants easily. Although the young people in our country may not fill the need for employees in technology companies, we will always be able to satisfy it by allowing those with the needed skills to emigrate from other countries, thereby maintaining our crucial competitive position in the world economy.

    By their statements, it can be most reasonably inferred that Wendy and Thomas would agree with which one of the following statements?

    (A) Efforts should be made to encourage the growth of the country's economy in areas that do not rely as heavily on technical knowledge.
    (B) Continued efforts to ensure that the country's future workforce includes those who have the skills needed by technology companies are warranted.
    (C) The quality of math and science education offered to the country's young people can be improved only if the rate of immigration is limited.
    (D) In the future, the country's economic stature is likely to decline.
    (E) Technology companies will adapt their business operations so that they can successfully employ people in many different countries who have needed skills.

EXPLANATIONS

26. This is most closely related to an INFERENCE question. We're looking for a choice about which Wendy and Thomas would both express the same opinion.

    (A) Neither participant expresses this opinion.
    (B) Yes. Both Wendy and Thomas would say that this is true.
    (C) Neither participant expresses this opinion.
    (D) It seems as though Wendy would say this is true; Thomas would definitely say it isn't.
    (E) Neither participant expresses this opinion.

SECTION III

QUESTIONS

1. Senator: For economic issues, I base my responses on logic. For political issues, I base my responses either on logic or gut instinct. For moral issues, I never base my responses on logic.

   Which one of the following can be correctly inferred from the statements above?

   (A) If the senator relies on logic, he may be responding to a moral issue.
   (B) If the senator relies on logic, he is not responding to an economic issue.
   (C) If the senator does not rely on logic, he is responding to a political issue.
   (D) If the senator does not rely on logic, he must be responding to an economic issue.
   (E) If the senator does not rely on logic, he might be responding to a political issue.

2. Social institutions are organized in such a way that they reinforce the need for their continued existence. Thus, although many political candidates claim that they will do away with certain social institutions that are not universally supported, it is unlikely that these candidates will be able to deliver on their promises.

   The statement that social institutions are organized in such a way that they reinforce the need for their continued existence functions in the argument in which one of the following ways?

   (A) It is a premise offered to lend support to the claim that political candidates will be unable to deliver on their promises to eliminate certain social institutions.
   (B) It is a conclusion supported by the premise that many political candidates claim that they will do away with some social institutions.
   (C) It is an assertion despite which the argument says that political candidates will succeed in doing away with the least popular of social institutions.
   (D) It is offered as evidence against the belief that political candidates are sincere when they promise to do away with certain social institutions.
   (E) It is the main conclusion of the argument.

EXPLANATIONS

1. This is an INFERENCE question. Your goal is to find the one choice that must be true based on the information in the passage.

   (A) No, the senator never bases moral issue responses on logic. Eliminate it.
   (B) No, the senator may very well be responding to an economic issue. Eliminate it.
   (C) No, the senator could be responding to a moral issue. Eliminate it.
   (D) No, the senator always uses logic to respond to economic issues. Eliminate it.
   (E) Bingo. Nice and wishy-washy, and accurate. With political issues, the senator might respond with a gut instinct. This is the answer.

2. This is a REASONING question. We want the choice that correctly describes the purpose of the indicated statement.

   (A) Yes. The statement in question is the only premise of the argument.
   (B) The statement in question is not supported by any other premise.
   (C) This choice contradicts the argument's conclusion.
   (D) The sincerity of political candidates is not an issue in this argument.
   (E) The main conclusion of the argument is that politicians will not make good on their promises.

SECTION III

QUESTIONS	EXPLANATIONS

3. An electronics manufacturer in financial trouble decided last year that, to survive, it needed to eliminate its least popular product lines to save on production costs. The product lines it eliminated accounted for 20 percent of all products produced by the manufacturer at that time. Yet, one year after their elimination, production costs directly related to the manufacture of their products have decreased by only 15 percent.

Which one of the following, if true, contributes most to an explanation of the difference between the reduction in manufacturing output and the cost savings achieved as a result of that reduction?

(A) The product lines eliminated by the manufacturer were also the most expensive products to produce.

(B) Production of products in the lines that were not eliminated were significantly cut back over the past year.

(C) Raw materials for the manufacturer's products constitute a far greater share of the products' direct production costs than expenses such as labor and maintenance.

(D) The total direct production costs associated with manufacturing components used in all of the manufacturer's products were not changed by the elimination of some product lines that used those components.

(E) The manufacturer's contract with the union to which its employees belong required the reassignment of workers who had previously been employed in producing the eliminated product lines to administrative departments not directly related to manufacturing operations.

3. This is a RESOLVE/EXPLAIN question. We're looking for the choice that describes how 20 percent of production could be eliminated while only reducing direct manufacturing costs by 15 percent.

(A) If anything, this would make the paradox worse.

(B) If anything, this would make the paradox worse. Cutbacks in addition to the ones mentioned should result in more savings, not less.

(C) This doesn't seem to offer a clear explanation of the unexpectedly low cost savings.

(D) Yes. This tells us that the costs of some part of the production process associated with the eliminated products were impossible to reduce.

(E) This choice describes costs not directly related to manufacturing, which are not relevant to the paradox here.

SECTION III

QUESTIONS

4. Advertisement: Professional exterminators will tell you that to rid your home of roaches, you must do more than kill all the roaches you see. This is why the system that professional exterminators use most includes a poison that inhibits the development of roach eggs already laid, as well as a chemical that kills all adult roaches. This same combination is now available to the nonprofessional in new Extirm. When you're ready to get rid of roaches once and for all, get Extirm in your corner.

All of the following are implied by the advertisement above EXCEPT:

(A) Professional exterminators asked about roach extermination recommended Extirm.
(B) Extirm contains a chemical that inhibits the development of roach eggs.
(C) More than one chemical is required to rid a home of roaches.
(D) Inhibiting the development of roach eggs may not eliminate roaches from the home.
(E) Roaches reproduce by laying eggs.

5. The use of genetically engineered bacteria to process some types of radioactive waste is preferable to the traditional method of burying it in sealed containers. Whereas waste disposed of by traditional means remains radioactive for thousands of years, the engineered bacteria can render radioactive waste safe within a matter of months. Also, breaches or flaws in the containment of buried waste can lead to harmful contamination of soil and water that may be extremely difficult to detect.

Which one of the following statements, if true, most weakens the argument?

(A) The by-products generated by the genetically engineered bacteria in processing radioactive waste are not more harmful to the environment than the radioactive waste itself would be.
(B) No type of genetically engineered bacteria has yet been discovered that can process all types of radioactive waste.
(C) The processes that produce radioactive waste also lead to radioactive contamination of equipment that cannot be reduced through the use of genetically engineered bacteria.
(D) The environmental conditions required by the genetically engineered bacteria in processing radioactive waste make harmful soil and water contamination likely.
(E) There is a risk that some of the genetically engineered bacteria, when used, will give rise toutant progeny that are unable to process radioactive waste.

EXPLANATIONS

4. This is an INFERENCE question. It is also an EXCEPT question, so your goal is to find the one choice that doesn't have to be true based on the information in the passage.

(A) We have no idea what they recommend. It's never mentioned in the passage. This is the answer.
(B) Yes, this is mentioned in the second sentence. Eliminate it.
(C) Yes, this is mentioned in the second sentence. One for eggs; one for adults. Eliminate it.
(D) Which is why we need two chemicals—see the second sentence again.
(E) This is a major part of sentence two. Eliminate it.

5. **Conclusion**: Engineered bacteria is a better way to dispose of some radioactive waste than is burying it in sealed containers.

Premises: Buried waste remains radioactive for much longer; burying waste can lead to contaminated soil or water.

Assumption: The cited advantages of bacteria are not outweighed by an unstated disadvantage.

This is a WEAKEN question. We're looking for the choice that tells us why bacteria might not be a better solution.

(A) This would strengthen the argument, if only slightly.
(B) This argument's conclusion doesn't state that bacteria are suitable for all types of radioactive waste.
(C) Like (B), this choice indicates that there are some types of radioactive contamination for which bacteria won't work, but the argument doesn't claim that they will work for all types of contamination.
(D) Yes. Bacteria have a more serious negative effect on soil and water than burying waste does, which casts doubt on the conclusion.
(E) As long as these mutants aren't harmful and don't render the method completely ineffective, this isn't relevant to the conclusion.

SECTION III

QUESTIONS

6. On Tuesday night we observed that comet X was moving in the direction of star P. On Wednesday night, a flare was observed that could have been caused by a comet colliding with a star. Therefore, the flare that was observed on Wednesday night was caused by comet X colliding with star P.

The questionable method of reasoning in the argument above is most similar to that in which one of the following arguments?

(A) At three o'clock, a trash can was standing upright at the corner of the intersection of Myrtle and Carleton. At four o'clock, a trash can was lying in the center of that same intersection. Because at four o'clock there was no longer a trash can standing upright on the corner, it is likely that a passing automobile collided with the trash can and knocked it into the intersection.

(B) This morning, Stewart was in downtown Frostburg. This afternoon, Stewart was in downtown Augusta. Because Stewart could not have traveled so far in so short a time without traveling by airplane, Stewart must have traveled in an airplane today.

(C) Yesterday, Misty expressed her intention to make an offer on a house that is for sale through realtor V. Today, an offer was made on a house that is for sale through a realtor. Therefore, that offer was made by Misty on a house that is for sale through realtor V.

(D) Either May or Kathleen will be the next CEO of Thiscorp. Because media reports suggest that the one chosen will not be May, Kathleen is certain to be the next CEO of Thiscorp.

(E) Ten minutes ago, a red car was moving down this country road at excessive speed. No one else has used the road all day. A car has just collided with a large tree along this country road; there can be no doubt that the car involved in the collision is red.

EXPLANATIONS

6. **Conclusion**: The flare was caused by comet X colliding with star P.

Premises: Comet X was observed heading toward star P, then later a flare was observed; a flare could have been caused by a comet colliding with a star.

Flaw: The fact that an observation could have had a particular cause is treated as positive proof that it did.

This is a PARALLEL-FLAW question. We're looking for the choice that makes the same mistake.

(A) The conclusion in the original is definite; the conclusion here is qualified.

(B) This is a good argument.

(C) Yes. This reproduces all of the features of the original.

(D) This argument involves an either/or that isn't similar to anything seen in the original argument.

(E) This is a good argument.

SECTION III

QUESTIONS	EXPLANATIONS

7. Sales representative: Our nutritional supplement treats mold allergies at least as well as any prescription drug does. Unfortunately, we have no study results to prove this claim, but the supplement is clearly effective: Our customer satisfaction surveys show that people with mold allergies who take our supplement all report a lessening of symptoms. No study conducted by any maker of a prescription drug has ever refuted this evidence.

The sales representative's argument is flawed because it reasons that

(A) the fact that the supplement is effective does not necessarily imply that it is as effective as any prescription drug
(B) the results of a survey conducted by an organization with commercial interest in its findings may be biased
(C) because no evidence demonstrates that a survey's results are inaccurate, the results must therefore be accurate
(D) the experiences of those who seek treatment for a condition are relevant to an evaluation of the relative efficacy of those treatments
(E) the lessening of symptoms does not necessarily constitute effective treatment of the malady responsible for those symptoms

8. It is widely believed that the consumption of certain cold medicines may impair a driver's ability to operate a vehicle safely. However, the results of examinations administered during the process of obtaining a driver's license show that this is a misconception. The rate at which examinees who were taking cold medicines were awarded driver's licenses was no different from the rate at which examinees in the population at large received driver's licenses.

The reasoning above is fallacious because it fails to consider the possibility that

(A) the number of those taking cold medicines during the examination process represented a relatively small proportion of the total number of examinees
(B) not all cold medicines have similar effects on a driver's ability to operate a vehicle safely
(C) an individual who is able to operate a vehicle safely may fail one or more of the examinations on which the decision to award a driver's license is based
(D) the belief that cold medicines impair coordination has been refuted by other studies not directly related to operating vehicles
(E) an individual who takes cold medicine may be able to operate a vehicle more safely than that individual would if he or she left the cold untreated

7. **Conclusion:** The supplement is at least as effective at treating mold allergies as any prescription drug.

Premises: Surveys show that all mold allergy sufferers who took the supplement improved; these surveys have never been refuted by the drug companies.

Assumption: The fact that the study has never been refuted indicates that its findings are correct; the improvement found in the study was at least as great as the improvements associated with those who are treated with prescription drugs.

This is a FLAW question. We're looking for a choice that describes or exploits an assumption.

(A) Careful. This would be a great answer to a weaken question, but this isn't something the argument says.
(B) Like (A), this is related to an error in the reasoning but doesn't correctly describe what the argument is saying.
(C) Yes. This indicates something that the argument does incorrectly.
(D) This doesn't seem like an incorrect thing to do.
(E) Again, this is a great weaken but doesn't fit the question asked

8. **Conclusion**: It is not true that certain cold medicines impair the ability to operate a car.

Premise: Applicants on cold medicine are no less likely to pass driver's license exams than are applicants generally.

Assumption: Performance on driver's license exams measures ability to operate a car; the cold medicines mentioned in the conclusion are the same ones the applicants in the survey were taking.

This is a FLAW question. We're looking for a choice that exploits an assumption of the argument.

(A) The size of the group taking cold medicine isn't relevant unless the number is very small.
(B) Yes. It's possible that only a few cold medicines have a detrimental effect; it seems likely that you wouldn't take them before taking a driver's license test, doesn't it?
(C) Close, but this indicates that those who fail may nevertheless operate a vehicle safely; it seems that this possibility would affect both groups equally.
(D) This doesn't appear to have any effect on the argument's conclusion.
(E) This is a side issue.

QUESTIONS	EXPLANATIONS

9. The fact that many animals preyed upon by large carnivores are herd animals does not therefore imply that their herding behavior confers protection from predation. When hunting prey that lives in herds, large carnivores routinely target the weakest members of the herd, and unless the targeted animal is a juvenile, even the closest relatives of the targeted animal do not act to protect it. The closest relatives of most juvenile animals, whether or not they live in herds, will most often act to protect them from predators.

Which one of the following most accurately expresses the main conclusion of the argument?

(A) The closest relatives of juvenile animals most often act to protect those animals from predators.
(B) Living in herds offers advantages that do not stem from the decreased likelihood of being killed by a predator.
(C) Large carnivores tend to prefer prey that lives in herds.
(D) The reason that many animals live in herds cannot be that herding behavior increases the number of animals that will act to protect the herd's members from large carnivores.
(E) The confusion engendered when a herd flees from a large carnivore provides protection for the targeted member of that herd, even when no other herd member actively protects that animal.

9. This is a MAIN POINT question. We're looking for what the argument wants us to believe.

(A) This is a premise of the argument.
(B) The issue here is not what advantages herding behavior offers so much as it is one particular advantage that it doesn't offer.
(C) The preferences of carnivores aren't what this argument is trying to tell us about.
(D) Yes. This is the choice that gets all of the significant pieces of the argument and tells us what the argument wants us to get from them.
(E) This would weaken the argument. It's certainly not the main point.

SECTION III

QUESTIONS

10. Recent history in many former dictatorships suggests that the introduction of democratic reforms and market reforms at the same time is ultimately counterproductive. Although many countries in which one of these types of reform was carried out independent of the other have in time embraced liberalization of both types, almost all countries in which both political and economic continuity are interrupted eventually slip back into authoritarian styles of government that exert strong control over the market. It can be concluded that the best strategy for reform in a country that was formerly a dictatorship is to promote increased democracy, or more freedom in the market, but not both.

Which one of the following statements, if true, would provide the greatest additional support for the argument above?

(A) Economic reform in countries that were not formerly dictatorships is usually more difficult to promote than is political reform.
(B) Some authoritarian governments oppress their populations by exerting control over their countries' markets.
(C) Reform efforts that do not address the fundamental humanitarian needs of a country's citizenry are unlikely to succeed.
(D) Reform in a former dictatorship cannot be successful without including aspects of political or economic continuity as well as political or economic liberalization.
(E) Countries with both democratic governments and market economies may also benefit from reform to one or the other of these systems.

EXPLANATIONS

10. **Conclusion**: The best strategy to reform former dictatorships is to propose democratic reform or market reform, but not both.

Premises: Many countries where one was introduced ended up adopting the other; most countries where the two were introduced simultaneously adopted neither.

This is a STRENGTHEN question. Because there are no obvious flaws, it's likely that our answer will directly support the conclusion.

(A) The difficulty of one route versus the other has no effect on this conclusion.
(B) The details of how authoritarian governments work do not appear to be relevant to this conclusion.
(C) Humanitarian needs are not directly relevant to the conclusion.
(D) Yes. This provides additional support for the fact that some type of reform must be advocated for, but advocating both will not be successful.
(E) These countries are not relevant to the conclusion.

SECTION III

QUESTIONS	EXPLANATIONS

11. In mathematics, different definitions of key concepts may be advanced, but no new definition is considered correct if it conflicts with the accepted definition. In some cases, however, it is possible that a new correct definition is able to solve some problem that the accepted definition cannot. In this case, because the accepted definition should always be the correct definition that is capable of solving the greatest number of problems, the new definition should become the accepted definition.

Which one of the following principles, if valid, most helps to justify the reasoning above?

(A) Any new definition of a mathematical concept that can solve some problem that the accepted definition cannot must be correct.
(B) No new correct definition that is able to solve some problem that the accepted definition cannot solve fails to solve any problem that the accepted definition can solve.
(C) It is possible that a new incorrect definition of some mathematical concept is capable of solving problems that the currently accepted definition cannot.
(D) The definitions of mathematical concepts cannot be evaluated in terms of their truth, only their correctness.
(E) Any existing correct definition of a mathematical concept that is not the accepted definition must fail to solve at least one problem that the accepted definition can.

11. **Conclusion**: A new correct definition that is able to solve some problems that the currently accepted definition cannot should become the accepted definition.

Premise: The accepted definition should be the correct definition that solves the greatest number of problems.

Assumption: A new correct definition that solves some problems that the currently accepted definition cannot must solve a greater number of problems than the currently accepted definition does.

This is a PRINCIPLE question. We're looking, more specifically, for the principle that would justify the conclusion.

(A) Determining whether a definition is correct is irrelevant to the conclusion; it covers only correct definitions.
(B) Yes. This would guarantee that the new definition really does solve more problems than the previous accepted definition.
(C) Incorrect definitions are not relevant to the conclusion.
(D) Truth is not relevant to this conclusion.
(E) This is a side issue; definitions of this sort are not relevant to the conclusion.

SECTION III

QUESTIONS

12. Computer Technician: This system has either a software problem or a hardware problem. None of the available diagnostic tests has been able to determine where the problem lies. The software can be replaced, but the hardware cannot be altered in any way, which means that if the problem lies in the hardware, the entire system will have to be scrapped. We must begin work to solve the problem by presupposing that the problem is with the software.

On which one of the following principles could the technician's reasoning be based?

(A) In fixing a problem that has two possible causes, it makes more sense to deal with both causes rather than spend time trying to determine which is the actual cause of the problem.
(B) If events outside one's control bear on a decision, the best course of action is to assume the "worst-case" scenario.
(C) When the soundness of an approach depends on the validity of an assumption, one's first task must be to test that assumption's validity.
(D) When circumstances must be favorable in order for a strategy to succeed, the strategy must be based on the assumption that conditions are indeed favorable until proved otherwise.
(E) When only one strategy can be successful, the circumstances affecting that strategy must be altered so that strategy may be employed.

EXPLANATIONS

12. This is a PRINCIPLE question. We are given five principles in the answer choices for this specific question, so we should come up with our own principle for the actions in the argument and match it to the answer choices.

(A) But they're not dealing with both causes—only the software cause. Eliminate it.
(B) They're not assuming that—if they were, they'd go out and replace the hardware. Eliminate it.
(C) They're not testing assumptions; they can't test anything. They just have to hope it's the problem that's cheaper to fix. Eliminate it.
(D) They're hoping that it's the software until it's really obvious it's not. This is the answer.
(E) They're not altering any strategy in the argument. Eliminate it.

SECTION III

QUESTIONS

13. To become a master at chess, a person must play. If a person plays for at least four hours a day, that person will inevitably become a master of the game. Thus, if a person is a master at the game of chess, that person must have played each day for at least four hours.

The error in the logic of the argument above is most accurately described by which one of the following?

(A) The conclusion is inadequate because it fails to acknowledge that people who play for four hours each day might not develop a degree of skill for the game that others view as masterful.
(B) The conclusion is inadequate because it fails to acknowledge that playing one hour a day might be sufficient for some people to become masters.
(C) The conclusion is inadequate because it fails to acknowledge that if a person has not played four hours a day, that person has not become a master.
(D) The conclusion is inadequate because it fails to acknowledge that four hours of playing time each day is not a strategy recommended by any world-champion chess players.
(E) The conclusion is inadequate because it fails to acknowledge that most people are not in a position to devote four hours each day to playing chess.

EXPLANATIONS

13. **Conclusion:** If a person is a master, she must have played chess at least four hours each day.

Premise: If a person plays four hours each day, she will become a master.

Assumption: Playing four hours each day is the only way to become a master.

This is a FLAW question. Try to come up with your own description of why the author's conclusion is flawed before you go to the answer choices, and then match your description to the choices.

(A) Whether other people think the player is a master is irrevelant. According to the argument, anyone who plays at least four hours a day "will inevitably become a master."
(B) Bingo. The author makes an invalid contrapositive in the argument. This is the answer.
(C) We have no idea whether this is true. Eliminate it.
(D) We don't care about chess champion recommendations. Eliminate it.
(E) We don't care about most people. The argument doesn't say everyone. Eliminate it.

SECTION III

QUESTIONS

14. Prescriptive grammar is not a natural science. We know this because prescriptive grammar relies upon a set of axiomatic principles, and no science that relies upon a set of axiomatic principles depends primarily on experimentation.

The conclusion of the argument follows logically if which one of the following is assumed?

(A) Some natural sciences rely on a set of axiomatic principles.
(B) All natural sciences depend primarily on experimentation.
(C) No science that depends primarily on experimentation relies on a set of axiomatic principles.
(D) All sciences that depend primarily on experimentation are natural sciences.
(E) No grammar that relies on a set of axiomatic principles is a science.

EXPLANATIONS

14. **Conclusion**: prescriptive grammar → natural science

Premises: prescriptive grammar → set of axiomatic principles; set of axiomatic principles → experimentation

This is a STRENGTHEN question. We want the choice that guarantees the truth of the conclusion by completing the chain from "prescriptive grammar" to "- natural science."

Note that the two premises given allow us to form part of such a chain: prescriptive grammar → set of axiomatic principles → experimentation. The most likely link we'll find in the choices is "- experimentation → natural science."

(A) No "some" statement can provide us the needed link.
(B) Yes. This reads "natural science → experimentation." Its contrapositive provides the link we're looking for.
(C) This reads "experimentation → set of axiomatic principles," which is the contrapositive of one of our premises. This choice doesn't add any new information.
(D) This reads "experimentation → natural science." This does not allow us to extend the chain.
(E) No grammar that does not rely upon a set of axiomatic principles is a science.

QUESTIONS

15. Last year, Marcel enjoyed a high income from exactly two places: his sporting goods store and his stock market investments. Although Marcel earns far more from his store than from his investments, the money he earns from the stock market is an important part of his income. Because of a series of drops in the stock market, Marcel will not earn as much from his investments this year. It follows then that Marcel will make less money this year than he did last year.

Which one of the following is an assumption necessary to the author's argument?

(A) Increased profits at Marcel's sporting goods store will not offset any loss in stock market income.
(B) Sporting goods stores earn lower profits when the stock market drops.
(C) Drops in the stock market do not always affect all of a particular investor's stocks.
(D) Marcel's stock market investments will be subject to increased volatility.
(E) If his income is lower, Marcel will not be able to meet his expenses.

EXPLANATIONS

15. **Conclusion:** Marcel will make less money this year than last year.

Premise: He made less from his investments.

Assumption: His other sources of income did not increase by enough to offset the decrease in profit from investments.

This is an ASSUMPTION question. The correct answer will be something necessary for the conclusion to be true, and, if made false, will make the argument fall apart.

(A) If they did offset, then Marcel could make just as much, which would make the argument fall apart. This is the answer.
(B) There is no connection between these two things except for the fact that Marcel is interested in both of them. Eliminate it.
(C) But we are specifically told in the argument that his portfolio WILL be affected. Eliminate it.
(D) Bummer, but we already know he's not going to make as much. Eliminate it.
(E) Bummer, but the argument never mentions his expenses. This is out of scope.

SECTION III

QUESTIONS

16. Efforts to encourage conservation by individuals are unlikely to address the world's most pressing energy problems, for although individuals have some knowledge of the amount of energy they use directly, there are hidden energy costs to everything an individual does. Every product purchased and every service received has an attendant energy cost, and the cumulative total of these costs far exceeds the amount of energy used directly by individuals.

    Which one of the following is an assumption on which the argument relies?

    (A) The most pressing energy problems involve consumption of energy that cannot be attributed to individual behavior.
    (B) The prices of goods and services do not incorporate the hidden energy costs involved in their production and delivery.
    (C) Conservation efforts are most effective when individuals have control over the amount of energy they consume.
    (D) The world's most pressing energy problems cannot be solved by reliance on the actions of individuals.
    (E) Individuals can effectively conserve energy in only those cases when they have some knowledge of the energy costs attendant upon their actions.

EXPLANATIONS

16. **Conclusion**: Efforts to encourage conservation by individuals are unlikely to solve the world's most pressing energy problems.

    Premise: The greatest proportion of energy consumption by individuals is in the form of hidden energy costs associated with products and services.

    Assumption: Individuals cannot act to conserve energy usage in forms where they cannot tell how much they are using; solving the most pressing energy problems involves reducing energy usage in forms that consume more energy than individuals directly consume.

    This is an ASSUMPTION question. We're looking for something on which the conclusion's truth depends.

    (A) The consumption that needs to be reduced is associated with individual behavior; the individuals just don't know how much they're consuming.
    (B) The prices of the goods with hidden energy costs aren't clearly relevant to the conclusion here.
    (C) Like (A), this choice doesn't make the needed distinction.
    (D) Like (A) and (C), this choice misses the fact that individuals are really consuming the energy; they just aren't aware of how much they're consuming.
    (E) Yes. If it's possible for individuals to engage in effective conservation even without this knowledge, then the argument's reasoning doesn't work.

SECTION III

QUESTIONS

17. Activist: All nations that base their economic policy on unbridled competition encourage dishonest business practices, and all nations in which dishonest business practices are common lose the trust on which international investment is based. Any nation that, because of factors beyond the government's control or because of shortsighted policies, loses the respect of its trading partners is unlikely to be able to secure needed aid in the event of economic hardship. Thus, if a nation wishes to maintain economic stability, it is essential that the activities of banks be heavily regulated.

Each of the following, if true, weakens the activist's argument EXCEPT:

(A) Moderate regulation of banks is adequate to ensure that dishonest business practices do not become commonplace.

(B) Unbridled competition, in the absence of other contributing factors, only leads to a low incidence of dishonest business practices in an economy.

(C) Those nations that lose the trust on which international investment is based do not necessarily lose the respect of their trading partners.

(D) It is possible for a nation to maintain economic stability without securing aid in the event of economic hardship.

(E) An economic policy based on unbridled competition is not the only shortsighted government policy that may lead to a loss of respect among a country's trading partners.

EXPLANATIONS

17. **Conclusion**: Banks must be heavily regulated if a nation wants to remain economically stable.

Premises: Unbridled competition encourages dishonest business practices; when dishonest business practices are common, a nation loses trust; a nation that loses respect cannot secure aid in times of economic trouble.

Assumptions: If banks are not heavily regulated, unbridled competition results; encouraging dishonest business practices leads to those practices becoming common; losing the trust of investors leads to losing the respect of trading partners; aid in times of economic hardship is needed to maintain economic stability.

This is a WEAKEN EXCEPT question. Four of these choices will attack assumptions of the argument; the odd choice out will be the answer.

(A) This weakens by pointing out that unbridled competition may not result even if banks are not heavily regulated.

(B) This weakens by pointing out that unbridled competition doesn't necessarily lead to dishonest business practices becoming common.

(C) This weakens by pointing out that a nation could lose trust without losing the respect of trading partners.

(D) This weakens by pointing out that securing aid in times of hardship isn't necessary to economic stability.

(E) Yes. Other shortsighted policies do not appear to be relevant to the conclusion.

SECTION III

QUESTIONS	EXPLANATIONS

18. Columnist: Labor unions claim that they take tough negotiating positions to secure fair treatment for workers, but they have self-interested motives in doing so. A union that gets higher wages for its members can collect higher union dues, thus allowing the union to make more political contributions and gain influence. There can be little doubt that the purpose of the labor movement is primarily to amass political power and only incidentally to help workers.

The reasoning in the columnist's argument is flawed because the argument

(A) incorrectly concludes that every union is interested in gaining political power based on the fact that many unions are interested in doing so
(B) improperly derives a conclusion about the labor movement as a whole on the basis of information concerning the behavior of individual labor unions
(C) assumes without warrant that two goals are mutually exclusive when a premise of the argument states that the pursuit of one goal may be furthered by pursuit of the other
(D) makes ambiguous use of the term "labor"
(E) rejects the arguments made by a group on the basis of information concerning the political preferences of that group

18. **Conclusion**: The labor movement's purpose is primarily to secure power and only secondarily to help workers.

Premise: Unions that secure better pay for workers serve their own interests by increasing their ability to wield political power.

Flaw: One of two potential motives for an effort is singled out as being the primary one; attributes of labor unions are ascribed to the labor movement as a whole.

This is a FLAW question. We're looking for a choice that describes or exploits an assumption.

(A) The relevant question isn't whether political power is in the unions' interest, but whether this is their primary interest.
(B) Yes. This refers to the part/whole flaw in the argument.
(C) The argument does not say that the two goals discussed are mutually exclusive.
(D) This term appears to be used in a consistent manner.
(E) No political preference is mentioned here.

19. In concluding that there has been a shift in the sense of parental responsibility in the United States since the 1960s, researchers point to the increase in the frequency with which fathers tend to the daily needs of their children. However, this increase cannot be attributed exclusively to a shift in parental mores, for during the same period there has been an increase in the percentage of mothers who have jobs. With this in mind, the increased participation of fathers in child-rearing may well be only a symptom of a more fundamental change in society.

The author of the passage criticizes the conclusion of the researchers by

(A) offering a clearer definition of the researchers' premises, thereby compromising their argument
(B) attacking the integrity of the researchers rather than their reasoning
(C) showing that the researchers have reversed cause and effect in making their argument
(D) pointing out that their criteria for "parental responsibility" are not a logical basis for their argument
(E) suggesting an alternative cause for the effect cited by the researchers

19. This is a REASONING question. Come up with your own description of how the author makes the argument and then match your description to the choices.

(A) Their argument is clear; it's their conclusion that stinks. Eliminate it.
(B) The author doesn't say that they are liars, just that their conclusion is wrong.
(C) No, the author is saying that there is a different cause. Eliminate it.
(D) Their criteria and premises are fine; it's their conclusion that is bad. Eliminate it.
(E) Yes—that it's not that fathers care more, it's just that they are exposed more to their children because mothers now work. This is the answer.

SECTION III

QUESTIONS

Questions 20–21

Upon exiting an exhibit, some visitors to art museums find it difficult to describe what it was that they liked and didn't like about the paintings. Yet because these visitors feel strongly about which art they believed to be good and which art they believed to be bad, appreciating a work of art obviously does not require the ability to articulate what, specifically, was perceived to be good or bad.

20. The argument above assumes which one of the following?

(A) The fact that some people find it difficult to articulate what they like about a work of art does not mean that no one can.
(B) If an individual feels strongly about a work of art, then he or she is capable of appreciating that work of art.
(C) The vocabulary of visual art is not a part of common knowledge, but rather is known only to those who study the arts.
(D) When a person can articulate what he or she likes about a particular painting, he or she is able to appreciate that work of art.
(E) Paintings can be discussed only in general terms of good and bad.

21. According to the passage above, all of the following could be true EXCEPT:

(A) Some museum visitors can explain with great precision what they liked and didn't like about a certain painting.
(B) If a person studies art, then that person will be able to articulate her opinion about paintings.
(C) If a person can't say why she likes a piece of art, it doesn't necessarily mean that she doesn't appreciate that piece.
(D) Some visitors can explain what they liked about a piece, but are unable to explain what they didn't like.
(E) The inability to express the reason for a particular preference indicates that the preference must not be strong.

EXPLANATIONS

20. **Conclusion:** Appreciating art does not depend on your ability to say what was good or bad.

Premise: Many visitors can't say what they liked or didn't like about art, yet they feel strongly about it.

Assumption: Strong feelings about art are the same as appreciating art.

This is an ASSUMPTION question. The correct answer will be something necessary for the conclusion to be true, and, if made false, will make the argument fall apart.

(A) We're looking for a connection between articulation and appreciation. This isn't it.
(B) Bingo. If it were not true that strong feelings can lead to appreciation, the argument would totally fall apart. This is the answer.
(C) This is classic LSAT babble. Vocabulary of visual art? Eliminate it.
(D) Always? What if the person hates it? Is that appreciation?
(E) We're not talking specific or general here; we're more concerned with whether we merely can or can't say anything at all. (B) is the best choice.

21. This is an INFERENCE question. Because it is also an EXCEPT question, your goal is to find the one choice that can't be true based on the information in the passage.

(A) This can be true—the argument only says that some can't. Eliminate it.
(B) This can be true—there could be some people who can do this. Eliminate it.
(C) Yes—as long as they feel strongly about it, they can still appreciate it. Articulation isn't necessary.
(D) This can be true also—there is no contradiction in the argument.
(E) This is the answer. It is the opposite of the argument, which says you can feel strongly and appreciate.

QUESTIONS

22. Evan: Earlier this year, the *Stockton Free Press* reported that residents consider Mayor Dalton more concerned with his image than with advancing the cause of the less fortunate of Stockton.

Dalia: But the mayor appointed a new director of the public television station, and almost immediately the station began running a documentary series promoting the mayor's antipoverty program.

Evan: Clearly the mayor has, by this appointment, attempted to manipulate public opinion through the media.

Evan's second statement counters Dalia's argument by

(A) disputing the relevancy of her statement
(B) suggesting that Dalia is less informed about the issue than he
(C) confusing the argument she presents with his own
(D) appealing to popular opinion that the mayor should not misuse his access to the media
(E) claiming that Dalia's argument is an example that actually strengthens his own argument

EXPLANATIONS

22. This is a REASONING question. Come up with your own description of how Evan's second statement counters Dalia, and then match your description to the choices.

(A) No, he attacks it directly, so he does think it's relevant. Eliminate it.
(B) He doesn't call into question the amount of information she possesses, but rather her interpretation of that information. Eliminate it.
(C) No, he's not confused at all. He's actually saying that her argument supports his argument.
(D) He doesn't appeal to anyone. Eliminate it.
(E) Bingo. He twists it around so it supports his argument. This is the answer.

QUESTIONS

23. Naturalist: Every year, thousands of animals already on the endangered species list are killed for their hides, furs, or horns. These illegal and often cruel deaths serve to push these species further toward the brink of extinction. The products made from these animals, such as articles of clothing and quack medical remedies, are goods no one really needs. What is needed is a large-scale media campaign to make the facts of the killings known and lessen the demand for these animal products. Such a campaign would be a good start in the effort to save endangered species from extinction.

Environmentalist: For the overwhelming majority of currently endangered species, the true threat of extinction comes not from hunting and poaching, but from continually shrinking habitats. Concentrating attention on the dangers of poaching for a very few high-visibility species would be counterproductive, leading people to believe that a boycott of a few frivolous items is enough to protect endangered species, when what is needed is a truly global environmental policy.

The point at issue between the naturalist and the environmentalist is which one of the following?

(A) whether the poaching of some endangered species actually increases that species' chances of becoming extinct
(B) whether a large-scale media campaign can affect the demand for some products
(C) whether more endangered species are threatened by poaching and hunting or shrinking of habitat
(D) whether some species could be saved from extinction by eliminating all commercial demand for that species
(E) whether a large-scale media campaign that lessens the demand for products made from endangered species is a good strategy for saving endangered species

EXPLANATIONS

23. This is a REASONING question. Come up with your own description of what they're arguing about, and then match your description to the choices.

(A) They both agree poaching is bad; they're arguing about whether it's the primary cause of extinction.
(B) Not whether this campaign will affect the demand, but whether it will affect extinction.
(C) We don't know the numbers. Eliminate it.
(D) They're arguing over the best method for saving as many species as possible.
(E) Yes—the environmentalist thinks that the strategy of saving habitats is more important than the naturalist's strategy of a media campaign. This is the answer.

SECTION III

QUESTIONS

24. Historian: Excavations in the ancient city of Ouz have uncovered a massive bronze statue. No other bronze object has ever been found in the city's ruins. Thus, because it appears that the ancient inhabitants of Ouz lacked either the ability to make bronze or the knowledge of how to shape it, it seems clear that the statue was looted and brought back during one of its many raids on neighboring cities.

Which one of the following, if true, most seriously weakens the historian's argument?

(A) Although all of Ouz's neighboring cities have been excavated, none has been found to include any bronze objects.
(B) The bronze statue is of a peacock, an animal that was widely found throughout the geographic region where Ouz was situated.
(C) No historical or archaeological evidence indicates that smaller bronze objects made in Ouz were removed by subsequent visitors to the site.
(D) A nearby city known to be frequently at war with Ouz contains signs that its inhabitants were able to shape bronze.
(E) Bronze was used in many regions as a material for making weapons throughout the era in which the city of Ouz was inhabited.

EXPLANATIONS

24. **Conclusion**: The statue found in the ancient city of Ouz was looted from a neighboring city.

Premises: There is no sign that the inhabitants of Ouz made anything out of bronze; the inhabitants at Ouz frequently raided other cities.

This is a WEAKEN question. Because there doesn't seem to be an obvious flaw to the argument, our choice will most likely attack the conclusion directly.

(A) Yes. Although this doesn't tell us with any certainty how the statue got there, it does cast significant doubt on the argument's explanation.
(B) This may lend slight strength to the conclusion; it doesn't weaken it.
(C) This may lend slight strength to the conclusion; it doesn't weaken it.
(D) This strengthens the conclusion.
(E) This is too general to have much impact on the conclusion.

SECTION III

QUESTIONS

25. Studies of fighter pilots reveal the surprising fact that they are much less likely to die of heart attacks than are members of the population at large, despite the stressful nature of their work and the rigorous selection process to which they are subjected. These results hold even when the data are adjusted to compensate for the fact that piloting fighter jets is dangerous work, and leads to some premature deaths. It seems doubtful, then, that recent studies purporting to show that job stress leads to an increased risk of heart attack can be correct.

Which one of the following, if true, lends the strongest support to the argument's conclusion?

(A) The average life expectancy of male fighter pilots is nearly five years shorter than the life expectancy of the general male population.

(B) The characteristics that allow fighter pilots to pass through the rigorous selection process to which they are subjected do not also allow them to avoid suffering the negative consequences of stress.

(C) Fighter pilots are in general fitter and more physically strong than are the members of the population at large, allowing them to survive more of the heart attacks they experience.

(D) Other studies of high-stress jobs outside the military have shown that the risk of heart attack triples for people who hold those jobs.

(E) Factors other than job stress, such as heredity, exercise, and diet, are known to be more important determining factors in whether or not an individual suffers a heart attack than is job stress.

EXPLANATIONS

25. **Conclusion**: It seems unlikely that job stress leads to increased risk of heart attack.

Premise: Despite the stresses to which they are exposed, fighter pilots are less likely to die of heart attack than are most people.

Assumptions: Comparisons concerning the likelihood of dying of a heart attack provide useful information about the incidence of heart attack; fighter pilots are representative of all those who have stressful jobs.

This is a STRENGTHEN question. We want a choice that will either shore up an assumption of the argument or support the conclusion directly.

(A) This seems most likely to be an effect of the hazardous nature of their work, which according to the argument was compensated for in the study. At best, this might weaken the conclusion.

(B) Yes. This concerns a characteristic of fighter pilots that may not be shared by the rest of the population. By eliminating a potential alternative explanation of the survey results, this strengthens the argument.

(C) This weakens the argument.

(D) This weakens the argument.

(E) Because the conclusion concerns only whether job stress increases the likelihood of heart attack, the fact that other factors may have more of an effect isn't truly relevant.

SECTION IV

QUESTIONS

EXPLANATIONS

Questions 1–6

An interior decorator is designing a color scheme using at least one of the following colors: red, orange, yellow, indigo, green, and violet. No other colors will be used. The selection of colors for the scheme is consistent with the following conditions:

If the scheme uses orange, then it does not use indigo.
If the scheme does not use green, then it uses orange.
If the scheme uses yellow, then it uses both indigo and violet.
If the scheme uses violet, then it uses red or green or both.

ROYIGV
O → –I
I → –O
–G → O
–O → G
Y → I and V
–V or –I → –Y
V → R or G
–R and –G → –V

Used	Not Used
(4) (G/O)	(O/I) VY

1. Which one of the following could be a complete and accurate list of the colors the scheme includes?

(A) yellow, indigo
(B) indigo, green
(C) yellow, indigo, violet
(D) yellow, green, violet
(E) orange, yellow, indigo, violet

1. (A) No. If Y is in, V has to be in.
(B) Yes.
(C) No. If V is in, R or G has to be in.
(D) No. If Y is in, I has to be in.
(E) No. If orange is in, I has to be out.

2. Which one of the following could be the only color the scheme uses?

(A) red
(B) yellow
(C) indigo
(D) green
(E) violet

2. (A) No. The scheme must use G or O.
(B) No. If Y is in, I and V have to be in.
(C) No. The scheme must use G or O.
(D) Yes.
(E) No. If V is in, R or G has to be in.

3. Which one of the following CANNOT be a complete and accurate list of the colors the scheme uses?

(A) orange, green
(B) green, violet
(C) red, orange, violet
(D) yellow, indigo, green, violet
(E) red, orange, yellow, indigo, violet

3. (A) This is possible.
(B) This is possible.
(C) This could happen.
(D) This is possible. Y, I, and V are all there, and either G or O is used.
(E) No. Both O or I cannot be used.

4. If the scheme doesn't use violet, then which one of the following must be true?

(A) The scheme uses orange.
(B) The scheme uses at least two colors.
(C) The scheme uses at most three colors.
(D) The scheme uses neither yellow nor indigo.
(E) The scheme uses neither yellow nor orange.

4. (A) Not necessarily. Watch your contrapositives.
(B) Not necessarily. Orange could be used alone.
(C) Right. There are at least three colors that have to be unused—V, Y, and either I or O—so at most three can be used.
(D) Not necessarily. It might use indigo.
(E) Not necessarily. It might use orange.

QUESTIONS	EXPLANATIONS

5. If the scheme uses violet, then which of the following must be false?
   (A) The scheme does not use red.
   (B) The scheme does not use green.
   (C) The scheme does not use indigo.
   (D) The scheme uses indigo but not yellow.
   (E) The scheme uses indigo but not green.

5. (A) This is possible.
   (B) This could happen.
   (C) This is true, when Y is also not used.
   (D) This is also possible if Y is out of the picture.
   (E) Bingo. This is impossible. If the scheme uses I, then O can't be used. If O isn't used, then G must also be used. So (E) must be false.

6. If the condition that if the scheme doesn't use green then it does use orange is suspended, and all the other conditions remain in effect, then which one of the following CANNOT be a complete and accurate list of the colors the scheme uses?
   (A) indigo
   (B) red, indigo
   (C) yellow, indigo, violet
   (D) red, indigo, violet
   (E) red, yellow, indigo, violet

6. (A) This is possible.
   (B) This is possible.
   (C) No. If V is in, R or G must be in, too.
   (D) This is possible.
   (E) This is possible.

SECTION IV

QUESTIONS

Questions 7–13

Five runners—Fanny, Gina, Henrietta, Isabelle, and Mona—are assigned to lanes numbered 1 through 5 on a track. Each runner has the option of wearing a knee brace during the competition. Two of the runners are from Palo Alto, two are from San Jose, and one is from Newcastle. The following conditions must apply:

Isabelle and Mona are assigned to the first two lanes, but not necessarily in that order.
The runner in the third lane is from Newcastle and wears a knee brace.
Neither runner from San Jose wears a knee brace.
Both Gina and Fanny are assigned higher-numbered lanes than that of Henrietta.
Neither Mona nor Fanny comes from San Jose.

EXPLANATIONS

FGHIM

S/K

H—G
H—F

M/S F/S

	1	2	3	4	5
Runner:	I/M	M/I	(H)	G/F	F/G
SSPPN:	S/P	P/S	N	S/P	P/S
Y/N Knee:	N/	/N	Y	N/	/N

(12)

M	I	H	G	F
P	S	N	S	P
Y	N	Y	N	Y

(13)

I	M	H	G/F	F/G
S	P	N	S/P	P/S
N	Y	Y	N/	/N

You can deduce that H must be third because two runners come before and two come after her. Because M and F can't be from San Jose, they must be from Palo Alto, and therefore I and G must be from San Jose and don't wear knee braces.

7. Which one the following could be an accurate list of the runners, in order from lane 1 to lane 5?

(A) Isabelle, Henrietta, Fanny, Mona, Gina
(B) Isabelle, Mona, Gina, Henrietta, Fanny
(C) Mona, Gina, Henrietta, Isabelle, Fanny
(D) Mona, Isabelle, Gina, Henrietta, Fanny
(E) Mona, Isabelle, Henrietta, Fanny, Gina

7. (A) No. H must be third.
(B) No. H must be third.
(C) No. I and M must be first and second.
(D) No. H must be third.
(E) Yes. This is possible.

8. Which one of the following could be true?

(A) Fanny runs in lane 5.
(B) Gina runs in lane 1.
(C) Henrietta runs in lane 2.
(D) Isabelle runs in lane 3.
(E) Mona runs in lane 5.

8. (A) Yes. See deductions above. Fanny can be in lane 4 or 5.
(B) No. Gina's in 4 or 5.
(C) No. H is in 3.
(D) No. H is in 3.
(E) No. M is in 1 or 2.

9. If the runner in lane 1 is from San Jose, then which one of the following could be true?

(A) Fanny runs in a lane numbered one higher than Isabelle's.
(B) Henrietta runs in a lane numbered one higher than Fanny's.
(C) Henrietta runs in a lane numbered one higher than Mona's.
(D) Henrietta runs in a lane numbered one higher than Isabelle's.
(E) Isabelle runs in a lane numbered one higher than Mona's.

9. (A) No. At least H is in between them.
(B) No. F comes after H.
(C) Right. M could be second.
(D) No. Isabelle is from San Jose, and is therefore in lane 1.
(E) No. Isabelle is from San Jose, and is therefore in lane 1.

SECTION IV

QUESTIONS	EXPLANATIONS

10. If a runner with a knee brace runs in lane 1, then which one of the following CANNOT be true?

(A) Fanny runs in lane 4.
(B) Gina runs in lane 5.
(C) A runner with a knee brace runs in lane 2.
(D) A runner with a knee brace runs in lane 3.
(E) A runner with a knee brace runs in lane 4.

10. (A) This could be true.
(B) This could be true.
(C) Right. It must be M in lane 1, so it must be I in lane 2, and I can't wear a knee brace.
(D) This is definitely true.
(E) This could be true.

11. Which one of the following must be true?

(A) Gina runs without a knee brace.
(B) Henrietta runs without a knee brace.
(C) Mona runs without a knee brace.
(D) Fanny runs with a knee brace.
(E) Isabelle runs with a knee brace.

11. Which one of the following must be true?

(A) Right. G must be from San Jose, and therefore can't wear a brace.
(B) This must be false.
(C) This could be true but doesn't have to be.
(D) This could be true but doesn't have to be.
(E) This must be false.

12. If runners wearing knee braces do not run in consecutively-numbered lanes, and runners not wearing knee braces do not run in consecutively-numbered lanes, then in exactly how many distinct orders could the runners be assigned to lanes?

(A) one
(B) two
(C) three
(D) four
(E) five

12. (A) Right. We can fill in the whole diagram.
(B) No. We can fill in the whole diagram.
(C) No. We can fill in the whole diagram.
(D) No. We can fill in the whole diagram.
(E) No. We can fill in the whole diagram.

13. If a runner with a knee brace runs in lane 2, then which one of the following CANNOT be true?

(A) The runner in lane 1 is from San Jose.
(B) The runner in lane 1 is from Palo Alto.
(C) The runner in lane 4 is from San Jose.
(D) The runner in lane 5 is from San Jose.
(E) The runner in lane 5 is from Palo Alto.

13. If a runner with a knee brace runs in lane 2, then which one of the following CANNOT be true?

(A) This must be true.
(B) Right. The runner in lane 1 must be from San Jose.
(C) This might be true.
(D) This might be true.
(E) This might be true.

SECTION IV

QUESTIONS

EXPLANATIONS

Questions 14–18

The Paulson, Rideau, Stevenson, Tisch, Van Pelt, and Wong families have each rented a time-share in a six-unit condominium. The condominium has three floors, labeled first to third from bottom to top. Each floor has an identical layout consisting of two units: a garden view apartment on the west side of the building and an ocean view apartment on the east side of the building. The following conditions must apply:

The Rideaus rent the unit immediately beneath the Paulsons's ocean-view unit.
If the Wongs rent an ocean-view apartment, the Rideaus occupy the same floor as the Van Pelts.
If the Paulsons and the Tisches occupy the same floor, the Wongs rent the unit immediately and directly beneath the Stevensons's unit.
If the Tisches rent a garden-view unit, the Wongs occupy a unit on the first floor.
If the Tisches occupy a first-floor unit, the Stevensons occupy a third-floor unit.

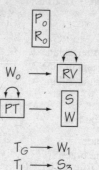

PRSTVW

P_o / R_o

$W_o \rightarrow$ RV

PT $\rightarrow$ S / W

$T_G \rightarrow W_1$

$T_1 \rightarrow S_3$

	Garden	Ocean
−R 3		
2		
−P 1		

14. Which of the following could be true?

(A) The Stevensons occupy a second-floor unit, whereas the Tisches occupy a first-floor unit.
(B) The Paulsons occupy a unit immediately and directly below the Wongs, and share a floor with the Tisches.
(C) The Paulsons rent a garden-view unit on the same floor as the Van Pelts.
(D) The Wongs rent an ocean-view unit on the same floor as the Van Pelts.
(E) The Tisches and Wongs both occupy the third floor.

14. (A) No. Try it.
(B) No. Try it.
(C) No. The Paulsons can never rent a garden-view unit.
(D) No. Try it.
(E) Right. See your diagram from question 18.

15. If the Van Pelts and the Tisches both rent garden-view units, then which of the following could be true?

(A) The Wongs rent the first-floor ocean-view unit.
(B) The Stevensons rent the first-floor garden-view unit.
(C) The Paulsons and the Tisches occupy the same floor.
(D) The Paulsons and the Wongs occupy the same floor.
(E) The Van Pelts and the Wongs occupy the same floor.

15. (A) Yes. This is possible.
(B) This isn't possible. Try it.
(C) This isn't possible. Try it.
(D) No. The Paulsons can never be on the first floor.
(E) This isn't possible. Try it.

SECTION IV

QUESTIONS	EXPLANATIONS

16. If the Wongs rent a third-floor unit, then which of the following must be true?

(A) The Rideaus rent a second-floor unit.
(B) The Stevensons rent a second-floor unit.
(C) The Stevensons rent a first-floor unit.
(D) The Tisches rent a third-floor unit.
(E) The Van Pelts rent a first-floor unit.

16. (A) No. The Rideaus would have to be in a first-floor unit.
(B) Not necessarily. They could be on the second floor, too.
(C) Not necessarily. They could be on the second floor, too.
(D) Right.
(E) Not necessarily. They could be on the second floor, too.

17. If the Tisches rent the first-floor ocean-view unit, then each of the following must be true EXCEPT:

(A) The Paulsons and the Stevensons occupy the same floor.
(B) The Rideaus and the Van Pelts occupy the same floor.
(C) The Van Pelts rent a garden-view unit.
(D) The Wongs rent a garden-view unit.
(E) The Paulsons rent a third-floor unit.

17. (A) This must be true. They're both on the third floor.
(B) Right. They could be on the same floor, but they don't have to be.
(C) This must be true.
(D) This must be true.
(E) This must be true.

18. If neither the Paulsons nor the Stevensons rent a third-floor unit, then which one of the following could be true?

(A) The Rideaus rent a second-floor unit.
(B) The Tisches rent a second-floor unit.
(C) The Wongs rent a second-floor unit.
(D) The Stevensons rent an ocean-view unit.
(E) The Wongs rent an ocean-view unit.

18. (A) No. They must be on the first floor.
(B) No. They must be on the third floor.
(C) Yes. This is possible.
(D) No. They must have a garden view.
(E) No. They must have a garden view.

SECTION IV

QUESTIONS

Questions 19–23

Four racehorses and their four jockeys are assigned to consecutive tracks at a racetrack—tracks 1, 2, 3, and 4. Each horse has exactly one jockey, and each pair is assigned to exactly one track. The horses are Ficklehoof, Galloper, Knackerbound, and Lackluster; the jockeys are Ramos, Simon, Tonka, and Urbach. The following conditions apply:

> Ficklehoof is assigned to a lower-numbered track than is Galloper, and at least one track separates the two.
> Knackerbound is assigned to track 2.
> Lackluster's jockey is Urbach.

19. Which one of the following horse and jockey teams could be assigned to track 1?

    (A) Ficklehoof and Ramos
    (B) Ficklehoof and Urbach
    (C) Galloper and Ramos
    (D) Galloper and Urbach
    (E) Lackluster and Tonka

20. If Ramos is assigned to a higher-numbered track than is Urbach, which one of the following statements cannot be true?

    (A) Ficklehoof is assigned to a lower-numbered track than is Simon.
    (B) Knackerbound is assigned to a lower-numbered track than is Ramos.
    (C) Knackerbound is assigned to a lower-numbered track than is Tonka.
    (D) Simon is assigned to a lower-numbered track than is Ramos.
    (E) Tonka is assigned to a lower-numbered track than is Knackerbound.

21. If Lackluster is assigned to a lower-numbered track than is Galloper, which one of the following statements could be false?

    (A) Ficklehoof is assigned to a lower-numbered track than is Urbach.
    (B) Galloper is assigned to track 4.
    (C) Either Ramos or Tonka is assigned to a lower-numbered track than is Urbach.
    (D) Simon is assigned to a lower-numbered track than is Urbach.
    (E) Urbach is assigned to track 3.

EXPLANATIONS

L / u

		1	2	3	4
FGKL	H:	F	K	G	L
rstu	J:				u
	OR				
	H	F	K	L	G
	J			u	

19. (A) Right.
    (B) No. Urbach must be paired with Lackluster.
    (C) No. Ficklehoof must be in track 1.
    (D) No. Ficklehoof must be in track 1.
    (E) No. Ficklehoof must be in track 1.

20. (A) This could be true. If R is higher than U, then R would be in 4 and L/U would be in 3.
    (B) This must be true.
    (C) Right. This can't be true. Tonka must be in track 1 or 2.
    (D) This must be true, because R is in track 4.
    (E) This could be true, because T must be in 1 or 2.

21. (A) No. This must be true. F must be in track 1.
    (B) No. This must be true. L and G must be in tracks 3 and 4.
    (C) No. This must be true. Only one track is higher than U, so one of them must be in a lower track.
    (D) Right. Simon could be on track 4.
    (E) No. This must be true. Same as (B).

SECTION IV

QUESTIONS

22. What is the maximum possible number of different horse and jockey teams, any one of which could be assigned to track 4?

(A) 2
(B) 3
(C) 4
(D) 5
(E) 6

23. If Simon is assigned to a higher-numbered track than is Lackluster, then which one of the following statements could be false?

(A) Galloper is assigned to a higher-numbered track than is Ramos.
(B) Galloper is assigned to a higher-numbered track than is Tonka.
(C) Lackluster is assigned to a higher-numbered track than is Tonka.
(D) Tonka is assigned to a higher-numbered track than is Ramos.
(E) Urbach is assigned to a higher-numbered track than is Ramos.

EXPLANATIONS

22. (A) No.
(B) No.
(C) Right. L and U, G and R, G and S, or G and T.
(D) No.
(E) No.

23. (A) No. Galloper has to be in track 4.
(B) No. Galloper has to be in track 4 with Simon.
(C) No. Lackluster is in track 3, and Tonka is in either 1 or 2.
(D) Right. They could each be in either track 1 or 2.
(E) No. Urbach is in track 3, and Ramos is in either 1 or 2.

NOTES

NOTES

NOTES

NOTES

NOTES

NOTES